The Politics of
Reproductive
Ritual

The Politics of Reproductive Ritual

Karen Ericksen Paige and Jeffery M. Paige

With the assistance of Linda Fuller and Elisabeth Magnus

UNIVERSITY OF CALIFORNIA PRESS

BERKELEY · LOS ANGELES · LONDON

University of California Press
Berkeley and Los Angeles, California
University of California Press, Ltd.
London, England
© 1981 by
The Regents of the University of California
Printed in the United States of America

1 2 3 4 5 6 7 8 9

Library of Congress Cataloging in Publication Data

Paige, Karen Ericksen
  The politics of reproductive ritual.

  Bibliography: p.
  Includes index.
  1. Birth customs. 2. Puberty rites. 3. Sex
customs. I. Paige, Jeffery M., joint author.
II. Title.
GN482.1.P34   392'.1   75-17289
ISBN 0-520-03071-0

Contents

Tables and Figures

TABLES

FIGURES

Acknowledgments

A work of comparative social science must necessarily build on the efforts of many others, and our debts, particularly to the ethnographers whose field work forms the starting point of our analysis, are substantial. Our study began as an analysis of women's pollution beliefs and menstruation practices but evolved into an analysis of the mechanisms used by men to control reproduction. This transition in focus was sparked by numerous conversations with the late Hortense Powdermaker who insisted that the preoccupation with reproductive events throughout the world could be best understood by studying the motives of men rather than women. Other ethnographers whose work was a necessary prelude to ours include John Whiting, Laura Bohannon, Frederik Barth and Jack Goody.

In order to develop an empirically-based theory about world-wide patterns of politics and ritual required the compilation, translation and coding of an enormous amount of ethnographic material. We would like to express our appreciation to our many coding assistants, especially Setha Low and Hartmut Guenther, and to the librarians at the University of California at Berkeley anthropology library for their many years of cooperation in locating and retrieving literally thousands of documents. The entire operation from its inception to the correction of page proofs and index construction could not have been completed without the daily assistance of Linda Fuller and Elisabeth Magnus who were so closely associated with every phase of this study that their names appear on the title page. Their endurance, dedication, and intellectual and personal flexibility were essential to the completion of this book. Both Ms. Fuller and Ms. Magnus supervised the entire coding operation, including the development of original codes used in our analysis, and kept track of all archival materials. Ms. Magnus was also responsible for typing and editing numerous drafts of the manuscript, assisting in the correcting of galleys and page proofs, the final compilation of all appendices and construction of the index. The entire manuscript was also edited by Cathy Brown, whose comprehension of the general theoretical perspective was invaluable in the translation of complex concepts into readable prose, and by Estelle Jelinek. Philip Brickman kindly responded to our editor's request to critique the entire manuscript before publication. Professor Brickman's broad understanding of ethnographic and statistical methods and of social exchange theory provided a critical review useful to important and necessary revisions in the final text. Our critique of psychoanalytic theories was aided by the careful reading and detailed comments of Nancy Chodorow and Alan Elms. Lively discussions with Guy E. Swanson and John Whiting about the theoretical model and methodological approach were always productive. Robert W. Hodge's conclusion that our statistical tests were indeed appropriate was encouraging. None of our assistants, colleagues, or reviewers are, of course, responsible for what appears in these chapters.

The enthusiasm and personal support of many friends was especially important during the writing phase of this project. In particular we are grateful to Ruth Dixon, Barbara Heyns, Kristen Luker, Gail Lapidus, Richard Ofshe, Philip Stone, Carol Tavris, Judith Tendler, and Norma Wikler. Most of all we would like to thank our editor, Grant Barnes, for his unfaltering support and endurance over the years, and our parents for emotional support and financial assistance. Finally, the financial aid of small grants from the University of California at Davis and a salary stipend from the Institute of Human Development at the University of California at Berkeley was gratefully appreciated.

Karen Ericksen Paige
Davis, California

Jeffery M. Paige
Ann Arbor, Michigan

1 Introduction

The physiological changes associated with the human reproductive cycle are the focus of intense emotions and almost obsessional interest in most human societies, and the biological indicators of these changes are often shrouded in ritual, myth, and folklore. In many preindustrial societies puberty, pregnancy, childbirth, and menstruation are the occasion for elaborate public ceremonies or are marked by ritual avoidance, physical or social seclusion, or dietary or other behavioral restrictions. The attainment of sexual maturity by both men and women may be accompanied by public rituals, sometimes called initiation rites. In some rituals the initiate becomes the central focus of a feast or celebration requiring months or even years of preparation and lasting from a few days to several months; the initiate may also be isolated in a specially constructed dwelling or partitioned area or be subjected to tattooing, body painting, genital mutilation, or severe hazing. Similarly, during pregnancy and parturition both women and men may be required to observe dietary restrictions, practice sexual abstinence, refrain from customary occupational activities, or stay in seclusion in a special birth hut or hammock. Menstruation is frequently believed to be a source of pollution and a threat to the health of men, to the success of the hunt, to the fertility of the soil, or to the welfare of the community. Contact with a menstruating woman, particularly sexual contact, is often strictly prohibited by behavioral taboos or prevented by physical segregation. Women may be sent to menstrual huts during their periods, and their

1

husbands may retreat to special men's societies, sweathouses, or lodges where they are protected from the dangerous properties of women's reproductive activities in general and menstrual pollution in particular.

The incidence and importance of these beliefs and practices vary widely from one society to another. Only a few societies observe most or all of these reproductive rituals, but most societies do have some behavioral restrictions or emotionally charged beliefs about the major events of the human reproductive cycle. Even in contemporary industrial societies menstruating women are widely regarded as irritable and emotionally unstable. The taboo on sexual intercourse during the menstrual period is widely observed, and a menstruating woman is expected to conceal her condition, especially from men, even if this requires restrictions on her normal activities. Pregnant women are also expected to restrict their activities, conceal their condition under loosely fitting garments, and refrain from sexual intercourse for some weeks before and after delivery. Male circumcision, once practiced almost exclusively by preindustrial peoples as part of a ceremonial initiation at puberty, has now been adopted, allegedly on hygienic grounds, in some industrial societies.

The behavior of women is much more constrained by reproductive rituals and beliefs than is the behavior of men, and these rituals and beliefs form the core of the mythology that surrounds women in all societies, including our own. Women are believed to be polluting, dangerous, and unstable in industrial societies because these beliefs, like those of preindustrial societies, are shaped by the intense emotions that surround the reproductive cycle. The rituals of preindustrial peoples express these beliefs in particularly vivid form. This book presents a theory to explain the nature and distribution of reproductive rituals in preindustrial societies and provides a starting point for analysis of beliefs about women and reproduction in industrial societies.

THEORIES OF REPRODUCTIVE RITUALS

The central role of reproductive rituals in preindustrial societies and the social and psychological importance of reproductive events in all societies have led to an extensive literature attempting to account for the form and distribution of these practices. In general, three major traditions can be distinguished in the literature: psychoanalytic theory, transition-rite theory, and structural-functional theory. Freudian and neo-Freudian theorists have interpreted ritual practices as expressions of underlying psychosexual personality conflicts; they view the elaborate rituals surrounding the reproductive cycle in preindustrial societies as an opportunity to apply their comprehensive theory of psychosexual development on a cross-cultural basis. Transition-rite theorists in the tradition of Arnold van Gennep have focused on the structure of ceremonies, seeking van Gennep's classic triad of separation, transition, and incorporation in ritual observances. As these theorists see it, ritual reinforces a society's age role and sex role structure by dramatizing individuals' transition to a new role and educating all members of the community about the role's rights and obligations. Theorists within the structural-functional tradition, inspired directly or indirectly by Emile Durkheim's view of ritual as reinforcing a society's collective view of itself and hence as increasing group solidarity, have attempted to locate sources of structural strain in the kinship or caste structure—strain that may lead to societal dislocations unless offset by the unifying power of ritual. All three traditions share the fundamental assumption that the purposes of ritual are seldom if ever the object of conscious knowledge. Widely differing interpretations of reproductive rituals are offered not only by those working within different traditions but by those within each major tradition as well. The most comprehensive interpretation of reproductive rituals is found in the vast psychoanalytic literature, in which analyses of each ritual rest on Freud's fundamental theory of psychosexual development. Although transition-rite theory can be classified as a structural-functional theory, in this book the interpretations of reproductive rituals that follow van Gennep's original formulation are discussed separately from the interpretations of reproductive rituals that are based on a structural-functional perspective more broadly defined.

Most theoretical debate and empirical research have focused on male circumcision because of Freud's theory that the Oedipal conflict is central to the psychodynamics of males in all societies. Since less attention has been devoted to the explanation of female reproductive rituals, most of the theoretical literature is derived from theories of circumcision and is far less original and complex. Our critique of the major theoretical explanations of the critical ritual events in the human reproductive cycle begins, therefore, with male circumcision; reviews of menarcheal and menstrual theories and explanations of the birth practices of both sexes follow later in the chapter.

Male Circumcision

Genital mutilations, particularly male circumcision, have been the subject of theories from the earliest days of the social sciences. These theories are probably more varied and certainly more bizarre than those advanced to account for other reproductive rituals. The explanations of circumcision proposed by Cebuan school girls in a survey conducted by Arthur Rubel and his associates are at least as plausible as much social science theorizing.[1] According to the Cebuan girls, circumcision was important in their society for the following reasons: it was a Christian custom; it made men physically strong; it was good for health and lessened susceptibility to cancer; it reduced embarrassing body odors; it improved sexual relationships and increased sexual satisfaction; and, finally, it was unnatural not to be circumcised.[2] It should be noted that the opposites of all these assertions have also been stated at one time or another. It has been argued that circumcision is a peculiarly Jewish, not Christian, custom; that it weakens men by turning them into menstruating women; that it has no effect on the incidence of cancer but may lead to hemorrhaging, infection, accidental amputation, and, in the absence of proper medical supervision, death; that antisocial body odors are a consequence of infrequent bathing, not an intact prepuce; that circumcision decreases sexual satisfaction and discourages masturbation; and, finally, that it is an unnatural, even barbaric, action.

Male genital mutilations and their associated ceremonies are important events in many cultures, sometimes the society's most important ceremonial occasion. As a result, the explanation of genital mutilation has been important in several major theoretical traditions.

Psychoanalytic Theories

Orthodox psychoanalytic theorists have viewed genital mutilations such as circumcision as a consequence of a universal male castration anxiety precipitated by the primary sexual attraction between mother and child and the competitive sexual jealousy between father and son which constitute the basic elements of the Oedipus complex.[3] According to the orthodox Freudian position, the development of genital eroticism during a boy's phallic stage leads to a narcissistic concern that the source of pleasure be protected against damage and to a consequent fear that the organ could be lost entirely. This fear is enhanced by adult taunts and by humorous threats of castration as a punishment for masturbation. Knowledge of female anatomy leads the boy to conclude that the organ could indeed be lost since he assumes that females must have been deprived of the penis they originally possessed. The child fears that his father will castrate him as punishment for desiring his mother and hating his father. In Freud's

1. Arthur J. Rubel, William T. Liu, and Ernest Branckwie, "Genital Mutilation and Adult Role Behavior Among Lowland Christian Filipinos of Cebu," *American Anthropologist* 73 (1971): 806–10.
2. Ibid., p. 807.
3. Otto Fenichel's *The Psychoanalytic Theory of Neurosis* (New York: Norton, 1945) is usually considered the definitive statement of the orthodox position; see in particular pp. 74–110.

well-known child-analytic case, "Little Hans," the Oedipal dilemma expressed itself in a childhood phobia against open places. Hans' underlying fear was castration by the bite of a horse which, according to Freud, bore several features that resembled his father.[4] In normal sexual development the boy resolves his Oedipus complex by renouncing his incestuous desires and identifying with his father, thereby adopting his father's values, including in particular the adult prohibition against incest. Fear of castration is the major element forcing the child toward this resolution. Circumcision, in this view, aids in the resolution of the Oedipal dilemma because it is a symbolic form of castration.

In order for the psychoanalytic theory of circumcision to apply to adult ceremonies rather than childhood fantasies, some theoretical linkage must be made between the two. In accounts of tribal initiation rites by such psychoanalytic theorists as Theodor Reik and Géza Róheim, the connection is made in two ways. First, it is argued that adult males continue to experience Oedipal anxieties that originated in their own childhoods and that these anxieties are heightened by the sexual maturation of their sons. Second, it is argued that a young man's Oedipal desires, which were repressed during childhood because of his powerless and dependent position, may erupt in the form of open rebellion against adult males once he is old enough to wield a weapon. For example, Reik asserts that "the unconscious memory of incestuous and hostile impulses of childhood which were turned upon his parents still lives in him. He fears [the] realization of these wishes, in which he might be the object injured at the hands of his own child."[5] Róheim, in his analysis of Australian tribal societies, also supports both the Oedipal origins of circumcision and the causal association between infantile experience and adult behavior.[6] Unfortunately for this argument, however, circumcision in Australia was invariably performed by a member of a boy's potential wife's marriage section and hence by his future father-in-law rather than his father. In fact, Róheim notes that the father was often protective of the boy during the initiation and might even kill the circumciser if the operation was bungled. Nevertheless, Róheim feels that the circumcision rites have the appearance of "a furious father attacking his son's penis"[7] and believes they are a result of paternal fears of an open Oedipal rebellion against the gerontocratic control of the band. Reik

4. Sigmund Freud, "Analysis of a Phobia in a Five-Year-Old Boy," (1909), pp. 47–184, in Freud's *The Sexual Enlightenment of Children* (New York: Collier, 1963).
5. Theodor Reik, *Ritual: Psychoanalytic Studies* (London: Hogarth Press, 1931), p. 105.
6. Géza Róheim, *The Eternal Ones of the Dream* (New York: International Universities Press, paperback edition 1969; originally published in 1945), pp. 68–79.
7. Ibid., p. 74.

and Róheim agree that the primary functions of the circumcision rite are the suppression of incest and the establishment of a strong identification with the male tribal leaders. These, of course, are also the putative consequences of the resolution of the Oedipus complex in all societies.

This explanation of the linkages between childhood sexual fantasies and adult ceremonial behavior is not without logical problems, even within the framework of orthodox psychoanalytic thought. Although it may be reasonable for a child to confuse fantasy and reality and to limit his sexual choices to members of his nuclear family, it is much less reasonable to suppose that fathers or mature sons might do the same. Circumcision does not seem necessary to repress mother-son incest since this is almost invariably punished by exile or death. Further, mother-son incest is extremely rare in all societies; when it does occur, it usually involves isolated family groups with limited access to sexual partners. Unless there is an extreme shortage of marriageable girls caused by female infanticide or hoarding by older males, a young man usually has ready access to female partners, and his sexual outlets are not limited to his aging mother. Since by puberty he is well aware of the punishment for incest and presumably old enough to distinguish fantasy from reality, it seems quite unlikely that he would try to realize his childhood dreams through an actual Oedipal revolt. Indeed, as Frederick Rose has pointed out, much of the tension in the initiation rites of Australians is a result of the absolute monopoly on nubile women held by the older men of the band and of the subsequent extended bachelorhoods of most young males.[8] This suggests that polygynous marriage might lead to initiation or circumcision, but the conflict would involve adult sexual competition rather than residual childhood fantasies. In many cases the father may, in fact, have a vested interest in the earliest possible marriage for his son in order to increase the strength of his own kinship faction or to contract a favorable alliance with affinal kin; he may, therefore, assist the son in solving his problems of adult object-choice. In any cases, the son's options do not seem so restricted that Oedipal revolts would be even a remote possibility, and there is no ethnographic evidence that the Oedipal revolt against the primal father described by Freud in *Totem and Taboo* ever, in fact, occurs in tribal or band-level societies.

The logic of psychoanalytic thought suggests that Oedipal conflicts are largely resolved by the end of the phallic stage at about age five so that it is strange to find them reappearing in adulthood with

---

8. Frederick G. G. Rose, "Australian Marriage, Land-Owning Groups, and Initiations," in *Man the Hunter*, ed. Richard B. Lee and Irven DeVore (Chicago: Aldine, 1968), pp. 200–08.

sufficient intensity to account for the months-long initiation ceremonies of Australian tribesmen. According to the orthodox position,
satisfactory resolution of the Oedipal dilemma is a necessary precondition of normal psychological development; conversely, incomplete
resolution is a source of neurotic behavior. If the circumcision rites of
tribal and band societies are expressions of unresolved Oedipal conflicts, then the adult males of these societies must be neurotic. This is
precisely the conclusion reached by Reik, who subtitled his chapter
on puberty rites, "Some Parallels Between the Mental Life of Savages
and Neurotics."[9] Similarly, Róheim claims that native Australian
groups are "autoplastic" rather than "alloplastic" like Western
societies: the Australians solve problems facing their society by manipulating their own bodies instead of by instrumental and presumably rational means.[10] This implicit equation between neurotic irra-
tionality and "primitives" has been thoroughly rejected by informed
anthropological opinion,[11] and, in any case, the psychoanalysts provide no explanation as to why the Oedipus complex should remain
unresolved among the Arunta or the Masai while it is so routinely
resolved by most Europeans and Americans.

The two principal causal elements in the psychoanalytic interpretation of circumcision, repression and identification, are to
some extent contradictory—a problem that some theorists have tried
to deal with, though without much success. As a symbolic castration,
circumcision assists in the repression of genital desires for the mother
by threatening emasculation; however, the operation is also alleged to
increase identification with virile adult males. Apparently reluctant to
argue that castration enhances masculinity, the psychoanalysts have
focused on other features of the surgical procedure in an effort to
resolve this contradiction. Róheim claims that the Australian rites
clearly indicate a psychological equation of the foreskin with both the
mother and the period of infantile sexuality and, hence, that the removal of the foreskin severs the boy's connection with his mother.[12]
In the Australian case this equation is bolstered by the fact that the
man who takes away the boy's foreskin must later provide him with a
wife so that circumcision represents a symbolic exchange of masculine and feminine characteristics. This theme, which is also present

9. Reik, *Ritual*, p. 91.
10. Géza Róheim, *Australian Totemism: A Psycho-Analytic Study in Anthropology*
(London: Allen & Unwin, 1915), p. 221.
11. See for example Mary Douglas' criticisms of this view in *Purity and Danger:
An Analysis of Concepts of Pollution and Taboo* (New York: Penguin Books, 1966), pp. 138-
-39. Douglas singles out Bettelheim and Róheim as examples of anthropological naïveté
among psychoanalysts but reserves her harshest words for Norman O. Brown, whose
description of the "anarchic primitive mentality" stands out even among
psychoanalysts as ethnocentric and fanciful ethnography.
12. Róheim, *Eternal Ones*, pp. 78–79.

in Reik's analysis of anthropological data,[13] has been elaborated by later clinical psychoanalysts. Herman Nunberg, for example, reports the case of a male patient whose son underwent circumcision during his analysis. On the basis of what appears to be rather liberal interpretations of his patient's dreams, Nunberg concludes that the patient equates the loss of the foreskin with the loss of his own mother and sees in the bleeding circumcision wound a similarity to the female vagina during menstruation.[14] Continuing this general line of argument, Frank Zimmerman asserts that the ritual elements of the traditional Jewish circumcision ceremony indicate a desire to increase virility by fashioning a new penis that resembles the adult male uncircumcised penis during erection.[15] Thus the circumcision operation serves a dual purpose. It threatens to take away the boy's penis through its symbolic association with castration, but, at the same time, it promises him a new and presumably more masculine identity by freeing him from the maternal foreskin and giving him a symbol of the male erection instead. Contradictory as these interpretations may seem, they are consistent with the Freudian description of the Oedipal dilemma. For example, Freud reports that Little Hans feared a plumber would come and take away his "widdler" with a pair of pincers, but then he would miraculously return to Hans a bigger replica of the missing organ.[16]

The most fundamental difficulties with the orthodox Freudian description of the origins of circumcision, however, are not in its internal logic but in its inability to account for cultural variations in circumcision practices, its emphasis on genital sexuality as the primary source of rivalry within the family, and its reliance on imaginative but subjective evidence from clinical cases and ethnographic examples. Although according to psychoanalytic theory the Oedipal dilemma is universal, circumcision occurs in less than a third of the societies in George Murdock and Douglas White's cross-cultural sample.[17] Although in theory the Oedipus complex is based exclusively on sexual rivalry, in matrilocal societies a boy's feelings of rivalry and conflict, as Bronislaw Malinowski has demonstrated, are focused on his sociological father, his mother's brother, rather than on his biological father, the husband and sexual partner of his mother. Although both Reik

13. Reik, *Ritual*, pp. 137–41.

14. Herman Nunberg, "Circumcision and the Problem of Bisexuality," *International Journal of Psychoanalysis* 28 (1949): 145–79.

15. Frank Zimmerman, "Origin and Significance of the Jewish Rite of Circumcision," *Psychoanalytic Review* 38 (1951): 103–12.

16. Freud, "Analysis of a Phobia," p. 136.

17. George Murdock and Douglas White, "Standard Cross-Cultural Sample," *Ethnology* 8 (1969): 329–69; presence of genital mutilation as coded by Murdock in his "Ethnographic Atlas, a Summary," *Ethnology* 6 (1967): 109–233.

and Róheim report a range of ethnographic examples, no attempt at systematic measurement of any kind is made by either.

The neo-Freudian theories and cross-cultural research of John Whiting and his students do not exhibit the major limitations of Freudian theory. Whiting accepted the general framework of the Freudian model, maintaining the orthodox Freudian connection between childhood experience and adult personality, but he also took into account cross-cultural variations in childhood experience and family dynamics. In their now-classic paper, "The Function of Male Initiation Ceremonies at Puberty," John Whiting, Richard Kluckhohn, and Albert Anthony argued that variations in the occurrence of male initiation ceremonies, particularly those involving genital mutilation, were a consequence of the relationship between mother and child in infancy.[18] According to Whiting et al., societies in which mother and infant sleep together apart from other family members and in which a postpartum taboo on sexual relations is maintained for a year or more encourage the establishment of a strong, exclusive tie of affection and dependency between mother and child. Whiting et al. denied that the connection was limited to genital sexuality but argued, nonetheless, that these strong ties increased the severity of Oedipal conflict later. Initially, Whiting et al. argued that an intense Oedipal conflict in childhood leads to a need for initiation at puberty for the same two reasons given by Reik and Róheim: to suppress a potential Oedipal rebellion and to establish a firm masculine identity. Thus, they contended, societies that foster close Oedipal ties often practice severe puberty rituals that include genital mutilation, trials of endurance, and seclusion from women. To support their argument, they cited Henri Junod's description of Thonga circumcision schools.[19] The Thonga periodically round up uncircumcised boys, distract them with a blow on the head with a club, and circumcise them in a brutal operation that frequently results in unconsciousness from shock. They proceed to beat, starve, torture, and harass the initiates, who have been isolated in a specially built camp from which they are forbidden to escape under penalty of death. According to Whiting et al., these measures are necessary to discourage the boys, who constitute age regiments in the king's army after initiation, from open rebellion and to bind them more strongly to the patriarchal Thonga culture. Using a selected sample of fifty-six societies, Whiting et al. succeeded

18. John W. M. Whiting, Richard Kluckhohn, and Albert Anthony, "The Function of Male Initiation Ceremonies at Puberty," in *Readings in Social Psychology*, ed. Eleanor Maccoby, T. M. Newcomb, and E. L. Hartley (New York: Henry Holt, 1958), pp. 359–70.

19. Ibid., pp. 361–62.

in demonstrating a strong empirical relationship between the presence of initiation rites having some or all of the characteristics of the Thonga ceremony and the presence of both separate sleeping arrangements for mother-infant pairs and long postpartum sex taboos. Since the two childrearing variables are highly correlated, the findings are not, of course, independent, but the empirical relationship has been consistently replicated in later studies.[20]

Whiting's later work gradually changed in focus from initiation ceremonies in which genital mutilation frequently but not always occurred to initiation ceremonies in which genital mutilation always occurred and finally to genital mutilation itself, even when not part of a formal ceremony. His theoretical framework changed gradually, too: he came to emphasize the establishment of a strong male identity rather than the threat of Oedipal rebellion. In the course of his research he has demonstrated a set of positive cross-cultural correlations among postpartum sex taboo, exclusive mother-son sleeping arrangements, genital mutilation, polygyny, patrilocality, patrilineality, and a tropical environment. In a 1964 article, he attempted to organize all these variables into a single causal chain that begins with the nature of the environment and ends with genital mutilation.[21] Tropical environments, he observes, are typically associated with the protein deficiency disease kwashiorkor; this indicates that diets in the tropics are likely to be deficient in protein. Extended nursing of infants is, therefore, necessary in tropical societies to compensate for this protein deficiency, and the postpartum sex taboo is necessary to prevent another pregnancy since nursing two children would overtax the milk production capacity of the mother. He demonstrates that societies which he classifies as having low-protein diets, largely cultivators of root crops, are, in fact, more likely to have long postpartum sex taboos. The postpartum sex taboo in turn leads the husband to seek sexual satisfaction from a second wife, thereby increasing the incidence of polygyny. Patrilocal residence develops to facilitate the control of polygynous co-wives. In patrilocal societies, especially those with patrilineal descent, a strong masculine identity and a loyalty to the patrilineal kin group are necessary. The strong mother-child bond fostered by exclusive mother-child sleeping arrangements

20. See William Stephens, *The Oedipus Complex: Cross-Cultural Evidence* (New York: Free Press, 1962), pp. 152–59; and Jean François Saucier, "Correlates of the Long Postpartum Sex Taboo: A Cross-Cultural Study," *Current Anthropology* 13 (1972): 238–49.

21. John W. M. Whiting, "Effects of Climate on Certain Cultural Practices," in *Explorations in Cultural Anthropology*, ed. W. H. Goodenough (New York: McGraw-Hill, 1964), pp. 511–44. For Whiting's research on the establishment of male identity, see Whiting, Kluckhohn, and Anthony, "Male Initiation Ceremonies"; and Roger V. Burton and John W. M. Whiting, "The Absent Father and Cross-Sex Identity," *Merrill-Palmer Quarterly of Behavior and Development* 7 (1961): 85–95.

must, therefore, be broken by genital mutilation ceremonies. In matrilocal-matrilineal societies that do not depend on male kin ties and local male loyalties, such rites are not needed.

The entire complex causal chain, therefore, leads from low-protein economics to postpartum sex taboo, polygyny, patrilocality, patrilineality, and, finally, genital mutilation. Whatever the merit of Whiting's explanations of the correlation between postpartum sex taboos, patrilocality, and genital mutilations, his nutritional theory of the origin of the postpartum taboo and hence his ultimate explanation of genital mutilation have been refuted by Jean Saucier.[22] Saucier demonstrates that postpartum sex taboos are associated with low-protein root crops only because of the correlation between extensive slash-and-burn cultivation and root crops. There is no relationship between high-protein cereal crops or low-protein root crops and postpartum sex taboo in societies based on extensive cultivation. Saucier suggests that the postpartum sex taboo is a consequence of polygyny, an idea at one time raised by Whiting himself,[23] and that the correlation with extensive cultivation reflects the high economic value of women workers in such societies and the economic advantages of polygyny.

Whiting's nutritional theory of genital mutilations is clearly wrong, as he himself admits,[24] but the pattern of associations he discovered remains a challenge to anthropological theory. As Yehudi Cohen said in a review of a book criticizing Whiting's views, "Whiting's interpretations leave much to be desired [but] thank heavens for John Whiting; were it not for him, some of us would have only windmills to tilt at."[25]

Despite Whiting's neo-Freudian emphasis on the relation between culture and personality and the emphasis in his later work on gender identification rather than sexual rivalry, he has remained within the general theoretical framework of the Oedipal dilemma. Bruno Bettelheim, though also committed to psychoanalytic principles, has proposed a radically different theory. He contends that genital mutilation serves to strengthen identification not with males but with females and that it is a consequence not of unresolved Oedipal fantasies but of envy of female sexual functions (womb envy) generated during earlier bisexual phases of infantile sexual development.[26]

22. Saucier, "Correlates," pp. 241–42.
23. John W. M. Whiting, "Comment," *American Journal of Sociology* 67 (1962): 391–93.
24. John W. M. Whiting. Personal communication, 1975.
25. Yehudi Cohen, review of *Initiation Ceremonies: A Cross-Cultural Study of Status Dramatization* by Frank W. Young, *American Anthropologist* 68 (1966): 776.
26. Bruno Bettelheim, *Symbolic Wounds: Puberty Rites and the Envious Male*, rev. ed. (New York: Collier, 1962).

According to Bettelheim, genital mutilation is not imposed on an unwilling son by a neurotic and vengeful father but is actually desired by the son, who covets the reproductive capacity of women. Bettelheim cites not only ethnographic examples but also clinical evidence from his own experience, cases in which schizophrenic boys attempted to mutilate their genitals out of envy of girls who had recently reached menarche. This theory, of course, completely reverses the positions of both Whiting and the orthodox Freudians, but Bettelheim's ethnographic examples are well chosen to support his argument.

Bettelheim's hypothesis was suggested earlier and in a more tentative form by M. F. Ashley-Montagu in an attempt to explain subincision ceremonies among Australian tribesmen.[27] Subincision is a radical surgical procedure in which a cut is made in the ventral aspect of the penis; in many cases, the incision is extensive enough to lay open the penile urethra from the meatus to the scrotum. The operation is practiced by many tribes in aboriginal Australia, several of whom also practice conventional circumcision (amputation of the foreskin). Ashley-Montagu suggested that the operation was instituted to cause the male to resemble the female both through the flow of blood from the wound and from the visual similarity between the subincised penis and the vagina. Ashley-Montagu grants that this theory may sound "somewhat fantastic"[28] (though comparison with some of the other psychoanalytic theories of genital mutilation might have reassured him). Indeed, the evidence from Australia in particular provides striking support for his hypothesis. The subincision wound and sometimes the subincised penis are referred to by the same term as the one used to describe the vagina or womb; origin myths attribute the operation or important elements in it to women rather than to men; and, as with circumcision, the operation is performed by members of the boy's future wife's marital section, who are referred to by the classificatory kinship term *mura*, which means mother. In addition, the subincision wound is frequently broken open after healing has begun, in an apparent attempt to simulate menstrual bleeding.

According to Bettelheim, the equation of bleeding from genital mutilation with women's menstruation is even more direct in Wogeo and closely related Papuan cultures, in which the penis is periodically slashed and the resulting bleeding is called "men's menstruation." Ian Hogbin even titles his definitive ethnography of the Wogeo *The Island of Menstruating Men*.[29] These genital operations do not resemble

27. M. F. Ashley-Montagu, "The Origins of Subincision in Australia," *Oceania* 8 (1937): 193–207.

28. Ibid., p. 204.

29. Ian Hogbin, *The Island of Menstruating Men: Religion in Wogeo, New Guinea* (Scranton, Pa.: Chandler, 1970).

conventional circumcision procedures, in which the prepuce is removed by means of a lateral incision, but they do resemble superincision: a longitudinal incision in the dorsal aspect of the prepuce, which is the dominant form of genital mutilation in the Insular Pacific. Bettelheim relies heavily on examples of superincision of both the Wogean and Insular Pacific varieties and on Australian subincision to support his theory. He pays considerably less attention to circumcision, though it is much more common and was the exclusive concern of earlier psychoanalytic writers.

The apparent conflict between the two versions of psychoanalytic theory, one stressing envy of men and the other of women, has been neatly resolved by Charles Harrington, who manages to protect the Whiting hypothesis against the Bettelheim onslaught while at the same time permitting Bettelheim a useful if somewhat peripheral role in the interpretation of genital mutilation.[30] Harrington, contrasting circumcision and superincision, demonstrates in a large cross-cultural sample that circumcision is correlated with strong differentiation in sexual socialization practices whereas superincision is correlated with the absence of sexual differentiation and a converging treatment of the sexes in childhood. His evidence is the more compelling because the scoring of sexual differentiation in childrearing was done by others for entirely different purposes. Curiously, however, Harrington classifies subincision with circumcision instead of with superincision on the grounds that most subincisers also practice circumcision. The logic of Ashley-Montagu's and Bettelheim's arguments, as well as their ethnographic evidence, clearly suggests that subincision and superincision should be regarded as equivalent. Nevertheless, Harrington's argument resolves the contradiction between Whiting and Bettelheim. Whiting is right because societies with strong sexual differentiation must use circumcision as a form of symbolic castration to establish a strong and distinct masculine identity for their boys; Bettelheim is right because societies with weak sexual differentiation are likely to demonstrate male envy of female sexual functions and, therefore, to attempt to reduce sexual differentiation through superincision. Unfortunately for Bettelheim, there are more than three times as many instances of circumcision in the Harrington sample as instances of superincision. Consequently, if the sample is representative of world societies, Bettelheim has explained not genital mutilation in general but only one rather specialized form. Furthermore, Bettelheim, like the earlier psychoanalysts, is handicapped by his assumption of universal psychological laws and by a set of ethnographic examples limited, in his case, almost exclusively

30. Charles Harrington, "Sexual Differentiation in Socialization and Some Male Genital Mutilations," *American Anthropologist* 70 (1968): 951–56.

to central and southern Australia and northeastern New Guinea. Whiting's theory has considerably more cross-cultural generality, though Harrington's work suggests that it is actually an explanation of circumcision rather than of superincision or subincision.

Transition-Rite Theories

Although psychoanalytic interpretations of genital mutilation have been influential in anthropological studies of culture and personality, the conventional anthropological view regards these mutilations as one of several common practices characterizing rites of transition between childhood and adulthood, between involvement in the family and wider kinship groupings, or between partial and full membership in a tribe or tribal organization. This perspective can, of course, be traced directly to the work of van Gennep.[31] The terms *rites de passage* and *initiation*, which he introduced, have become such a standard part of the anthropological lexicon that they are used even by such theorists as Whiting, who were advancing distinctly different theoretical positions. In van Gennep's original formulation, *rites de passage*, or rites of transition, involved three distinct ceremonial elements: separation from the original status, a designated state of transition, and, finally, incorporation into the new status. The transition-rite theory of male genital mutilation parallels that explaining female puberty rites. It stresses the transition from boyhood, with its commitment to the immediate family, to the status of adult male, with its commitments to wider sexual, lineage, and tribal groups. According to van Gennep, circumcision was a frequent part of *rites de passage* because it symbolically severed the connection with childhood and left an indelible sign of adult status. It was therefore no different from several similar practices that accomplished the same objectives. According to van Gennep, "Cutting off the foreskin is exactly equivalent to pulling out a tooth (in Australia, etc.), to cutting off the little finger above the last joint (in South Africa), to cutting off the ear lobe or perforating the ear lobe or the septum, or to tattooing, scarifying, or cutting the hair in a particular fashion."[32]

According to van Gennep, the practice of circumcision by the Jews has confused the analysis of initiation rites by focusing the attention of biblical commentators solely on circumcision. "If the Jews had linked themselves with Yaweh by perforating the septum, how much fewer would have been the errors in ethnographic literature."[33] Van Gennep's casual equation of genital and other body mutilations raises

31. Arnold van Gennep, *The Rites of Passage* (Chicago: University of Chicago Press, 1961).
32. Ibid., pp. 71–72.
33. Ibid., p. 72.

some obvious questions which have not been overlooked by psycho-analytic critics.[34] Men in all societies are considerably more attached to their penis than to their septum, if indeed they know the location of this obscure part of their anatomy. Films of subincision operations have been sufficient to make even medically trained males blanch.[35] Of all the mutilations listed by van Gennep, only genital mutilation involves a functionally important and emotionally charged organ and a potentially dangerous and sometimes fatal surgical procedure. As Bettelheim has pointed out,[36] the transition-rite theory does not account for why some societies focus their attention on the emotionally charged sexual organs while others do not. Van Gennep's version of transition-rite theory cannot even account for cross-cultural variation in initiation as he defines it since it does not provide the slightest suggestion about why initiation rites should dominate social life in some socieites and be entirely absent in others.

Two transition-rite theorists since van Gennep have attempted to explain cross-cultural variation in male initiation rites by arguing that certain cultural conditions produce a greater need for the dramatization of role transitions than others. Frank Young attempts to demonstrate that male initiation rites and the associated genital mutilations are a consequence of the presence of solidary male groups and of the need to dramatize male status in order to protect this solidarity.[37] He claims to have demonstrated empirically that the presence of male solidarity as measured by exclusive male organizations and activities is correlated with initiation rites and that when this variable is controlled, Whiting's association of these rites with patrilineality and patrilocality proves spurious. But Young's work, including both his original article and his later book, proves nothing of the kind and is based to a large extent on tautological reasoning. Young is aware of this problem: "Is the relation between male solidarity and initiation ceremonies tautological?" he asks, and later answers the question by admitting that, on the conceptual level if not the empirical level, "there is room for doubt."[38] After examining his indices of male solidarity and initiation rites, we find considerable room for doubt on both levels. Young's scales of male solidarity and initiation rites, which he terms "male sex-role dramatization," contain identical cul-

34. See Bettelheim, *Symbolic Wounds*, pp. 16–18.
35. Philip Singer and Daniel E. Desole, "The Australian Subincision Ceremony Reconsidered: Vaginal Envy or Kangaroo Bifid Penis Envy," *American Anthropologist* 69 (1967): 355.
36. Bettelheim, *Symbolic Wounds*, p. 16.
37. Frank W. Young, "The Function of Male Initiation Ceremonies: A Cross-Cultural Test of an Alternative Hypothesis," *American Journal of Sociology* 67 (1962): 379–96; and Frank W. Young, *Initiation Ceremonies: A Cross-Cultural Study of Status Dramatization* (New York: Bobbs-Merrill, 1965).
38. Young, "Alternate Hypothesis," p. 504.

tural elements. Although *all* the elements in the two scales do not overlap, enough of them do to render his results suspect. Young seems to have established that the presence of male initiation rites is positively correlated with the presence of male initiation rites.

Another attack on Whiting's work was launched by Yehudi Cohen, who, like Young, defended the conventional transition-rite hypothesis. According to Cohen, male initiation rites are a result of the functional need to separate boys from their families and incorporate them into lineage organizations in unilineal societies.[39] His theory analyzes the rites according to the classic triad of separation, transition, and incorporation. Cohen attempts to prove his theory by demonstrating a correlation between male initiation rites in childhood or adolescence and unilineal descent, which he contrasts with cognatic and duolineal descent. Although he finds a strong relationship in the predicted direction, it can be argued that his results are spurious. Unilineal descent groups must, of course, ensure the loyalties of their members or cease to exist, but broader kin-group obligations also exist in cognatic or duolineal societies. It could even be argued that kinship obligations beyond the nuclear family are *more* extensive in cognatic and duolineal than in unilineal societies because ties extend to both matri- and patrikin rather than only to one or the other. Although these ties do tend to be looser, ambilineal descent groups and bilateral kindreds are perfectly capable of uniting for action, especially when unified by a virilocal residence rule. Apparently Cohen is confusing the bilateral, neolocal, isolated nuclear family of industrial societies with the considerably more extensive bilateral organizations in preindustrial societies. Both duolineal and cognatic societies usually require loyalty to a group of kin wider than the nuclear family; rarely are organized kin groups entirely absent. Hence, according to Cohen, initiation rites should also be present. According to his findings, however, these rites are almost never (one out of eighteen cases) present in cognatic or duolineal societies, even though on the average one would expect a substantial percentage of cognatic descent groups in a random sample of preindustrial societies.[40]

Even overlooking this theoretical problem, Cohen's results replicate rather then refute Whiting's original research. Since Whiting demonstrated that male initiation rites were positively correlated with patrilocal residence and patrilineal descent, the positive association between unilineal descent and initiation rites in Cohen's data must be a result of the correlation between patrilineal descent and initiation

39. Yehudi A. Cohen, "The Establishment of Identity in a Social Nexus: The Special Case of Initiation Ceremonies and Their Relation to Value and Legal Systems," *American Anthropologist* 60 (1964): 529–52.

40. Cohen, "Identity," Table 6, p. 544.

rites. Thus, he seems to have proved that patrilineal descent is associated with initiation rites, a finding perfectly consistent with Whiting's male-identity hypothesis but contradictory to his own unilineal-descent hypothesis. Both matrilineal and patrilineal descent systems, according to Cohen, should have an equal need to sever childhood ties to the nuclear family, but only patrilineal descent systems apparently do so. Whiting, on the other hand, argues that the patrilocal-patrilineal complex requires initiation ceremonies to establish male identity and that there is no corresponding need for initiation in matrilocal-matrilineal societies. Thus, Whiting's results (and, for that matter, his theory) emerge unscathed from the critical research of Young and Cohen. Apparently challenges to Whiting's findings have led to little empirical or theoretical progress.

There seems little reason to accept transition-rite theories as explanations of circumcision or other forms of genital mutilation since this is at best a peripheral concern of cross-cultural researchers like Young and Cohen. Such researchers are interested in circumcision only insofar as it is part of something that can be designated a transition rite; consequently, their definitions of initiation broaden the theoretical focus from genital mutilation to numerous other initiation practices.

Structural-Functional Theories

The recent attempt of M. R. Allen to apply the sex antagonism theory developed by Robert Murphy to the study of initiation rites also provides little insight into the causes of genital mutilation because Allen is primarily concerned with initiation into secret men's societies and not with the presence or absence of genital mutilation. The causes of circumcision in particular are ignored in Allen's work since he surveys only Melanesian societies; although some of these societies practice superincision, none practices circumcision.

Murphy had argued that the antagonism between the sexes expressed by residential segregation of adult males was a consequence of exogamous unilocal societies that kept consanguines of one sex together while sending those of the other sex to become affines in other villages.[41] Murphy thought this pattern particularly likely in patrilocal societies because most matrilocal societies show a distinct tendency toward local endogamy. Allen argued that exogamous unilineal communities should also have initiation rites, though it is difficult to find any theoretical connection between sex antagonism as described by Murphy and initiation rites as described in Allen's book. The closest Allen comes to postulating a theoretical connection is to

41. Robert F. Murphy, "Social Structure and Sex Antagonism," *Southwestern Journal of Anthropology* 15 (1959): 89–98.

state that male initiation serves the "function" of "providing the participants with an institutionalized means of acting out sentiments that
might otherwise have undesirable social or psychological consequences."[42] What these consequences might be is never fully
described. Whatever the value of Murphy's initial hypothesis in understanding antagonism between the sexes, Allen's attempt to apply
the theory to male initiation rites provides no theoretical illumination
or empirical evidence on the relationship between exogamous communities and initiation. Although Allen clearly intends to provide an
alternative or at least a complementary theory to Whiting's, neither
his hypotheses nor his data provide any help in understanding Whiting's findings.

In sum, there seems to be no theory other than Whiting's that
can account for the known social correlates of circumcision. Although
this state of affairs causes considerable discomfort to critics of the
culture-and-personality school, who cannot accept the relationship
between childhood experience and adult institutions on which the
theory is based,[43] the findings refuse to go away. Neither transition-
rite nor other structural-functional theories of circumcision have en-
joyed similar empirical support.

Menarcheal Ceremonies

Menarcheal ceremonies, unlike male circumcision, have not
produced an abundant theoretical and research literature. Ceremonies associated with sexual maturity in women are usually referred
to as puberty rites and with few exceptions are interpreted as transition rites according to van Gennep's original scheme. There are,
however, important case studies of menarcheal ceremonies in single
societies that illustrate orthodox psychoanalytic and structural-
functional approaches. Like male circumcision, menarcheal ceremonies have been explained by psychoanalytic thinkers as behavioral
expressions of psychodynamic conflicts, by transition-rite theorists as
mechanisms for initiating individuals into adulthood, and by
structural-functional theorists as symbolic indicators of structural
cleavages in a society.

Psychoanalytic Theories

Two different theories to explain menarcheal ceremonies have
been proposed by orthodox psychoanalytic thinkers. The first focuses
on the psychological conflicts that menarche arouses in women by

42. M. R. Allen, *Male Cults and Secret Initiations in Melanesia* (Victoria: Melbourne
University Press, 1967), p. 121.
43. See Marvin Harris, *The Rise of Anthropological Theory: A History of Theories of
Culture* (New York: Crowell, 1968), pp. 449–63.

modifying and extending Freud's original thesis about the origin of men's fears of deflowering a virgin. While Freud himself never specifically addressed the psychodynamic implications of menarche, he did claim that a woman's sexual initiation released powerful pre-Oedipal aggressive impulses toward the man who robbed her of her virginity.[44] Later psychoanalytic thinkers have suggested that such impulses are first aroused by the onset of menstruation rather than by sexual initiation. According to these writers, genital bleeding at menarche is interpreted as a narcissistic injury: it revives pre-Oedipal fantasies of having been robbed of a penis[45] and, consequently, arouses anger and resentment toward men. The menarcheal seclusion, social segregation, and personal taboos that are important aspects of many menarcheal ceremonies are social control mechanisms to hold women's unconscious aggressive impulses in check.[46]

The second theory focuses on psychological conflicts that menarche arouses in men. According to this explanation, men desire a virginal menstruating woman but fear castration by her jealous father.[47] Menarcheal ceremonies are a mechanism for relieving men's unconscious anxieties about castration.[48] The most impressive application of this latter theory is Kathleen Gough's analysis of tali-tying rites among the Nayar and Tiyyar castes on the Malabar Coast of southern India.[49] Until the late nineteenth century young girls participated in a mock menarcheal-cum-marriage ceremony just before menarche. During this elaborate ritual they were secluded for three or four days as if they were actually experiencing menarche, then publicly "married" to a male, or symbol of a male, who represented the ideal future husband from the appropriate caste. This rite was not an actual marriage ceremony, and the person or object serving as the "ritual husband" in the ceremony was not recognized as the woman's legal future husband. Gough proposes that these ceremonies were a consequence of unusually intense Oedipal conflicts produced by

44. Sigmund Freud, *Sexuality and the Psychology of Love* (New York: Collier, 1963), pp. 70–86.

45. Helene Deutsch, *Psychology of Women, Vol. I: Girlhood* (New York: Grune and Stratton, 1944), pp. 149–84.

46. Marie Bonaparte, *Female Sexuality*, tr. John Rodker (New York: International Universities Press, 1953), pp. 191–208; and C. D. Daly, "The Psycho-Biological Origins of Circumcision," *International Journal of Psychoanalysis* 31 (1950): 217–36.

47. William Stephens, "A Cross-Cultural Study of Menstrual Taboos," *Genetic Psychology Monographs* 64 (November 1961): 385–416; and Deutsch, *Psychology of Women*, pp. 149–84.

48. Sybille Yates, "An Investigation of the Psychological Factors in Virginity and Ritual Defloration," *International Journal of Psychoanalysis* 31 (1950): 167–84.

49. Kathleen E. Gough, "Female Initiation Rites on the Malabar Coast," *Journal of the Royal Anthropological Institute* 85 (1955): 45–80; Gough bases much of her analysis on the theories of Ernest Jones, *On the Nightmare* (London: International Psycho-Analytic Library, No. 20, 1931), and Melanie Klein, *The Psycho-Analysis of Children*, trans. A. Stachey (London: International Psycho-Analytic Library, No. 22, 1932).

economic and political conditions in the region during the nineteenth century, particularly the elder males' immense political authority and personal control over communal property and lineage activities. She contends that this monopoly of power and wealth made younger males feel particularly intense fears of castration by their elder kinsmen and correspondingly strong incestuous desires toward their mothers. The appearance of mature sexuality in the young virgin women of the lineage aroused these unconscious conflicts because of the association between a virgin woman and one's own mother. In order to keep these Oedipal desires in check, the men of these castes publicly relinquished sexual rights to their sisters and daughters before menarche, that is, before incestuous seduction was likely to occur. Their ambivalence about relinquishing control over their kinswomen to another male is evidenced by the fact that only sexual rights were ritually renounced. Some degree of authority over a woman and her future offspring was retained either through adherence to matrilineal rights of social paternity to her offspring, as among the Nayar and northern Tiyyar, or by the custom of polyandrous marriage, as among the southern Tiyyar.

When cash wages and personal property replaced communal lineage ownership during the twentieth century, the authority of the gerontocracy collapsed, and tali-tying rites were simultaneously eliminated. According to Gough, the elimination of the communal property system strengthened men's bonds to their wives and weakened their bonds to their mothers and sisters, thereby removing the need for ritual expressions of Oedipal conflicts.

Transition-Rite Theories

Van Gennep's *rites de passage* theory remains the most widely accepted explanation of female puberty ceremonies. His interpretation of these ceremonies as mechanisms to initiate women into adulthood has provided the basis for most current cross-cultural research, especially comparative research on socialization practices.[50] Van Gennep insisted on a distinction between ceremonies associated with the attainment of biological maturity and those associated with social

---

50. In *Patterns of Culture* (Boston: Houghton Mifflin, 1959), pp. 24–30, Ruth Benedict sets out clearly the main theme of later research: the overriding importance of cultural values in determining the criteria used to admit women and men into adult status. She emphasized that "in order to understand puberty institutions [we need to know] . . . what adulthood means in that culture, not biological puberty." She does recognize that female puberty rites tend to coincide with menarche. But she argues that since menarcheal rituals do not occur in all societies, they cannot be a direct consequence of the biological event itself. She suggests that menarcheal rituals probably celebrate social distinctions such as marriageability that are connected with sexual maturity but does not examine this hypothesis in detail in her analysis.

puberty, which theoretically could take place at any time between childhood and marriage depending on the specific ages a society used to distinguish adulthood from childhood. Menarcheal ceremonies, he argued, were merely ritual responses to the first appearance of an event; only ceremonies intended to announce a woman's social, not biological, maturity constituted true female *rites de passage*. Since ethnographic data collected subsequent to van Gennep's formulation have shown that, in fact, most puberty ceremonies for women do coincide with the onset of menstruation, current researchers no longer emphasize the distinction between menarcheal ceremonies and "true" puberty rites. Recent empirical studies group menarcheal ceremonies with other puberty ceremonies and often view menarche merely as a convenient benchmark to indicate a woman's readiness to enter social adulthood rather than as a central focus of puberty ceremonies. The main focus of research has been to modify van Gennep's theory to account for the fact that female puberty ceremonies are by no means universal. Empirical research has been aimed primarily at specifying the social characteristics that best predict cross-cultural variations in female puberty practices. Little effort has been made to explain why the onset of menstruation is usually the focus of the ceremony.

Judith K. Brown's survey of female initiation rites probably best illustrates the van Gennep perspective. She accepts his theory that puberty ceremonies are mechanisms to initiate women into adulthood, but proposes that such a dramatic transition is necessary only among societies in which a woman lives her adult life among the same people with whom she has lived as a child.[51] When a woman leaves her natal community after marriage to live in her husband's community, the move itself designates her change of status, making a special ritual announcement unnecessary. In Brown's study, a puberty rite is defined broadly as "a ceremonial event which is mandatory for all girls in a society which takes place any time between the years of eight and twenty";[52] the study excludes betrothal and marriage ceremonies and menarcheal rites that are the same as rites at subsequent menses. The results of her survey showed that ceremonies during this age period were significantly more likely to occur among societies with matrilocal or bilocal residence patterns than among societies with patrilocal or neolocal residence patterns. Since the majority of women in matrilocal and bilocal societies remain in one community throughout their lives, the greater incidence of puberty ceremonies in

51. Judith K. Brown, "A Cross-Cultural Study of Female Initiation Rites," *American Anthropologist* 65 (1963): 837–53.
52. Ibid., p. 838.

these societies confirms Brown's hypothesis. The relationship between the two residence clusters and the presence or absence of puberty ceremonies is strong and statistically significant.

Brown's study has stimulated a series of challenges and rebuttals, focused not so much on her theory of female puberty rites as on
her use of the cross-cultural survey method of data collection. Controversy continues to rage over this method's validity, particularly its
challenge to cultural diffusion theories of social customs.[53] Harold
Driver has compiled a detailed description of the specific ritual elements found in female puberty rites in western North America in an
effort to trace the process by which these elements might have dif-
fused historically.[54] The most widely distributed ritual elements (such
as ritual seclusion, food and work taboos, and avoidance of men) he
considers historically older, probably brought to North America by
the first migrants from Asia. Later immigrants picked up, or "bor-
rowed," these traits as they came into contact with the older residents. Drawing on these data, and also on data he collected on North
American residence patterns, Driver argues that female puberty rites
cannot be a consequence of residence, as proposed by Brown. Of the
198 groups in his own sample of one world region, he finds that *all*
practice puberty rites as defined by Brown. Only among the societies
in northern California and the Athabaskan Southwest is there a statistical relationship between matrilocal residence and ritual as Brown
would predict. But even among these societies, Driver argues, a functional relationship between residence and rites is unlikely since the
rites *preceded* the adoption of matrilocal residence. He cites historical
and archeological data to show that these peoples brought their rites
with them during their migration from the north and that matrilocal
residence, at least among the Apacheans, was acquired *after* contact
with matrilocal groups already living in the Southwest.[55] Morris
Opler, the noted authority on the Apacheans, has challenged Driver's

---

53. Driver's challenges and Brown's rebuttals begin with Harold Driver, "Girls'
Puberty Rites and Matrilocal Residence," *American Anthropologist* 71 (1969): 905–08,
which contains his major criticisms of the functional theory of ritual. Brown replies in
"Girls' Puberty Rites: A Reply to Driver," *American Anthropologist* 72 (1970): 1450–51.
This is followed by a remark about Brown's analysis of "painful" rites in Driver's
"Brown and Driver on Girls' Puberty Rites Again," *American Anthropologist* 73 (1971):
1261–62, and Brown's rejoinder, "Initiation Rites for Girls: A Further Reply," *American
Anthropologist* 73 (1971): 1262–63. See also Morris Opler, "Cause and Effect in Apachean
Agriculture, Division of Labor, Residence Patterns, and Girls' Puberty Rites," *American
Anthropologist* 74 (1972): 1133–46; and Harold Driver, "Reply to Opler on Apachean
Subsistence, Residence, and Girls' Puberty Rites," *American Anthropologist* 74 (1972):
1147–51.

54. Harold Driver, "Girls' Puberty Rites in Western North America," *University
of California Anthropological Records* 6 (1941): 21–90.

55. Ibid.

interpretation of Athabaskan puberty rites and matrilocality,[56] and since then the diffusionist debate over Brown's hypothesis has died down (though the general controversy surrounding cultural diffusion theories continues).

Frank Young provides another interpretation of female puberty ceremonies within the theoretical framework proposed by van Gennep. He describes them as "sex role dramatization" rites because, he says, they teach women how to assume a role in female work groups.[57] Young proposes that the most important determinant of female initiation rites is the degree of female solidarity within the household unit. He hypothesizes that rites are more likely to occur in societies in which women must learn to cooperate within a group of all-female workers. Female solidarity is measured by an interaction variable purported to measure the presence of a "crystallized group image" among women workers: the presence of cooperative female work groups within the domestic unit, or the presence of a barrier around the domestic quarters (to indicate "institutional household unity"), or both. Although Young's interpretation of female puberty rites is not flawed by tautological reasoning like his interpretation of male initiation rites, it remains unvalidated: there is no significant statistical relationship between his measures of female solidarity and puberty practices.[58]

Structural-Functional Theories

Structural-functional analyses of menarcheal ceremonies are best illustrated by two well-known case studies of individual puberty ceremonies in two different world regions. Both theorists, Nur Yalmon and Audrey Richards, attempt to demonstrate how structural characteristics of social groups, namely lineage and caste structure, create social tensions concerning a daughter's mate choice and thereby have political implications for social solidarity. Menarcheal ceremonies are viewed as symbols of structural cleavage.

Kathleen Gough's psychoanalytic analysis of tali-tying rites has been challenged by Yalmon, whose structural-functional analysis of

56. Opler, who is a noted authority on the region Driver uses to support his arguments on matrilocal residence and puberty rites, criticizes some of Driver's generalizations about ritual practices, economy, and social evolution in the region—particularly his assertions about the acquisition of matrilocal residence after arriving in the region and the dominance of female puberty rites; see Opler's "Agriculture, Labor, Residence, Rites," pp. 1133–46.

57. Young, *Initiation Ceremonies.*

58. When the statistical calculation is carried out to judge the probability that there is a proportional difference in rites between societies with high female solidarity and societies with low female solidarity, it yields a weak association, p less than .10; see Young, *Initiation Ceremonies*, Table 25, p. 110.

these rites in southern India and Ceylon (Sri Lanka) suggests two alternative explanations.[59] He argues, first, that in the castes discussed by Gough the rites may be a mechanism for legitimizing a woman's future offspring as members of the matrilineal clans. While matrilineal descent is a more important organizing principle among the Nayar than the Tiyyar castes, Yalmon points out the existence of dispersed matrilineal clans among the Tiyyar as well. In this region, then, rites could serve to dramatize matrilineal claims to a woman's future offspring. Second, after noting the similarity of Nayar and Tiyyar rites to certain rites performed by the bilateral Kandyan Sinhalese of Ceylon, Yalmon suggests that tali-tying rites may also reflect anxiety about the future caste status of spouses and offspring. In both southern India and Ceylon, lineage and caste may co-exist, but social status depends much more on the caste status of one's parents than on their lineage status. Status is determined by the caste status of both parents, and since it is essential that one's father have equal or higher status than one's mother, there is a rigid prohibition against hypogamy. Yalmon hypothesizes that it is the intense concern with preserving "caste purity" that prevents a woman from marrying or even coming into social contact with a lower-caste male. If a woman has sexual contact with a lower-caste male, not only she and her future offspring but her entire caste will be polluted. To guard against this risk, a public announcement of the woman's intentions to marry a man of the correct caste is made, in the form of the tali-tying rites, just before she becomes sexually mature and thus before seduction and pregnancy are real possibilities.

Audrey Richards' study of the matrilineal Bemba of Central Africa also proposes a connection between menarcheal ceremonies and the preservation of familial ascriptive status.[60] In the case of the Bemba, however, concern is focused on securing an offspring's affiliation to its mother's lineage rather than on maintaining caste purity by ensuring an appropriate father for her offspring. Richards argues that both the elaborate Bemba puberty ceremony, called the *chisungu*, and concern about attaching a kinswoman's future offspring to its mother's lineage are consequences of the so-called matrilineal puzzle: the inevitable conflict that the marriage of daughters produces in a matrilineal social system.[61] In such systems a daughter's marriage produces the problem of how to persuade the husband to establish

59. Nur Yalmon, "On the Purity of Women in the Castes of Ceylon and Malabar," *Journal of the Royal Anthropological Institute* 93 (1963): 25–58.

60. Audrey I. Richards, *Chisungu* (New York: Grove Press, 1956).

61. Audrey I. Richards, *African Systems of Kinship and Marriage*, ed. A. R. Radcliffe-Brown and C. D. Forde (London: Oxford University Press, 1950), pp. 207–51.

his household matrilocally under the authority of her kinsmen while at the same time denying him jural authority over his own children. Since the Bemba are too poor to offer large economic inducements to a husband to remain in the wife's natal village, there is a real likelihood that after the marriage is consummated he will remove her and her future offspring to his own community. Richards describes how the sequence of events and symbolic structure of the *chisungu* demonstrate both the kinsmen's concern about persuading the husband of the advantages of living in their village and, even more importantly, the woman's attainment of the ability to produce offspring for the lineage. The *chisungu*'s ritual attempt to dramatize lineage claims to a woman's future offspring is reflected in the timing of the rite within the long marriage process. A woman's future husband has already been given both sexual and domestic rights during the time of his groom service. The relationship is not considered a legitimate marriage, however, until the *chisungu* is completed. Once a woman begins to menstruate, she leaves her husband's quarters and begins preparing for the month-long ceremony. Her husband is not permitted access to her again until completion of the ceremony, when he consummates the marriage in public. This sequence, Richards says, shows that a husband is not permitted to have access to a *fertile* woman until after her fertility and lineage claims to any offspring produced have been publicly dramatized. Before menarche, of course, sex relations could not produce offspring at all, so ambiguous lineage status is not a problem. Richards supports the connection between puberty rites and the problem of marriage in matrilineal descent systems, at least in Africa, by documenting similar ceremonies in other Bantu matrilineal societies and the absence of such rites in patrilineal societies.

Menstrual Pollution and Sex Segregation Practices

Psychoanalytic theories of menstrual practices, like psychoanalytic theories of menarche, focus on the psychological responses to menstrual bleeding and the psychodynamic causes of menstrual ritual practices. Theorists within the structural-functional tradition, in contrast, view menstrual practices as expressions of a more general sex antagonism and frequently group them with a larger complex of customs emphasizing the polluting quality of female sexuality and restricting men's interaction with women not only during menstruation but throughout women's reproductive span. There has been no attempt to explain menstrual practices within the transition-rite framework, perhaps because van Gennep did not consider them "true" rites, that is, rites that aid in social role transitions, despite the empirical similarities between menstrual practices of some societies (such as entry into seclusion and purification upon emergence) and other so-called transition rites.

Psychoanalytic Theories

Psychoanalytic theories of ritual practices associated with menstruation extend the concepts already discussed in connection with menarche. Again, one school of thought focuses on psychological conflicts that menstruation arouses in women. Menstrual bleeding is held to represent a loss of body control, mutilation, loss of a penis, and the sadistic aspects of sexuality, and to arouse intense conflicting emotions, both passive (shame and disappointment) and active (anger and resentment toward men and toward the mother, who is held responsible for the woman's lack of a penis). Menstrual social restrictions are thus interpreted as realistic mechanisms for protecting others from the menstruating woman's infantile aggressive impulses.

The other, more orthodox, psychoanalytic interpretation emphasizes male rather than female psychodynamics. It argues that female sexuality, particularly menstruation, continues to arouse intense ambivalence in men throughout their adult lives. The absence of menstrual theories in Freud's own work has not prevented later analysts from including the role of menstrual bleeding in modified explanations of the male Oedipus complex.[62] These explanations require an acceptance of an even more elaborate fantasy life and complex psychodynamics on the part of men than are described in Freud's classic Oedipal model. They say, first, that men equate menstrual bleeding both with bleeding of their own genitalia after paternal castration and with the aggressive assault upon the mother that parental coitus represents to children. Second, men have a fantasy, well known in clinical research and appearing in numerous myths and folktales, that a woman's vagina contains teeth that will bite off the penis during coitus.[63] Thus, they also fear castration by women. Male fears of paternal castration and castration by women have sometimes been linked to the fantasy of the "phallic mother": the infantile belief that after intercourse the mother still has the father's penis inside her so that if the son were to act on his incestuous desires, his father's penis might attack him during coitus.[64]

62. C. D. Daly, "The Psycho-Biological Origins of Circumcision," *International Journal of Psychoanalysis* 31 (1950): 15–236; and C. D. Daly, "Der Menstruation Komplex," *Imago* 14 (1928): 11–75; Yates, "Ritual Defloration"; and Róheim, *Eternal Ones*.

63. Wolfgang Lederer, *The Fear of Women* (New York: Harcourt Brace Jovanovich, 1968), pp. 44–52; Robert Murphy, "Social Structure and Sex Antagonism," *Southwestern Journal of Anthropology* 15 (Spring 1959): 95; and Morris Opler, *An Apache Life-Way* (Chicago: University of Chicago Press, 1941), p. 81.

64. Yates, "Ritual Defloration," and Gough, "Female Initiation Rites."

Psychoanalytic theories of male responses to menstruation, then, argue for multiple castrators: the father, the phallic mother, and women in general. To reduce their anxiety, men must take the drastic protective measure of isolating menstruating women.

The classic castration anxiety theory of menstrual restrictions requires only fear of castration by the father. This formulation has been tested empirically by one of Whiting's students, William Stephens, who proposes that the childrearing practices producing the most severe Oedipal conflicts in males should also produce the most severe menstrual restrictions.[65] The severity of menstrual restrictions was measured by a four-item scale ranging from sex taboos (low) to menstrual huts (high). Stephens analyzed childrearing conditions producing variations in the severity of Oedipal conflicts and castration anxiety and also noted the frequency of genital injury and general physical injury themes in the societies' folktales. Of the ten childrearing variables measured, four were significantly associated with the severity of menstrual restrictions: length of the postpartum sex taboo, father as main disciplinarian, punishment for masturbation, and severity of sex training. Thus, severity of menstrual restrictions was strongly associated with only one important empirical indicator of Oedipal conflicts and castration anxiety from Whiting's model, the postpartum sex taboo. Menstrual restrictions did not correlate with polygyny or male initiation rites, two of Whiting's other critical preconditions. If male initiation rites and menstrual taboos are consequences of the same childrearing conditions, then practices predicting male initiation in Whiting's studies should also predict menstrual taboos. Stephens does not account for this inconsistency. Moreover, if male initiation and menstrual taboos both represent castration anxiety, they should be strongly associated with each other. Stephens does not examine this possibility; nor does he test an association between menstrual taboos and the most direct measure of castration anxiety, circumcision.

A third psychoanalytic theme considers menstrual fears and social restrictions as stemming from taboos associated with bodily discharges generally. According to the so-called cloacal theory of menstruation, menstrual bleeding arouses associations between infantile theories of childbirth through the anal opening and the feces as a phallic symbol.[66] Men fear menstruating women because of their unconscious anxiety that the penis in intercourse will be held responsible for robbing the woman of blood, baby, and feces. In his survey of

65. William Stephens, "A Cross-Cultural Study of Menstrual Taboos," *Genetic Psychology Monographs* 64 (1961): 388–416.

66. Deutsch, *Psychology of Women;* Klein, *Psycho-Analysis of Children;* and Karen Horney, *Feminine Psychology* (New York: W. W. Norton, 1967).

reproductive practices, Clellan Ford attempted to support the cloacal theory by asserting that menstrual restrictions and abhorrence are less severe in societies in which women use menstrual pads to prevent the flow from becoming public.[67] This assertion is not supported by his data: of the nineteen societies in which women used some method of hiding menstrual bleeding, seven (37 percent) permitted "freedom of activity" during the menses while the majority (63 percent) practiced menstrual restrictions.

Bettelheim has applied his womb envy theory of male genital mutilations without modification to emotional and behavioral responses to menstruation.[68] Relying heavily on George Devereux's analysis of Mohave menstrual beliefs and customs,[69] Bettelheim argues that menstrual practices worldwide are based on veneration rather than fear of a woman's reproductive capacity. For Bettelheim, men's attempts to make their own genitalia bleed are critical evidence in support of his thesis. But since self-inflicted genital mutilations to create menstrual-like bleeding are exceptional in world societies, they do not explain the widespread belief in female pollution, horror of menstrual blood, and social avoidance practices of men as well as women. It is difficult to accept the notion that such beliefs and practices derive from veneration, or womb envy, as Bettelheim argues.

Structural-Functional Theories

Researchers and theorists within the structural-functional tradition have interpreted menstrual practices as expressions of a basic sexual antagonism resulting from exogamous marriage, either directly or indirectly through exogamous marriage's effects on male solidarity, community solidarity, and male dominance over women. This view challenges Freud's basic model of the development of social institutions which proposed that exogamous marriage, totemism, and incest prohibitions were all a consequence of Oedipal conflicts, particularly fear of paternal castration and guilt about aggressive fantasies of killing and eating the powerful father. Durkheim's speculation about incest and exogamy, which preceded Freud's own theory, reverses the Freudian causal chain.[70] Durkheim suggested that incest prohibitions were a consequence rather than a cause of exogamy. He considered men's fear of women and menstrual blood to be central to the development of social solidarity of the clan, totemism, and exogamous marriage practices. He claimed that members of "primi-

---

67. Clellan Ford, *A Comparative Study of Human Reproduction* (New Haven: HRAF Press, 1964), pp. 18–19.
68. Bettelheim, *Symbolic Wounds.*
69. George Devereux, "The Psychology of Feminine Genital Bleeding," *International Journal of Psychoanalysis* 31, part 4 (1950): 237–57.
70. Emile Durkheim, *Incest: The Nature and Origin of the Taboo* (New York: Lyle Stuart, 1963; originally published in 1898).

tive" clan societies believe literally that they share the same blood and that their identity as a social unit is endangered if any of that blood is spilled by one of their members. Since kinswomen spill blood periodically, they are particularly threatening to clan solidarity and to each of the individual clan brothers. For Durkheim, the fear of contacting menstrual blood because of its equation with spilled clan blood is the major source of sexual antagonism.[71] Menstruation's connection with sexuality further intensifies the "type of repulsion that the two sexes have for one another,"[72] leading men to marry women who possess the blood of another clan which is not dangerous.

Claude Lévi-Strauss has criticized Durkheim's analysis on two points.[73] First, he asserts that while incest taboos and exogamy are widespread, menstrual prohibitions are not and that the role of menstrual blood in the analysis of incest and exogamy must, therefore, be questioned. Here he not only underestimates the prevalence of menstrual taboos but uses examples that contradict or refute some of his criticism. For instance, he speaks of Winnebago youths breaking menstrual restrictions by visiting their lovers in menstrual huts but fails to mention that such violations are considered extremely dangerous and likely to lead to violent consequences.[74] He also suggests that the in-marrying women of the patrilineal Chagga, who of course are not clan members, are more threatened by their daughters' menstruation than are the clan members themselves. The quote he uses to support his criticism, however, is quite explicit on the danger of menstrual blood to Chagga men. While Chagga say, "Do not show it to your mother, for she would die!"[75] they also say, as the quotation continues, "Protect the blood from the gaze of your father, brothers, and sisters. It is a sin to let them see it."[76] Lévi-Strauss's second criticism—that a woman's menstrual blood is as dangerous to her husband as to members of her own clan—is more crucial to Durkheim's theory and less easy to refute. It is well known that husbands, and men in general regardless of their clan membership, are endangered by menstrual blood. The fear of kinswomen's menstrual blood, then, cannot be a cause of exogamy as Durkheim theorizes. Lévi-Strauss does not, however, offer an alternate explanation of menstruation fears and rituals.

Recent theory and research have modified Durkheim's theory in an attempt to explain cross-cultural variations in intensity of

71. Ibid., p. 85.
72. Ibid.
73. Claude Lévi-Strauss, *The Elementary Structures of Kinship* (Boston: Beacon Press, 1969).
74. Paul Radin, *The Winnebago Tribe* (Lincoln: University of Nebraska Press, 1923), pp. 88–90.
75. Lévi-Strauss, *Elementary Structures*, p. 21.
76. Ibid., p. 22.

menstrual pollution practices by examining structural causes of broader sexual antagonism. On the basis of his observations of the Mae-Enga and other patrilineal societies in the New Guinea Highlands, M. J. Meggitt has proposed a causal relationship between the practice of marrying women from enemy kin groups and an aggravated fear of women.[77] In these societies, marriages customarily take place between hostile, feuding kin groups so that in-marrying women are enemies as well as spouses. This situation not only produces an intense fear of female pollution, especially menstrual pollution, but also leads to the practice of almost total structural segregation of the sexes and to the development of men's cults whose purported aim is to strengthen men's resistance to contamination by in-marrying wives. During menstruation women are referred to as "she with the evil eye"[78] and are segregated in menstrual huts or in a special part of their own houses. Wives are especially polluting during menstruation, but they are also considered dangerous any time they approach men. Men even fear touching their skirts since these are thought to be polluted through their contact with the female genitals. Copulation is always dangerous and is supposed to take place only often enough to produce children. Mae-Enga bachelors prepare for the inevitable threat of marital contamination through a special dramatic ceremony just before marriage, and both bachelors and married men all sleep together in a men's house apart from women. Meggitt summarizes his main hypothesis as follows: "We might expect . . . to find the notion of feminine pollution emphasized in societies where affinal groups are seen . . . as inimical to one's own groups, but absent or of little significance where marriages usually occur between friendly groups."[79]

In his study of Melanesian cults and initiation rites, M. R. Allen proposes that a pollution ideology and sex segregation practices and associations should occur not only in the patrilineal societies described by Meggitt but in any society in which unilineal descent is combined with unilocal residence.[80] In both matrilineal-matrilocal and patrilineal-patrilocal societies there is a local core of consanguines who marry members of outside kin groups. Whether the local core of consanguines is female or male, choosing spouses from other communities should be associated with pollution beliefs and segregation

77. M. J. Meggitt, "Male-Female Relationships in the Highlands of Australian New Guinea," in *Cultures of the Pacific,* ed. Thomas G. Harding and Ben J. Wallace (New York: Free Press, 1970), pp. 125–43.

78. Ibid., p. 129.

79. Ibid., p. 140.

80. M. R. Allen, *Male Cults and Secret Initiations in Melanesia* (Victoria: Melbourne University Press, 1967).

practices. Allen attempts to support his theory through descriptions of Melanesian societies with either type of descent-residence combination, but he does not present a systematic analysis of how unilineal-unilocal groups differ in the degree of sexual antagonism and segregation practices from nonunilineal or nonunilocal groups.

The Mundurucu of Brazil are an exception to both Meggitt's and Allen's hypotheses: they have the unusual combination of patrilineal descent and matrilocal residence and do not engage in feuds with affines, but they demonstrate intense sexual antagonism and fear of women's pollution. All males over thirteen years of age live in exclusive men's houses. In these houses are kept sacred musical instruments which are continuously guarded so that women will not see or touch them. Any woman caught spying on the sacred instruments is gang-raped. Men are cold and aloof toward their wives and jokingly speak of using sex to dominate women. Robert Murphy proposes that structural sexual segregation and fear of women among the Mundurucu are mechanisms by which men preserve their dominance over women while still maintaining sex-based solidary work groups.[81] Murphy agrees with Meggitt and Allen that sex segregation and antagonism are consequences of exogamous marriage customs, unilineal descent, and unilocal residence but contends that they are more directly related to economic structure. The division of labor among the Mundurucu is based solely on sex, but daily cooperation between men and women is also required. Since a sexual division of labor creates female groups that are potentially as solidary as male groups, the ideology of sexual antagonism and structural segregation is a useful way of maintaining male dominance. Murphy recognizes that the simplest band societies typically have a division of labor based solely on sex but are less directly antagonistic toward women. He suggests that hostility toward women is less intense in these simplest societies because the work units are not in daily cooperative contact.

Mary Douglas' analysis of the symbolic structure of social systems offers an additional interpretation of female pollution beliefs and practices.[82] According to her theory, pollution beliefs are used to regulate social relations; thus, an analysis of the patterns and significance of these beliefs reveals the underlying tensions in a society. Douglas, like Murphy, contends that when pollution beliefs are applied to women, they can be used to "bind men and women to their allotted roles."[83] According to Douglas, pollution beliefs and sexual antagonism should be most pronounced in what she calls "strictly ar-

81. Robert F. Murphy, "Social Structure and Sex Antagonism," *Southwestern Journal of Anthropology* 15 (1959): 95.
82. Mary Douglas, *Purity and Danger* (London: Pelican, 1966), pp. 166–87.
83. Ibid., p. 167.

ticulated"[84] social systems: those in which a husband's ability to dominate and control his wife conflicts with other equally important needs such as the need to acquire wealth and prestige. This conflict is strongest in systems in which women are important sources of currency between men since women can use this to their advantage, playing men off against each other. Douglas illustrates the conflict by describing the importance of women, wealth, and dominance among the Mae-Enga, Lele, and Yurok, all groups with well-articulated pollution beliefs and elaborate menstrual restrictions.

Douglas argues that pollution beliefs and sexual antagonism should be less important under two different conditions, either of which eliminates the conflict between male dominance and the acquisition of wealth through wives. First, she agrees with Murphy that pollution beliefs should be less pronounced in the simplest societies, those in which a husband's dominance over his wife is complete and undisputed. The Australian Walbiri are used to illustrate the first condition: any woman who deviates from the normative pattern of sex role behavior is punished with direct physical force. Since sexual behavior cannot undermine other aspects of the social system that rely on marriage relations, pollution practices are unnecessary. The Nuer are used to illustrate the second condition, in which strictly enforced lineage principles determine mate choice and paternity, thereby reducing the contradiction between a husband's dominance over his wife and his acquisition of power and wealth. Nuer husbands and wives may never even live together, and if the wife commits adultery, her husband's dispute with her seducer is commonly settled through a fine rather than death or banishment. Although Nuer husbands do not sleep with their menstruating wives, menstruating women are not segregated and female sexuality is not viewed as particularly dangerous to men. Douglas does not attempt to link these two conditions to such antecedent structural characteristics as residence, descent, or division of labor, as do Meggitt, Allen, and Murphy. Nevertheless, she describes tensions producing pollution beliefs and antagonism and two conditions under which they should be reduced. She summarizes her hypotheses as follows: "When . . . dominance is accepted as a central principle of social organization and applied without inhibition and with full rights of physical coercion, beliefs in sex pollution are not likely to be highly developed."[85]

Two cross-cultural surveys have examined the empirical association between pollution practices and sex antagonism proposed by the Meggitt, Allen, and Douglas theories. Alice Schlegal has examined

---

84. Ibid.
85. Ibid., pp. 168–69.

the relationship between patterns of male authority and menstrual restrictions in a sample of matrilineal societies; Frank Young and Albert Bacdayan have tested a causal association between social rigidity, male dominance, and menstrual taboos.

Schlegal proposes that in matrilineal societies, the greater the dominance of husbands and brothers the lesser the autonomy and social status of women. One of her measures of female status is the severity of menstrual restrictions.[86] She therefore proposes that menstrual restrictions should be less elaborate in societies in which neither husbands nor brothers are dominant. Schlegal's measure of male dominance in matrilineal societies is the type of marriage preferred: matrilateral cross-cousin marriage indicates that husbands are more dominant over women than brothers; patrilateral cross-cousin marriage indicates that brothers are more dominant over women than husbands; and mixed or random marriage preferences indicate that neither husbands nor brothers are dominant.[87] Schlegal's analysis shows significant associations between types of cousin marriage and other measures of husband versus brother dominance over women (such as divorce rates, whether or not brothers disrupt sisters' marriages, and control over children), suggesting that cousin marriage may in fact be a valid index of types of male dominance in matrilineal societies. She finds no statistically significant relationships, however, between preferred marriage type and her main measures of female autonomy (polygyny, sexual restriction, menstrual restriction, and avoidance patterns). She concludes, "We can safely put to rest the hoary notion that menstrual restrictions indicate low female status, or any status position whatsoever."[88] Reexamination of her raw data on the distribution of menstrual restrictions across the three types of dominance suggests that this conclusion may be unwarranted. When menstrual restrictions are dichotomized into presence or absence of husband dominance, matrilineal societies with husband dominance are only half as likely (26.3 percent) to seclude menstruating women as are societies in which husbands are not dominant (52 percent). The proportional distribution of menstrual restrictions across these two dominance patterns could not have occurred by chance ($p<.06$). This reanalysis supports Douglas' theory, which argues that pollution beliefs should be least pronounced when husbands' dominance over women is complete and undisputed.

The main goal of Young and Bacdayan's study is to challenge the neo-Freudian Whiting model by reexamining Stephens' castration

86. Alice Schlegal, *Male Dominance and Female Autonomy* (New Haven: HRAF Press, 1972).
87. Ibid., pp. 10, 13.
88. Ibid., p. 93.

anxiety theory about menstrual taboos. As in their argument pertaining to male initiation rites, they propose that such taboos can be better accounted for by a "social rigidity" explanation.[89] That is, the less solidary a social group, the more likely it is to manifest male dominance and menstrual restrictions. This causal model, like their model for male initiation rites, is tautological, as the inclusion of a male solidarity measure in the construction of measures of social rigidity and male dominance demonstrates. Young and Bacdayan admit the tautology of their argument but assert that it is still preferable to a castration anxiety theory which does not consider structural causes: "The rigidity interpretation asserts a tautology and leaves it at that. The castration anxiety hypothesis asserts the more difficult link between a cultural pattern and a dimension of the personality system."[90] Despite Young and Bacdayan's methodological and logical shortcomings, their statistical data correlate the severity of menstrual restrictions with community exogamy, secret societies, and men's houses—a result predicted by Meggitt and other structural theorists.

From the many theories of menstrual pollution and sexual antagonism there emerge two general approaches that can be tested empirically. Stephens' castration anxiety hypothesis suggests that sexual antagonism in the form of menstrual restrictions should be correlated not only with the cluster of castration anxiety measures developed by Whiting but also with the most significant indicator of castration fear, circumcision. Structural theories propose that pollution practices should be associated with exogamous marriage practices, particularly when marriages take place between hostile groups: with unilineal descent and unilocal residence regardless of the sex of the core local lineage group; or with sexual division of labor, especially when male and female groups must work cooperatively on a daily basis.

Birth Practices: Couvade and Maternal Restrictions

Most of the literature on rituals associated with pregnancy and birth has been devoted to the male practice of couvade rather than the variety of maternal restrictions even though couvade is far less common. Although transition-rite theories and psychoanalytic theories within the Whiting tradition interpret certain maternal restrictions as ritual, they have usually interpreted maternal restrictions as measures to protect the health of the mother and child. Couvade has been interpreted either as a "protective rite" or as a manifestation of Oedipal conflicts, womb envy, or cross-sex identity. It has also been the focus

---

89. Frank Young and Albert Bacdayan, "Menstrual Taboos and Social Rigidity," *Ethnology* 4 (April 1965): 225–40.
90. Ibid., p. 237.

for debate about the function of rituals in general, and during the nineteenth century it was used to demonstrate the validity of theories about the evolution of social institutions.

Psychoanalytic Theories

Most psychoanalytic speculation and research on birth practices have focused on couvade, though attempts have been made to explain aspects of the widespread customs pertaining to women, particularly food and sex taboos. Psychoanalysts have offered two major explanations of couvade. Reik, basing his interpretations to a large extent on Freud's theory of taboo and the ambivalence of emotions outlined in *Totem and Taboo*,[91] says that male observance of food taboos and seclusion are rituals used to repress unconscious aggressive impulses toward both mother and child.[92] Imitations of labor and post-delivery recuperation are attempts to force the newborn to fixate on the father instead of the mother, thereby preventing it from developing incestuous desires for her. The husband in his unconscious fantasies also equates the newborn with his own feared authoritarian father. Paternal fasting is an attempt to suppress the urge to devour the child and an expiation for being guilty of this urge. Reik adds that although the newborn represents the husband's father, it simultaneously represents the husband's victory over fears of castration by his father as punishment for Oedipal desires.

Bettelheim suggests that couvade, like circumcision and practices associated with female genital bleeding, reflects men's unconscious desire to actualize the feminine aspects of their bisexual nature.[93] Simulated childbirth by men emphasizes men's contribution to childbearing and minimizes women's contribution. It represents an extreme form of empathy in which the husband identifies so closely with the maternal role that he feels the need for special care. As Bettelheim suggests, "Such an aping of the superficials only emphasizes the more how much the real, essential powers are envied . . . men enact couvade to fill the emotional vacuum created by their inability to bear children."[94] It is important to the womb envy theory of couvade as a sex-role reversal that there be little or no ritual surrounding pregnant and parturient women; unfortunately for Bettelheim this is rarely the case.

Roger Burton and John Whiting's research based on Whiting's neo-Freudian status envy theory of identification[95] also explains

91. Sigmund Freud, *Totem and Taboo* (New York: Vintage Books, 1918), pp. 26–97.

92. Theodor Reik, *Ritual: Psychoanalytic Studies* (London: Hogarth Press, 1931), pp. 27–89.

93. Bettelheim, *Symbolic Wounds*, pp. 109–13.

94. Ibid., p. 11.

95. Roger Burton and John Whiting, "The Absent Father and Cross-Sex Identity," *Merrill-Palmer Quarterly of Behavior and Development* 7 (Winter 1961): 85–95.

couvade as an expression of male identification with the female role. As in Whiting's model of all reproductive rituals, these researchers propose that two important structural preconditions have a significant impact on the process of identity development through status envy: mother-infant sleeping arrangements and residence patterns. In societies in which the mother and child sleep together away from the father, the child will perceive the mother as the all-powerful determinant of how resources are distributed; he or she will form a primary identification with the female role and begin to envy women. In male children this can produce a "cross-sex optative identity." (It is hypothesized that when the father sleeps with the mother and child, the child will form an "adult optative identity" rather than a sex-based one since in this situation the child differentiates between self and adult rather than between self and male or female.) As the child develops, he or she enters into contact with the larger community and begins to form a "secondary identification" with the sex perceived as the more powerful. In patrilocal societies the child perceives males as the more powerful sex; in matrilocal societies, females have the envied status. Societies in which structural conditions lead to both primary and secondary identification with females—that is, societies with both exclusive mother-child sleeping arrangements and matrilocal residence—should be most likely to practice rituals like couvade which enable men to act out the female role. From their investigation of sixty-four world societies, Burton and Whiting find some evidence to support their model, although not all of the data are presented in the published paper. Of the twelve societies with couvade, ten had exclusive mother-child sleeping arrangements and nine had matrilocal residence. Burton and Whiting do not indicate how many societies have exclusive mother-child sleeping arrangements but not couvade; nor did they test the main hypothesis predicting that an interaction between sleeping arrangements and residence produces the greatest likelihood of couvade. Reanalysis of their published data does show that the relationship between exclusive mother-child sleeping arrangements and couvade is statistically significant at the .07 level.

A later investigation by Robert Munroe, Ruth Munroe, and John Whiting[96] has tested the same hypotheses on a sample of seventy-four world societies. Of the ten societies with both exclusive mother-child sleeping arrangements and matrilocal residence, 70 percent were found to observe couvade. Of the twenty-one societies with neither exclusive mother-child sleeping arrangements nor matrilocal residence, only 10 percent were found to observe couvade. The pres-

96. Robert L. Munroe, Ruth H. Munroe, and John W. M. Whiting, "The Couvade: A Psychological Analysis," *Ethos* 1 (Spring 1973): 30–44.

ence of one of the two antecedents produced an intermediate effect: of societies with exclusive mother-child sleeping arrangements but not matrilocal residence, 35 percent observed couvade, and of societies with matrilocal residence but not exclusive mother-child sleeping arrangements, 25 percent observed couvade. Overall, the association between couvade and its hypothesized antecedents was found to be significant (p<.005). Further research has attempted to confirm the cross-sex identity hypothesis by studying the determinants of individual variations in couvade symptoms and practices within a single society, testing the association between the number of couvade taboos that an individual considers it necessary to obey or the number of couvade symptoms he experiences and the salience of males in the household during infancy and childhood or "femininity" of responses to psychological tests.[97] Despite these efforts, the validity of Whiting's fundamental assumption of an association between salience of the father in the early socialization process and ambivalence in gender identity in the growing male continues to be regarded with skepticism.[98]

The single empirical study of world patterns of maternal birth practices was conducted by one of Whiting's students, Barbara Ayres.[99] She hypothesizes that cross-cultural variability in the extensiveness of maternal food and sex taboos during pregnancy reflects cultural differences in childhood socialization practices, particularly those pertaining to dependency and sexual behavior. Though she agrees with Ford and Whiting that food restrictions during pregnancy are probably instituted for health reasons, she suggests that the number of foods tabooed and the severity of sanctions for violating taboos are psychological in origin. She argues that pregnant women have special food cravings which are manifestations of increased dependency needs. In societies which reward dependency behavior

97. Ibid., pp. 44–74; S. B. Nerlove, "Trait Dispositions and Situational Determinants of Behavior Among Gusii Children of Southwestern Kenya," unpublished doctoral dissertation, Harvard University, 1969; R. L. Munroe, R. H. Munroe, and S. B. Nerlove, "Male Pregnancy Symptoms and Cross-Sex Identity: Two Replications," *Journal of Social Psychology* 89 (1973): 147–48; R. L. Munroe and R. H. Munroe, "Male Pregnancy Symptoms and Cross-Sex Identity in Three Societies," *Journal of Social Psychology* 84 (1971): 11–25.

98. See Seymour Parker, Janet Smith, and Joseph Ginat, "Father Absence and Cross-Sex Identity: The Puberty Rites Controversy Revisited," *American Ethnologist* 2 (November 1975): 687–706; C. Harrington, *Errors in Sex-Role Behavior in Teenage Boys* (New York: Teachers' College Press, 1970); H. B. Biller, *Father, Child, and Sex Role* (Lexington, Mass.: Heath-Lexington Books, 1971); and E. Herzog and Cecelia Sudia, *Boys in Fatherless Families*, U.S. Dept. of Health, Education, and Welfare, Office of Child Development, Children's Bureau, #(OCD) 72–33 (Washington, D.C.: 1971).

99. Barbara Ayres, "Pregnancy Magic: A Study of Food Taboos and Sex Avoidances," in *Cross-Cultural Approaches: Readings in Comparative Research*, ed. Clellan Ford (New Haven: HRAF Press, 1967), pp. 111–25.

during childhood, pregnancy evokes the greatest dependency needs and potentially the most harmful food cravings; thus, these societies should have the greatest number of pregnancy food taboos. Moreover, societies with the severest punishments for violating pregnancy food taboos should be those with the most severe punishments for childhood dependency behavior. Applying Whiting and Irvin Child's codes for cross-cultural variation in socialization practices to a sample of forty world societies,[100] Ayres first calculated the extent to which the number of foods tabooed during pregnancy and the severity of sanctions for violation of the taboos were associated with aspects of dependency socialization. As she predicted, the greater the initial indulgence of dependency behavior in children, the greater the number of food taboos during pregnancy. Similarly, a significant statistical relationship was observed between the punishment of childhood dependency and the severity of penalties a society imposed for violations of pregnancy food taboos.

Ayres interprets pregnancy sex taboos as a reflection of cultural anxiety about sex behavior. She views a long pregnancy sex taboo as a cultural mechanism for relieving women's unrealistic anxiety about the potentially harmful consequences of sex relations. Thus, she hypothesizes that the greater the sex anxiety in a society, the longer the pregnancy sex taboo will be. Her results lend some support to this contention. She found that the length of the pregnancy sex taboo was significantly associated with Whiting and Child's measure of the severity of punishment of sex behavior in childhood, as well as with George Murdock's classification of the restrictiveness of premarital sex norms.[101]

Other theorists in the psychoanalytic tradition have argued that restrictions on women's behavior, particularly a taboo on sexual intercourse during pregnancy and parturition, reflect psychological conflicts aroused in men or women by the birth event, particularly by genital bleeding at birth. Thus, pregnant and parturient women are segregated from men and required to abstain from sexual intercourse either because men unconsciously dread the genital bleeding that occurs at birth,[102] or, as Devereux argues, because blood at childbirth activates the parturient woman's castration complex and arouses unconscious hostile impulses from which men must be protected.[103] These arguments parallel the psychoanalytic interpretations of

100. John Whiting and Irvin Child, *Child Training and Personality* (New Haven: Yale University Press, 1953).

101. George P. Murdock, *Ethnographic Atlas* (Pittsburgh: University of Pittsburgh Press, 1967), p. 59, col. 78.

102. William Stephens, *The Oedipus Complex: Cross-Cultural Evidence* (New York: Free Press of Glencoe, 1962).

103. Devereux, "Bleeding," p. 225.

menarcheal ceremonies and menstrual pollution practices as unconscious defenses against the perceived danger of female genital bleeding.

Transition-Rite Theories

Van Gennep considered couvade to be only a "protection rite," but he regarded the practice of segregating women during childbirth as a classic *rite de passage*.[104] He classified social segregation, food taboos, and sex taboos during pregnancy as belonging to the rites of separation and the period of isolating women during delivery and afterwards (when the taboos are gradually lifted) as the transition stage. Rites of incorporation, which he termed the social return from childbirth, might be represented by a purification rite some time after birth.

Young, however, has interpreted the birth process as a *rite de passage* for both parents. He hypothesizes that the real focus of attention during childbirth is not the newborn but the parents and that the ritual activities of both spouses before and after delivery are a sort of parental social initiation into the larger community of relatives.[105] Again, the explanatory variable proposed to account for cross-cultural variation in the extent to which parenthood is dramatized is "solidarity." This time, the solidarity in question is that of the larger family unit, or corporate family. It is assessed by the political organization of the society—by whether or not the society is organized into exogamous or clan communities. When children are born, it is in a "solidary" community's best interest to integrate the nuclear family into the larger group since children are important for the survival of the group as a whole. Young measures the intensity of parenthood dramatization rites by a six-point Guttman scale, with the most elaborate dramatization indicated by postpartum rituals involving both husband and wife, such as the seclusion of mothers at or after delivery and the practice of couvade by husbands. To test his hypothesis, Young observed the distribution of parenthood dramatization scores across three kinds of communities: those without clan organization, segmented communities, and clan or exogamous communities. Although 46 percent of the solidary clan and exogamous communities had the most elaborate parenthood rituals, so did 30 percent of the least solidary communities, those without clan organization. This difference could be produced by chance alone. The weak statistical association between the intensity of parenthood ceremonies and Young's indicator of degree of solidarity within the larger corporate unit raises questions about the validity of his interpretation.

104. Van Gennep, *Rites of Passage*, pp. 41–49.
105. Young, *Initiation Ceremonies*, pp. 111–21.

Couvade, Anxiety Reduction, and Social Evolution

Yet another explanation of birth practices, in this case couvade, involves the connection between the performance of ritual activities and anxiety reduction, as discussed by Bronislaw Malinowski,[106] A. R. Radcliffe-Brown,[107] and George Homans.[108] Although Malinowski did not discuss couvade in his theory, Radcliffe-Brown refers specifically to couvade to illustrate the superiority of his own theory over Malinowski's. According to Malinowski, individuals perform rituals to reduce anxiety produced by uncertainty about the outcomes of certain acts or events. Radcliffe-Brown argues that rituals produce anxiety: individuals worry about whether they are performing the ritual properly according to social expectations. He uses the example of adherence to food taboos by Andamanese men during their wives' pregnancy to illustrate his point.[109]

Homans suggests that each of these ideas about ritual has merit and that the two are not in fact contradictory; Radcliffe-Brown merely goes one step further than Malinowski. Malinowski's theory as applied to couvade suggests that a man feels anxious about the birth of his child and that certain rituals—if he performs them correctly—help reduce this anxiety or at least keep it latent. According to Homans, Radcliffe-Brown's argument adds that if the rituals are performed incorrectly or not at all, the individual continues to be anxious. Although Homans grants that improper performance of couvade may itself create anxiety, he believes that the practice retains its original purpose of reducing male anxiety about the uncertainties of birth.

A final theory of couvade, though actually the first to be proposed, has been largely ignored by contemporary anthropologists because of its association with discredited nineteenth-century theories of the evolution of cultural institutions. In 1865, J. J. Bachofen proposed a theory about the sequence of stages of cultural development which argued that the custom of couvade arose during humankind's evolution from matriliny to patriliny.[110] He interpreted couvade as a rite of adoption that a woman's husband performed in order to gain social recognition of his legal rights over her offspring. Although Ed-

106. Bronislaw Malinowski, *Magic, Science, and Religion* (New York: Doubleday Anchor Book, 1954; originally published in 1948), pp. 17–92.
107. A. R. Radcliffe-Brown, "Taboo," in *Structure and Function in Primitive Society,* ed. A. R. Radcliffe-Brown (New York: Free Press Paperback, 1965), pp. 133–52.
108. George Homans, "Anxiety and Ritual: The Theories of Malinowski and Radcliffe-Brown," *American Anthropologist* 43 (1941): 164–72.
109. Radcliffe-Brown, "Taboo," pp. 148–49.
110. David M. Schneider and Kathleen Gough, *Matrilineal Kinship* (Berkeley: University of California Press, 1962), pp. 7–8, summarizing J. J. Bachofen, *Das Mutterecht* (Stuttgart: Krais and Hoffman, 1861).

ward Tylor had earlier accepted the notion that couvade was a form of sympathetic magic, he later became convinced that Bachofen's theory was the correct one. In his famous essay, "On a Method of Investigating the Development of Institutions," Tylor discarded his earlier theory on the basis of an analysis of 350 social groups, twenty-eight of which practiced couvade.[111] He classified all societies into three categories according to their postmarital residence pattern: matrilocal, patrilocal, and matrilocal-patrilocal. Of his twenty-eight cases of couvade, none was observed in matrilocal societies, twenty occurred in matrilocal-patrilocal societies, and eight were found in patrilocal societies. Although there is of course no evidence to support Tylor's theory of social evolution, his report of a relationship between residence and couvade anticipates the more recent findings of Burton and Whiting, who found couvade to occur more frequently in matrilocal societies. Well after the evolutionary schemes of nineteenth-century anthropologists had been discarded, in 1930, Malinowski defined the function of couvade in the same way as Bachofen and Tylor: "The function of couvade is the establishment of social paternity by the symbolic assimilation of the father to the mother."[112] He rejects the notion that it is a survival trait, or vestige, however, seeing it instead as integral to maintaining the institution of the family.

SUMMARY

The events in the human reproductive cycle which are examined in the chapters to follow have been the focus of much speculation and theory and some empirical research since the late nineteenth century. Psychoanalytic theories have presented the most comprehensive framework for explanations of reproductive rituals, arguing that they are behavioral consequences of inherent psychodynamics within either sex that produce conflicts about castration, penis envy, womb envy, or unconscious sexual hostility and aggression toward the opposite sex. Reproductive rituals, then, are caused by basic invariant psychological processes shared by all individuals in all societies. Because these rituals vary considerably cross-culturally, researchers using psychoanalytic principles have modified orthodox theory by arguing that psychodynamic conflicts may vary in their intensity from one society to the next. Transition-rite theories, like those of orthodox psychoanalysis, assume that all societies share at least the latent ritual

111. Edward B. Tylor, "On a Method of Investigating the Development of Institutions: Applied to Laws of Marriage and Descent," *Journal of the Royal Anthropological Institute* 18 (1889): 245–72.
112. Bronislaw Malinowski, "Culture," in *Encyclopedia of the Social Sciences*, vol. 4, ed. Charles G. Seligman (New York: Macmillan, 1930), p. 631.

sequence of true *rites de passage*, even if they do not dramatize each stage with equal intensity. Van Gennep believed that all societies performed *rites de passage* at critical reproductive events since such events represented an important status transition for the individual that had to be dramatized in the community. His original theory has also been modified by later empirical researchers such as Judith K. Brown and Frank Young, who suggest that the cross-cultural variability in reproductive rituals may be explained by differences in the need for dramatic role transition rites rather than differences in the expression of a universal latent structure shared by all societies. Finally, theories within the structural-functional tradition argue that rituals associated with reproductive events are symbolic indicators of certain structural tensions in a society, particularly the tensions produced by exogamous marriage patterns, which threaten caste purity, disrupt systems of unilineal descent, particularly matrilineal descent, or create the potential for disputes with the in-marrying group. Some theorists within the structural-functional framework also argue that the significance of reproductive events depends on the authority relationship between spouses so that the degree to which a woman's husband or her own kin can exert authority over her and use her as a pawn leads to differences in beliefs and practices pertaining to her reproductive capacity. According to another structural argument, sexual antagonism is produced by a sexual division of labor that requires equal but separate participation by both sexes in subsistence activities, thereby giving women a potential power over men that men wish to deny them. Within each of these frameworks, then, rituals are indicators or consequences of structurally and psychologically produced tensions rather than attempts to resolve such conflicts.

2 Reproductive Ritual: A Continuation of Politics by Another Means

The three major theories of reproductive ritual reviewed in Chapter 1 all assume that ritual has well-defined social or psychological functions even when the precise meaning of a ritual act is left unspecified. In this chapter we will outline a new theory that interprets reproductive rituals as political tactics used to solve social dilemmas that become crucial at certain points in the human reproductive cycle. This theory, based on a bargaining-exchange theory, makes assumptions about the nature of intratribal social relations and the significance of ritual that are somewhat at variance with psychoanalytic, Durkheimian, and traditional anthropological interpretations of tribal politics and ritual. This interpretation of reproductive ritual is based on three interrelated arguments. First, those events in the human reproductive life cycle marked by ritual observances—birth, puberty, and menstruation—pose potential crises for preindustrial societies; at such times the issue of kinship loyalties, particularly the loyalties of new or potential members of the society, may be subject to transfer, renegotiation, or dissolution. Each of these potential crises we term a "dilemma." Second, the solution to each of these dilemmas is often a ritual because in preindustrial societies direct political or legal solutions are often not possible. Ritual is not simply an alternative to politics; it is a continuation of politics by another means. Third, the prospects for resolving a dilemma without recourse to ritual depend on the political and economic resources of a society; these resources in turn are determined primarily by its mode of production. At any particular stage of the life cycle (and, according to our theory, during any particular life cycle dilemma), political resources determine both the use and form of ritual, and economic resources determine political resources. Economy leads to polity leads to ritual. The direction of the causal arrow is clear, but the specific causal linkages are neither simple nor obvious. It is the purpose of this chapter and the ones that follow to demonstrate the validity of this general causal scheme, to trace these intervening causal linkages, and to test the specific hypotheses the theory generates. In this chapter we attempt only an outline of the general theory. The complete argument depends on the detailed analysis of the dilemmas of female and male puberty (Chapters 3 and 4), birth (Chapter 5), and menstruation (Chapter 6).

Each of these dilemmas actually represents a special case of a more general problem in band and tribal societies. In such societies, women and their offspring represent important economic and political assets; gaining rights to such important assets in the absence of centralized legal authority can be a source of intense and sometimes irresoluble conflict. The potential claimants are usually though not invariably males, who exercise control over women and children in all societies even if childcare is under the control of women. Fathers and husbands are the major claimants to women although rarely does a single individual hold exclusive social and legal rights to a woman and her offspring. In theory and often in practice, relatives of a woman's father and husband share these rights, and there are other males in the society who may wish to establish competing claims to her reproductive capacity.

Since the distribution of rights to women and children is determined not by biology but by social opinion, tradition, and individual bargains, competition over control of women's reproductive capacity poses problems in all societies. Even in our own society, sexual competition and the protection of nubile daughters are major male preoccupations, and litigation over divorce, child custody, paternity rights, and abortion is chronic. But these conflicts are likely to be particularly acute in preindustrial societies, in which the allegiance of children is the major determinant of wealth, social status, and political power. In such societies, gaining a new member of a kin group or the reproductive capacity to produce an additional member means gaining an actual or potential contributor to the communal economy, a new supporter in a political faction, or an additional ally in a feud. In these societies, a woman's lifetime fertility is an important capital asset. Since societies organized at the band or tribal level have no police, no standing armies, and no formal legal system independent of any one claimant or group of claimants, disputes over rights to women must be settled directly by bargains among the interested parties themselves. In the absence of any binding authority these bargains may always be upset and new bargains made.

This fundamental difficulty confronts any man or group of men attempting to assert or defend rights to women's reproductive capacity in the absence of centralized authority. In no society does a woman's biological father retain exclusive sexual and procreative rights to her throughout her reproductive span or even relinquish those rights to his sons; he must transfer them to someone outside his own immediate conjugal unit. Since the man to whom these rights are transferred is not a close kinsman, the father is essentially relinquishing some or all control over his daughter and her future children to a potential enemy: children that might have strengthened the father's own domestic group will instead strengthen another's.

Although conflict over the control of women's fertility is a continual problem, it becomes particularly critical at four points in the human reproductive cycle—female and male sexual maturity, childbirth, and menstruation. At these times, agreements, whether implicit or explicit, over rights to fertility may be disputed, ignored, or renegotiated. After a daughter's menarche, control must be transferred to another male outside the conjugal family before seduction or elopement diminishes the daughter's value to her father as reproductive capital. Elopement, seduction, or even a reputation for promiscuity can jeopardize a father's ability to contract a favorable bargain with his daughter's future husband. Access to a woman's fertility without a father's consent reduces the value of the daughter in a legitimate marriage bargain primarily because the paternity of any offspring she produces will be ambiguous. Anyone claiming sexual access to the woman could assert rights to her offspring.

Before a son reaches sexual maturity, some means must also be found to ensure that the additional power represented by another potential competitor for female reproductive capacity does not upset the established relationships of adult males in the community. Sons mature, marry, and leave home just at the time when their increased authority over a wife and children of their own make them increasingly valuable as allies. The marriage of a child may split the original family and cause it to contract through fission; the new family splits off from the old, forming new patterns of kinship loyalty. The dilemma of fission from the original conjugal family, particularly by sons, is an inevitable consequence of sexual maturity.

At childbirth, when a woman's reproductive capacity is realized, conflict shifts to control over the actual rather than the potential allegiance of offspring and is focused on the questions of legitimacy and fulfillment of marriage bargain terms by the birth of healthy offspring with unambiguous paternity. But paternity is not always beyond dispute, and allegiance is never final. Legitimate rights to a child in preindustrial societies are established by informal agreements and social consensus, but agreements may be broken and consensus may vanish. The birth of a child tests agreements and threatens consensus because it immediately transfers the question of legitimate rights from the hypothetical to the actual. This is the dilemma of legitimacy posed by childbirth.

After marriage, evidence of a woman's continued fertility poses a potential dilemma for her husband. While a wife's fertility gives a man economic and political power, it confronts him with difficulties in choosing how to represent his power to others. If he deemphasizes it, he may gain the good will and trust of his affines and consanguineal kin, but he puts himself at a disadvantage in bargaining over rights to women and children and other economic and political resources. If he displays his power, he may make himself respected, gain more power, and improve his bargaining position, but he also stands to alienate and threaten others—a danger in societies where powerful men are highly dependent on the good will of others in the community. Short of pregnancy and childbirth themselves, the clearest indication of a woman's fertility is her periodic menses. As long as a woman menstruates, she may produce children; and as long as she produces children, the dilemma posed by her husband's increasing power remains.

Each of these events in the human reproductive cycle presents opportunities for males to assert new claims or renegotiate old claims to women's fertility. Since in the absence of centralized authority no bargain is ever final, there may, in fact, be no effective means of establishing or defending rights to women and their offspring and, hence, no solution to the dilemmas of each of these critical reproductive events. What cannot be accomplished through law or contract may, however, sometimes be accomplished through ritual.

WHAT IS RITUAL?

It is not immediately apparent from ethnographic accounts of reproductive rituals how each could be a continuation of politics by another means. The ambiguity about how such rituals should be defined within the traditional theoretical frameworks is less the fault of individual theorists than a demonstration of the ambiguity in anthropology generally about how a ritual should be defined.

Jack Goody has recently attempted to clarify the term "ritual" in anthropology and to extend the concept to cover a broad number of social customs.[1] Based on an analysis of the underlying assumptions of theories of magic, religion, and reason, particularly those of Durkheim, Malinowski, and Talcott Parsons, Goody's argument questions the polar oppositions of sacred-profane and rational-irrational upon which most distinctions among magic, religion, reason, and their ritual expressions are based. Durkheim, for example, views religion as "sacred" and expressive of consensus by an assembled group to reaffirm social solidarity. Magic, however, is a private, optional ritual rather than a public, obligatory one (as is religion), and if magical rites are not carried out, the likely result is bad luck, not "sin." Malinowski, on the other hand, distinguished between rituals that are magical and rituals that are religious by arguing that the former have "practical" value known to all while the latter are simply "expressive" (symbolic) in value. Parsons distinguishes magical and religious rituals on the basis of the rational-irrational dimension. A ritual is religious if its goal, or function, is irrational, such as the expression of group solidarity, but magical if its goal is rational, or empirical.[2]

According to Goody, the term "ritual" applies to a variety of customary behaviors, whether they be magical, religious, scientific, or daily social customs. He focuses on the perceptions and interpretations of an act by the observer and argues that information is being communicated in rituals by the performers. First, he asserts that whether or not a ritual is "expressive" (that is, nonempirical or irrational) depends on whether or not the observer of the activity perceives a connection between means and end; a ritual is irrational if the observer believes that the actions being performed "stand for something other than they seem." Rituals may be symbolic communication, but what they symbolize depends on the observer's interpretation, not necessarily the performer's intent. Goody then argues that a variety of secular customary acts, such as language, are also symbolic so that symbolic action in the form of magical or religious ritual alone cannot really be clearly distinguished from any other type of social behavior.

"Ritual" cannot be used only to describe special social acts to which an observer attaches meaning. For Goody, then, rituals are best defined simply as a "standardized form of behavior/custom"[3] in which the acts being performed are not interpreted by the observer as

1. Jack Goody, "Religion and Ritual: The Definitional Problem," *British Journal of Sociology* 12 (1961): 142–64.

2. See especially Emile Durkheim, *The Elementary Forms of Religious Life* (New York: Free Press, 1965); Bronislaw Malinowski, *Magic, Science, and Religion* (New York: Doubleday Anchor Books, 1954; originally published in 1948); and Talcott Parsons, *Essays in Sociological Theory* (Glencoe, Ill.: Free Press, 1954).

3. Goody, "Religion and Ritual," p. 159.

leading empirically to the goals that are professed by the performer. Ritual elements are not themselves instrumental acts although they do have intent. They are clearly a mechanism by which the performer is attempting to convey information, to communicate something to the observer, such as a change in his power relations.

This definition of "ritual," which emphasizes the role of observers' own evaluations of the activities and the significance of ritual as a mechanism by which performers attempt to convey information, certainly provides the necessary theoretical framework to interpret reproductive rituals as implicit bargaining tactics. We agree that rituals are performed with the intent of conveying information to observers but argue in addition that the performer of the ritual is himself gathering information. Rituals are political tactics by which, in the absence of more direct political tactics, both performers and observers may gauge each other's future intentions and attempt to manipulate and monitor current public opinion. Reproductive rituals, in particular, attempt to influence public opinion about one's claims to a woman's fertility, monitor kin-group loyalty despite the potential for individual power and wealth that rights to reproductive capital represent, and assess one's potential ability to challenge successfully any competing claims.

The form that ritual politics takes depends fundamentally on the availability of other strategies that might be more effective in establishing claims, monitoring loyalty, and manipulating social opinion. A potential claimant would be ill-advised to spend two weeks in a hammock avoiding food and work during his wife's childbirth, to sponsor a menarcheal ceremony for his daughter, or to subject his son to the circumciser's knife if he could claim or defend his rights to reproductive assets by hiring a lawyer, calling the police, or signing a binding contract. When more effective tactics are not available, however, a claimant has much to gain by making ritual claims and, since other claimants are in no position to oppose him except by engaging in public ritual themselves, nothing to lose.

Reproductive rituals, then, can be viewed as a form of psychological warfare, or puffery, used when opportunities for more direct forms of conflict and more explicit bargaining are restricted. Even if claimants have the backing of a powerful military force to protect their interests, in the absence of a centralized authority to bind parties to a bargain, agreements about the distribution of rights to women's fertility or the loyalty of sons to the kin group are not legally enforceable. Ritual demonstrations of good faith in respect to previously negotiated bargains and also the ritual monitoring of behavior demonstrating good faith are both mechanisms used to assure all interested parties that bargains will indeed be fulfilled.

Although all tribal societies can be expected to resort to ritual bargaining tactics during critical reproductive events, the particular form that ritual takes and the reproductive events that pose the most serious dilemmas for individuals depend on the political resources at the disposal of adult males. In most tribal societies, the status and wealth of potential competitors are fairly similar so that the political resources available to each interested party are roughly the same. As a result, each claimant resorts to similar bargaining strategies. In most cases, differences within a single society are not large. Across the range of tribal social organizations, however, there are substantial differences in political and economic power and, therefore, important differences in the kinds of ritual tactics employed to resolve reproductive dilemmas. Three different forms of ritual politics can be distinguished.

Ritual surveillance of competing claimants should be most typical of societies with a high, stable resource base that encourages the development of large cohesive kin groups that act as political units to exploit and defend those resources. In these societies, individuals have the wealth and the unconditional kin-group backing to make explicit agreements about rights to women and offspring. Ritual surveillance ensures that parties to these agreements fulfill the terms required of them and that those individuals not party to an agreement do nothing to upset its terms.

Social mobilization rituals should be typical of societies which lack a high, stable resource base and large cohesive kin groups. In these societies, individuals cannot rely automatically on a large kin group to defend their interests and must instead create and maintain kin-based factions to side with them in disputes over rights to women and offspring. Explicit agreements are lacking because there is no mechanism to enforce them. The performer of a social mobilization ritual tries to enlist supporters by persuading them of his power, his generosity, his popularity, and the justice of his cause. At the same time he gauges, through community response or participation, the extent of the support that he already has. Some societies that lack a high, stable resource base are so poor that expensive ceremonies are not possible and there is no wealth to hold political factions together. Others have a more productive resource base but one that is inherently unstable since surpluses are fluctuating and perishable. In these unstable societies, an individual can create a powerful faction but can only hold it together as long as his wealth endures. He can gain support at critical reproductive events by sponsoring ceremonies and feasts that put others in his debt.

Unstable societies are characterized by a third form of ritual, displays of *ritual disinterest* in accumulated wealth and power or in the control over women's fertility that brings wealth and power. Ritual disinterest in a woman's fertility is an attempt to convince others that the wealth and power represented by a woman's fertility will not be used to default on obligations to consanguines, affines, or the larger community. It is particularly characteristic of unstable societies because the loyalties of their most powerful individuals are particularly uncertain. In the poorest societies, which completely lack political and economic sanctions to enforce loyalty, default is more probable; in the high resource base societies, with strong political and economic motives for loyalty, default is less probable. But in the unstable societies, the possibility of default is maximally uncertain and must be regularly assessed and denied through ritual disinterest.

Reproductive rituals, then, are attempts to gain political advantage in conflicts over women and children rather than mechanisms for satisfying the psychological needs of individuals or for symbolically reducing social conflict and tension. Reproductive rituals are motivated by self-interest; their sentimental and religious symbolism merely cloaks their true objectives.

The classic textbook examples of political uses of ritual—song duels, spear-throwing contests, competitive feasts, and potlatches—have usually been interpreted as prelegal mechanisms of maintaining social control or as adaptive mechanisms. But such rituals can also be interpreted as political bargaining tactics for defending claims, influencing public opinion, and monitoring the intentions of potential competitors.

The use of ritual to mobilize a temporary political faction is most apparent in the Eskimo song duel and the Tiwi spear-throwing contest. These rituals allow each party to state his grievance publicly and allow other community members to decide which side they favor.[4] It has been argued that such rituals minimize the possibility that each disputant will mobilize his respective kinsmen with resulting general feuding and violence since a disputant who feels he has no backing from his kinsmen would stop pressing his claims.[5]

The Eskimo song duel, for example, is used to judge which disputant is right or wrong by mobilizing community opinion on the side of one or the other decisively enough to prevent a feud.[6] The common reason for this ritual is one man accusing another of seducing his wife. The dispute is settled by a large public meeting where the two disputants take turns singing insulting songs at each other instead of giving their side of the story. The community responds to each song

4. Elman Service, *The Hunters* (New York: Prentice-Hall, 1966), pp. 54–57.
5. Marvin Harris, *Culture, Man, and Nature* (New York: Crowell, 1971), p. 358.
6. Ibid.; see also Knud Rasmussen, *The Intellectual Culture of the Ingulik Eskimo*, Report of the Fifth Thule Expedition 1921–24, vol. 7, no. 1, tr. W. Worster (Copenhagen: Gyldendal, 1929), pp. 231–32, quoted in Harris, *Culture*, p. 379.

with different amounts of laughter, and eventually one of the singers gives up as it becomes clear that he is losing the contest.

Ritual bargaining among the Tiwi is somewhat more aggressive since it involves the dodging of spears thrown at a defendant by an accuser and has been known to result in death.[7] As with the Eskimo song duel, the most frequent reason for Tiwi spear-throwing contests is the seduction of wives. Since Tiwi women are likely to be married to senior elders of the society, the accuser of seduction is usually a senior male who is much older and less agile than the defendant. This "duel" starts off the night before with the elder's making a public charge against the young man. The next day everyone in the community gathers in a circle in an open space. The accuser stands at one end of the circle and the defendant at the other. The elderly accuser is ceremonially painted and is carrying a ceremonial spear in one hand and hunting spears in the other. The young defendant is not painted and is holding either one or two hunting spears or throwing sticks depending on how defiant he is (the throwing sticks are less defiant). The ritual begins with the accuser reciting in minute detail the life history of the defendant, including the many favors that he and his relatives have done for him and his relatives, even the most remote of favors to the most remote of kin. This procedure, dramatizing the antisocial character of the defendant's alleged behavior, lasts for at least twenty minutes. Then the elder man throws aside his ceremonial spear and begins throwing the hunting spears at the defendant, who dodges them. The defendant is not allowed to throw his spears at the elder. The skill required of the defendant is to lose artfully to the elder without being hurt or making his loss seem too feigned. He is not to embarrass the elder accuser or else community opinion would be against him, but if he has any ambitions of gaining prestige and success he must also beware of making a fool of himself. A skillful young defendant may allow the old man to throw spears for some time, then finally let one of them draw blood without causing great injury. If this occurs, the audience considers the defendant to have behaved admirably and the elder to have retained his honor. The defendant is almost forced to conform to this ritual since if he chose to engage in a real fight or allowed the elder accuser to be embarrassed, steps would be taken by the community, including his own relatives.

Another form of ritual is large elaborate feasts and giveaways. The sponsor attempts not only to demonstrate his great wealth and political power but also to cause his political rivals to lose power. By sponsoring large feasts and giveaways, a man can make it impossible for his rival to reciprocate equally and thus humiliate and defeat him.

7. C. W. Hart and Arnold R. Pilling, *The Tiwi of North Australia* (New York: Holt, Rinehart and Winston, 1960), pp. 80–83.

The potlatches of the Northwest Coast Indians (which have been called "fighting with property")[8] and the yam and pig feasts of Melanesian societies (which have been called "fighting with food")[9] are the best known examples of this form of ritual conflict. The potlatch rituals became most elaborate when overt conflict among the Northwest Coast Indians was outlawed by the Canadian government. According to Helen Codere, they were a replacement of direct hostility with ritual rivalry.[10] A wealthy chief, for example, will burn hundreds of blankets and canoes and damage the most valuable prestige object, a copper, in order to indicate his disregard for his property and to demonstrate that he is wealthier than his rival. If the rival is not able to destroy an equal amount of property soon after, he loses influence in the tribe and the victor gains influence. The most feared rivalry involves the breaking of the coppers. A chief may break his copper and give the broken parts to his rival. If the rival wants to maintain his status, he must break a copper of equal or higher value and then return both his broken copper and the fragment received from the aggressor. The latter must then pay for the copper received. The chief who received the first copper fragment may also break his own copper and throw both into the sea. By this act he is considered superior to the aggressor and therefore the victor in the dispute. When the rivalry between chiefs progresses to the stage of breaking coppers, outright violence is common.

The competitive feasts of many Melanesian societies are strikingly similar to the potlatch.[11] Competitive feast-giving usually occurs among men of prestige and influence ("big men") who are often the war leaders in a society. Acquiring such power does not depend entirely on kinship ties and is based to a large extent on success in establishing a group of followers through personality, manipulative ability, and social indebtedness. The political life of the Siuai of Bougainville, described in detail by Douglas Oliver, illustrates ritual conflict through feast-giving among rivalrous big men.[12] Siuai leaders use pig feasts to challenge rivals, who in order to keep their power and influence must follow the challenger's feast with one of equal or better quality. When a big man initiates a challenge through feast-

8. Helen Codere, *Fighting with Property: A Study of Kwakiutl Potlatching, 1792–1930* (New York: J. J. Augustin, 1950).

9. Michael W. Young, *Fighting with Food: Leadership, Values, and Social Control in a Massim Society* (Cambridge: Cambridge University Press, 1971).

10. Helen Codere, ed., *Kwakiutl Ethnology* (Chicago: University of Chicago Press, 1966), p. 77.

11. For an analysis of the politics of competitive feasting in Melanesia, see Marshall Sahlins, "Poor Man, Rich Man, Big-Man Chief: Political Types in Melanesia and Polynesia," *Comparative Studies in Society and History* 5 (April 1963): 285–303.

12. Douglas L. Oliver, *A Solomon Island Society* (Boston: Beacon Press, 1967; originally published in 1955), pp. 386–95.

giving, the major work of supplying and preparing the food is the responsibility of his loyal supporters, such as members of his men's society. The sponsor of the feast also invites a "resident-defender," an allied political leader who acts as a kind of co-host.[13] An ambitious host attempts to invite as many other allied big men as possible along with their factions to demonstrate his far-reaching prestige. The rival, who is the object of the feast, is called the "guest-of-honor." Rivals are chosen very carefully since the host must choose a man who is not powerful enough to retaliate successfully but who is powerful enough so that his loss will increase the host's power.

ANTECEDENT CONDITIONS
OF REPRODUCTIVE RITUALS

The form of reproductive rituals in preindustrial societies de-pends on the political resources individual claimants have available to establish and protect claims to women's reproductive capacity. The ability to make explicit bargains concerning women and offspring de-pends on the ability to assure that such bargains are enforced. En-forcement power in preindustrial societies requires that males of a consanguineal kin group act as a corporate unit, using force if neces-sary, to defend their interests and resolve disputes. Such groups have been termed *fraternal interest groups*, a theoretical construct describing the social bases of power first defined by Thoden van Velzen and W. Van Wetering but based on Robert Murphy's analysis of residence and conflict among the Mundurucu.[14]

The concept of fraternal interest groups has been increasingly used in studies of political organization and internal conflict in prein-dustrial societies, but it has not yet been applied to the understanding of reproductive ritual. Van Velzen and van Wetering, Keith Otterbein and Charlotte Otterbein, Melvin Ember and Carol Ember, and Wil-liam Divale have demonstrated correlations between the presence or absence of fraternal interest groups and the incidence of violence, feuding, and internal warfare in samples of preindustrial societies.[15] Jeffery Paige showed that the presence of fraternal interest groups

13. Ibid., p. 392.
14. H. U. E. Thoden van Velzen and W. van Wetering, "Residence, Power Groups, and Intra-Societal Aggression," *International Archives of Ethnography* 49 (1960): 169–200, and Robert Murphy, "Intergroup Hostility and Social Cohesion," *American Anthropologist* 59 (1957): 1018–35.
15. Van Velzen and van Wetering, "Residence"; Keith F. Otterbein, "Internal War: A Cross-Cultural Study," *American Anthropologist* 70 (1968): 277–89; Keith F. Otter-bein and Charlotte S. Otterbein, "An Eye for an Eye, a Tooth for a Tooth: A Cross-Cultural Study of Feuding," *American Anthropologist* 67 (1965): 1470–82; Melvin Ember and Carol R. Ember, "The Conditions Favoring Matrilocal Versus Patrilocal Residence," *American Anthropologist* 73 (1971): 571–94; and William Divale, "Migration, External War-fare, and Matrilocal Residence," *Behavioral Science Research* 9 (1974): 75–134.

was associated with kin-based political subunits in tribal societies and suggested that the segmentary political system as described by Meyer Fortes and E. E. Evans-Pritchard, and John Middleton and David Tait was also associated with the presence of fraternal interest groups.[16] John Whiting and Beatrice Whiting demonstrated an association between fraternal interest groups and structural aloofness between husbands and wives and suggested that sexual segregation facilitated the high levels of internal conflict reported in these societies.[17]

Residential Bases of Fraternal Interest Group Organization

Murphy has argued that rules of matrilocal residence distribute consanguineally related males throughout a society while those of patrilocal residence concentrate related males in a single location.[18] In a matrilocal society a core group of females is married to a heterogeneous group of affinal males who are in essence strangers in their wives' villages. In other words, matrilocal residence patterns prevent males from forming localized kinship groups. Since men are the most important political actors in preindustrial societies, matrilocal residence, by separating male kinsmen, inhibits unified political action while patrilocal residence, by uniting male kinsmen, facilitates the formation of political factions. These factions, or fraternal interest groups, include not only brothers but also kinsmen of varying degrees of consanguinity and from all living generations.

Avunculocal residence patterns produce the same overlapping kin-group ties as patrilocal residence, and, therefore, they too should be associated with politically effective fraternal interest groups. Just as patrilocal residence localizes fathers and sons in the same community, avunculocal residence localizes uncles and grown nephews. Bilocal and neolocal residence patterns produce the same political conditions as matrilocal residence and similarly inhibit the formation of fraternal interest groups. In matrilocal societies, sons live with their wives' families; in neolocal societies, they live separately in another community; and in bilocal societies, they may or may not live with their consanguineal kin. All three residence patterns are thus characterized by the absence of a core group of consanguineally related males.

16. Jeffery M. Paige, "Kinship and Polity in Stateless Societies," *American Journal of Sociology* 80 (1974): 301–19; Meyer Fortes and E. E. Evans-Pritchard, *African Political Systems* (London: Oxford University Press, 1940); and John Middleton and David Tait, eds., *Tribes Without Rulers: Studies in African Segmentary Systems* (London: Routledge & Kegan Paul, 1958).

17. John Whiting and Beatrice Whiting, "Aloofness and Intimacy of Husbands and Wives: A Cross-Cultural Study," *Ethos* 1 (1975): 184–207.

18. Murphy, "Intergroup Hostility."

In patrilocal and avunculocal societies, groups of related males with similar interests in disputes can act as a unit to challenge any competitors. In societies that do not localize related males in the same community, men are likely to have conflicting loyalties since they have close ties of kinship and economic interdependence with their wives' families, their natal households, and any other households with which they interact for daily support in subsistence and political activities. Since every man has some loyalties to each household, any conflict involving these households is a matter of serious concern. Therefore, matrilocal, ambilocal, and neolocal societies attempt to repress overt conflict and inhibit individuals from stating their griev-ances in the form of overt violence. Such an act would place one's friends in a vulnerable position since they are in all probability also friends of one's challenger. Among patrilocal and avunculocal societies, overt conflict is not only more likely but may produce even greater fraternal interest group solidarity by adding new members through successful feuding and minimizing the potential for further challenges from those groups with which they feud.

According to van Velzen and van Wetering, a fraternal interest group is a localized group of consanguineal kin united for concerted action by shared interests; it is not limited to brothers but may include an entire lineage or clan.[19] They assume that fraternal interest groups will exist in all patrilocal (and avunculocal) societies since these resi-dence rules localize kinsmen in one community. In using residence alone as a measure of fraternal interest group strength, they estab-lished a convention that has been followed in most later research al-though Keith Otterbein included polygyny as an additional index on the grounds that sons of the same father would usually share a com-mon interest and location, and the Whitings suggested that important capital assets under kin-group control should also be considered.[20] Despite the increasing use of the fraternal interest group concept, however, no researchers have yet examined the possible *economic* bases of fraternal interest group formation or developed direct mea-sures of variability in the *strength* of fraternal interest groups.

Economic Bases of Fraternal Interest Group Formation

We contend that a society's economic organization determines its political organization and, therefore, also determines the strength of fraternal interest groups. Three economic factors are most crucial. The first factor is the *presence or absence of valuable economic resources that*

---

19. Van Velzen and van Wetering, "Residence."
20. Keith Otterbein, "Internal War," and Whiting and Whiting, "Aloofness."

can be controlled by adult males in the society. The more valuable the economic assets, the greater the likelihood that they can be converted into political resources that provide incentives for kinsmen to form and maintain a cohesive political faction united by a common interest in the control or defense of these valuable assets. The second critical factor is the *military vulnerability of valuable economic assets* to attack or confiscation by other organized groups of males. The greater the potential gains from attacking other individuals' property or the potential losses of assets to the successful attacks of others, the greater the incentive for adult males to keep their sons and other male relatives under their direct control by localizing them in the same community throughout their lives. The third critical factor is *access to valuable economic assets only through the mediation of fathers and other adult males* by sons at maturity so that there is no opportunity for sons to form an independent resource base.

There have been numerous attempts to develop typologies of preindustrial economies. Economies have been categorized according to evolutionary schemes that focus on technological developments facilitating control over nature, ecological schemes specifying the caloric energy produced by various ecosystems, and ad hoc schemes clustering societies with similar economic and social structures.[21] None of the major economic typologies evaluates the effect of an economic structure on the strength of fraternal interest groups although the technological distinctions that have been developed are useful for this purpose.

The classification of economic systems described below groups the major economic systems in terms of the three factors that we consider critical in accounting for fraternal interest group organization and strength: the value of the dominant economic resources available in a society, military vulnerability of those resources, and the extent to which sons must rely on fathers for access to wealth. These factors determine the extent to which men can command and reinforce the loyalty of large numbers of kinsmen and, thus, the society's potential for producing a strong political force capable of contracting and protecting explicit bargains.

Societies with Stable Valuable Resources

Societies in which the dominant economic activity is based on *herding* of domesticates, such as cattle, horses, and camels, or the *cultivation of land by hoes, plows, and irrigation* have the most stable and

---

21. Gerhard Lenski, *Human Societies* (New York: McGraw-Hill, 1970) contains the author's own evolutionary scheme and those preceding his own. See also Marvin Harris, *Culture, People, Nature* (New York: Crowell, 1975), especially Chap. 12; and David Aberle, "Matrilineal Descent in Cross-Cultural Perspective" in *Matrilineal Kinship*, ed. David Schneider and Kathleen Gough (Berkeley: University of California Press, 1961).

valuable economic resources and, therefore, are the most likely to form large kin-based factions.

Hoe agriculture, when used in slash-and-burn, or shifting, cultivation, produces a substantially higher yield per unit of cultivation than less technologically efficient techniques such as the digging stick. As a food cycle analysis of a Gambian society has shown, hoe cultivation can support a substantially larger population than the digging-stick shifting cultivation techniques used among the Tsembaga Maring.[22] Use of the hoe also allows the sowing of high-yield cereals such as wheat and barley; with the less efficient digging stick, the cultivation of roots is dominant. The use of a *plow* increases still further the amount of land that can be cultivated, and the yield. With the hoe, the problems of weeding and maintaining soil fertility become increasingly severe the longer the plot is cultivated; the plow reduces these problems and allows for the permanent cultivation of fields. Plow cultivation has another advantage over hoe cultivation: it replaces human energy with animal energy, increasing economic surplus and releasing laborers for other productive pursuits such as manufacturing, trade, and politics. The use of *irrigation* in conjunction with the plow further increases the yield, thereby making the land exceedingly valuable. Fertile lands do not always need a plow so that irrigation does not necessarily reduce the labor force, but irrigation has the significant advantage of controlling the water necessary for cultivation, whether by natural flood waters or by man-made channels.

While *pastoralists* cultivate only on a small scale, if at all, they control valuable capital assets in the form of animals, which can be stolen if not protected. Competition with sedentary agriculturalists for pasture land creates the potential for conflict and violence. Lands must be protected for both grazing and water holes, the latter being a common focus of dispute and violent feuding.

The military vulnerability of each of the economic assets of these subsistence economies is clear. When valuable economic assets take the form of herds, as in pastoral societies or plow agricultural societies in which animals provide the essential capital implement of production, the asset is not only scarce but also valuable and easily stolen. Similarly, the land itself, when providing a high yield through the use of hoes, plows, or irrigation, is scarce and valuable enough to be worth fighting for. Both herds and valuable land can be obtained only from the men who own them, thereby making it essential and profitable in the long run for sons to maintain allegiance to their fathers.

22. See Harris, *Culture, People, Nature,* pp. 236–37, 239–41, describing the research of M. R. Haswell, *Economics of Agriculture in a Savannah Village: Report on Three Years' Study Among the Gambia.* (London: H.M. Stationery Office, 1953).

For example, a camel-breeding culture in a barren environment provides almost no opportunities for sons to establish an independent resource base: camels are scarce, reproduce slowly, and can be obtained only from other men who control them. Thus, these economic systems provide considerable incentive for fraternal interest group formation.

Societies with Unstable and Low-Value Resources

Societies in which the dominant subsistence activity is diggingstick shifting cultivation, buffalo hunting, fishing, or hunting and gathering command resources of considerably less value. Some of these societies have a very low subsistence level. Others have periodic large surpluses that are too perishable to have any long-term value.[23] In neither type of society is there much incentive for the formation of strong fraternal interest groups.

Digging-stick shifting cultivation is practically confined to areas where knowledge of or access to iron does not exist, such as the South American and African tropical regions and the Insular Pacific. Since in these regions there is no prolonged drought and the harvest season is long, yams, taro, and manioc can be dug for an extended period and food need not be stored for any length of time; in fact, storage in such regions would be nearly impossible given the humid climate. In the swidden-pig economies of the larger islands of the Insular Pacific, shifting cultivation is supplemented by pig-raising, but since pigs compete with humans for the food cultivated, yams, they must be periodically slaughtered.[24] All these digging-stick shifting cultivation societies, then, are characterized by periodically abundant, perishable resources. The land itself is of low value because it must be abandoned after a few years of cultivation, once the soil is exhausted and the forest and weeds begin to take over. It may take up to fifteen or twenty years for the plot to become fertile enough to use again. Preparing and cultivating land does not require a large labor force. The burning and clearing of tropical forest is nearly always done individually or by small family units, and anyone can obtain and maintain a garden plot simply by doing some clearing, planting, and weeding. Individuals or groups may try to take each other's already cleared plots rather than going through the effort of preparing plots from

23. See especially Marshall Sahlins, *Tribesmen* (Englewood Cliffs, N.J.: Prentice-Hall, 1968); C. Daryll Forde, *Habitat, Economy, and Society* (New York: Dutton, 1963), p. 407; Richard B. Lee and Irven DeVore, eds., *Man the Hunter* (Chicago: Aldine, 1968); and Harris, *Culture, People, Nature* for discussion of political economy of diggingstick cultivation, buffalo hunting, fishing, and hunting-gathering societies.

24. Roy Rappaport's *Pigs for the Ancestors* (New Haven: Yale University Press, 1967) is devoted to a large extent to discussing the usual implications of the human vs. pig competition for food.

virgin forest. But plots must be so frequently left fallow that they do not justify large-scale military occupation. These features of digging-stick shifting cultivation offer little incentive for the formation of strong fraternal interest groups. Sons need not rely on adult males to obtain economic resources, and fathers need not rely on large numbers of sons for their labor. The resource level, while not as high as that of pastoralists or complex agriculturalists, is in many societies high enough to encourage the formation of temporary kin-based factions that leaders maintain by distributing surplus resources among their followers.

Buffalo hunting and fishing societies, like societies based on digging-stick cultivation, have an unstable resource base, Food is periodically plentiful but cannot be stored and is not valuable enough to enforce loyalty of kinsmen through promises of sharing or inheriting wealth derived from communal property. Nor can buffalo or fish be owned and guarded from attack. Both buffalo hunters and fishermen, like digging-stick cultivators, can easily obtain economic resources individually, without the mediation of older kinsmen.

Buffalo hunting in the North American plains began with the introduction of the horse, which allowed individuals to search for herds with considerable efficiency. However, buffalo migrate seasonally in search of grazing lands and appear on the plains only periodically. Among buffalo hunters, therefore, effective political and military units are formed for only that part of the year when food is abundant; for the rest of the year they divide up into smaller units better adapted to the winter season. These groups retain some continuity throughout the seasonal cycle but do not necessarily constitute single kin groups. Individuals can join or leave depending on personal circumstances and group desirability. As among digging-stick cultivators, some men can attain leadership through exceptional skill, luck, or energy in their short-term exploitation of resources. Thus, a political faction may develop around a skillful hunter although membership loyalty is difficult to maintain.

Fishing societies, particularly those of salmon fishermen of the Northwest Coast of North America, also rely on abundant but perishable and unpredictable resources. Although some fish are taken at sea, the major subsistence base of the society, salmon, are caught during their annual upstream spawning runs. Salmon fishermen, like buffalo hunters, do not occupy the same settlement throughout the year but move in small groups to a number of different fishing sites. The principal villages are occupied mainly during the winter season when most fishing ceases. When salmon runs begin in the spring, fishermen stake out their sites, often fighting fiercely over them. The value of the sites fluctuates with the density of the salmon flow from year to year. Families theoretically control certain sites, and wealth depends to a large extent on the ability to retain or steal the most productive sites. Social leadership in fishing societies is based largely on accrued wealth, especially as manifested by the ability to sponsor successful potlatches. While fishing economies provide relative abundance, the unpredictable fluctuations of this resource from one year to the next, its relatively equal accessibility to all members of the society, and its perishability provide little incentive for the formation of fraternal interest groups.

Hunting-gathering economies are the least likely to produce fraternal interest groups, or even temporary political factions based on personal influence. These societies have scant, perishable resources; unlike unstable societies, they do not even have periodic large surpluses. Such societies are extremely small in comparison with those of other ecotypes, seldom exceeding a hundred members. Small bands, sometimes made up of only three or four families, migrate in search of food and water and only occasionally join with other bands. The band implicitly claims a territory, but this claim by no means implies a monopoly. Families in a band are likely to group together only during certain seasons; in the dry season they congregate near water, but in the rainy season they scatter widely to search for food. Each family produces its own food, with men typically hunting and women gathering. A man usually hunts alone or with his sons or other relatives, but if game is found it must be shared equally with everyone in the band. In most extractive societies, food supplies represent the only important form of economic wealth. They can be obtained by anyone who wants them and are seldom valuable enough to trade or inherit. Thus, there is little incentive for sons to remain under their fathers' authority or for fathers to require the services of a large number of sons. The development of even temporary factions is very weak, and egalitarianism is stressed to a greater degree than in any other type of preindustrial society.

ASSESSING THE STRENGTH OF FRATERNAL INTEREST GROUPS

The dominant economic resource base of a society, we have argued, should have a substantial impact on the political dynamics within the society. But economy does not provide a direct measure of the political power of a fraternal interest group. The following variables provide a sensitive index of variation in fraternal interest group strength: (1) demonstrated ability to make explicit contractual agreements involving substantial wealth with other kin groups in the society; (2) size of the fraternal interest group; and (3) an ideological base, namely, descent reckoning that reinforces the loyalty of fraternal interest group members. Together these variables constitute an intervening link mediating the effects of the economic resource base on ritual bargaining tactics observed at critical reproductive events. The strength of a society's fraternal interest groups depends on the extent to which all three factors are present. Societies with valuable, stable economic resources should have larger fraternal interest groups that are more able to contract explicit bargains and to reinforce the allegiance of their members. In contrast, societies that do not have the economic resources to keep sons localized should have smaller fraternal interest groups that are more likely to resort to implicit bargains and less likely to mobilize their members to take political action.

The Ability to Contract Explicit Bargains

The ability of kin groups to contract explicit bargains with each other, particularly for rights to reproductive capacity, is central to our theory of reproductive rituals. We measure it by the ability to contract explicit marriage bargains: marriage arrangements that involve the transfer of valuable resources from one kin group to another and the stipulation that property be returned in cases of default such as barrenness, divorce, or death. Murdock's classification of the seven types of customary marriage arrangements in preindustrial societies[25]—*absence* of significant material consideration or bridal gifts only, *token brideprice, brideservice, dowry, gift exchange, exchange,* and *brideprice*—can be used to determine ability to contract explicit marriage bargains.

In a large number of societies, a man becomes the legally recognized husband of a woman without transferring goods to her parents; that is, they exhibit what Murdock classifies as *absence* of significant material consideration or bridal gifts only. Frequently, a marriage becomes recognized when a woman simply moves in with a man or when her father or legal guardian grants permission for the marriage. In our sample, most such societies were among the least productive economically and the weakest politically. This marriage arrangement, like *token brideprice*, in which the husband gives his affines a small or symbolic payment only, is clearly not an explicit bargain.

In *brideservice*, the husband performs services for his father-in-law in return for rights to the daughter, though not always to her offspring. The terms of the agreement vary considerably; usually either a specified number of days, months, or years of labor is re-

---

25. George P. Murdock, *Ethnographic Atlas* (Pittsburgh: University of Pittsburgh Press, 1967), p. 47, col. 12.

quired before the marriage is legally recognized, or services must be performed continually throughout the marriage. Labor is a valuable resource in exchange for a wife, but unlike capital, it cannot be retrieved by the husband if his wife's family defaults on their side of the bargain.

Dowry, or the transfer of substantial wealth from the bride's relatives to the bride, is relatively rare in tribal and band societies. As Jack Goody and S. J. Tambiah have made clear in their analysis of dowry marriage, the wealth goes to the daughter, not the groom's kinsmen (although the groom may have some control over the property) as a conjugal fund.[26] Thus, dowry does not involve two kin groups, and although it may take the form of an explicit contract, it cannot be considered an indicator of fraternal interest groups' ability to contract explicit bargains with other groups.

Gift exchange is the exchange of gifts of substantial value between the relatives of the bride and groom or a continuing exchange of goods and services in approximately equal amounts. It is actually unequal in that the groom and his kin are receiving not only the gifts but also the most valuable resource—the bride's reproductive capacity. Although gift exchange may involve contractual agreements, the goods are often perishable, and their return in case of default is not specified.

Exchange marriage, practiced by relatively few societies,[27] is the transfer of a sister or other female relative of the groom in exchange for the bride. Laura and Paul Bohannan's description of exchange marriage among the Tiv of Central Nigeria illustrates the complexities that inevitably develop with such a practice.[28] In theory, a man practicing exchange marriage takes his younger sister as a marriage ward and exchanges her for rights to the younger sister of another man; the two women should then bear the same number of children of the same sex. In practice, of course, the probability that a man will have a younger sister available for trade when he is looking for a wife is not very great, and the probability that wife and sister will produce matching offspring is even more remote. Often, Tiv men must bargain for kinsmen's sisters or daughters to use as marriage wards at the same time that they are bargaining for a wife. Since the kinsmen may also be planning marriages—for themselves, their sons, their daughters, or their sisters—finding a female to exchange can be exceedingly difficult.

---

26. Jack Goody and S. J. Tambiah, *Bridewealth and Dowry* (Cambridge: Cambridge University Press, 1973), pp. 1–58.

27. See Table 3 in ibid., p. 22.

28. Laura Bohannan and Paul Bohannan, *The Tiv of Central Nigeria* (London: International African Institute, 1953), pp. 69–71.

Some forms of cousin marriage also trade the fertility of one woman for another, though not always through direct exchange. Such trades have been widely researched by anthropologists partly because some of the more elaborate systems for exchanging women occur among societies long thought to be among the most "primitive," such as the Australian aborigines. Among the Arunta, for example, a man can marry a woman from only one of two sections in the opposite moiety.[29] A man of one moiety relinquishes rights to his sister's fertility only temporarily when he agrees to her marriage because any daughter she bears during the marriage must marry someone within the mother's moiety section—specifically, a son of the mother's brother. Any sons that she bears are retained by her husband's father's group: they must marry a daughter of the father's brother. Cross-cousin marriage occurs in many other societies in somewhat different form, but it still accomplishes the same purpose: it allows a man to retain certain jural rights over his kinswoman's offspring so that her fertility may be viewed as being on temporary loan, to be regained when her children marry.[30] While both sister exchange and cross-cousin marriages involve the reciprocal exchange of capital assets between kin groups, ethnographic data on societies practicing these marriage forms do not make clear whether compensation is required if either group does not fulfill the terms of the contract (for example, if either of the women exchanged is barren or dies or divorces, or if brides do not produce the same number of offspring of the same sex).

In a *brideprice* arrangement, the kinsmen of the bride relinquish rights to her and her offspring in return for other valuable capital goods paid by the groom or his relatives. This wealth takes the form of relatively valuable nonperishable assets such as animals, hoes, and, in some cases, wage earnings. It is transferred in a series of installments throughout the marriage rather than in a single transfer at the time of marriage. Installments are frequently contingent on the birth of offspring. Fathers and other kinsmen commonly lend a young husband much or all of the wealth he needs to contract a marriage, thereby indebting him to them for quite some time. Since the bride-

29. Marvin Harris, *Culture, Man, and Nature* (New York: Thomas Y. Crowell, 1971), pp. 335–40.
30. The practice of father's brother's daughter cousin marriage among the Bedouins also reserves certain women—patrilateral parallel cousins—to whom men have customary first claims in a marriage. According to Murphy and Kasdan, this system, while keeping a man's kinswomen as closely tied to his fraternal interest group as possible without violating the incest taboo, may also undermine group solidarity by creating the potential for segmentation and fission through too severe an isolation of each agnatic unit in the society. See Robert Murphy and Leonard Kasdan, "The Structure of Parallel Cousin Marriage," in *Marriage, Family, and Residence*, ed. Paul Bohannan and John Middleton (Garden City, N.Y.: Natural History Press, 1968), pp. 185–201.

price is a large investment for both the groom and his kin, parties to a brideprice bargain almost always insist that some specified amount of property be returned in cases of default such as barrenness, divorce, or death. The value of the resources and the stipulation of compensation for default indicate that brideprice marriage is an explicit marriage bargain by our definition. It is, in fact, the only one of Murdock's seven marriage types that fulfills our definition. Therefore, our measure of fraternal interest groups' ability to contract explicit agreements is the presence or absence of brideprice as coded by Murdock. Ideally, we would include a consideration of the value of brideprice in our measure since this varies considerably within societies and between societies, and over time. Although some ethnographic accounts do detail the content of each brideprice installment and evaluate its economic worth in terms of its proportion of a man's total assets,[31] developing our own codes to measure value in this way would substantially reduce our effective sample size since ethnographic sources usually do not include such detailed information.

Size of the Fraternal Interest Group

The presence or absence of brideprice may provide a measure of bargaining ability, but it does not, of course, measure the capacity of a kin group to defend the bargain and monitor its terms. A group cannot successfully enforce explicit bargains unless it has the military strength necessary to demand contract compliance through force or the threat of force. The larger the military unit backing a bargain, the greater the success in enforcing contract compliance.

The extent to which the economic resource base determines the size of a political unit has been demonstrated indirectly in studies of family structure in preindustrial economies. A group that considers all of its members to belong to the same domestic unit should be more likely to defend the interests of the domestic unit if its rights are challenged or if military action is necessary. Family units, of course, vary considerably in size and structure, ranging from small, independent, monogamous families to large, extended, polygamous ones. A family may live in more than one household, and a household may include people who are not family members. Anthropologists have used many systems of classifying family types, placing greater or lesser weight on the number of wives married to the same husband (monogamous, polygamous), the number of conjugal units under the authority of one or more elders of a senior generation (independent families, stem, extended), and whether these related individuals live

31. See especially Walter Goldschmidt, "The Economics of Brideprice Among the Sebei and in East Africa," *Ethnology* 13 (1974): 311–31.

within the same household or share the household with others (mother-child households, homesteads, and compounds versus family longhouses).

The first attempt to examine systematically the extent to which different family types were associated with different economic systems was M. F. Nimkoff and Russell Middleton's analysis of 549 societies, contained in Murdock's 1967 *Ethnographic Atlas*.[32] They dichotomized family structures into "independent" and "extended," with the former including independent monogamous and polygynous families under the authority of a single male, and the latter including stem and extended families of varying sizes. They found that independent families tended to be associated with hunter-gatherer economies and extended families with settled agricultural economies. The two types tended to occur with equal frequency in societies with combined extractive and agricultural economies. Nimkoff and Middleton interpreted this relationship by postulating that four characteristics of preindustrial economic systems influenced family structure: (1) the reliability and abundance of the food supply; (2) the demand for labor; (3) the extent to which the economy demanded geographic mobility; and (4) the availability of real property (land) for family exploitation. The more reliable and abundant the food supply, the less mobility demanded, the greater the demand for labor and property controlled, and the larger the family size.

Rae Blumberg and Robert Winch also report an association between family size and economy using a somewhat different dichotomous measure of family size (independent monogamous families versus all other), with the smallest, or least "complex," families associated with extractive economies and the most complex associated with complex agriculture.[33] Family size was also associated with patterns of inheritance and descent reckoning, with the largest families associated with patrilineal inheritance and descent systems. In fact, they conclude that the presence of corporate patrilineal ownership and inheritance of property was the strongest predictor of family complexity, though they do not explain why this should be so.

Although there are data on both family and household structures that could be used to measure the size of the fraternal interest group, such a measure is less reliable than actually counting the number of individuals that form a political subunit in a society. Therefore, we constructed our own measure and coded the original ethno-

32. M. F. Nimkoff and Russell Middleton, "Types of Family and Types of Economy," *American Journal of Sociology* 66 (1960): 215–25.
33. Rae Blumberg and Robert Winch, "The Rise and Fall of the Complex Family: Some Implications for an Evolutionary Theory of Societal Development," paper presented at the Annual Meeting of the American Sociological Association, New York, August 1973.

graphic sources used in this study (see Appendices I–III for discussion of methods, codes, and source material). Earlier we defined a fraternal interest group as a consanguineal kin group that acts as a corporate unit, using force if necessary, to defend their interests and resolve disputes. The size code measures the average size of the society's largest consanguineal kin group that meets these criteria. For coding purposes, the criteria are defined in greater detail.

The kin group acts as a corporate unit if its leaders must meet from time to time to consider kin group affairs. These meetings may include formal councils of elders, ceremonial gatherings, audiences with kin-group heads, courts presided over by a single lineage-group head, or informal meetings of localized groups of kinsmen even when such meetings are not regularly scheduled or organized. The leadership may consist of one man or many, but it must meet periodically to consider the welfare of the kin unit. Moieties and implicit exogamous marriage groups which order marital choice but do not have a corporate existence or make decisions are not corporate kin groups. The leadership of a corporate kin group must be selected largely or entirely on the basis of ties of consanguineal kinship, or such kinship must exercise veto power over selection. In many cases the members of the kin group in its entirety constitute the leadership.

The kin group defends its interests and resolves disputes if it makes decisions about adjudication of disputes within the group or accepts collective responsibility to the dictates of higher authorities; it must also make decisions about the military organization and deployment of the kin group in internal warfare with other kin groups.

Enforcing Loyalty and Allegiance

Even if a large fraternal interest group can make explicit bargains and has a large military force to compel compliance to them, the ability to mobilize that force depends on the loyalty of its members to each other's interests. There is always the possibility of defections, or fission (as Chapter 4 will demonstrate). But the belief that members of a fraternal interest group share a common ancestry not shared by other groups can reinforce individual loyalty to the group and inhibit defection to an opposing group. Continuing loyalty of succeeding generations of fraternal interest group members is particularly likely if kinsmen hold to the belief that their wives' offspring are descended from, and therefore allegiant to, only their own fraternal interest group and that a wife's own kin group has no ideological claims whatsoever to her offspring. This, of course, describes patrilineal descent reckoning; it is distinguished from matrilineal descent, in which offspring owe allegiance to their mother's lineage only, and from cognatic systems, in which offspring owe allegiance to the kin groups of both parents.

In summary, then, the strength of a fraternal interest group depends on the marital transactions, numbers, and loyalties of its members, and these qualities depend on the nature of the economy. Our theory, which assumes that ritual is a form of politics, predicts that the nature and use of ritual at each of the major events of the human reproductive cycle are determined by the strength of fraternal interest groups.

METHOD

The utility of our bargaining theory of reproductive ritual, and of the alternative explanations offered by psychoanalytic, transition-rite, or structural-functional theories, is ultimately determined by their ability to account for the pattern of empirical relationships between ritual and other cultural elements observed in actual societies. In the analyses of the rituals of circumcision, menarcheal ceremonies, birth practices, and menstrual restrictions and sex segregation reported in the chapters that follow, specific hypotheses derived from our bargaining theory were tested, using data derived from ethnographic accounts of preindustrial societies. The results were then compared with those obtained from testable predictions derived from other theoretical perspectives. Our analysis is based on the cross-cultural method developed by Murdock and his colleagues. Compared with past cross-cultural survey analyses, however, ours relies much less heavily on the Human Relations Area Files as a source of data. We used an improved world sample, recently published recodes of selected cultural elements, and sophisticated statistical techniques to estimate the extent to which observed relationships between variables results from functional association as compared with historical diffusion. These recent improvements in sampling and analysis have eliminated many of the methodological difficulties encountered in cross-cultural surveys.

Selection of Sample

A sample of 108 tribal and band societies was selected from the Standard Cross-Cultural Sample (SCCS) recently developed by George Murdock and Douglas White;[34] this sample provides the data

34. George Murdock and Douglas White, "Standard Cross-Cultural Sample," *Ethnology* 8 (1969): 329–69.

on which the empirical analyses of politics and reproductive rituals are based. The SCCS is a stratified sample of world societies. It is designed to minimize the effects of historical diffusion by including only one society from each of 186 distinct sampling provinces relatively equally distributed across the six major world regions. Each sampling province consists of a cluster of societies with similar cultures, languages, and geographical locations.[35] The society chosen to represent each province in the SCCS was the one we found to be best described in the ethnographic literature, most frequently included in past cross-cultural samples, and most likely to be included in the Human Relations Area Files. Another society from the same sampling province was sometimes substituted for that appearing on the SCCS list since the basic sampling unit is the province rather than a single society. The 186 societies in the SCCS have been listed as they appear along a continuous geo-cultural arc so that statistical tests of the influence of historical diffusion may be applied.

The procedure used to select our study sample involved four steps. First, every second society on the SCCS list was selected although in cases where ethnographic materials were more abundant on an adjacent society than on the society selected by this rule, the better-described society was substituted. Second, we oversampled societies with matrilineal descent by adding any matrilineal society that was adjacent to a nonmatrilineal society selected by the every-other-case rule. Matrilineal descent was oversampled because of its strong association with avunculocal and matrilocal residence, residence patterns that have significant facilitating or inhibiting effects on the formation of fraternal interest groups. Third, thirteen societies on which data for a pilot study had already been collected previously were substituted for the SCCS societies representing their sampling provinces. In no case was more than one society from the same sampling province included. These procedures yielded a sample of 114 societies. Finally, an empirical definition of peasant agriculture was developed, and all societies in our sample that fit the definition were excluded from the statistical analyses. It has already been recognized that including "large states" in cross-cultural surveys can result in spurious correlations since the kinds of social and cultural characteristics investigated by most cross-cultural studies appear infrequently in complex societies. Although some peasant communities within large states have rituals similar to those observed in tribal and band societies, the theory we have developed makes no predictions about the antecedent conditions of reproductive rituals in communities under the authority of organized legal and military institutions of

35. George P. Murdock, "World Sampling Provinces," *Ethnology* 7 (1968): 305--26.

large states. In order to test the hypothesis that ritual is a form of political bargaining that takes place in the absence of more formal mechanisms for asserting claims and adjudicating disputes, we had to limit our sample to social groups in which such formal mechanisms are either absent or unlikely to influence the individual or kin-group bargains that are the focus of the study. The statistical analysis, then, excludes peasant societies within large states—that is, agricultural societies whose political complexity, as defined by Murdock and White, is greater than that of independent local communities, petty paramount chiefdoms, or "small states" organized into districts.[36]

Table 1 compares the distribution of societies by world region for the SCCS and our study sample with and without peasant societies. When peasant societies are included, the sample is reasonably representative of the six world regions except for an underrepresentation of the Circum-Mediterranean. This is primarily because matrilineal societies are rare in this region and therefore could not be oversampled. Matrilineal societies make up 21 percent of our sample but only 14 percent of the SCCS. Of the twenty-four matrilineal societies appearing on the SCCS list, twenty-three of these or substitute societies from the same sampling province are included in our sample. Eliminating six peasant societies from the sample further underrepresents the Circum-Mediterranean and to some extent East Eurasia, and further overrepresents the other four world regions. With the exception of the Circum-Mediterranean underrepresentation, the differences in the distribution of societies between the sample upon which the statistical analyses are based and the SCCS are not great. Further inspection of the remaining Circum-Mediterranean societies in the SCCS showed that including additional societies from this world region in the study sample would not eliminate the problem of their underrepresentation. With three exceptions, the remaining Circum-Mediterranean societies either were peasant societies or were not included in the *Ethnographic Atlas*, which is the source of our codes for economic base, residence, and other antecedent conditions of reproductive rituals. The remaining three societies were excluded because their ethnographies contained inadequate information on the variables for which we had devised original codes. The extent to which this and other biases in the sample influence the statistical relationships can be ascertained through statistical methods for estimating the effects of historical diffusion. Appendix II lists our complete sample of societies and gives the sampling province, language, group, location, principal ethnographic authorities, and period of observation for each.

36. Murdock and White, "Standard Cross-Cultural Sample," p. 353.

TABLE 1. Regional Distribution of Societies (percentages)

	Sample Excluding Peasants (n=108)	Sample Including Peasants (n=114)	SCCS (n=186)
Africa	17	16	15
Circum-Mediterranean	9	11	15
East Eurasia	16	17	18
Insular Pacific	20	19	17
North America	19	19	18
South America	19	18	17

Coding

Each society's scores on the measures developed for the study, such as the size of the group's political units and the type of reproductive rituals practiced, were coded from ethnographic sources describing the society by three graduate assistants, each of them trained in coding ethnographic materials and fluent in at least one foreign language. When a coding decision was not unanimous, we used the score obtained by two out of three coders. All ethnographic sources cited by Murdock and White in the SCCS were coded in the original language when that language was English, French, Spanish, or German. Supplementary sources not cited by Murdock and White were also consulted, with the exception of those written in Russian, Danish, and Arabic. In cases in which the Human Relations Area Files (HRAF) microfiche collection was consulted, only the complete text of sources was used rather than the precoded materials so that our coders would not be biased by the coding categories devised for the Files. The coded data used in this study, then, should be more representative of the true distribution of world culture traits under investigation than they would be if we had followed the more common procedure of basing the analysis on HRAF or English language sources only.

All variables, or traits, were coded for the time period and locale specified by Murdock's 1967 *Ethnographic Atlas* and Murdock and White's SCCS.[37] Therefore, the original codes devised for the analysis of reproductive rituals refer to the same time period and place as the codes already developed and published by Murdock and his colleagues. This made it possible to include the published codes and the original codes in the same analysis. Our illustrative material was drawn from these same ethnographic sources whenever possible, though information on societies that have been described by a trained ethnographer but are not included in the study sample is also used at some points in the development of the argument. The ethnographic

---

37. Murdock, *Ethnographic Atlas*.

evidence in the chapters that follow has, therefore, been selected from a carefully defined sample of tribal and band societies, and only those sources that have passed Murdock and White's scrutiny have been used in the quantitative analysis. The complete bibliography of ethnographic sources used is presented in Appendix III, and the scores obtained for each society on each of the original codes or indices are presented in Appendix I.

Controlling for Historical Diffusion

Our selection of a sample from the SCCS list permitted the use of recent statistical solutions to Galton's problem, or the problem of historical diffusion, which has been the most serious impediment to the acceptance of findings produced by cross-cultural surveys. The main criticism of cross-cultural findings has been that since neighboring societies may share traits because of diffusion or common histories, the statistical associations identified are likely to be inflated. A number of statistical techniques have been developed to partial out the effects of diffusion so that the "true" functional association between cultural traits may be ascertained.[38] Most methods, such as the linked-pair method developed by Raoul Naroll,[39] depend on the alignment of sample societies along a diffusion, or geo-cultural, arc (as in the SCCS). A coefficient of similarity is computed for each variable under investigation by correlating the score obtained for each society with the score obtained for the adjacent society on the list, usually in descending order. The zero-order correlation between two variables and the two similarity coefficients can then be inserted into a partial correlation formula so that the effects of diffusion, or geographical adjacency, on the observed relationship can be partialed out. According to this method, the partial correlations obtained should be reasonable estimates of the functional relationships between the two variables. Colin Loftin and Dean Simonton have argued convincingly, however, that the underlying assumption of the linked-pair method (and similar methods)—namely, the assumption that diffusion inflates correlations—is inaccurate.[40]

According to Loftin, historical diffusion or geographic propinquity produces correlations that are unreliable rather than inflated. Because of the possibility of historical similarities and diffusion

38. Murdock and White, "Standard Cross-Cultural Sample," pp. 348–52.

39. Raoul Naroll, "A Fifth Solution to Galton's Problem," *American Anthropologist* 66 (1964): 863–67.

40. Colin Loftin, "Galton's Problem as Spatial Autocorrelation: Comments on Ember's Empirical Test," *Ethnology* 11 (October 1972): 425–35; and Dean Keith Simonton, "Galton's Problem, Autocorrelation, and Diffusion Coefficients," *Behavior Science Research* 10:4 (1975): 239–48.

among adjacent societies, a sample of world societies will contain redundant information. The redundancy problem, according to this argument, is overlooked by statistical solutions to the diffusion problem
but can be corrected. Instead of correcting the zero-order correlation
between variables, one must correct the degrees of freedom. The degrees of freedom are inflated because of redundant information in a
cross-cultural sample since the true number of independent cases is
inflated. Simonton concludes that the linked-pair and similar
methods merely "convert unbiased but unreliable raw correlations
into biased 'downward' and equally unreliable partial correlations."[41]
The statistical solution Simonton has devised for the redundancy
problem estimates the *effective* number of cases in a sample. In this
procedure what is manipulated is not the zero-order correlation between any two variables but instead the number of cases upon which
the correlation is based and, therefore, the degrees of freedom determining the significance level of the correlation. Historical diffusion
does not change the size of zero-order correlation coefficients between two variables, but it can reduce the effective sample size and,
therefore, lead to statistically nonsignificant correlations.

The possible effects of historical diffusion on the empirical relationships obtained in this study were estimated by applying Simonton's technique for estimating the effective n for each correlation that
appeared to be statistically significant prior to correction. First, the
similarity coefficients for each of the correlated variables were computed. To estimate the effective n, the variance (V) of the correlation
(r_{AB}) was first calculated, in which $V = (1 + r_{AA} r_{BB}) / N (1 - r_{AA} r_{BB})$. Next,
the effective degrees of freedom were estimated by $n = (V + 1) / V$, which
was then used to obtain the t values needed to judge the significance
level of each correlation.

RESIDENCE, RESOURCE BASE, AND FRATERNAL
INTEREST GROUP STRENGTH: AN EMPIRICAL ANALYSIS

In this chapter two variables in addition to residence patterns
have been proposed as measures of fraternal interest group strength
in tribal and band societies. First, a more sensitive indicator of fraternal interest group strength is a group's ability to contract explicit bargains and to protect those bargains through the military action of a
large and loyal group of kinsmen. Second, the strength of fraternal
interest groups depends on the characteristics of the economy in addition to residence patterns. Before discussing our empirical analyses
of the ability of these three indices to explain cross-cultural patterns of

41. Simonton. "Galton's Problem," p. 242.

reproductive rituals, the methods by which the three measures were devised must be described and the extent to which they are associated statistically examined.

Measures

Our measure of the *residence* patterns that promote or inhibit the formation of fraternal interest groups was simply the dominant residence pattern of a society as coded by Murdock and Suzanne Wilson in 1972 and by Murdock in 1967.[42] If the dominant residence pattern was either avunculocal or patrilocal, the society received a score of 1; if it was matrilocal, ambilocal, or neolocal the society received a score of 0.

To measure *resource base*, the dominant subsistence economies of the societies in our sample were clustered into eight categories, formed by combining Murdock's codes for the relative dependence of a society on five major types of subsistence activity, on animal husbandry, and on the presence or absence of the plow and animal traction.[43] An additional variable, the presence or absence of metal hoes, had to be coded from the original ethnographic materials because Murdock codes only the presence or absence of metalworking without specifying whether this activity includes the manufacture of hoes.

The first of the eight categories, *hunting-gathering* economies, are those based primarily on hunting or gathering or both, with 45 percent or less of subsistence activities devoted to fishing; no mounted hunting; and 25 percent or less of subsistence activities devoted to any kind of agriculture or animal husbandry. The second category, *fishing* economies, are defined as those in which 46 percent or more of subsistence is based on fishing (excluding the collecting of food from water or the pursuit of aquatic mammals); 25 percent or less of subsistence is based on agriculture and animal husbandry; and there is no mounted hunting. In *mounted hunting* economies, hunting contributes 36 percent or more to the economy; fishing 35 percent or less; agriculture and animal husbandry combined contribute less than 25 percent; and hunting is from the backs of horses, camels, or reindeer. *Pastoral* economies are those in which animal husbandry contributes at least 26 percent to the subsistence economy, and the predominant species kept are cattle, camels, deer, sheep and goats, or horses; and 25 percent or less of subsistence activity is devoted to

42. George P. Murdock and Suzanne F. Wilson, "Settlement Patterns and Community Organization: Cross-Cultural Codes 3," *Ethnology* 11 (July 1972): 261, col. 9; Murdock, *Ethnographic Atlas*, p. 48, col. 16. Murdock and Wilson's codes were used for all societies in the sample that appear on the 6CCS list; Murdock's early codes were used for all substitute societies not coded by more recent recodes.

43. Murdock, *Ethnographic Atlas*, p. 46, col. 7; p. 51, col. 28; p. 53, col. 39.

agriculture. The last four categories cover societies based primarily on agriculture, the society's placement depending to a large extent on the nature of its agricultural technology. *Simple horticultural* economies include groups in which 25 percent or more of the subsistence activity is devoted to casual or extensive (shifting) agriculture in the absence of metal hoes, and also agricultural societies based on intensive and irrigated cultivation without metal hoes when the proportion of subsistence activity devoted to agriculture and animal husbandry combined is between 26 percent and 45 percent. *Advanced horticultural* economies are those based on intensive or irrigated agriculture or on extensive cultivation with metal hoes, when Murdock's codes indicate that agriculture and animal husbandry combined account for 46 percent or more of the subsistence activity. *Agricultural* economies are those in which the combined contribution of agriculture and animal husbandry is 26 percent or more when Murdock's codes also indicate that plows with animal traction are used in cultivation. Agricultural economies that meet these criteria but have a high level of political complexity, indicating that they are part of what Murdock calls "large states," are classified as *peasant* economies. As reported earlier, there were six peasant economies in our original sample of 114 societies, and these societies have been excluded from our analyses of political and reproductive rituals.

The economic systems represented in our sample form discrete categories and exhaust the various combinations of subsistence activities that are observed among societies in the Murdock and White SCCS. For purposes of analysis, the hunting-gathering, fishing, mounted hunting, and simple horticultural economies were collapsed into a single category, Low Value Resource Base, and given a score of 0. The pastoral, advanced horticultural, and agricultural societies, excluding those that are part of large states, were collapsed into a second category, High Value Resource Base, and given a score of 1.

Each of the three variables used to measure the strength of fraternal interest groups—ability to contract explicit bargains, group size, and descent ideology—has been described in detail earlier. Murdock's classification of modes of marriage[44] was used to construct a measure of the ability to contract explicit bargains: societies that practice brideprice received a score of 1, and all other forms of marriage received a score of 0. The size of the largest politically effective consanguineal kin group was measured by estimating from the original ethnographic sources the actual number of individuals belonging to a group that could be described as corporate and that made decisions regarding the adjudication of disputes, the obedience of mem-

44. Ibid., col. 12.

bers, and the operation of internal wars. Since the size of the effective political subunits in the sample varied substantially, the scores obtained by each society were collapsed into three categories. Societies with political subunits of 1,000 or more were given a score of 2, those with subunits containing between 100 and 999 members received a score of 1, and those with subunits containing fewer than 100 members were given a score of 0. The ability to reinforce the loyalty and allegiance of kinsmen was measured by a dichotomous code of descent reckoning as coded by Murdock and Wilson,[45] with societies described as patrilineal receiving a score of 1 and societies with all other forms of descent receiving a score of 0.

Our composite index of fraternal interest group strength was obtained merely by adding the scores on each of the components for each society, with the scores ranging from a maximum of 4 to a minimum of 0. More detailed descriptions of code construction of these and all other variables used in the empirical analyses are presented in Appendix I.

Results

The relationships between each of these variables for the 108 tribal and band societies in our sample are presented in Table 2. Inspection of the zero-order correlations in the matrix shows, first, that the three measures that make up the index of fraternal interest group strength (strength index) are highly correlated with each other. The trichotomized measure of the size of political subunit is correlated .48 with the measure of the ability to contract explicit bargains and .48 with the measure of loyalty. The bargaining measure and the loyalty measure are correlated .51. After the possible effects of historical diffusion are taken into account, using Simonton's method, each of the correlation coefficients remains statistically significant at the .001 level. The matrix also indicates that the components of the strength index make nearly equal contributions to it: both loyalty and bargaining correlate .78 with the index, and the size measure correlates .86. These correlations also remain statistically significant at the .001 level after the possible effects of diffusion are controlled by reducing the effective n.

Second, the data in the matrix indicate that the dichotomous measure of the value of the economic resource base is a much stronger predictor of fraternal interest group strength ($r=.66$) than is the dichotomous measure of residence patterns promoting or inhibit-

45. Murdock and Wilson, "Settlement Patterns," col. 10; for all substitute societies Murdock's *Ethnographic Atlas*, p. 49, cols. 20, 22, 24 were used.

TABLE 2. **Relationship between Resource Base, Residence Patterns, and Measures of Fraternal Interest Group Strength (n=108)**

Variable	2	3	4	5	6
1. Resource Base[1]	.31[b]	.66[c]	.60[c]	.57[c]	.46[c]
2. Residence Patterns[2]		.39[b]	.33[b]	.27[a]	.44[c]
3. Strength Index			.86[c]	.78[c]	.78[c]
4. Size of Political Unit[3]				.48[c]	.48[c]
5. Bargaining[4]					.51[c]
6. Loyalty[5]					

[a] $p < .05$.
[b] $p < .01$.
[c] $p < .001$.
[1] High value resource base = 1; low value = 0.
[2] Residence patterns that localize kinsmen (patrilocal and avunculocal) = 1; patterns that disperse kinsmen (matrilocal, ambilocal, neolocal) = 0.
[3] Size less than 100 = 0, between 100 and 999 = 1, over 1,000 = 2.
[4] Brideprice present = 1, absent = 0.
[5] Patrilineal descent present = 1, absent = 0.

ing the formation of fraternal interest groups ($r = .39$). Even so, both correlations remain statistically significant after the effects of diffusion have been taken into account. Both residence and resource base are significantly associated with two of the three components of the strength index once the effects of diffusion are reduced. The size of the correlation coefficient and the significance level are higher between each component of the strength index and resource base than between each component and residence. The multiple correlation coefficient between the strength index, residence, and resource base is .69, which is only insignificantly greater than the zero-order correlation between resource base and strength ($r = .66$), suggesting that retaining residence in the model does not increase the ability of structural measures to predict fraternal interest group strength. Resource base alone is an adequate predictor of strength. However, the residence variable has been retained in the model and in subsequent empirical analyses because its effect on the dependent variables— reproductive rituals—is unknown.

STRENGTH OF FRATERNAL INTEREST GROUPS AND THE FORM OF REPRODUCTIVE RITUAL

The empirical data indicate that resource base is a better predictor of fraternal interest group strength than is residence pattern although the relationship between residence and strength is in the predicted direction. When a society has resources that are both stable and valuable (that is, herds or land cultivated by hoes, plows, or the use of irrigation), its ability to make explicit bargains concerning women and children and to protect such bargains through the military action of a large and loyal political faction is maximized. When a society lacks valuable resources, fraternal interest groups are either weak or absent. The society's capacity to engage in explicit bargains regarding rights to women's fertility is substantially reduced without valuable capital assets or a large, loyal faction. If resources of some value (such as fish, buffalo, or land suitable for rudimentary shifting cultivation) are available, temporary political factions can be established; but if the resources available have little value, the possibility of developing even a temporary faction is remote, and the likelihood of effective bargaining is correspondingly reduced. In the absence of many loyal kinsmen or valuable resources, individual bargaining for women and children must be implicit, and the individual's claims must remain problematic. Without enforcement power, there is little that anyone can do to assure that his rights are recognized by others and protected against challengers.

The political uses of ritual at the critical events of the human reproductive cycle—sexual maturity, childbirth, and menstruation—depend ultimately on fraternal interest group strength. We have argued that at each of these critical events customary patterns of control over reproductive assets are threatened: by the need to transfer rights over a woman from one group of men to another, by the competition for access to women from newly mature claimants, by the ambiguities surrounding attribution of paternity, and by the opportunity for a husband to take advantage of the wealth and power based on his wife's reproductive capacity by defaulting on obligations to his kin. The sexual maturity of both women and men, childbirth, and menstruation present problems of control in all preindustrial societies, but the society's response to those problems is determined by the nature of the political economy.

In societies in which there are stable and valuable economic resources, strong fraternal interest groups are likely to develop, and the dilemmas posed by the major events of the human reproductive cycle are responded to by the form of ritual bargaining characterized earlier in this chapter as surveillance rituals. In strong fraternal interest groups, ritual politics focuses on monitoring existing bargains and on preserving the loyalty and size of the fraternal interest group itself. Ritual solutions to social dilemmas in societies in which fraternal interest groups are weak or absent take a different form. Ritual bargaining is used to construct and maintain temporary political coalitions or to gauge community opinion. We have termed this form of ritual behavior social mobilization. Some of these societies have little or no economic surplus to hold a faction together or to serve as a basis for acquiring personal power. Others have considerable surpluses of

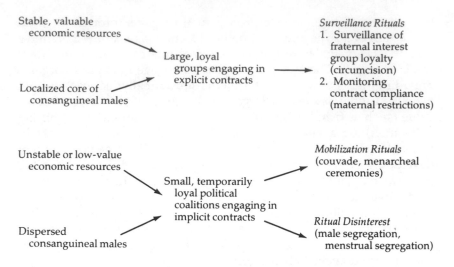

Figure 1. Economic and Political Predictors of Forms of Reproductive Rituals

resources that are unpredictable and perishable; political factions based on these surpluses are equally unstable. In this latter type of society, men are likely to show ritual disinterest in wealth and power or in the wealth and power that their wives' reproductive capacity represents. Through this kind of ritual they declare their willingness to comply with obligations to kin and community that they are acquiring the power to ignore.

Figure 1 summarizes the hypothesized relationships of reproductive rituals to economic and political variables. In the chapters that follow, the dilemmas posed by reproductive events and the ritual responses of the weak and the strong are examined in detail. In each case, ritual provides only a partial solution to the problem at hand, and in no case is the solution final. In the shifting world of ritual politics, in which appearances often overshadow substance, apparent loyalties can easily dissolve and allegiances frequently change. But in preindustrial societies that lack strong centralized political systems, ritual solutions to the dilemmas of the human reproductive cycle are often the only ones available.

3 The Dilemma
of Menarche:
Female Puberty Rites

Since the appearance of the menstrual flow is widely regarded as the first positive indication that a woman is able to bear
children, menarche represents the earliest point in the life cycle at
which bargaining over rights to a woman's fertility becomes critical.[1]
In societies in which a man's wealth, power, and prestige are largely
determined by the number of children he controls, acquiring rights to
a woman who can produce many children is essential. Although
theoretically a woman should be able to produce a child every nine
months throughout a reproductive span of up to thirty years,[2] fetal,
infant, and maternal mortality rates make actual fertility much lower
than the number of possible conceptions. Demographic estimates
show that even under conditions most favorable to high fertility, few,
if any, women produce more than twenty children. According to John
Peel and Malcolm Potts, the highest average rate of child production
per female in any society is eleven, with six being the overall average
across societies.[3] Therefore, a man who wants many children to survive to maturity must maximize his chances by obtaining rights to a
woman who becomes fertile at an early age and by gaining sexual
access to her as soon as she becomes fertile.

1. Moni Nag, "Factors Affecting Human Fertility in Nonindustrial Societies: A
Cross-Cultural Study," *Yale University Publications in Anthropology* 66 (1962): 104.
2. Ibid., pp. 104–14.
3. John Peel and Malcolm Potts, *Textbook of Contraceptive Practice* (Cambridge:
Cambridge University Press, 1969), pp. 18–19.

This task is made difficult by the unpredictable timing of a woman's biological development. The time at which girls reach menarche is highly variable and cannot be accurately predicted on the basis of associated physical changes such as breast development and the appearance of pubic hair. A compilation of ethnographic estimates of average menarcheal ages among our sample societies, for example, produced a range from thirteen to seventeen years.[4] Moni Nag indicates that intrasocietal variations in menarcheal age are even greater than those between societies.[5] Thus, the average, or modal, age at menarche in a society provides little basis for an accurate prediction of the age at which an individual woman in that society will begin to menstruate. Nor does the attainment of menarche guarantee immediate fertility. The period of time between menarche and ovulation, sometimes referred to as "adolescent sterility," is highly variable in length and impossible to predict for any single woman.[6] There are some data to suggest that the period of adolescent sterility is recognized in a number of societies. The Jivaro, for example, believe that a woman should not be expected to bear her first child until a certain tree, which blossoms every six months, has bloomed three times since the woman's first menses—in other words, until at least eighteen months after menarche.[7]

If a man marries a girl before she has reached menarche, he is running the risk that she may remain infertile for many years to come. Among the Andaman Islanders, for example, the average age at menarche has been estimated at fifteen years, with a range of eleven to nineteen years.[8] If a young Andaman wife-seeker settled a marriage on a fifteen-year-old woman on the guess that she would begin menstruating at the same time as most other women her age, but if in fact she did not do so, he might have to wait four years or longer before she acquired the capacity to reproduce. Each of these years would represent a loss of potential offspring. Because of this risk, it is in the suitor's best interest to marry a woman who has already started menstruating, preferably at or soon after menarche so that he has sexual rights to her throughout her entire reproductive span. Menarche is therefore usually a prerequisite to the final settlement of a marriage bargain.

4. Raymond Pearl, *The Natural History of Population* (London: Oxford University Press, 1939). Additional research on menarcheal age distribution in industrialized countries is summarized in Chap. 1 of *The Female Reproductive Cycle: An Annotated Bibliography* by Karen Paige, Elisabeth Magnus, Susan Hahn, and Cher Carrie (Boston: G. K. Hall, forthcoming).

5. Nag, "Human Fertility," p. 107, citing Paul Popenoe, *Problems in Human Reproduction* (Baltimore: Williams & Wilkins, 1926), p. 165.

6. Nag, "Human Fertility," p. 107.

7. Michael Harner, *The Jivaro* (Garden City, N.Y.: Anchor Press, 1973), p. 83.

8. Edward H. Man, "On the Aboriginal Inhabitants of the Andaman Islands," *Journal of the Anthropological Institute of Great Britain and Ireland* 12 (1877): 79.

MANIPULATING THE APPEARANCE
OF SEXUAL MATURITY

The social importance of an early menarche is illustrated by parents' attempts in many societies to stimulate its onset or to suggest that it is forthcoming by altering the daughter's physical appearance. Ethnographers have recorded numerous medicinal recipes that combine herbs and foods believed to produce menarche[9] and have described such mechanical methods as massaging a woman's stomach.[10] One common mechanical method, usually the prerogative of the fiancé or husband, is breaking the hymen: manually, by coitus, or by piercing with a weapon.[11] In some societies, a spirit medium is called in to encourage the appearance of menarche.

Alteration of physical characteristics most closely associated with sexual maturity is also a common practice. Promoting a mature appearance of the external genitalia may be attempted by constant massage, stretching, and tattooing of the labia.[12] Attempts to increase the size of the breasts through constant rubbing, stroking, and pul-

9. See ethnographic summaries by Janet Schreiber, "Cross-Cultural Study of Menstrual Perceptions," World Health Organization Task Force Report on the Acceptability of Fertility Regulating Methods AFT 3:6, April 1974. Among the Mayans, for example, women were given a hot drink made out of the mashed roots of guaco, roots of basamite, and chinanco, all of which were boiled together and mixed with honey. Among the Burmese the mixture was jaggerty and ginger; the Malays thought flow would be induced by a combination of betel nut and pieces of an insect taken for seven days in succession; and the Serbs either wore red flowers or drank them in a special concoction.

10. The Nama, according to Isaac Schapera, believe that menstrual flow can be encouraged by massaging a woman's stomach (*The Khoisan Peoples of South Africa* [London: George Routledge & Sons, 1930], p. 408).

11. For example, John Honigmann reports that the Kaska believe that sexual intercourse causes menarche; he suggests that this belief may be a convenient way of forcing a man to marry a particularly undesirable daughter by forcing the daughter to publicly point out the man who "started her" ("The Kaska Indians: An Ethnographic Reconstruction," *Yale University Publications in Anthropology* 51 [1954]: 132). Among the Gros Ventre, the burden of producing menarche is again shifted to the husband; Regina Flannery suggests that they believe menarche is produced by coitus, which should occur only after marriage (*The Gros Ventres of Montana: Part 1. Social Life* [Washington, D.C.: Catholic University of America, 1953], p. 127). John Roscoe describes how a Ganda husband unlucky enough to have married a woman who has not yet begun to menstruate will attempt to begin her flow himself by piercing her with his weapon, enough so as to draw blood, each time he goes to war (*The Baganda* [London: Macmillan, 1911], p. 80).

12. Young women among the Marquesans (Robert Suggs, *Marquesan Sexual Behavior* [New York: Harcourt, Brace and World, 1966], pp. 39–42), Nyakyusa (Monica Wilson, *Rituals of Kinship Among the Nyakyusa* [London: Oxford University Press, 1957], p. 87), and Nama (Schapera, *Khoisan Peoples*, p. 243) are encouraged throughout childhood to practice elongating the outer labia. Young women among the Maori (Elsdon Best, *The Maori* [Wellington, New Zealand: Polynesian Society, 1941], II, 557), Mongo (Gustave-E. Hulstaert, "Le mariage des Nkundó," *Institut Royal Colonial Belge, Mémoires* 8 [1938]: 60), and Trobrianders (Bronislaw Malinowski, *The Sexual Life of Savages* [New York: Harcourt, Brace and World, 1929], p. 305) design special tattoo markings along the labia.

ling are common, as are painted designs that give the illusion of greater size. Among the Arunta, the kinsmen most likely to profit from early marriage play important roles in a special breast-growing ceremony. These kinsmen, the mother's brothers, play a significant role in selecting the woman's husband and have first marriage rights over her future daughters. Baldwin Spencer and F. J. Gillen's account of the ceremony suggests the great social importance of early sexual development:

> To promote the growth of the breasts of a girl, the men assemble at the *Ungunja*, or men's camp, where they all join in singing long chants, the words of which express an exhortation to the breasts to grow, and others which have the effect of charming some fat and red ochre, which men who are *Gammona*—that is, brothers of her mother—have brought to the spot, as well as head and arm bands of fur-string. . . . At daylight one of them goes out and calls her to a spot close to the *Ungunja*, to which she comes, accompanied by her mother. Here her body is rubbed all over with fat by the *Gammona* men, who then paint a series of straight lines of red ochre down her back and also down the center of her chest and stomach. A wide circle is painted around each nipple and straight lines below each of these circles.[13]

Altering a woman's physical characteristics to suggest sexual maturity may indeed convince some suitors that she is ready to produce children and therefore to marry. After all, a suitor often has only the family's word that a daughter has begun to menstruate. Even if he demands physical proof of menstruation, he cannot be sure that the blood was produced by menstruation and was not the blood of a chicken, goat, or pig smeared on the daughter just before his inspection.

PROTECTING A DAUGHTER'S MARRIAGE VALUE AFTER MENARCHE

Menarche represents not only the time when a woman is of maximum value in a marriage bargain but also the beginning of a period during which she will become especially vulnerable to seduction and rape. Many men may find it more profitable to "steal" a nubile young woman, even at the risk of retaliation, than to negotiate a formal but expensive marriage contract with her father. Young single men are particularly likely to attempt to avoid a formal marriage bargain in this way since they are more likely than older married

13. Baldwin Spencer and F. J. Gillen, *The Arunta* (London: Macmillan, 1927), II, 480–81.

men to lack the necessary wealth. The grossly unequal bargaining position of young men relative to older and wealthier ones among the Tiwi illustrates the conditions that can make elopement or abduction of a nubile woman a successful solution to the problem of obtaining a wife.[14] Because young Tiwi men are competing with older wife-hoarding polygynous men, they may have to wait until they are forty years old before they gain enough wealth and prestige to enter into a formal marriage bargain. For younger men, seducing or abducting a newly fertile woman may be a wiser solution than settling for a widow who is near the end of her reproductive period. Not only does the seducer acquire a woman with a long career as a child producer ahead of her, but by seducing her, he diminishes her value to other suitors. His success in acquiring one wife illegally through seduction may even increase his chances for acquiring additional ones legally, for some fathers are eager to bargain with men who have shown their power by acquiring wives.

Even a man who has already entered into preliminary marriage negotiations and made some payments in goods or labor may find elopement to be the best solution. Through elopement he can eliminate competing suitors who might outbid him in the final marriage contract, and he can shorten the period of gift-giving and bride-service. He can also demonstrate the father's inability to control his own daughter and his lack of authority over his potential son-in-law, thereby possibly shaming the father into lowering the amount of compensation demanded.[15]

The effects of seduction or abduction on a woman's marriage value depend on the ability of her father to retrieve her and force the seducer to compensate for what he has stolen.[16] If the father has sufficient political and military backing, he may be able to coerce the seducer into marriage and full compensation. More commonly, he re-

---

14. C. W. Hart and Arnold Pilling, *The Tiwi of North Australia* (New York: Holt, Rinehart and Winston, 1960), pp. 79–83.

15. See for example Roy Rappaport, "Marriage Among the Maring," in *Pigs, Pearlshells, and Women*, ed. R. M. Glasse and M. J. Meggitt (Englewood Cliffs, N.J.: Prentice-Hall, 1969), pp. 127–30.

16. Elopement among the Gisu, described below, is typical of many other societies: "The young man waits with some of his age mates . . . by a spring or river. When the girl comes to fetch water, the young men leap out and carry her off. Propriety demands that she should struggle and make a show of resistance, but unless she is genuinely surprised, she will not make herself heard. She is taken to the house of a senior maternal kin of her captors . . . and placed under his care. This relative must then send messengers to both fathers and arrange for bridewealth discussion to take place" (Jean la Fontaine, "Gisu Marriage and Affinal Relations," in *Marriage in Tribal Societies*, ed. Meyer Fortes [Cambridge: Cambridge University Press, 1962], pp. 102–03)

ceives only part of the compensation he could have expected from a legal marriage, and in some instances he may receive none of it.[17] If the seducer cannot be found or pressured into marriage, the father's chances of marrying off his daughter profitably to another man are greatly diminished. A woman's chastity is in many societies a crucial determinant of her marriage value because a prospective husband wants the assurance that no other man will be able to challenge his paternity rights by claiming prior sexual access to her once she is fertile.

Even if a woman does not behave promiscuously, accusations of promiscuity can diminish her value in a marriage bargain and cause her father economic loss. As Lucy Mair points out, the importance of a woman's virtue in a marriage bargain has just as much to do with her reputation for chastity as with the more technical issue of the presence of an intact hymen.[18] Gossip can undermine the prospective husband's assurance of paternity as much as a seduction. As the Tikopia put it, "In this land, if a man is sensible, and hears that a woman is going with another man, he does not wish to marry her."[19] A woman's damaged reputation can have more serious consequences for her father than actual seduction since if it is not founded in fact, there is no obvious culprit to pressure into marriage.[20] A bad reputation will ward off some suitors and provide ammunition for the rest in their campaign to lower the father's compensation demands. The implication that a man is too weak to control his daughter makes him more vulnerable to pressure during negotiations.

17. Like the Maring, Tallensi fathers lacking family backing have little recourse but to harangue and threaten the seducer until he finally gives in. According to Meyer Fortes, "A girl's father resorts to all sorts of devices to coerce her abductors. He may use ritual pretexts, exploit ties of cognatic kinship with the abductor's lineage or clan, even, in extremity, threaten to kill himself on their doorstep, or, in the old days, to stir up war against their clan" (*The Web of Kinship Among the Tallensi* [London: Oxford University Press, 1949], p. 91). As a consequence of this outburst, a father may receive a gift to placate him and perhaps in a few years finally receives at least an installment of the customary wealth compensation.

18. Lucy Mair, *Marriage* (Harmondsworth, England: Penguin Books, 1971), Chap. 10.

19. Raymond Firth, *We, the Tikopia* (Boston: Beacon Press, 1936), p. 451.

20. See especially illustrations in Robert Felkin, "Notes on the Fur Tribe of Central Africa," *Proceedings of the Royal Society of Edinburgh* 13 (1884–86): 235; Virginia Gutiérrez de Pineda, "Organización social en la Guajira," *Revista del Instituto Etnológico Nacional* 3 (1948): 56; Verne Ray, "The Sanpoil and Nespelem," *University of Washington Publications in Anthropology* 5 (1932): 136–37; Melville Herskovits, *Dahomey* (Evanston, Ill.: Northwestern University Press, 1967), I, 285; Morris Opler, *An Apache Life-Way* (Chicago: University of Chicago Press, 1941), p. 143; Pliny Goddard, "Life and Culture of the Hupa," *University of California Publications in American Archaeology and Ethnology* 1 (1903): 54–55; Carleton S. Coon, "Tribes of the Rif," *Harvard African Studies* 9 (1931): 135; and Honigmann, "Kaska Indians," p. 132.

THE FATHER'S DILEMMA AT MENARCHE

From a father's point of view, there are many advantages in marrying off a daughter as soon after menarche as possible. The longer the delay between a woman's menarche and her marriage, the greater the chance that her marriage value will decline because of seduction, rape, or accusations of promiscuity. If she remains unmarried for too long after menarche, suitors begin to pass her over in favor of younger fertile women with a longer exploitable reproductive span. Finally, the longer she remains unmarried, the longer her father must bear the costs of supporting her.

Although delaying marriage past menarche has its drawbacks, it also has its advantages. Since the timing of menarche is unpredictable, a father may be suddenly confronted with the task of selecting a son-in-law from the small group of suitors available at any given moment. Ideally, a father would like to take advantage of good marriage prospects as they present themselves. A time extension would give him a wider field of potential sons-in-law to choose from and would allow him to seize on current opportunities to form an important political alliance with another family. Economically, a time extension would mean that the father could arrange to receive compensation at the time when he needed it most to pay off pressing debts or invest in other marriages for his sons or himself. Once he entered into marriage negotiations, he could draw them out for months or years, extracting payment after payment from the suitor before relinquishing his daughter. Finally, he could settle the bargain at a time when the going rate of marriage compensation was highest. As Mair illustrates, the going rate of compensation in a society can fluctuate widely, and taking advantage of its fluctuations can be crucial, especially for fathers whose own sons' marriages depend entirely on the fathers' ability to contract profitable marriages for the daughters of the family.[21]

A father's dilemma at menarche, then, is his choice between marrying off his daughter at or shortly after menarche without being able to take advantage of the best economic and political conditions for a marriage, and delaying the marriage long past menarche to take advantage of economic and political conditions while running the risk of losing his daughter's marriage value through her seduction, loss of reputation, or depreciation over time.

21. Mair, *Marriage*, pp. 54–67; and Lucy Mair, "African Marriage and Social Change," in *A Survey of African Marriage and Family Life*, ed. Arthur Phillips (London: Oxford University Press, 1953), p. 52.

PREMENARCHEAL BETROTHAL

Premenarcheal betrothal, an option practiced in 82 percent of our sample societies, allows mate selection and preliminary marriage negotiations to occur before menarche even though a final marriage settlement is usually not reached until after menarche. Generally, the suitor and his kin must make some sort of investment in the future bride. There are three common types of betrothal investment: "rearing" or adopting the potential wife;[22] performing services for the potential father-in-law; and paying gifts or portions of property which may later be counted as installments of marriage compensation.[23] Two or more of these practices often occur simultaneously; for example, the woman's potential affines care for her while the suitor lives and works for her family. Both father and suitor can break the agreement at any time although the suitor may incur some economic loss by doing so. Investments of laboring for the potential father-in-law or supporting the potential wife during her stay with the suitor or his kin are obviously not returnable; gifts and property are generally returned.[24]

Premenarcheal betrothal would appear to resolve the father's dilemma since it gives him a time extension before menarche during which he can choose a son-in-law at his leisure, receive some payments as he needs them, and keep his daughter's marriage value relatively safe. That it does not resolve the father's dilemma is due to menarche's unpredictable timing.

Let us consider again the example of the Andaman Islanders, among whom the average age at menarche is fifteen years and the range is eleven to nineteen years. If a father waits until his daughter is thirteen or fourteen, a year or two before the average age at menarche, before betrothing her, he may be taken by surprise when she begins menstruating at age eleven. If he decides to take no chances and betroth her at age nine or ten, he may be staking her

22. For examples of "rearing the bride," see Man, "Andaman Islands," p. 136; H. Ian Hogbin, "Marriage in Wogeo, New Guinea," *Oceania* 15–16 (1944): 329–30; Henri Junod, *The Life of a South African Tribe* (New Hyde Park, N.Y.: University Books, 1962), I, 104–06; and Viviana Pacques, "Les Bambara," *International African Institute Ethnographic Survey of Africa* 1 (1954): 125.

23. In some societies, the time at which the series of payments begins is a matter of ceremony, as among the Riffians, who seal the payment by tattooing the daughter (Coon, "Tribes of the Rif"). Among the Azande, the suitor may take the young daughter to his own home prior to payment, but the relationship is not considered a legal marriage until he has paid ten spears. See Charles G. Seligman and Brenda Z. Seligman, *Pagan Tribes of the Nilotic Sudan* (London: Routledge & Kegan Paul, 1932), p. 512.

24. Such is the case among the Lau Fijians, who may make partial gifts and payment of property to a father for up to twenty years. If the marriage never takes place, however, the father is obligated to return all the gifts accumulated during the betrothal period. See Laura Thompson, "Southern Lau, Fiji: An Ethnography," *Bernice P. Bishop Museum Bulletin* 162 (1940): 90–91.

future marriage on a promise that must be kept over a period as long as ten years. Since child mortality rates in most world societies are high[25] and since an early betrothal can entail a long and expensive engagement with no guarantees of the woman's fertility, a suitor is understandably reluctant to enter into such an agreement. If he does and the woman does not reach menarche soon afterward, he may break off the agreement.

Even if the fiancé does not tire of waiting for the woman to mature or trying to meet the father's compensation demands, the father may decide that alliance with the fiancé's family is no longer advantageous because of war, shifting allegiances, or a change in family fortunes. The longer a betrothal period, the more likely are political and economic changes that make the envisioned marriage less advantageous than it was at the time it was first proposed. Therefore, even with the precaution of premenarcheal betrothal, many women reach menarche with no fiancé or with a fiancé whom the father now considers unsuitable. Delay in marriage for a period past menarche is still often necessary to allow the father to take advantage of the economic and political conditions that best serve his interests.

MENARCHEAL STRATAGEMS AND FRATERNAL INTEREST GROUP STRENGTH

We hypothesize that the dilemma created by a daughter's menarche should be more serious in societies in which fraternal interest groups are weak or absent than in societies with strong fraternal interest groups. A father defends his daughter's marriage value after menarche by preventing theft of her reproductive capacity and by maintaining a strong bargaining position during negotiations over her value. In most societies, the father guarantees the husband unambiguous paternity rights, the critical determinant of marriage value, by protecting his daughter's virginity and her reputation for virginity until marriage.[26] In strong fraternal interest group societies, a father has the backing of a large corporate group of kinsmen to defend his daughter's marriage value by force or force threat. Often kinsmen have an economic motivation because they receive a share of the

25. Nag, "Human Fertility," Table 77, pp. 223–25.
26. With the exceptions of polyandrous societies and societies in which husbands are powerful enough to thwart any challenges to their rights, husbands usually expect to be the sole biological father to a wife's offspring through the duration of the marriage contract. Even in the case of secondary marriages, such as leviratic marriages, children produced during a woman's subsequent marriage are recognized as the biological children of the original husband. Similarly, in bilateral, some patrilineal, and especially matrilineal societies, a woman's husband is expected to be recognized as the biological father of his wife's children although his jural authority over them may be shared with other males.

bridewealth. Politically, their reputation may suffer if an outsider can dishonor one of their kinswomen with impunity. Since they are corporate, they can be readily mobilized as needed. Their backing allows the father to extend the process of mate selection and marriage negotiations well past menarche with minimal risk. In weak fraternal interest group societies, a father cannot rely on the unconditional backing of a corporate kin group to protect his interests. Once his daughter reaches menarche, he can defend her marriage value only by drawing together a temporary coalition of supporters. Ritual becomes necessary to gather and assess political support at the critical time of a daughter's menarche. Menarcheal ceremonies serve this purpose. They are therefore likely to be characteristic of weak rather than strong fraternal interest group societies.

Defending Marriage Value in Strong Fraternal Interest Group Societies

The Importance of Virginity

In strong fraternal interest group societies, parties to a marriage make an explicit contract involving large transfers of wealth. Because the contract is enforceable by all kin groups concerned and because either the wealth or the woman can be retrieved if one side does not satisfy the contract conditions, marriage bargains in strong fraternal interest group societies include formal procedures for verifying the daughter's marriage value. Such procedures as infibulation and virginity tests illustrate the importance of virginity in a marriage bargain.

Infibulation. Infibulation is an operation that consists of scarifying the sides of the vulva, then holding them together so that they fuse during the healing process. This operation is carried out by the pastoral Somali and a number of other strong fraternal interest group societies in northeast Africa and adjacent regions. Among the Somali, infibulation takes place when a girl is between the ages of six and eight, or sometimes earlier.[27] The Somali state explicitly that its purpose is to prevent intercourse. I. M. Lewis describes how a serious suitor insists on being shown a potential wife's fused genitals before completing a marriage bargain so that he may be assured of her virginity.

Probably the most detailed description of infibulation is presented by John G. Kennedy in his discussion of genital mutilation rit-

---

27. I. M. Lewis, *Peoples of the Horn of Africa* (London: International African Institute, 1955), p. 135.

uals among the Egyptian Nubians. The Nubians perform clitoral excision in association with infibulation. The operation proceeds as follows:

> On the night before the operation, [the girl] is adorned with gold and dressed in new clothes. . . . With little fanfare or preparation, the midwife quickly performs the operation. As several women spread her legs, a bowl is placed beneath the girl to catch the blood, and the clitoris, the labia minora, and part of the labia majora are excised with a razor or knife. The women meanwhile chant, "Come, you are now a woman." "You became a bride." "Bring her the groom now." "Bring her a penis, she is ready for intercourse," etc. . . . According to some informants, this chanting and shouting serves partially to drown the screams of the child. . . . After the ordeal, the mother and nearest female relatives serve dates, candy, popcorn, and tea to the visiting women, and the hostess sprinkles them with perfume. . . . Sometimes the child's legs remain tied together for forty days. More typically she is regarded as healed seven to fifteen days after the operation. This healing process generally provides the scar tissue for the complete closure of the vulva except for a small urination orifice which is kept open by a match or a reed tube.[28]

According to Kennedy, the woman's defloration at marriage is traumatizing for both bride and groom since the groom must consummate the marriage by penetrating his wife's sealed vagina. (In some instances, a midwife reopens the woman's vagina with a knife or razor before the couple have intercourse.)[29] Like the Somali, the Nubians state explicitly that the purpose of this surgery is to prevent loss of virginity. Infibulation is an essential prerequisite for marriage.

Virginity Tests.   Like infibulation, a virginity test gives the husband and his kin proof of the bride's virginity. Final compensation may be contingent on this proof, which usually takes the form of a public display of the bloody sheet upon which the couple consummated their marriage. If the daughter is not a virgin, the father may be forced to pay back some of the bridewealth or, if a husband insists, to take back his daughter and declare the marriage invalid. Failure of the test brings great shame on the father's family and may impair their ability to contract marriages for other daughters.[30]

28. John G. Kennedy, "Circumcision and Excision in Egyptian Nubia," *Man* 5 (1970): 175–91.
29. Ibid., p. 182.
30. Coon, "Tribes of the Rif," p. 141. In this sample, virginity tests were taken most seriously among the Riffians, Hausa, Dahomeans, Basseri, Ashanti, Tarasco, Bambara, Kazak, Hebrews, and Nyakyusa although they also play an important role in the weddings of many other societies.

Among the Basseri, for example, the consummation and public witnessing of the bride's virtue is the primary focus of an elaborate wedding ceremony:

> At sunset [the couple] re-enters the nuptial tent, where their hands are joined by a prominent man in the community, and then are left alone. The only equipment in the tent is the bride's bedding and a clean white cloth for sleeping on, and perhaps some sweets or fruits for a breakfast. A male relative of the groom stands guard outside the tent; when the marriage has been consummated, he shoots a gun into the air, and the women of the camp greet the news with their high-pitched trilling. Next morning the white sheet is inspected by both familes together; if the girl was not a virgin, her husband may divorce her without giving her the *mahr* dowry and may even if his family is strong succeed in getting back the brideprice.[31]

Among the Kazak, the husband is given a special robe and a horse decorated with ceremonial trappings on the wedding day. On the morning after the wedding night, the husband, if he has found his bride to be a virgin, puts on the robe, jumps on horseback, and rides to the father-in-law's, where he is warmly welcomed and congratulated. If, on the other hand, he finds that his bride is not a virgin, he has the right to kill the horse, tear apart the robe, and rip up the bridal tent with his saber. After having thus humiliated his bride, he can force the father to return the compensation or to give him another daughter without payment.[32]

The serious consequences of a virginity test among the Hebrews are described in detail in the Bible.[33] If the husband and his family can prove that the daughter came to the marriage already deflowered, she is stoned to death. However, if her father can prove that he has been tricked and that his daughter was in fact a virgin, the groom and his family must pay 100 shekels for causing the father such humiliation and loss of status.

If a husband himself has deflowered the woman prior to the wedding, he and his family may be less than rigid about the virginity requirement. Among the Riffians, for example, a husband may try to postpone the defloration portion of the wedding until he and his bride can arrange to falsify proof of her virginity, perhaps by waiting until a subsequent menstrual flow provides the required stained sheet.[34]

---

31. Fredrik Barth, *Nomads of South Persia* (Boston: Little, Brown, 1961), pp. 141–42.
32. Alfred Hudson, "Kazak Social Structure," *Yale University Publications in Anthropology* 20 (1964): 46–47.
33. Deut. 22:13–21.
34. Coon, "Tribes of the Rif," p. 141.

A nonvirgin bride may also attempt to pass the test unassisted. Ashanti women, for example, may apply ants to the vagina the day before marriage to irritate the tissue so that at the moment of consummation the tissue begins to bleed.[35]

A Father's Tactics for Protecting Virginity and the Reputation for Virginity

As the practices of infibulation and virginity tests illustrate, guaranteeing unambiguous paternity rights to a husband by giving him a virgin daughter is crucial in marriage bargains. While fathers in most societies attempt to prevent seduction of an unmarried daughter by supervising her conduct and restricting her contacts with men, this surveillance is most effective in strong fraternal interest group societies since it requires the assistance of many people, who protect the father's interests as their own. In these societies, kinsmen may guard the daughter so strictly and continuously that no man can gain access to her. Among the Riffians of Morocco, for example, the time between the signing of the betrothal agreement and the wedding is considered an extremely dangerous period for all parties to the bargain. The betrothed daughter is hardly ever allowed to leave the house. When she does go out, she must be accompanied by a group of companions, called *thiuziren*.[36] Among the Dahomeans, a young woman is isolated from men and watched continually until she marries. Surveillance protects the daughter not only from seduction but also from accusations of promiscuity. Displays of strict chaperonage encourage others to believe that the daughter cannot possibly be involved in any sexual activity.[37]

A Father's Tactics for Dealing with Seduction and Premarital Pregnancy

If seduction does occur despite the father's precautions, the father must force the seducer to marry because the woman would otherwise be unmarriageable or would command a much lower brideprice. With strong kin-group backing, a father can effectively extract payment from the seducer by force or force threat. In some societies, a daughter's seduction may damage a father's bargaining position so severely that she or the seducer is killed. Children produced outside marriage may be seized by the father as payment for use of the daughter's reproductive capacity. In some societies, their ambiguous paternity may render them so valueless or so divisive to the community that they are aborted or killed.

35. Herskovits, *Dahomey*, I, 284n.
36. Coon, "Tribes of the Rif," p. 134.
37. Herskovits, *Dahomey*, I, 291–95, 282–83.

Among the Thonga, "marriage by abduction," as described by Henri Junod, is practiced by poor men who cannot afford bride-price.[38] The young suitor arranges for one of his friends to tell the woman to meet him in the bush. There the couple consummate their union, then run off, usually to the village of one of the woman's mother's relatives. They include maternal relatives in the intrigue be-cause in Thonga these kin receive none of the bridewealth and thus have no interest in protecting the woman's marriage value. The woman's father makes an effort to retrieve her, but he settles on a compromise if he finds her determined to continue the relationship since in Thonga girls are known to commit suicide or run away if they do not like their father's marital choice.[39] According to Junod, com-pensation is almost always paid eventually. The "thief" can attempt to pay the necessary brideprice over a long period of time; or he can relinquish the first female offspring born to the woman if he cannot or does not want to pay the full compensation. As the Thonga describe this practice, "the child will pay for her mother."[40] If the couple goes to the seducer's kin for refuge instead of the kin of the woman's mother, the father resorts to violence. He and his kinsmen "go as enemies" to the village of the seducer's kinsmen. There they kill live-stock and destroy property until the seducer's kin agree to pay the brideprice.

Among the Nuer, a woman's father and brothers protect her marriage value by not allowing any man to have sexual intercourse with her unless he is wealthy and definitely plans to marry her.[41] If a less suitable man seduces the daughter despite their precautions, they may demand full compensation for the transgression in the form of a heifer and a steer or, in the case of pregnancy, go to the seducer's cattle kraal and confiscate the number of cattle they consider adequate marriage compensation. If the seducer later marries the woman, he will try to convince the father to count any cattle taken toward the marriage payment. If he does not marry her but she bears a child, her relatives keep the confiscated cattle as payment for the child. E. E. Evans-Pritchard makes clear that only powerful families can be sure of getting adequate compensation for any damage to their daughters' marriage value. "If the father is strong and has the backing of a pow-erful lineage he is not resisted, since he has right on his side."[42]

---

38. Junod, *South African Tribe*, I, 119–20.
39. Ibid., 281.
40. Ibid., 120.
41. E. E. Evans-Pritchard, *The Nuer* (London: Oxford University Press, 1940), pp. 166–67.
42. Ibid., pp. 166–68.

If an unmarried woman is seduced among the Kazak, her parents force the seducer to marry her with full compensation.[43] If she is pregnant and the seducer cannot be found or cannot pay, she and her child have little value. She is forced to abort, at the risk of her own life, by drinking mercury or breathing the vapors of mercury within a sweat house. If the child survives to term and is delivered, it is abandoned on the steppe.[44]

The Nama Hottentot punish the seducer of an unmarried woman by cutting off one of his testicles,[45] thrashing him and confiscating his property or, if the woman is still a child, killing him.[46] If he impregnates the woman, however, he is expected to marry her; if he does not, he must give the family cattle or money to pay for feeding the child. If he refuses, he is taken before the tribal council and flogged. Once he has finished paying for the child's upbringing, he is given full paternity rights.

Both the Gheg Albanians and the Basseri murder a seducer of an unmarried girl without risk of retaliation.[47] Fredrik Barth notes that of the two cases of homicide during his stay with the Basseri, one was the result of a man's attempt to elope with someone's daughter. Among the Rwala, if an unmarried woman becomes pregnant, both woman and child are taken outside the camp area and killed; Robert S. Rattray notes that Ashanti women may also be killed for premarital pregnancy.[48]

Societies in Which Virginity Is Not Important

In a few strong fraternal interest group societies, seduction prior to marriage does not ruin a woman's marriage value and may even increase it. This is possible because unambiguous paternity rights are ensured not by virginity until marriage but by explicit contract: children produced by a seduction are awarded to the future husband regardless of their biological paternity. This practice, to be truly effective, requires strong kin-group backing to retrieve a woman who has

43. Hudson, "Kazak Social Structure," p. 47.

44. Ibid., citing S. I. Rudenko, *Ocherk Byta Severo-vostochnykh Kazakov*, no. 15 (Leningrad: Materialy Komissii Ekspeditsionnykh Issledovanii Akademii Nauk, 1930), p. 49.

45. Leonhard Schultze, *Aus Namaland und Kalahari* (Jena: G. Fischer, 1907), p. 119.

46. Schapera, *Khoisan Peoples*, p. 242.

47. M. E. Durham, *Some Tribal Origins, Laws, and Customs of the Balkans* (London: Allen & Unwin, 1928), p. 69; and Barth, *Nomads*, p. 139.

48. Alois Musil, *The Manners and Customs of the Rwala Bedouins* (New York: Czech Academy of Sciences and Arts, 1928), p. 240; and Mair, "African Marriage," p. 120, citing Robert S. Rattray, *Ashanti Law and Constitution* (London: Oxford University Press, 1929), p. 298.

eloped, seize and maintain custody of the children she produces, award them to the future husband by contract, and back up that contract if necessary.

The Masai, for example, are not concerned with the biological origins of a woman's children since the marriage contract clearly specifies that the future husband be recognized as the sole sociological father of any children produced. Premarital pregnancy is so valued that if a father offers a husband a virgin daughter, the husband may send her back immediately to her father's village, demanding a heifer and refusing to deflower the woman until the heifer has been received. Marriages often take place while the husband is away at war since young men must enter the warrior class and perform a stint of military service. The new wife takes up residence in the husband's village and produces children by other men until the husband returns. This practice allows the husband to begin building up his power by having children even though he is away fulfilling his military obligations.[49]

The Kipsigis also consider childbirth prior to marriage advantageous. As J. G. Peristiany puts it: "[A] future husband will usually be glad of the proof of his fiancée's fertility and also of the young baby which will become his. A baby is in reality more of an asset than a handicap to an unmarried girl."[50] Similarly, the Shilluk consider the biological origins of a child to have little bearing on paternity rights.[51] The payment of bridewealth at marriage certifies the husband as the undisputed sociological father of all children produced by his wife.[52] As Charles Seligman and Brenda Seligman describe it, "If a girl has one child before marriage, the child belongs to the husband who provides the bridewealth, which would be the same as if she had no child."[53] If she has two or more children, however, her father may choose to keep them as members of his own kin group instead of relinquishing them as part of a marriage bargain. In such cases the father demands less bridewealth from the husband.

Menarcheal Stratagems of Weak Fraternal Interest Group Societies

Among societies in which fathers lack the political resources of a strong fraternal interest group to protect a daughter's marriage value,

49. L. S. B. Leakey, "Some Notes on the Masai of Kenya Colony," *Journal of the Royal Anthropological Institute of Great Britain and Ireland* 60 (1930): 199–203.

50. Mair, "African Marriage," p. 51, quoting J. G. Peristiany, *The Social Institutions of Kipsigis* (London: George Routledge & Sons, 1939), pp. 46, 52–54.

51. Seligman and Seligman, *Pagan Tribes*, p. 68.

52. Ibid.

53. Ibid.

the dilemma produced by the onset of menstruation is far more serious and the tactics available to resolve it are considerably less potent.
Without the military force of a large and loyal group of kinsmen, a
man's newly fertile daughter is especially vulnerable to seduction and
elopement since her father lacks the power to command kinsmen to
chaperone her or to deter potential seducers by threatening violent
retaliation. Without the backing of a strong fraternal interest group, a
father must develop a temporary community-based faction that will
hold together and protect his daughter's fertility until marriage. To
employ this strategy effectively, he must have developed his faction
by the time his daughter reaches sexual maturity.

Menarche, then, takes on immense social significance in societies
that lack strong fraternal interest groups. It not only marks the time
by which a father must have developed public support for his rights
to negotiate a formal marriage contract but also indicates that he must
settle the marriage very soon. The length of time he has available to
select the most valuable suitor and negotiate the marriage depends
entirely on the strength of his temporary faction and on his own ability to keep it together. The weaker the faction, the greater the pressure for the father to contract an early and perhaps less suitable
marriage before he loses the ability to bargain at all. Without the
support of community opinion, his newly fertile daughter can be easily seduced, abducted, or impregnated without compensation.

The public ceremonies, feasting, and observance of taboos associated with the onset of menstruation, then, are implicit bargaining tactics by which a father attempts to develop community support strong
enough to protect his daughter's value in a marriage bargain. Such
public ceremonies could be used to develop political support in any
society, but they are especially important in societies in which men
lack the support of large and powerful kin groups. In these societies,
sponsoring a public ceremony or engaging in other forms of public
ritual at a daughter's menarche can serve several political purposes.
First, the giver of the ceremony states unequivocally that the newly
fertile woman belongs to him and that he has the right to negotiate
the terms under which he will relinquish her reproductive capacity to
another man. Second, by accepting his hospitality, those who attend
the ceremony implicitly recognize his rights and renounce any illegitimate designs on her. Third, if the ceremony is large and successful, the father demonstrates his command of community opinion to
both potential suitors and potential seducers, who will hesitate to
risk offending him and his large circle of friends. Marshall Sahlins,
Douglas Oliver, and Roy Rappaport have shown that sponsoring
public ceremonies is a way of accruing prestige and political influence

based on social indebtedness.[54] Accruing prestige and influence is particularly crucial when a man's most valuable resource is most susceptible to seduction. If a father is too poor to give a public ceremony, he can at least attempt to make his daughter as inaccessible as possible perhaps by secluding her in a special hut and warning that dire supernatural consequences await any man who dares touch her. Although such strategies are not as impressive as a public feast, they may discourage potential seducers long enough for the father to settle the marriage. If all else fails, the father may take advantage of a daughter's seduction by calling in the community to witness it and proclaiming the seducer as her legal husband. This technique, though crude, may be the most convenient method for forcing the marriage of a daughter who is promiscuous, unattractive, or otherwise difficult to marry.

Preparing a Successful Menarcheal Ceremony

In his efforts to develop support from a large segment of the community, a father wants many people not only to attend the menarcheal ceremony itself but to join his temporary faction earlier by helping to prepare for the ceremony ahead of time. The more elaborate the preparations, the larger and more successful the ceremony will be. Large numbers of people can help grow food, make special costumes, prepare dances, songs, and special performances, and manufacture whatever equipment will be needed to entertain numerous guests for many days or weeks. Thus, preparations may begin months or even years in advance. The father first enlists the aid of close relatives in the initial planning and long-term preparations and later, with their help, encourages friends and neighbors to donate food, costumes, and other goods and services. During this critical preparatory period, the father wants community members to begin declaring their intentions so that he can predict just how much support will be available to him when he needs it most. One important group whose assistance is often sought is potential affines, whose participation in the preparations (as well as attendance at the ceremony) can indicate serious intentions to settle a marriage bargain. In many societies, the aid of potential affines is actively sought as soon as a daughter shows the first signs of sexual development in order to facilitate marriage soon after the menarcheal ceremony.

The more wealthy and prestigious a father is before his daughter's menarche, the more successful he will be in preparing an impres-

54. Marshall D. Sahlins, *Tribesmen* (Englewood Cliffs, N.J.: Prentice-Hall, 1968), pp. 86–95; Douglas L. Oliver, *A Solomon Island Society* (Boston: Beacon Press, 1967), pp. 361–95; and Roy Rappaport, *Pigs for the Ancestors* (New Haven: Yale University Press, 1967).

sive celebration. A father with less renown may be able to count only on close relatives and affines who live in the community; he must hope that this small core group will amass enough food and equipment to impress the larger community when the ceremony takes place. Among the Marshallese, for example, ceremonial preparations for a member of the royal family begin two or three years in advance, with all the women on the island aiding in the preparation of special menstruation mats and many people helping to build a large seclusion house for the young princess. Preparations for a commoner take much less time. Only relatives and close friends are willing to help make menstrual mats, and male kinsmen are called on to build a small seclusion house next to the house of the woman's parents.[55]

The most critical problem in preparing a public menarcheal ceremony is judging exactly when menarche will take place. Given its unpredictable timing, a father could easily be caught unprepared by an unusually early menarche or, if his daughter matures late, be unable to halt a waning of interest on the part of community members in a ceremony that has been repeatedly postponed. Often, a daughter's physical development is closely watched for clues that menarche is imminent. Breast development is the physical sign most often mentioned in ethnographic accounts as indicating that menarche will soon occur although it is by no means foolproof. The Lesu estimate that after the breasts reach a certain size, menarche will follow within "the next eight to ten moons." Hortense Powdermaker found that Lesu women were often quite accurate in predicting which of the girls in the village would be the next to attain menarche.[56]

The elaborate menarcheal ceremonies of the Chiricahua Apache illustrate the heavy reliance on implicit bargaining and temporary community support in societies without fraternal interest groups. According to Morris Opler, the chief ethnographer of the Chiricahua, menarcheal ceremonies are the major ceremonial occasions in the society.[57] The elaborate and careful maneuvers that fathers use to encourage communitywide assistance with the preparations, which take an entire year, begin with efforts to win support from those who will play important ceremonial roles in the menarcheal ceremony. Discreet inquiries among various members of the community and sometimes neighboring communities are used to identify those who might be willing to commit themselves not only to participation in the ceremony but, in some cases, to a life-long personal responsibility to the young woman and her family. About a year before the family assumes

55. Camilla Wedgwood, "Notes on the Marshall Islands," *Oceania* 13 (1942): 8–12.
56. Hortense Powdermaker, *Life in Lesu* (New York: W. W. Norton, 1971), p. 141.
57. Opler, *An Apache Life-Way.*

their daughter's menstruation will begin, they start searching for the female attendant who will accompany the daughter throughout the proceedings. "This woman must be personally approached and asked to lend her help, and she may even refuse to participate. She must always be rewarded if she does perform this function."[58] A second important person, the "singer," will play a large part in the supervision and execution of the dramatic rituals in the ceremony. He must be approached with even more care because his commitment to perform as singer involves a series of gift exchanges that may continue long past the rite itself. "If you choose one of these men, you are brothers for life, even if you are not related to him. . . . After the ceremony is over, you give each other some valuable things— saddles, horses, anything that is worth something."[59]

While important supervisors of the ceremony are being drawn into the preparations, the daughter's relatives begin making her an elaborate dress out of buckskin, which may be donated by friends:

> If you were out [hunting deer] with a thoughtful man and you had a daughter who was going to have a feast next summer, this man you're hunting with might say, "Your daughter is going to have a feast, and you haven't enough buckskin. You keep all the hides." He would do that because maybe that might be your last chance to get buckskin [for the girl's ceremonial dress].[60]

Yet another important task that must be taken care of in advance is obtaining help of mask makers. Sometimes the mask makers are relatives of the father; other times, according to Opler's informant,

> A man whose girl is going to have her ceremony would come out [into the center of a common camping area] and say, "All you people, listen! I'm going to give a feast for all you people. I need your help. I want all you men who know the ceremony of the masked dancers and you men who know songs to help. I'm paying for your good time. I'm having plenty to eat for all of you. I am a poor man but still I'm doing this. Let's all help and have a good time. . . ." Afterwards he might ask more definitely to be sure he'd have somebody.[61]

This informant said that his father was continually being urged to make masks and perform all sorts of services in preparation for menarcheal ceremonies. His description illustrates the ambivalence that is typical of the "helpers" enlisted and demonstrates the father's

58. Ibid., p. 84.
59. Ibid., p. 86.
60. Ibid., p. 83.
61. Ibid., pp. 87–88.

need to engage in constant urging and pleading.[62] On one occasion, the informant's father reluctantly agreed to try to enlist men as dancers for the ceremony. First he asked his son, who refused, then another man, who also refused. At this point, he referred the problem back to the family planning the ceremony. They approached the son again, this time promising food from the ceremony and other valuables as inducements. Finally, the girl's father began begging: "I'm a poor fellow. This feast is for everybody. You can dance better than anyone else." The young man gave in, explaining to Opler, "So you have to sympathize with them sometimes. If they must have to have you and it looks as though you are not going to do it, they call you 'brother' even though you're no relation to them. They say, 'Don't refuse!' "[63]

The Menarcheal Ceremony

Once a daughter's first menstruation arrives, there is a great flurry of activity and last-minute preparations. The daughter's family calls on friends and neighbors to announce the great event, encouraging them to join in celebration either during the period of ritual menstrual seclusion or upon the daughter's emergence from seclusion. The particular sequence of activities and ritual events varies from one ceremony to another, just as the particulars of American wedding ceremonies vary despite a similar general format. Menarcheal ceremonies usually include a period of ritual seclusion for the daughter and a public ceremony with much food, singing, and dancing. At the onset of menstruation, the daughter is usually secluded in her parents' house or in a specially built seclusion hut. Her seclusion may last a few days, a few months, or in some cases more than a year.[64] The public ceremonies either coincide with the daughter's se-

---

62. Opler's informant describes his father's reaction to requests for making masks for the ceremony: "He can see more at the feast grounds, have his meals like anyone else, and have a better time than he can spending his time at his camp painting dancers. I think that many times it looks as though the old man doesn't want to do it. But these feast makers ask in such a way that he can't refuse. Sometimes he goes away, and when he comes back, there is someone waiting for him begging him to help . . . my father used to complain, 'Those people ask me to paint masked dancers. But they don't help me out with the equipment. They don't know how much work it is doing this for four days. It's tiring.' The people who were giving the feast had to scurry around and get equipment if my father was short of things. They sometimes had to ask other people for buckskin and things that were needed" (*Apache Life-Way*, p. 88).

63. Ibid.

64. Beatrice Blackwood, *Both Sides of Buka Passage* (Oxford: Clarendon Press, 1935), p. 253; Clement Doke, *The Lambas of Northern Rhodesia* (London: George G. Harrap, 1931), p. 156; Gustaf Bolinder, *Indians on Horseback* (London: Dennis Dobson, 1957), p. 81; and T. O. Beidelman, *The Matrilineal Peoples of Eastern Tanzania* (London: International African Institute, 1967), p. 33.

clusion or occur when the daughter emerges from seclusion as a dramatic climax. The elaborate Kurtatchi ceremony illustrates a typical ritual sequence and shows how successful a family can be in getting village and even intervillage recognition of a daughter's nubility.[65]

The Kurtatchi Menarcheal Ceremony. At the moment a mother finds out that her daughter's menstrual flow has appeared, she announces the event to her closest friends and relatives, who respond by jumping and shouting, "By and by we shall eat a big pig and have a dance." They begin helping the family prepare food and special equipment to carry the food. Several men are persuaded to build the platforms and other ceremonial equipment needed for the rite. For a little less than a week, the menstruating daughter and her young attendants are secluded in the mother's house, where they must fast, observe taboos, and have their heads painted red and white. Fasting during this period is also required of the woman's nearest relatives or of the entire village if she is from a wealthy family. On the fourth or fifth day, all the women of the village perform a dance, sound a conch shell, and call out, "Tomorrow we shall eat a big pig. It will be cut into pieces," naming the parts of the pig they prefer as they chant.[66] Then they send word to neighboring villages, urging them to collect and prepare food for the ceremonial puddings to be eaten at the feast. Beatrice Blackwood's informants said that as many women from other villages as can attend will accept the invitation to the ceremony. After the neighboring villages have been alerted, the men in the menstruating woman's village begin building a special walkway to be used by the woman and her attendants during one of the most dramatic episodes of the ceremony though this elaborate and expensive part of the ceremony is omitted by poorer families.

After the feast, which is attended by the entire community and many neighbors, the guests gather up the food that has been collected and take it home with them. Men are supposed to have brought a supply of fish to the members of the woman's family, who may prepare it and give it away to the villagers. At the close of the festivities, in a final community-wide ritual, the menarcheal woman is released from her seclusion. A special brew is prepared for her to drink; it is supposed to "fasten her belly" so that her menstrual periods will not appear again until after her marriage.[67] While the concoction cooks, the community is supposed to observe a fast and a work taboo.

65. While the Kurtatchi ceremony is less elaborate than the Apache, it is more typical of the kinds of successful menarcheal ceremonies described in the ethnographic literature (Blackwood, *Buka Passage*, pp. 248–70).

66. Ibid., pp. 253–54.

67. Ibid., p. 258.

> All the . . . people in the village must stay in their huts, and must on no account go out, even to relieve themselves. They must not speak, and children must not cry. If anyone were to speak, the pot in which the concoction is brewing might break . . . and this would be very bad for the girl, causing her always to have an excessive flow at her periods.[68]

To end the taboos, the men explode heated bamboo as a signal to the surrounding villages that the brew is ready and everyone is to gather round as the woman emerges from the house. Once they have all observed her, they gradually disperse.

This last phase of the ceremony offers a final opportunity for the father to size up the amount of his community support in protecting his daughter until her marriage is settled. Blackwood notes, for example, that during the final phase of a ceremony, she witnessed one young man saying that he did not intend to obey the fast. The women became extremely angry with him, saying that if he did not obey the fast, he would be held responsible for some terrible disaster in the village.[69] Insisting that everyone in the village observe stringent work and food taboos while the brew is being made allows the father to judge the degree of community support that he has accrued by means of the ceremony.

The woman's family takes the bowls containing the special concoction and hangs them up in the rafters of their house as a way of stopping her menstruation until marriage. When the woman first sleeps with her husband, her family is supposed to take down the bowls, slash them open, and throw them into the sea. This act releases her family's influence over her fertility and allows her to have children. If her family decides that they want to keep her from getting pregnant, even after her marriage, they "forget" to take the dishes down from the rafters.[70] Kurtatchi women usually marry soon after the menarcheal ceremony although they occasionally take up residence with a potential husband before the ceremony. In these cases the affines play a more significant role in the ceremonies, which become a sort of public confirmation that the woman's fertility has already been spoken for.

A Ceremony That Failed. An expensive and elaborate menarcheal ceremony creates a sizable political faction for the father in two ways: by involving many people in the preparations and by providing food and entertainment for many guests. Even if preparations go smoothly, the ceremony will fail to serve its purpose if it is

68. Ibid.
69. Ibid, p. 260.
70. Ibid., p. 265.

poorly attended. Poor attendance is very damaging to the father's position, for it suggests to the whole community that he lacks the political support necessary to protect his daughter against seduction and to arrange a suitable marriage. A father takes a sizable risk if he plans a large, expensive ceremony without being sure that many people will come. In such a situation, less dramatic bargaining tactics may be more successful.

Colin Turnbull's first-hand account of the "elima" ceremony among the forest Mbuti, a hunting-gathering society, describes several incidents indicating that one father's attempt to celebrate his daughter's menarche failed miserably.[71] Normally, when a Mbuti attains menarche, she and all her friends enter a seclusion hut together for weeks of celebration. The whole event is carefully chaperoned and supervised by an older man and woman who are designated the "father" and "mother" of the ceremony. While the girls inside the hut sing and chant, the young men outside respond with their own songs. Mbutis from all around the hut watch as certain men attempt to enter the seclusion hut: this is a mock battle, carefully orchestrated and supervised by the "father" and "mother" of the ceremony, which ensures that only men who are considered eligible suitors succeed in entering. Entry into the hut is interpreted as an implicit declaration of serious interest in marriage to the menarcheal woman.

The ceremony observed by Turnbull, however, was marked by low attendance. As it proceeded, men began showing more interest in returning to the hunt and daily work than in the festivities. The man whom one of the two menarcheal women in the hut wanted to marry did not even show up. Finally, all the women inside the seclusion hut emerged and went from camp to village, searching for him and other eligible men. After some time, they found him and urged him to follow them back to their hut to declare his intentions. He agreed but reluctantly, and when he entered the hut, he chose to betroth a different woman. Turnbull's informants told him that they were very upset about the unorthodox way in which the ceremony had been conducted. They "felt it was wrong for the girls to go wandering about from village to village, sometimes sleeping overnight in camps several miles away. This was unheard of."[72] A final indication of failure was that one of the menarcheal women for whom the rite was being held never did get a betrothal offer. She married later as part of a sister-exchange arrangement when one of her male relatives

---

71. Colin Turnbull, *The Forest People* (New York: Simon & Schuster, 1962), pp. 184–200.
72. Ibid., p. 199.

needed someone to marry into the family from which he was obtaining a bride.

Less Elaborate Rituals

In many societies, such as those of some hunting bands and marginal shifting cultivators, a lack of surplus resources makes the sponsoring of expensive elaborate ceremonies economically and politically impracticable. Fathers in these societies must resort to simpler and less costly rituals to protect a daughter's marriage value: sponsoring a public dance-and-song fest, finding community members to agree to act as sponsors guiding a daughter through a public ordeal, or insisting that a daughter be called by a different name during and after menarche. These measures may or may not be as successful politically as the elaborate menarcheal celebrations previously described, but they do allow a father to assess the extent of his political support at this critical time by giving him the opportunity to observe the willingness of community members to adhere to these cultural traditions now that they pertain to his own daughter.

The Warrau of South America, who do not sponsor large feasts and elaborate celebrations like those of the Apache and Kurtatchi, have devised an alternate strategy for assessing public commitment. [73] A menarcheal Warrau woman is secluded in a special hut during her menstrual flow. Two "blood parents" are asked to act as ceremonial sponsors in presenting the daughter to the community at the end of the menstrual seclusion. The female "blood parent" carries the young woman from the menstrual hut to a bench specially made for her by the male "blood parent" and designed by friends in the community. In a later ceremony, the woman's hair is cut, first by her "blood father" and then by anyone in the village who wishes to participate. In a final rite, called the "fruits of blood," the woman's parents sell food to any members of the community who care to come to the father's house and buy it, either through "donations" of money or with special ornamental gifts to be worn by the girl. [74] This ritual exchange allows the father to determine the success of prior displays and rituals in garnering community support for his efforts to protect his daughter's fertility long enough to contract a legal marriage.

Other groups conduct even less elaborate ceremonies. Among the Nambicuara, for example, a menarcheal woman is isolated for two

73. María Suárez, *Los Warao* (Caracas: Instituto Venezolano de Investigaciones Científicas, 1968), pp. 207–08.
74. Ibid., p. 208.

to four months inside a shelter especially built for the occasion.[75] During this seclusion, she observes food taboos and is fed by her mother. When it is time for her to emerge, family members do some dancing and singing and tear down the seclusion hut. According to Lévi-Strauss, the menarcheal woman usually marries as soon as she emerges from her seclusion. If she marries, there is a feast and more dancing and singing. Among the !Kung Bushmen, a menarcheal woman is put in a specially built hut, around which designated men and women dance for the duration of the flow.[76] Among the Andaman Islanders, the parents of a girl who has reached menarche begin weeping over her, then send her to the sea to bathe. Afterwards, she is put either in her parents' house or in a specially built shelter near their house, where she must remain strictly secluded and tabooed for three days. During the entire three days, she is completely wrapped in long strands of leaves and must sit in a special position, with her legs doubled up beneath her and her arms folded. For twenty-four hours she is not permitted to speak or sleep. Throughout her seclusion she is guarded by her parents and their friends, one of whose tasks is to keep her from falling asleep.[77] During this period, her parents also insist that she be called by a new name. People in the community must not refer to her by any other name until after she has borne her first child.

Menarche and Ritual Defloration.   Ceremonies associated with the attainment of sexual maturity among the Arunta of central Australia are particularly noteworthy in that they demonstrate both the social importance of menarche in politically weak societies and the use of ritual as a strategy for asserting rights to a woman's reproductive capacity. The ceremonies begin with the "breast-growing" ritual described earlier in this chapter, continue with a menarcheal rite, and end with a defloration ceremony, which takes place just before the young woman is handed over to her husband. Since Freud based his theory about the virginity taboo on such a ceremony, this final portion of the ceremony is particularly important in the psychoanalytic literature on female sexuality.

75. Claude Lévi-Strauss, "La vie familiale et sociale des indiens Nambikwara," *Journal de la Société des Américanistes de Paris* 37 (1948): 109.

76. Lorna Marshall, "The !Kung Bushmen of the Kalahari Desert," in *Peoples of Africa*, ed. James Gibbs, Jr. (New York: Holt, Rinehart and Winston, 1965), p. 261.

77. A. R. Radcliffe-Brown, *The Andaman Islanders* (New York: Free Press, 1922), pp. 92–94. A photograph of an Andaman woman during her menarche ordeal is included in Radcliffe-Brown's monograph (see Plate 16).

The onset of menstruation itself is celebrated in a relatively simple manner. The woman, her mother, and her mother's sisters set up a special camp outside the main women's camp, where they remain until the menstrual flow has ceased. No men or children are allowed to come near them during these days. The menstruating woman digs a twelve-to-eighteen-inch hole over which she must sit while her mother and aunts provide her with food. At the end of the flow, the hole is filled up and the woman and her relatives return to the main camp.[78]

When the woman's future husband hears that his fiancée has reached maturity, the defloration ceremony is arranged. All those who take part in the defloration have a special interest in the woman's newly acquired reproductive capacity: they represent the woman's own moiety, the section of the moiety into which she will marry, and the section of the moiety that has customary rights to marry her future children. The first part of the ceremony is the physical removal of the hymen, which is perforated with a stone knife by the representative from her own moiety. Next, the three men have sequential sexual intercourse with the woman, the man from her own moiety first, the representative from the section that will marry her children second, and the representative from her future husband's section third. Not until the completion of this ceremony is the husband allowed intercourse with her.[79] Freud theorized that defloration by someone other than the husband was a method for protecting the husband from the pre-Oedipal outrage of his wife as she was robbed of her virginity, but fraternal interest group theory offers an alternate explanation.

Without the political resources of strong fraternal interest groups, none of the Arunta men with customary rights to the woman's fertility has sufficient military force to protect those rights. Sexual intercourse with the young woman immediately after her menarche is an alternate strategy by which all three men, especially the one representing the woman's own kinsmen, attempt to protect those rights for their group by impregnating her before her husband can do so. From Spencer and Gillen's description of the ceremony, defloration of a newly fertile woman by representatives of these three groups is in their own interest and not, as Freud suggests, in the interest of the future husband, who would surely be better advised to endure his wife's rage at defloration than to allow ambiguity about the paternity of her first child. Since the first man to have sex with her

78. Spencer and Gillen, *Arunta*, II, 481.
79. Ibid., 472–74.

is a representative of her own father, the true genitor of her first child may be a member of her own kin group; if the genitor's rights are disputed, her kinsmen can call on those who witnessed the defloration ceremony to support their claims. Her kinsmen can also uphold the rights of the group with customary rights to marry her future offspring since they also saw its representative have intercourse with the woman. Among the Arunta, the claims of the husband's group and the husband himself seem to come last. (In our sample, the Arunta ceremony offers the only clear case of physical defloration by someone other than the husband though there is some evidence that Marshallese chiefs practice a variant of *droit de seigneur*.)[80]

STRENGTH OF FRATERNAL INTEREST GROUPS AND MENARCHEAL CEREMONIES: AN EMPIRICAL ANALYSIS

Measure of Menarcheal Ceremonies

The presence or absence of the ceremonial recognition of menarche and the ceremony's degree of elaborateness were coded from the ethnographic sources on each sample society listed in Appendix III. A ceremony or ritual activity was classified as a menarcheal ceremony if the ethnographic data indicated that it was associated with the onset of menstruation, sometimes referred to indirectly as the "advent of adulthood," "maturity," "sexual maturity," or "transition into puberty." Menarcheal ceremonies were first divided into two different categories to distinguish elaborate ceremonies, such as those of the Kurtatchi or Apache, from less elaborate ones, such as those of the !Kung or Warrau. A score of 3 was assigned to the "elaborate" ceremonies if they had one or both of the following characteristics: (1) The daughter must observe ritual seclusion (with or without food and social restrictions) or other form of segregation from the community for a week or more (that is, longer than the length of the menstrual flow); (2) a public ceremony is held that includes members of the community at large. In the majority of the cases, these two characteristics occurred jointly although there were some cases in which the public celebration was actually a wedding ceremony fused with a menarcheal ceremony and others in which the daughter was submitted to a lengthy seclusion period without a community-wide ritual. A score of 2 was assigned to the less elaborate, or "limited," ceremonies if feasting, dancing, or singing was either absent or limited to close family members and if menarcheal

---

80. P. A. Erdland, "Die Marshall-Insulaner, Leben und Sitte, Sinn und Religion eines Sudsee Volkes," *Ethnological Monographs Anthropos Bibliothek* 2 (1914): 82.

seclusion lasted only during the length of the menstrual flow (less than a week). Cases in which information was too ambiguous to make a good distinction between a score of 3 and 2 were always classified as "limited." For example, if the ethnographer simply stated, "At puberty girls are paraded through the village," the society would be given a score of 2.

Menarcheal ceremonies were coded as absent for a society if women took part in some ceremony between childhood and marriage but the ceremony did not coincide with menarche or if the ethnographic sources indicated that no menarcheal practices occurred. A coding distinction was made between societies practicing some female ritual and societies practicing none. A society received a score of 1 if ceremonies or other special activities included women but were described as age-set rites, lineage celebrations, or male initiation rites in which women played an auxiliary ritual role. Private family activities marking a daughter as marriageable, such as handing her a special veil to wear in public or tying up her hair on social occasions, were assigned a score of 1. Societies practicing genital surgery, such as clitoral excision, received a score of 1 if the surgery was a prerequisite to marriage but not performed in association with menarche. A score of 0 was assigned to those cases in which the ethnographic data clearly indicated that menarcheal ceremonies were not held either during the first menstruation or shortly before or after menarche. Cases in which the ethnographers did not discuss female puberty were assigned a score of 0, rather than a missing data code, if there was a discussion of life cycle events, marriage, menstruation, or child development without mention of menarcheal ceremonies specifically. In such cases, additional ethnographic sources not specifically mentioned by Murdock were always consulted for additional information. Societies in which only royalty or special classes of women celebrated menarche were also coded 0 when there was no evidence that commoners or other classes practiced a less elaborate ceremony.

The classification and ordering of these customs are described in Table 3. As the table indicates, only the two highest categories (2 and 3) represent menarcheal ceremonies and for the purpose of statistical analysis have been collapsed into a single category. The lowest two categories representing the absence of menarcheal ceremonies were also collapsed into a single category. In our sample, 51.9 percent (n=54) of the societies celebrated menarche, and of these, 75.9 percent were classified as "elaborate." Of the fifty societies without menarcheal ceremonies, 20 percent had some ceremony in which women participated before marriage, excluding betrothal, marriage, or naming ceremonies, and 80 percent observed no general ceremonies. Coder reliability for the differentiation between the presence,

TABLE 3.   **Measure of Menarcheal Ceremonies**[a]

Custom	Score	Percentage (*n*)	Category Description
Menarcheal Ceremonies Present			
Elaborate	3	39.4% (41)	Onset of menstruation marked by (1) ritual seclusion, observance of taboos, and avoidance of men for more than one week; or (2) extensive communitywide public feasting and ceremonies; or (3) both 1 and 2. Customary guarding or segregation of female children throughout late childhood and adolescence not included.
Limited	2	12.5% (13)	Onset of menstruation marked by ritual seclusion, taboos, and male avoidance during length of flow (less than one week). Parents may also observe taboos. Public feasting and ceremonies either limited to close family members or absent.
Menarcheal Ceremonies Absent			
Other	1	9.6% (10)	Attainment of sexual maturity not marked by special public ritual, but (1) unmarried females may play role in male rites or lineage rites; or (2) marriage requires genital surgery or ritual observances (such as wearing veil, tying up hair) but not in association with menarche.
None	0	38.5% (40)	No special ritual practices associated with attainment of puberty. Category includes cases of rites for special classes of females only (such as royalty).

[a]Missing data: Iban, Aweikoma, Tikopia, Ainu.

absence, and "missing data" was .877, with the major source of error contributed by the ambiguity between missing data and absent and the ambiguity about how to classify lengthy seclusion of two years or more without an emergence celebration. The coder reliability is reduced to .812 when distinctions among all four categories are made, with the major source of error due to the distinction between the two "absent" categories 0 and 1.

Relationship Between Menarcheal Ceremonies and Fraternal Interest Groups

The zero-order correlations between menarcheal ceremonies, the strength of fraternal interest groups, and two structural condi-

TABLE 4. Correlates of Menarcheal Ceremonies

Variable	2	3	4
1. Resource Base	.31[a]	.66[b]	−.46[a]
2. Residence Patterns		.39[a]	−.31[a]
3. Strength Index			−.44[a]
4. Menarcheal Ceremonies			

[a]p<.01.
[b]p<.001.

tions facilitating the formation of fraternal interest groups are presented in Table 4. These data support the hypothesis that menarcheal ceremonies are more likely to occur among societies in which residential patterns and economic resource base inhibit the formation of fraternal interest groups and among those having weak fraternal interest groups, as measured by the ability to contract and defend explicit bargains through the action of numerous loyal kinsmen. After the effects of historical diffusion have been taken into account, the correlation coefficients between menarcheal ceremonies and each of the three antecedent conditions remain statistically significant. Menarcheal ceremonies are significantly negatively associated with residence patterns ($r = −.31$), resource base ($r = −.46$), and the strength index ($r = −.44$).

The extent to which the composite measure of fraternal interest group strength mediates the effects of residence and resource base can be examined in the path diagram in Figure 2, which describes the effects of each of the three predicted antecedents of menarcheal ceremonies, controlling for the others, when the strength index acts as an intervening link between the two structural characteristics and menarcheal ceremonies. The statistical significance of each path coefficient in the diagram is determined by the actual number of cases upon which each coefficient is calculated rather than by the effective n since the Simonton method cannot be used to estimate the true t's for standardized beta (or path) coefficients.[81] Since paths that are not statistically significant before correcting for diffusion will not, of course, become statistically significant once such a correction is made, inspection of this path model allows us to reject certain hypotheses about the causes of menarcheal ceremonies. The path diagram indicates that neither residence nor fraternal interest group strength alone exerts significant effects on menarcheal ceremonies. Only the direct path between resource base and ceremonies is statistically significant. These results suggest, first, that a bargaining theory model of menarcheal ceremonies need not include residence patterns and, sec-

81. D. K. Simonton, personal communication, 1977.

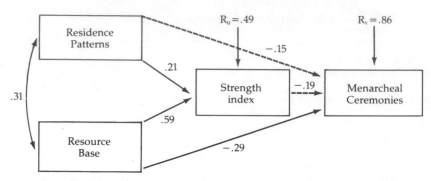

Figure 2. Path Diagram for Menarcheal Ceremonies Including
All Three Indicators of Fraternal Interest Group Solidarity
(prior to correcting for diffusion effects)

ond, that the strength index is not a powerful mediator between
resource base and ceremonies. The standardized beta coefficients
presented in Table 5, however, suggest that measuring fraternal interest group strength does provide a better model of menarcheal ceremonies than one that emerges from considering resource base alone.
The two models described in Table 5 show that the inclusion of residence in the model masks the effect of fraternal interest group
strength on menarcheal ceremonies. When residence is included, the
strength index does not exert a statistically significant unique effect
on menarcheal ceremonies. When residence is excluded, the unique
effect of strength on menarcheal ceremonies does reach statistical significance. Inspection of the beta coefficients in both models shows
that eliminating residence has only a minimal effect on the size of the
coefficient for resource base (an increase from $-.29$ to $-.30$) but has a
significant effect on the size of the strength coefficient, which increases from $-.19$ to $-.24$. The results in Table 5 also show that
eliminating residence from the model does not significantly reduce
the power of a fraternal interest group model in predicting
menarcheal ceremonies. The two-variable model accounts for 25 percent of the variance in ceremonies cross-culturally compared with
26 percent explained by a three-variable model. One percentage point
of explained variance is worth sacrificing since the two-variable
model includes a direct measure of political bargaining. The multiple
correlation ($R=.50$) remains statistically significant at the .005 level
after the effects of diffusion are accounted for.

    The important question, however, is the role of fraternal interest
group strength as the crucial intervening link between resource base
and menarcheal ceremonies. To what extent is the strong association

TABLE 5. **Standardized Regressions for Menarcheal Ceremonies (prior to correcting for diffusion effects) ($n=94$)**

Variable		Beta	t	p
Residence Patterns		−.15	1.503	ns
Resource Base		−.29	2.417	<.01
Strength Index		−.19	1.526	ns
	MR=	.51		
	R^2=	.26		
Resource Base		−.30	2.512	<.01
Strength Index		−.24	2.000	<.025
	MR=	.50		
	R^2=	.25		

between weak resource base and menarcheal ceremonies due to the strong relationship of each variable with politically weak fraternal interest groups? The appropriate empirical test is simply the partial correlation between resource base and menarcheal ceremonies when fraternal strength is held constant. The results of this test show that the association between resource base and ceremonies drops substantially, from −.46 to −.25, and that the amount of variance in ceremonies explained drops from 21 percent to 6.3 percent. This reduction demonstrates that a substantial proportion of the effects of resource base on the presence or absence of menarcheal ceremonies is due to the effects of resource base on fraternal interest group strength. Weak resource base is correlated with menarcheal ceremonies because a weak resource base inhibits the development of strong fraternal interest groups. This analysis lends strong support to our bargaining theory of menarcheal ceremonies. Individuals in societies with economic resource bases of little political value, such as hunting-gathering, fishing, or shifting agricultural economies, resort to implicit bargaining mechanisms in the form of public menarcheal ceremonies because such economic systems produce societies with weak fraternal organization.

Alternate Explanations of Menarcheal Ceremonies

Three major alternate explanations of menarcheal, or "puberty," ceremonies outlined in Chapter 1 can also be tested empirically: the *rites de passage* theory, represented by Judith Brown's research, the structuralist theories of Nur Yalmon and Audrey Richards, and Kathleen Gough's psychoanalytic theory. Brown's cross-cultural survey suggests that "puberty" ceremonies are associated with matrilocal and bilocal residence patterns, and Yalmon and Richards, on the basis of analyses of single cultural areas, propose that social rules about kinship affiliation, or descent, explain menarcheal ceremonies. The extent to which Gough's psychoanalytic interpretation of the Malabar tali-tying rites explains worldwide patterns of menarcheal ceremonies can also be tested by analyzing the relationship between politically and economically powerful kin groups, a measure of the intensity of the Oedipus complex, and menarcheal ceremonies in our world sample.

Rites de Passage and Residence

Basing her conclusions on the analysis of seventy-five world societies, Brown argues that "puberty" ceremonies are performed to help a young woman and members of her natal community adjust to her new status as an adult when such a status transition does not take place less dramatically through the removal of the woman to her husband's community after marriage. The greater statistical likelihood of "puberty" ceremonies in matrilocal and bilocal societies, in which a woman is most likely to remain in her natal community, than in patrilocal and neolocal societies, in which she is likely to leave her natal community after marriage, offers strong support for this view ($X^2=12.67$, $\phi^2=.17$, $r=.41$). Brown's transition-rite theory and our fraternal interest group theory both make predictions about dominant residence patterns and menarcheal, or "puberty," ceremonies although the correlation between Brown's dichotomous residence measures and "puberty" rites ($r=.41$) is much stronger than the correlation between our residence measure and menarcheal ceremonies ($r=.31$). However, the two theories predict an opposite relationship between the ceremonies and neolocal residence, and this difference could account for the difference in size of correlations. Brown predicts that puberty ceremonies should be absent in neolocal societies since women move from their natal community after marriage; fraternal interest group theory predicts that the ceremonies should be positively associated with neolocality since this residence pattern disperses adult kinsmen through the society, making the formation of fraternal interest groups difficult. Of the six neolocal societies in our sample, five (83.3 percent) celebrate menarche as our theory would predict. Inspection of Brown's results shows that in her sample the distribution of puberty practices among her neolocal societies confirms her theory as well.[82] Of the eleven neolocal societies in her

---

82. Judith K. Brown, "A Cross-Cultural Study of Female Initiation Rites," *American Anthropologist* 65 (1963): 840, Table 2.

sample, only four (36.3 percent) celebrated female puberty.

There are three possible explanations for the difference in the relationship between neolocality and ceremonies found in the two studies. First, sampling bias may misrepresent the true proportions of different residence patterns, or bias may have been introduced by dropping from the sample cases that contain inadequate information on the variables to be studied. Second, there may be differences in the coding of ceremonies due to differences in the definition of "puberty" and menarcheal ceremonies. Finally, there may be differences in the coding of residence patterns.

Sampling bias by Brown cannot account for the differences in the neolocal findings. A comparison between the distributions of societies in Brown's sample with those in the Murdock and White Standard Cross-Cultural Sample (SCCS)[83] and our study sample shows rather modest biases, such as an underrepresentation of the Insular Pacific and Circum-Mediterranean by 4 percent and 3 percent, respectively, and an overrepresentation of South American and African societies by 4 percent each (see Table 6 below). A more plausible source of bias is Brown's need to drop 25 percent of the cases in her original sample due to inadequate information on residence and female puberty practices.[84] This strongly biases her sample by underrepresenting patrilocal societies, which are less likely to have puberty ceremonies. According to Brown's residence codes, 49 percent of the societies in her sample are patrilocal, a substantially lower proportion than the 66 percent in Murdock's 1967 world sample or the 63.8 percent in the recent SCCS.[85] In fact, if Brown had scored the entire original 100 cases by devising a method for estimating female puberty practices from poor information, her findings would most likely be stronger than those reported. The differences in the neolocal findings, however, cannot be due to the underrepresentation of patrilocal societies.

The differences in our definitions of what constitutes a ceremony also cannot account for the discrepant neolocality findings. Inspection of the coding discrepancies of puberty or menarcheal ceremonies between Brown and our coders revealed only three discrepancies out of the thirty-nine cases both samples share, produc-

83. George P. Murdock and Douglas White, "Standard Cross-Cultural Sample," *Ethnology* 8 (1969): 329–69.

84. Brown, "Female Initiation Rites," p. 838.

85. Roy d'Andrade, "Sex Differences and Cultural Institutions," in *The Development of Sex Differences*, ed. Eleanor Maccoby (Stanford, Calif.: Stanford University Press, 1966), p. 182.

ing a correlation of .92 between the two estimates. None of the three societies coded differently is neolocal.[86]

Another difference between the two samples that could account for the discrepant findings regarding menarcheal practices in neolocal societies, and therefore for different correlations between dichotomized residence patterns and menarcheal ceremonies, is the difference in the methods used to code residence patterns. Whereas Brown coded the residence patterns of each of her societies on the basis of unpublished codes developed at Harvard University's Human Development Lab,[87] we used the more recent refined codes published by Murdock and Wilson and Murdock.[88] A recalculation of types of residence for seventy-two of Brown's societies according to these more recent codes showed nineteen discrepancies, producing a correlation of .76 between Brown's and Murdock's residence estimates. If "true" residence is in fact associated with puberty practices, as both Brown and the present study predict, then a more reliable estimate of dominant residence patterns should only improve Brown's original findings if her theory is correct. Use of the more recent, refined Murdock residence codes, however, does not alter the neolocal-rite relationship reported by Brown. Of the five cases coded as neolocal, two hold menarcheal ceremonies, an estimate much lower than that produced on our own sample to the trend produced by Brown.

One major difference between Brown's sample and our own could account for the differences in the relation between neolocality and ritual. Unlike Brown, we eliminate societies, or communities within societies, that are considered "large states." Inspection of Brown's sample indicates the inclusion of eight large states, of which only two (25 percent) have "puberty" rites. More importantly, three of the seven neolocal as well as three of the twenty-one patrilocal societies in which rites are absent are large states. Not only may the inclusion of large states in Brown's study inflate her correlation—since so few large states perform rituals of interest in both our

86. The differences in coding of the Ainu, Samoyed, and Thonga may be due to the following factors. First, our Ainu sources only mention that puberty rites are held without any indication of sex being initiated, timing of rite, or if women are initiated separately from men. All of these omissions made for insufficient data to judge the presence or absence of a menarcheal ceremony. Second, we used a different time period and locale for coding the Samoyed. Third, Brown coded the menarcheal ceremonies of the northern clan of the Thonga as representative of the Thonga as a whole whereas we coded the specified group of Thonga, who did not hold menarcheal ceremonies.

87. Brown, "Female Initiation Rites," p. 841.

88. George P. Murdock, *Ethnographic Atlas* (Pittsburgh: University of Pittsburgh Press, 1967), p. 48, col. 16; and George P. Murdock and Suzanne F. Wilson, "Settlement Patterns and Community Organization: Cross-Cultural Codes 3," *Ethnology* 11 (July 1972): 261, col. 9.

studies—but the inclusion of three large neolocal states in which rites are absent could explain the different relationships between neolocality and rites produced by the two studies. When large states are eliminated from Brown's sample, using Brown's residence codes, 50 percent of the neolocal societies have "puberty" rites; using Murdock's more reliable codes, 66.7 percent of the neolocal societies have puberty rites. The latter trend is much higher than the 36.4 percent found in Brown's original study and is in the same direction observed in our study. It seems then that the inclusion of large states in Brown's sample and their exclusion in ours best explains our discrepant findings regarding the neolocal-rite relationship. A critical test of the relative statistical power of Brown's residence dichotomy and the two-step model combining resource base and fraternal strength need therefore not be performed.

In addition, omitting large states from Brown's sample reduces her correlation between residence patterns keeping or sending away women and "puberty" rites from .41 to .35, the latter being only slightly higher than our correlation between a different residence dichotomy and menarcheal ceremonies ($r = .31$). A correlation of .35, however, is significant, and Brown's theory still accounts for 12.3 percent of the variability in "puberty," or menarcheal, ceremonies among tribal and band societies. The extent to which Brown's relationship holds up once the possible effects of historical diffusion are taken into account must also be inspected.

Before Simonton's test for estimating the effects of diffusion could be applied to Brown's results, her sample of seventy-five societies had to be ordered along the same geo-cultural arc as the SCCS. The sampling provinces of each of her societies were pinpointed, with the exception of three cases that could not be located in the 1967 *Ethnographic Atlas*. The remaining seventy-two societies were arranged in descending order in the same sequence as that of societies in the SCCS. Six societies in Brown's sample had to be eliminated because they were located in the same sampling province as the six societies chosen to represent the province. Therefore, the Lamba, Ganda, Tallensi, Goajiro, Yagua, and Choroti were retained; and the Bemba, Gusii, Mossi, Cagaba, Cayapa, and Chama were dropped. In two cases, the society chosen to represent the sampling province in cases of overlap was arbitrary; and in four cases, the society used in our sample was chosen so that the relationships obtained would be based on similar world societies. Table 6 describes the effects of this correction on the world distribution of Brown's sample. As the table shows, when the proportions of societies in each of the six world regions contained in Brown's original and corrected samples are compared with the SCCS distribution, eliminating societies that du-

TABLE 6. Comparison of Regional Representatives between Brown's Original and Corrected Samples and SCCS (percentages)

	SCCS	Brown (original sample)	Brown (corrected)	Difference (Brown original vs. SCCS)	Difference (Brown corrected vs. SCCS)
Africa	15	19	16	+4	+1
Circum-Mediterranean	15	12	13	−3	−2
East Eurasia	18	17	19	−1	+1
Insular Pacific	17	13	14	−4	−3
North America	18	17	19	−1	+1
South America	17	21	20	+4	+3

plicate sampling provinces represented does produce a more representative sample, especially for Africa. It should be noted, however, that Brown's original sample was already fairly representative.

The effective n's were obtained for a sample with and without cases that Murdock and White code as large states so that the effects of diffusion on Brown's original findings could be examined. Table 7 describes the relationship between Brown's scores for menarcheal, or "puberty," ceremonies and residence patterns that determine whether women stay home or leave home after marriage, using Murdock's codes for dominant residence. The distribution of "puberty" ceremonies across the two residence clusters in the upper table shows that even when redundant cases are eliminated from Brown's original sample and Murdock's more reliable residence codes are used, the relationship originally established by Brown is replicated so that the correlation between ceremonies and residence patterns that tend to determine whether women stay or leave home after marriage is still .41, with Brown's residence dichotomy accounting for 17 percent of the variance in "puberty" ceremonies. After the potential effects of historical diffusion are taken into account, the relationship remains statistically significant ($t=2.982$, p<.01). The lower table presents the distribution of ceremonies across the two residence patterns after large states have been eliminated from the sample. The statistical relationship is not nearly as strong without the large states ($X^2=6.994$, $X^2=11.114$), partly reflecting the fact that of the eight large states in Brown's sample only two had ceremonies and that the six without ceremonies were all societies in which women tend to leave home after marriage. The reduction in the strength of the statistical relationship illustrates how correlations between cultural traits can become spuriously high when complex societies are included in a cross-cultural sample. After the effects of diffusion are controlled, the correlation between ceremonies and residence patterns among tribal and band societies ($r=.35$) is still statistically significant ($t=2.561$,

The Dilemma of Menarche: Female Puberty Rites 117

TABLE 7. Relationship between "Puberty" Ceremonies and Residence Configurations Determining whether Women Stay or Leave Home after Marriage on Brown's Corrected Sample

"Puberty" Ceremonies	Stays Home (matrilocal, bilocal)	Leaves Home (patrilocal, avunculocal, neolocal)
	Including Large States[a]	
Present	89.5%	44.7%
	(17)	(21)
Absent	10.5%	55.3%
	(2)	(26)
Total	100.0%	100.0%
	(19)	(47)
	Excluding Large States[b]	
Present	88.2%	51.2%
	(15)	(21)
Absent	11.8%	48.8%
	(2)	(20)
Total	100.0%	100.0%
	(17)	(41)

[a] $X^2 = 11.114$; $r = .41$; $\phi^2 = .17$; $t = 2.982$, $p < .01$, effective $n = 46$.
[b] $X^2 = 6.994$; $r = .35$; $\phi^2 = .12$; $t = 2.561$, $p < .02$, effective $n = 49$.

$p < .02$). This result suggests that whether neolocal residence is collapsed with matrilocal and bilocal residence, as in our model, or with patrilocality, as in Brown's model, a statistically significant relationship between residence configurations and "puberty," or menarcheal, ceremonies can be produced. This holds true even when large states are excluded from the sample and the effects of historical diffusion estimated although the power of the relationship is reduced.

It must be recognized, however, that Brown's transition-rite theory of "puberty" ceremonies does not include hypotheses about the political complexity of societies. Her theory concerns only residence patterns that might necessitate public dramatizations of a change in women's social identity. Although our analysis shows that the political complexity of societies has an important effect on the statistical relationships, particularly after the effects of diffusion are considered, Brown's original theory is confirmed when methodological deficiencies in her original sample and codes are corrected. Our analysis of the effects of historical diffusion on Brown's empirical results should meet Harold Driver's objections to her findings, summarized in Chapter 1. Although Driver was dubious about the functional association between residence and "puberty" ceremonies, an estimate of the potential effects of diffusion on Brown's results was not performed on the entire sample. The results of our analysis of

Brown's relationship support Brown's functional hypothesis rather than Driver's diffusion hypothesis.

The analysis also showed, however, that a bargaining theory of menarcheal, or "puberty," ceremonies explains considerably more of the variance than Brown's transition-rite theory. Our theoretical model explains 25 percent of the cross-cultural variance in menarcheal ceremonies, compared with only 12 percent of the variance accounted for by Brown's theory when large states are eliminated from her sample and 17 percent when large states are included. When the analysis of menarcheal ceremonies is confined to tribal and band societies, then, our bargaining theory accounts for twice as much of the variance as Brown's theory.

Descent

Nur Yalmon's theory of tali-tying rites in Sri Lanka and among the Nayar in southern India argues that the obsession with "caste purity" and "female purity" reflected in the rites is related to the strict custom of determining the status of offspring by the status origins of both parents and particularly to the social requirement that one's father's status be equal to or higher than one's mother's status. Yalmon therefore interprets the tali-tying rites as ritual mechanisms by which a daughter's intention to marry a man of appropriate status is publicly announced. Tali-tying ceremonies, then, reflect concern about the social affiliation of future offspring. Audrey Richards' interpretation of Bemba menarcheal ceremonies also emphasizes the importance of social affiliation, but the source of tension produced by a woman's sexual maturity among the Bemba is the inevitable conflict—the "matrilineal puzzle"—that marriage creates in all matrilineal societies. In these societies, marriage threatens the woman's matrilineal kin group's authority over her potential offspring.

Although neither Yalmon nor Richards attempts to generalize about the causes of menarcheal ceremonies beyond the world regions that each is investigating, the two explanations have an underlying theme that could be tested on a world sample. Both explanations suggest that menarcheal ceremonies reflect the tensions produced in societies in which the social affiliation of a woman's husband is of serious consequence to the woman's own kin group, particularly affecting the social, political, and economic ties between her kin group and her future offspring. Although there are no caste societies in our sample, this general hypothesis can be tested by examining the extent to which menarcheal ceremonies are associated with descent rules that allow a woman's kin group to have important social rights to any offspring produced by the marriage. In such societies, there is always the possibility that a daughter's marriage will alter those customary ties through attempts by the husband or his kin group to assert exclu-

TABLE 8. **Relationship between Menarcheal Ceremonies and Descent**[a]

Menarcheal Ceremonies	Patrilineal	Matrilineal	Bilateral	Other Nonunilineal[b]
Present	18.4%	58.3%	78.6%	71.4%
	(7)	(14)	(22)	(10)
Absent	81.6%	41.7%	21.4%	28.6%
	(31)	(10)	(6)	(4)
Total	100.0%	100.0%	100.0%	100.0%
	(38)	(24)	(28)	(14)

[a]Missing data: Ainu, Iban, Tikopia, Aweikoma.
[b]Quasilineal, ambilineal, and duolineal.

sive claims to offspring. Both bilateral and matrilineal kinship systems recognize the legitimacy of claims of a woman's kin group to her future offspring; only patrilineal descent systems do not.

Inspection of the distribution of menarcheal ceremonies among societies with different descent systems in Table 8 shows that the majority of societies with matrilineal and bilateral descent rules celebrate menarche, as do the other nonunilineal systems (that is, quasilineal, ambilineal, and duolineal systems). In contrast, only 18.4 percent of patrilineal societies have menarcheal ceremonies. These results support a hypothesis about the determinants of menarcheal ceremonies that encompasses both Yalmon's and Richards' observations.

If descent systems are dichotomized into patrilineal and nonpatrilineal categories, the ability of nonpatrilineal descent to predict menarcheal ceremonies may be examined statistically and compared with results produced by the bargaining model. The zero-order correlation between patrilineal descent and menarcheal ceremonies is .41, which remains statistically significant after the potential effects of historical diffusion are considered ($t=4.071$, $p<.001$). Patrilineal descent is one of the three components of our measure of fraternal interest group strength, in which it is used as a measure of fraternal loyalty. It is possible, then, that part of the negative relationship between patrilineality and menarcheal ceremonies could be accounted for by the association of each of these variables with a low-value resource base. It has already been observed that the association between resource base and menarcheal ceremonies is reduced substantially when the effects of the fraternal strength index are partialed out. The relationship between resource base and ceremonies could be similarly affected by the relationship of each to patrilineality alone. The correlation between resource base and menarcheal ceremonies is reduced to .31 when the effects of patrilineality are held constant. However, the critical test of the relative power of a descent theory and bargaining theory is to compare the proportion of variance in menarcheal ceremonies explained by each. The absence of patrilineal descent explains only 16.8 percent of the variance in menarcheal ceremonies, a figure substantially lower than the 25 percent explained by the bargaining model. Although societies in which a woman's kin group retains legitimate authority over her offspring may indeed be anxious about the consequences of women's sexual maturity, our theory argues that the public celebration of menarche in these societies is not simply a symbol of that anxiety but also an active political tactic by which the rights of the woman's kin group may be protected through a ritual show of force. The empirical evidence lends strong support to that interpretation.

Oedipal Conflicts

A third interpretation of menarcheal ceremonies can be derived from Gough's analysis of the psychological bases of Nayar tali-tying rites. Like Yalmon and Richards, Gough does not attempt to generalize about the causes of menarcheal, or "puberty," ceremonies on the basis of her observations. She does, however, describe a set of testable preconditions of tali-tying rites that could also explain world patterns of menarcheal ceremonies. Gough proposes that the ritual celebration of female sexual maturity is an expression of the intense Oedipal conflicts among Nayar males created by social characteristics of Nayar society that give elders a monopoly of power over important economic resources. Gough's psychoanalytic theory thus leads to precisely opposite predictions from our own about the relationship between political economy and menarcheal ceremonies.

Whatever the psychodynamic consequences of elders' monopoly of power over valuable resources, they do not express themselves in menarcheal ceremonies in our sample. Our data show instead that menarcheal ceremonies are characteristic of societies in which economic resources do not provide assets that would promote formation of political factions to protect them, are not vulnerable to military attack, and can be obtained without the mediation of elders in the society. The data also show that these conditions inhibit the development of loyal fraternal interest groups with the capacity to make and defend explicit bargains and that, in the absence of strong fraternal interest groups, ritual bargaining (here, in the form of menarcheal ceremonies) is a political necessity.

What, then, explains the intense interest in female sexual maturity among the Nayar (prior to British administration) and the elaborate menarcheal rites? If the Nayar had appeared in our sample, their economic resource base would have been classified as advanced agriculture, which should lead to the development of strong fraternal interest groups. According to our operational definition, however, the Nayar would be coded as having weak fraternal interest groups. Unlike most of the advanced agriculturalists in our sample, the Nayar have small, kin-based political subunits (the property-owning group, consisting of brothers, sisters, and sisters' children living in a common household), and they have neither an organized patrilineal descent system nor brideprice.[89] In fact, the Nayar are a classic example of a society in which the traditional definition of marriage does not apply. It could be argued that the tali-tying rites are bargaining tactics by which the weak Nayar political unit attempts to protect a daughter's reproductive assets and therefore its claims to complete authority over her offspring. Although the absence of traditional marriage among the Nayar eliminates the chronic problem of competing claims by a socially recognized husband and his kin group, it does not prevent the assertion of paternity claims by undesirable males, specifically those from inferior castes or subcastes. Since there will never be a marriage ceremony to demonstrate paternity rights, the Nayar must ensure before a daughter's sexual maturity that any future offspring she produces are publicly recognized as legitimate members of the appropriate lineage segment and subcaste. The degree of community participation in the rites could be a mechanism for gauging future public willingness to support kin group efforts to prevent illicit paternity claims. This interpretation of the Nayar ceremony would support the contention that menarcheal ceremonies are directly determined by the political strength of a fraternal interest group and only indirectly by economic resource base, which is the causal sequence confirmed in our empirical analysis of world patterns. The case of the Nayar shows that if the political organization is weak, then reproductive rituals, such as tali-tying rites, are practiced even in the presence of valuable economic resources such as advanced agriculture.

89. See Murdock's notes for the Nayar in *Ethnographic Atlas*.

4 Male Circumcision: The Dilemma of Fission

The theory of politics and ritual outlined in Chapter 2 provides an explanation of ritual practices associated with sexual maturity that is not dependent on the connection between childhood socialization, adult personality structure, and social institutions as the three major alternative theories propose. As in the case of menarcheal ceremonies, the theory of male circumcision rituals begins with the idea that rituals are used politically, first, to gain by informal social influence what cannot be gained by direct action and, second, to determine the possibilities for successful action by revealing prevailing community sentiment and the possible future political actions of others before a given political course is adopted. By implication, ritual political strategies are most frequent in situations in which more direct political solutions are unavailable or likely to fail. Public ritual, whether female menarcheal ceremonies or male circumcision, is a response to insoluble social dilemmas.

In the case of menarcheal ceremonies, the dilemma occurred in societies that lacked strong fraternal interest groups capable of protecting the honor and virginity of nubile daughters or enforcing strict adherence to accepted forms of marital negotiations. In such societies, fathers resorted to dramatic appeals to public opinion through feasts or seclusion ceremonies. These ceremonies enabled them to enlist a sizable, if temporary, coalition in support of their control over their daughters at a particularly critical time and to ascertain possible sources of opposition or subversion by thorough scrutiny of ceremo-

122

nial attendance lists and the behavior of guests, particularly young unmarried men who might be contemplating elopement. Needless to say, this method of protecting a daughter's fertility and future marriageability is markedly inferior to, for example, murdering seducers or forcing them to marry, but, then, ritual is always a last resort in a situation that has no practical solution.

Similarly, the ritual practice of circumcision can be seen as an attempt to solve an insoluble dilemma by both influencing public opinion and gauging the future intentions of others. In none of the cases of circumcision in our study sample is the act simply carried out in privacy by the immediate family of the initiate; on the contrary, in most cases it is marked by elaborate ceremonies, extensive feasts, and participation by religious and secular authorities. Indeed, for some societies, such as the Rwala Bedouin, it is the most important public ceremony regularly observed in the society. A glance at some societies practicing circumcision—the Thonga, Tiv, Rwala, Kazak, and ancient Hebrews—indicates that the ceremonies are typical not of weak fraternal interest group societies but of societies with powerful and sometimes massive fraternal interest groups, chronic internal warfare and feuds, and tight contractual control over women and marriage. These societies confront a political problem that is shared by all societies but that involves the most serious consequences for strong fraternal interest groups. We have called this problem the dilemma of fission.

THE DILEMMA OF FISSION

As Meyer Fortes has pointed out, the dilemma of fission is inherent in the growth of the domestic or family group, which over time shows distinct phases of expansion and then fission and contraction.[1] The expansion phase of a family unit begins with the birth of its first child. The family's total social and political resources continue to expand as more children are born, assuming that the family head maintains complete economic, affective, and, most importantly, jural control over all the children. The marriage of the first child, on the other hand, marks the beginning of contraction as the family of orientation begins to divide into new families of procreation headed by children who have now attained the rights of adulthood and jural authority both over themselves and over their own future children. The marriage of children is, therefore, an ambivalent occasion for the original family head, the first step in the gradual contraction of the

1. Meyer Fortes, "The Developmental Cycle in Domestic Groups," in *Kinship*, ed. Jack Goody (London: Penguin Books, 1971), pp. 85–98.

domestic group as formerly dependent children split off to form their own households. Fortes argues, in fact, that parents may fear and resent the need to grant the rights of adulthood to their children, for example, at initiation ceremonies and that "their resistance may be strengthened by the knowledge that initiation is the thin end of the wedge that will ultimately split the family."[2]

Although the domestic group is necessarily split when a grown child establishes an independent household, the loss of formerly dependent children through marriage is a matter of degree as expressed in the proverbial nuptial reassurance, "You're not losing a son (daughter); you're gaining a daughter (son)." The reassurance that parents draw from such folk wisdom depends partly on how badly they need the resources represented by ties of kinship and partly on their actual prospects for maintaining some control over their offspring's future families. In advanced industrial societies, neolocal residence and monogamous nuclear families are the expected family pattern, and fissioning is usually accepted, perhaps with some grumbling about the ingratitude of children on one side and the meddling of parents on the other. But in societies in which large lineage segments are the most important determinants of wealth, social status, and political power, fission is unlikely to be dismissed with simple grumbling. The allegiances of fissioning family groups, particularly to their family of orientation and that family's kin, are of critical interest to both the family of orientation and the new family of procreation. The more important the military and political power of kin groups, the more critical the question of fission becomes.

The dilemma of fission bears some resemblance to the dilemma of the Oedipus complex, but it differs in ways that are crucial to an understanding of adult kinship rituals. Like the Oedipal dilemma, fission involves conflict between fathers and sons, that is, between the heads of the families of orientation and of procreation; also like the Oedipal dilemma, the conflict is inherent in the organization of the domestic family unit. The Oedipal dilemma, however, takes place within the family of orientation. Jural authority remains in the hands of the father, and sexual objects are limited to mother or female siblings. In addition, the Oedipal dilemma occurs at a time when the male child is economically and emotionally dependent and when his ability to distinguish fantasy from reality is limited. The dilemma of fission, on the other hand, occurs when the family of orientation is beginning to break up. The father must relinquish jural authority over his son, and the son himself acquires jural authority over his future

2. Ibid., p. 94.

children and hence over the source of kin-based power. The conflict is not primarily a sexual one since the son's marriage breaks the close Oedipal confines of the original domestic group and thus eliminates sexual conflict as a source of friction. It is instead a political conflict of loyalty and allegiance between the two now-independent family heads. In short, the conflict concerns adults, not children, and rational questions of power and success, not children's dreams of omnipotence and revenge. The dilemma of fission, then, unlike the dilemma of Oedipus, is a problem for adults and is rooted in the social structure of adult society. If the dilemma of fission is the source of circumcision or any other ritual practice, it will not require a theoretical detour through infant personality, Oedipal rebellions against the primal father, or neurotic primitives.

Although all people in all societies, whether "primitive" or "civilized," confront the dilemma of fission, the severity of the problem varies considerably from society to society. Fission occurs least often in societies with stable valuable resources requiring military defense, in which allegiance can be compelled through the threat of force and the promise of inheritance—that is, in societies based on strong fraternal interest groups. But since the strength of these interest groups is based on the allegiance of offspring, including not only the first filial generation but frequently several descending generations, fission in these societies represents a serious loss, not merely of a son but of the son's sons and their sons, along with their wealth, women, and weapons. In such societies, fission is not a cause for grumbling but a major political crisis. In societies in which low-value, perishable, and fluctuating resources can attract the allegiance of much smaller and less stable groups of kin, fission occurs more frequently but involves a smaller loss since the political and economic power of concentrated groups is not great to begin with. In a loosely organized agamous band like that of the Mbuti hunters, a fissioning son takes with him only what he can carry. In this relatively egalitarian society, the political and economic power of any married man is the same as that of all others, and a young man who establishes a new domestic unit represents no threat to his father. The loss suffered by the original family head is not substantial since the departure of the son neither drastically reduces his fund of kin-based political power nor adds dramatically to that of his enemies. In societies with strong fraternal interest groups, however, the fissioning of adult family heads can radically upset the existing balance of power by altering the political structure of a major lineage or clan. In these societies, fissioning becomes a particularly critical dilemma.

FISSION IN SOCIETIES WITH STRONG FRATERNAL INTEREST GROUPS

Societies based on strong fraternal interest groups are capable of pyramidizing unified local lineage segments into gigantic maximal lineages, and these in turn become even more extensive clans which are at least for some purposes capable of unified military, political, or economic action. The size of these units dwarfs any comparable kinship organization in weak fraternal interest group societies. The largest Somali clans composed more than 100,000 individuals, who could operate as a unit in clan feuds and disputes over grazing rights and water.[3] The Thonga clans averaged more than 22,000 individuals, and larger clans such as the Ronga might mobilize as many as 2,000 warriors under a centralized military command and a strict regimental structure.[4] Even among the anarchic Tiv, a large lineage segment might number some 8,000 individuals, and for some purposes the tribe itself could be considered a single large lineage.[5] The ancient Hebrew clans included thousands, if the Bible (Num. 26) is to be believed. These massive military and political units were all built up from smaller lineage segments, usually by degree of patrilineal affinity, with descendents of common ancestors forming subfactions within the larger clan structure. An idealized picture of a lineage organization such as that approximated by the Tiv would show all members of the tribe descending from the same apical ancestor and would branch at each male ancestor of each descending generation until the minimal lineage segment (the *tar* among the Tiv) was reached. Although such an idealized branching structure seldom exists in practice, partly because by definition clansmen cannot trace their individual genealogical linkages, the segmentary structure of these immense kinship organizations is the source of both their immense potential military strength and their greatest weakness. Each apical ancestor at every generational level may be viewed either as a link between two or more lineages of his descendents or as a potential point of fission within the lineage structure. Frequently he may be both; the Tiv, for example, may mobilize to the level of the clan for some disputes, but disputes are equally likely between neighboring *utar* (plural of *tar*) made up of people who belong not only to the same clan but to the same lineage segment.

3. I. M. Lewis, *A Pastoral Democracy: A Study of Pastoralism and Politics Among the Northern Somali of the Horn of Africa* (London: Oxford University Press, 1966), p. 5.
4. Average clan sizes estimated from population size and clan enumeration provided by Henri Junod, *The Life of a South African Tribe*, vol. 1 (New Hyde Park, N.Y.: University Books, 1962), pp. 16–20; fighting strength estimated by Junod, *South African Tribe*, p. 459.
5. Laura Bohannan and Paul Bohannan, *The Tiv of Central Nigeria* (London: International African Institute, 1953), p. 23.

Although the power of a lineage or clan is ultimately determined by the number of men of military age it can muster, this number is in turn determined by the number of women of childbearing age it can control; fertile women in turn can only be purchased by brideprice, frequently paid in animals; animals in turn must be protected by males of military age. Thus, there is often a more or less explicit equation between male warriors, wealth measured in herds, and women representing potential reproductive power; and the actual and potential power of a kin group changes with fluctuations in any of these resources. This equation is apparent, for example, in the Somali institutions of blood money and bride wealth. Blood money in the amount of 100 camels must be paid by those responsible for the death of a kinsman, but only fifty camels must be paid for the death of a kinswoman, reflecting the distinct Somali preference for fighting men.[6] The brideprice, which should be viewed as a payment not for the bride but for the usufruct rights to her reproductive capacity, varies considerably but seems to average approximately twenty-five camels.[7] The size of a man's herd is closely correlated with the number of wives he has not only because camels are required to buy women but because large polygynous families tend to produce many males who can be used in herding, guarding, raiding, and defense of grazing rights.

Since military power and political power depend on the continual expansion of the numbers of males in the clans, strong fraternal interest groups place an overwhelming value on fecundity. God's instructions to Jacob, the eponymic ancestor of the twelve tribes of Israel, were: "be fruitful and multiply; a nation and a compass shall be of thee and kings shall come out of thee" (Gen. 35:11). This directive typifies the political thought not only of the Hebrew patriarchs but of men in most strong fraternal interest group societies. According to Musil, among the Rwala it is the duty of every man capable of procreation to marry:

> This duty is laid upon him by his connection with his kinsmen. The more numerous these are, the more power and influence they possess. The individual who refused to defend the rights of his kin would be expelled, and whoever deliberately declined to multiply its defenders would meet the same fate. Without his kin, *ahl* (minimal lineage segment), the Bedouin would be the most wretched of beings.[8]

6. Lewis, *Pastoral Democracy*, p. 84.
7. I. M. Lewis, *Marriage and Family in Northern Somaliland* (Kampala, Uganda: East African Institute of Social Research, 1962), pp. 15–16.
8. Alois Musil, *The Manners and Customs of the Rwala Bedouins* (New York: American Geographical Society, 1928), p. 135.

Similarly, Lewis claims that the Somali are fond of observing, "when a son is born the clan extends."[9] Procreation and the expansion of lineage segments are as essential to political and military survival in strong fraternal interest group societies as steel production is in industrial societies, and they are assigned a similarly high priority.

On the other hand, the faster a lineage segment multiplies, the greater the number of its male offspring; the greater its generational depth and military power and wealth, the greater the rewards for fissioning. Ambitious family heads with their own descendents may decide—because of population pressure on the available land, tyrannical control by lineage elders, or disputes over the distribution of lineage resources—that it would be advantageous for them to separate their interests from those of their kinsmen. Such a fission means the division of herds of cattle, camels, or other movable wealth; partial or complete physical segregation of the resulting groups; and increasing unwillingness to settle disputes peacefully. Thus, the very process of lineage growth that is the only route to political power is also the road to political dissolution. The strong centrifugal tendencies of fraternal interest group societies are reflected in their political systems, which can be intensely individualistic or even anarchic. In a strong fraternal interest group, every man is a potential lineage head and, therefore, also a potential traitor to his lineage. In the words of an Arab proverb, "I against my brother; I and my brother against my cousin; I, my brother, and my cousin against the next village; all of us against the foreigner."

Fission in Pastoral Societies

Anarchic tendencies toward lineage fission are most apparent in pastoral societies, where the absence of settlement, the presence of a highly portable form of wealth, and problems of overgrazing and pressure from adjacent sedentary peoples all lead to intense individualism and facilitate internal lineage cleavages. As Jane Schneider has pointed out, in pastoral societies the ownership of herds is vested in the heads of families, and as soon as sons marry, they begin to establish an independent "selfish identity." This creates intense competition between "fathers and sons, and among the sons and their sons who are patrilateral first cousins."[10] According to Schneider, in pastoral Circum-Mediterranean groups it is typical that "the father-son relationship is somewhat strained and potentially competitive;

---

9. Lewis, *Marriage and Family*, p. 35.
10. Jane Schneider, "Of Vigilance and Virgins: Honor, Shame, and Access to Resources in Mediterranean Societies," *Ethnology* 10 (1971): 11.

that brothers are not emotionally close after they marry; [and] that the most enduring and solidary bonds are those uniting a mother and her children and, in lesser degree, those [bonds] between cross-cousins and between a mother's brother and his sister's children."[11] Relations with affinal relatives may be more cordial than those with consanguineal kin because affines do not represent major sources of political power and, therefore, are not directly involved in the conflicts that may lead to fission.

Pastoral societies differ among themselves in their pastoral base, their degree of nomadism, and the extent of their contact with agricultural peoples, and these ecological differences lead to different patterns of lineage organization and different patterns of fission. In general, pastoral societies can be ordered along a continuum according to the durability of their principal herd animal and their requirements for grazing land. The pure pastoral nomad, the Bedouin or man of the desert, typically depends exclusively on camels for subsistence but may also possess horses for raiding. Since camels can survive in extremely inhospitable environments, the Bedouin typically have little contact with sedentary peoples and instead move over vast areas in which pasturage rights are not well defined. The aridity of the land means that many acres are needed to support even a small family group; under these circumstances, lineages frequently split up into small segments which operate independently. In slightly more hospitable areas with greater rainfall, goats and sheep can be combined with camels, but the former require much more frequent watering and better pasturage, increasing the importance of kin-based coalitions for defending wells and grazing routes. The greater wealth in herds and the greater incentive for military alliances lead to greater lineage depth, but they also create a considerably more competitive system in which fissioning may take place by the liquidation of lineage groups or by their absorption into more successful, which is to say more fruitful, lineages. Since these groups generally live in areas more favorable for agriculture, they are more often in contact with sedentary peoples, and unsuccessful lineages may spin off and settle among the cultivators. When cattle are added to sheep and goats, true nomadism is usually lost, and the population becomes to some extent sedentary. Some subgroups may migrate to seasonal pasturage while others become increasingly concerned with tillage agriculture. This expands the group's resource base considerably and leads to larger and more cohesive lineages. When fissioning occurs, it is likely to occur either through sedentary spin-offs or through military conquest

11. Ibid.

by the more successful lineages, who drive poorer ones back into the deserts.

Although in each pastoral society the process of fission is somewhat different, the problem is common to all. In our study sample, the Rwala represent the pure Bedouin camel herders; the Somali represent the transhumant camel, sheep, and goat herders; and the ancient Hebrews represent the semisedentary cattle herders and agriculturalists.

The Rwala: Routinized Fission

The camel-herding Rwala pride themselves on being the only true Bedouins of northern Arabia. They have a well-established contempt for all sedentary peoples and even for other Arabs who pursue a less pure form of nomadism.[12] Fissioning is inherent in the Rwala minimal lineage segment, the *ahl*. The *ahl* is the basic unit in the settlement of blood debt, and its members share obligations of mutual aid and defense. In the event that a member of an *ahl* commits murder, for example, the entire *ahl* may seek protection in a neighboring tribe, taking their camels, tents, women, and horses with them and remaining collectively until the murder is avenged or a blood payment arranged.[13] The membership of the *ahl* is limited to a total of seven generations, traced through the male line in a peculiar fashion that creates different *ahls* for fathers and sons. A man's *ahl* consists of his patrilineal relatives in the first three ascending generations and their collaterals and descendents for three generations. It also includes three descending generations so that a young man will typically have a small and therefore weaker *ahl* than an older man; the speed with which he can increase his power depends on how rapidly he has sons and his sons have their own sons.[14] Since the father and son are in different generations, the son's *ahl* will contain the collaterals and descendents of an apical ancestor one ascending generation below the apical ancestor of his father's *ahl*. With each succeeding generation, then, the *ahl* automatically fissions by declaring the descendents of a common patrilineal ancestor to be no longer part of the *ahl*.

The process of fission is followed with cold-blooded logic by the Rwala. Alois Musil's companion Blejhan traced his ancestry to Zeri, one of two sons of Nassar, who was part of Blejhan's father's *ahl* but not part of Blejhan's. The descendents and collaterals of Nassar's other son, Abdallah, were not part of Blejhan's *ahl* either, and, consequently, an entire patrilineal segment had been severed. As Blejhan described the situation, "My father's *ahl* reached as far back as Nassar

---

12. Musil, *Rwala*, p. 45.   13. Ibid., pp. 489–96.   14. Ibid., p. 48.

the father of Zeri and Abdallah, but the descendents of Abdallah do not concern me at all; they will not protect me and I shall not protect them."[15] In practice this meant that Blejhan's father could be subjected to death in retaliation for a murder committed by Abdallah's descendents, but Blejhan could not intervene and, in fact, would have no interest in the dispute whatsoever. The fissioning of the *ahl* and the subsequent cleavages in the Rwala political organization are made possible by the barren desert ecology and the consequent dispersion of grazing herds and by the extremely high death rate of adult males, which keeps the population from increasing. More than 80 percent of Rwala males die of wounds suffered in battles with other tribes[16] so that any attempt by an ambitious Rwelji to expand his *ahl* into a larger and more powerful lineage segment will inevitably be drowned in blood.

The Somali: Competitive Fission

The pastoral Somali are transhumant camel, sheep, and goat herders who follow a complex annual migratory cycle in order to take advantage of seasonal variations in pasturage and water. Although territorial rights to pasturage are not exclusive, permanently fixed, or even well defined, there is recognition of customary rights to certain grazing routes, and watering places may be held by groups or individuals if considerable effort is put into their maintenance.[17] Although the Somali environment is barren, it is less so than the desert lands inhabited by the Rwala; protection of grazing rights and herds within the tribe and, consequently, internal military advantage have considerably greater importance for the Somali than for the Rwala. The Somali's greater wealth and collective resources make it worthwhile for relatively large lineage groups to form contractual alliances in defense of their interests. As a result of these differences in ecology and wealth, the Somali lineages have considerably greater genealogical depth than those of the Rwala, and the size of parallel lineage segments also varies much more than among the Rwala.

Although Rwala can seldom trace their patrilineage beyond four generations and scarcely care about the name of any ancestor beyond the third ascending generation, the Somali are genealogical fanatics: they trace their ancestry back as far as twenty ascending generations. According to I. M. Lewis, even children of seven or eight could recite the entire genealogy back to the eponymic ancestor of their clan family[18] even though clan families have little military or political importance. The next level of kinship segmentation is the clan, which may

---

15. Ibid.   16. Ibid., p. 666.
17. Lewis, *Pastoral Democracy,* pp. 31–55.   18. Ibid., p. 128.

extend back fifteen generations and is an effective unit in feuds over grazing and watering rights. Below the level of the clan is the primary lineage, tracing its ancestry back eight to ten generations. The primary lineage, which is usually an exogamous marital group, is the effective unit of political allegiance. Primary lineages in turn are divided into smaller contractually bound groups of agnatic kinsmen called *dia*-paying groups, which are responsible for paying blood money and for collective vengeance and mutual aid.

Like all pastoral peoples, the Somali are obsessed with fecundity and explicitly recognize the importance of large lineage organization both in internal political jockeying for advantage in disputes and ultimately for strength in battle. The Somali distinguish between "long" or prolific lines and "short" or nonprolific lines, and they refer to the latter in insulting terms that indicate powerlessness and worthlessness.[19] The concept of a "short" or "long" line, though a bit complicated, is essential for understanding Somali politics and feuding. A "long" line is one that traces many intervening ancestors between living members and the eponymic ancestor; a "short" line is one in which there are relatively few intervening links. For example, the Dubalhante clan was divided into lineage segments of very uneven numbers of members, counting very different numbers of intervening links back to the clan eponym. The descendents of one of Dubalhante's sons outnumbered the descendents of another more than forty to one, giving the former group overwhelming military and political superiority even though the two groups occupied exactly parallel positions in the segmentary kinship structure since both groups were descendents of men in the first filial generation after Dubalhante himself. The smaller lineage counted only five members between itself and Dubalhante whereas the larger might count as many as fifteen intervening ancestors.[20] Lewis regards this difference as a result of Somali forgetfulness and assumes that ancestors who were not important points of segmentation are dropped from the genealogy.[21] Lewis' reasoning is apparently based on the idea that since the same temporal period separates the living ancestors of Dubalhante from the lifetime of the eponym himself, they must necessarily have had the same number of intervening generations even if each generation in the "short" line had fewer offspring. The Somali, according to Lewis, "heatedly denied" that they had forgotten any ancestors. They pointed out, logically enough, that even children knew every one of their ancestors and that some living men had as many as five generations of descendents while others had one.[22] On logical grounds the Somali would seem to have the best of the argument.

19. Ibid., p. 144.   20. Ibid., pp. 144–49.   21. Ibid., p. 148.   22. Ibid., pp. 182–86.

Such genealogical structures indicate the basic dynamics of power in Somali society. The founder of a "long" lineage might, for example, get off to an early start by marrying at age fifteen. By acquiring additional wives and herds, he might succeed in marrying his eldest son to a wealthy family so that his son's son would also be able to marry at the relatively early age of fifteen. If the family continued to acquire wives early and expand its wealth and numbers, it is possible that by age eighty the founder of the "long" line could have five generations of sons, and his line would be a major military power. A poor man, on the other hand, might be unable to accumulate sufficient wealth to marry until his middle thirties. Since his wife would likely be from a poor family herself, his ability to find a bride for his own son would also be diminished. If his son was similarly unsuccessful, the founder of the "short" line would have only two generations of sons at his eightieth birthday, and his line would be a weak power in the Somali kinship and political systems.

The drive to build a "long" lineage through the acquisition of women, herds, and sons leads to uneven growth within the lineage structure and to the subordination or virtual extinction of "short" lines. As the Somali are fond of observing, a man must either "be a mountain or attach himself to one."[23] Weaker lineages are either extinguished, forced out of Somali society by their inability to meet blood-debt obligations, or absorbed on unfavorable terms by the "long" lineages. Thus the race to be part of a "long" lineage begins early in a man's life, and his closest agnatic kin are among his principal competitors. Within the "long" lines, however, the process of growth is also unequal. Some lineages dominate a particular clan, and some *dia*-paying groups are much larger than others. A *dia*-paying group in a strong lineage is always in a position to get a better deal in its negotiations with other *dia*-paying groups than is one which is a member of a numerically weak lineage. This leads to attempts by the strong to dominate the weak and enhance their position further, resulting in factional splits within the long lines and increasing the hostility of collaterals.

At the base of the structure, in the *dia*-paying group itself, fission typically occurs over the allocation of blood debts within the group.[24] The group as a whole is typically responsible for the payment of 100 camels, but stronger groups may distribute the share to the disadvantage of poorer members or resent the poorer members' inability to pay. In either event, fission is likely, and it occurs most frequently when a blood payment must be made. The defecting agnatic faction separates its camels from the herds of the other *dia*-paying group members and announces that it is no longer responsible for

23. Ibid. 24. Ibid.

their debts. Similar tensions exist throughout the segmented Somali lineage structure. The substantial opportunities for aggrandizement at the expense of weak lineages lead to intense internal lineage conflict and eventually to fission between closely allied agnatic groups. While continuing to ally themselves against outsiders, they may become engaged in chronic blood feuds even though they formerly considered themselves part of the same primary lineage or even the same *dia*-paying group. Then, despite frequent Somali insistence that agnatic ties are "like iron," competitive pressures within the Somali lineage organization lead to fissioning and anarchic lineage fragmentation.

The Ancient Hebrews: Fission and Sedentarization

The ancient Hebrews were never true pastoralists. From the time of the Patriarchs, cattle as well as sheep and goats are regularly mentioned as constituting family wealth,[25] and by the time of their settlement in Canaan, they had become at least to some extent sedentary agriculturalists, raising vines, fruit trees, and cultivated field crops. Thus, the historical development of ancient Israel, from the time of the Patriarchs through the conquest of Canaan to the golden age of David and Solomon's Dual Monarchy, represents a transition from semipastoralism to settled agriculture. Although a parallel change took place in political and lineage organization as the Hebrews developed from a loose tribal confederation toward a centralized state, even at the apex of its power under David, the unified kingdoms of Israel and Judah were never tightly integrated despotic states like ancient Egypt and Assyria but instead remained subject to strong tribal and lineage influences. As Max Weber has observed, the relatively inhospitable agricultural environment of Canaan restricted the economic base of the Israelite monarchy, and the lack of fertile and easily irrigated areas such as the Nile or Tigris and Euphrates deltas limited its growth.[26] Even in the time of the Patriarchs (ca. 2000–1600 B.C.), however, the Hebrews had developed a much more substantial pastoral base than either the Rwala or the Somali, and their patterns of tribal and lineage organization differed accordingly.

In the period of the Patriarchs the fundamental grazing animal was the cow, and the presence of this animal along with sheep and goats had profound effects on the growth of lineage organization and the pattern of lineage fission. Cattle require better range and more watering than do sheep or goats. Consequently, questions of ownership rights to land and water resources became more critical than was

---

25. See for example the description of Abraham's possessions in Gen. 13:1–7.
26. Max Weber, *Ancient Judaism* (New York: Free Press, 1952), pp. 5–10.

the case among either sheep or goat herders with their transhumant migratory patterns, or certainly the Bedouins with a vast empty but essentially barren desert over which to roam. The cattle herders of the Patriarchal period had a considerably greater incentive to form large military alliances than did either the Rwala or the Somali since control of particularly favorable grazing areas was critical in determining the size of herds. The cattle in addition to sheep and goats also provided a much larger source of capital wealth so that the ability of a patriarchal family head to bind sons or even unrelated servants and herdsmen to him was greater. Even the earliest patriarchs had hired herdsmen and servants;[27] in contrast, among the Somali and Rwala, herding is basically the duty of immature sons. Finally, the grazing requirements of cattle inevitably brought the Hebrews into contact with sedentary peoples since good pasture land was inevitably close to or overlapping with good agricultural land. Thus, throughout the wandering of the Patriarchs from Ur to Chaldes to Beersheba in the land of Canaan, they were inevitably in close contact with settled agricultural peoples, many of whom had already formed city- or even nation-state organizations built on an agricultural base. Neither the Rwala, who remained in the desert, nor the Somali, who had limited contacts with settled cultivators, were similarly constrained by enveloping agriculturalists. Pressure from adjacent cultivators and predatory raiding and warfare with them are a constant theme in the Pentateuch, and the Israelite conquest of agricultural Canaan was as much a process of infiltration by initially alien herdsmen as it was a formal military conquest.[28] These ecological characteristics led to larger and more cohesive lineages and clan organizations, increased conflict with sedentary peoples, and greater territorial integrity of individual clan units among the Hebrews than among the Somali or Rwala, and also to a distinct pattern of fission.

The basic structure of the Israelite kinship organization, like that of the Somali and Rwala, was based on primary agnatic lineage segments three or four generations in depth. Each segment was termed a *go'el*.[29] The *go'el* was responsible for the administration of property and, more importantly, for avenging death or injury to its members by retaliating in kind against the offender or a member of his *go'el*. Even during the period of centralized control under David, blood vengeance continued to be exacted though central administrative control attempted to limit it.[30] The primary lineage segments (*go'alim*) were

27. See Gen. 13:7.
28. Roland de Vaux, *Ancient Israel: Its Life and Institutions* (New York: McGraw-Hill, 1961), pp. 214–15.
29. Ibid., pp. 21–22.
30. Ibid., p. 160.

united into localized agnatic groups by patrilocal residence and the tendency of collaterals to remain together. After settlement in Canaan, these clans took on the form of particular villages or clusters of villages. The clans in turn were integrated into clan families, which are the tribes referred to in the biblical accounts. Strictly speaking, the Israelites as a whole might be considered a tribe and the twelve "tribes" clan families descended from a single eponymic ancestor. During the period in which Canaan was divided into a tribal confederacy (1200–1021 B.C.), these clan families held distinct territories, and there was little of the overlapping that characterized the more fluid Somali structure. Even in the Patriarchal period, Hebrew clans seem to have greater territorial integrity than the Somali clans of the twentieth century.

These patterns of lineage, tribe, and clan organization and the greater sedentary nature of the Israelites even in the Patriarchal period led to a different pattern of fission which can perhaps best be illustrated by considering the specific accounts of fission described in Genesis. Figure 3 shows a simplified genealogy of the biblical patriarchs from the first generation above Abraham to the eponymic founders of the Israelites and adjacent tribes. The crossed lines indicate major points of fission as described in Genesis. A study of each indicates the principal causes of kin-group fission in the Patriarchal period.

Terah had three sons, Abraham, Nahor, and Haran, who initially formed a primary lineage segment in the wider tribal kinship organization. Although no account of the fissioning of Nahor is presented in Genesis, fission presumably did occur since the descendents of Nahor are later referred to as Arameans or Syrians (Gen. 28:5) and lived outside the Israelite tribal boundaries. The Bible does provide clear accounts of the other major fissions of the Patriarchal period. Abraham and his nephew Lot originally formed a common herding unit, and Abraham took Lot, whose father Haran had died, with him on his migration into Canaan (Gen. 11:31). Eventually, the grazing land was unable to support the growing herds and flocks of both Abraham and Lot, and the shortage of land was complicated by pressures from the Canaanites, who were settled cultivators eager to acquire additional agricultural land themselves (Gen. 13:6–7). The result was open conflict between Abraham's and Lot's herdsmen (Gen. 13:7), followed by a decision to separate in order to avoid escalated hostilities. Abraham remained where he was, and Lot chose to settle among the sedentary agricultural peoples of the Jordan plain, where he presumably abandoned the seminomadic patterns that Abraham continued (Gen. 13:10–11). Since sedentary life, particularly urban sedentary life, is despised as corrupting by all nomads, it is not

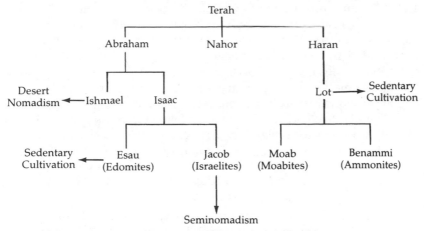

Figure 3. Simplified Genealogy of Hebrew Patriarchs Showing
Principal Lines of Fission Described in Genesis

surprising that Lot found himself in Sodom and Gomorrah while the
seminomadic Abraham became the patriarch of God's chosen people.
This distinction between the sinful life of the sedentary cultivator and
the purity of the nomad would be revived by the Rechabites, who
disdained wine and other products of cultivation and founded a
splinter sect to establish the old nomadic verities amidst the settled
population of Canaan in the period of the Prophets. According to the
spokesmen of the lineage of Rechab (Jer. 35:7):

> Neither shall ye build house, nor sow seed, nor plant vineyard,
> nor have *any*; but all your days ye shall dwell in tents; that ye may
> live many days in the land where ye be strangers.

At this point, return to nomadism was a hopeless millenial dream,
and the sons of Rechab became a religious cult rather than a fissioning
lineage segment.

As is well known, Lot did not fare well among the settled cultivators, barely escaping with his life when their cities were destroyed
and losing his wife through salinization. Lot's fate represents the
dominant method of fissioning among seminomads—the separation
of an agnatic group and its spin-off into settled cultivation. Despite
the separation, agnatic ties were still strong enough for Abraham to
intervene on Lot's behalf when Lot was captured during an intercity
war in the Transjordan (Gen. 14:14–16). Lot did not return unscathed
from his Transjordan sojourn, however, and having lost his wife and
having no sons, seemed to have founded not only a "short" but an
extinct lineage. According to the biblical account, Lot's daughter
saved his line from imminent extinction through primary incest
(Gen. 19:30–38). Their two sons became the eponyms of the Moabite

and the Ammonite tribes. Lot retained an implicit military alliance with Abraham during his lifetime, but twelve generations later the Moabites and Ammonites went to war against the Israeli armies commanded by Abraham's lineal descendent David, and the two tribes eventually became vassal states under David and Solomon.[31] The former members of a primary lineage had become subject to warfare and conquest, and fissioning was complete.

The fissioning of the Ishmaelites followed an opposite pattern, though it too led to military rivalry. At the insistence of Abraham's first wife, Sarah, Ishmael and his mother, Hagar, Sarah's Egyptian maid who had been married to Abraham in desperation because of Sarah's apparent barrenness, were driven into the desert to become outcasts after Sarah miraculously bore a son (Isaac) herself (Gen. 21:9–21). This alternative to fission by sedentarization might be called fission by forced expulsion into primary desert nomadism. While biblical commentators may have had some ambivalence about urban sedentary life, their opinion about desert nomads is clear. Doomed to a life of pure desert nomadism, Ishmael will be "a wild man; his hand will be against every man and every man's hand against him" (Gen. 16:12). The fissioning of the first filial generation of Abraham, then, was accomplished by the strong driving the weak into the desert in much the same way as the "long" Somali lineages drove out the "short." When Abraham died, his property passed entirely to Ishmael's half brother, Sarah's son Isaac, who had the distinct advantage of affinal backing since Ishmael's mother was Egyptian and hence beyond the pale of kinship or tribal loyalty.

A similar animosity characterized the fission of the sons of Isaac: Jacob, in customary pastoral fashion, found his brother Esau to be his most dangerous enemy and sought refuge among his mother's brother's kin (Gen. 28:1–5). Jacob's cunning attempt to become Isaac's designated heir and the consequent resentment of the displaced Esau led to fission and eventual military confrontation between their respective descendants; by the time of David, Esau's sedentary descendants, the Edomites, were at war with the Dual Monarchy.[32]

The two patterns of fission among the Patriarchs — spin-offs into sedentarization and forced fissions in which the stronger party drove the weaker one back into the deserts — can both be traced to the pressures and proximity of sedentary peoples, the value of grazing land in a cattle-based economy, and the desire to inherit a family head's wealth. The intensity of the struggle between Jacob and Esau was a direct result of their father's rather considerable wealth, a disproportionate share of which passed to the eldest son under Hebrew law.

31. De Vaux, *Israel*, pp. 96, 247.   32. Ibid.

Among the Hebrews, as in all pastoral societies, brothers can become each other's most dangerous enemies, and father-son relationships can be strained to the breaking point. On the other hand, kinship is the basis for powerful alliances; the unity of the twelve tribes descended from Jacob becomes the foundation for the strength of Israel.

As pastoral societies progress toward sedentarization, the pattern of fission moves from the automatic and relatively amicable dispersion of the Rwala *ahl* to the competitive lineage growth-and-absorption patterns of the Somali to the fratricidal fissioning of the Hebrews. As the amount of wealth controlled by lineage heads increases and pressures from agricultural peoples become more intense, control of grazing lands becomes critical; fission, therefore, has increasingly important political consequences and is attended by greater conflict.

Fission in Sedentary Societies: Sorcery and Expansion Among the Tiv

The Tiv of northern Nigeria are shifting horticulturalists who cultivate yams, sweet potatoes, other root crops, and maize; keep small domestic animals such as sheep and goats; and possess small numbers of dwarf cattle. Despite the presence of small flocks and herds, animal husbandry contributes only approximately 10 percent of Tiv subsistence. Horticulture contributes half, and the remainder is derived from fishing, hunting, and gathering.[33] Although the fallow cycle of swidden horticulture creates some residential instability, there are no permanent migratory patterns, and migration occurs through sporadic short-range moves to new farmland. Land, not flocks or herds, is the principal source of wealth among the Tiv. Its value and its scarcity make it the major focus of both internal and external military and political conflict. Tiv ideas on land tenure are summed up in their own customary observation, "We don't have a boundary, we have an argument."[34] As was the case in pastoral systems, sons are valuable for their military potential; before the Pax Britannica, when individual compounds were ringed with defensive stockades, they were even more important. Land can be acquired only through inheritance in the agnatic line or by displacing other Tiv or foreign tribes. Taking land from others, however, requires kin backing and cannot be undertaken by individual sons. Thus the Tiv economy, like pastoral economies, sets up strong incentives for large

---

33. George P. Murdock, *Ethnographic Atlas* (Pittsburgh: University of Pittsburgh Press, 1967), p. 74.

34. Paul Bohannan, *Tiv Farm and Settlement* (London: H.M. Stationery Office, Colonial Research Studies No. 15, 1954).

agnatic kin groups, and in fact the Tiv lineage structure and fission process in some ways closely resemble those of pastoralists. Each lineage segment is part of a larger lineage segment one generation back in time and, ultimately, part of the maximal lineage: the entire tribe, descended from the original ancestor, "Tiv." In fact, had the neat segmented structure of the Tiv not existed, it is likely that anthropology would have had to invent it since the complete division of the entire tribe into segmented agnatic branches is a great aid to textbook illustrations of patrilineal kinship structure. The minimal lineage segment *(tar)* consists of the living descendants of an apical male ancestor who is from four to six generations removed from the eldest living members of the *tar*. Since residence is patrilocal and the members of the *tar* form a primary agnatic lineage, there is an almost complete correspondence between geographic and genealogical proximity, a situation that has no parallel in the more fluid pastoral tent groups. The same principle applies to higher order lineages in the kinship structure: members of two *utar* descended from a common ancestor live next to one another, and the members of this large lineage segment live adjacent to descendants of a common ancestor still another generation removed. This pattern repeats itself at every genealogical level up to that of large clans numbering in the tens of thousands.[35]

The *tar* is the fundamental unit of the Tiv system of internal conflict. Within the *tar*, violence of any kind is denied although putatively lethal sorcery is both expected and feared. Members of adjacent *utar* descended from a common ancestor also deny conflict; although it does occur, weapons are limited to clubs and stones. As genealogical distance increases, conflicts become increasingly frequent and violent, and spears, bows, and arrows (in extremely remote groups, poison arrows) may be used.[36] Outside the Tiv tribe as a whole, warfare and conquest are considered the natural state of affairs.

As the members of a *tar* increase, they require additional lands and attempt to take it from adjacent groups. The Bohannans note that this problem has become even more acute since the Tiv began growing cash crops.[37] Tiv expansion usually occurs when a kin group moves into new territory occupied by as remote a kin group as possible. The members of two adjacent *utar* which are descended from the same ancestor will seldom expand into one another's territories but will move against the lands of another lineage segment at a higher order of lineage segmentation. This tactic allows them to count on

35. Bohannan and Bohannan, *The Tiv*, pp. 19–25.
36. Ibid., p. 25.
37. Ibid., p. 57.

each other for military support. The same principle holds true for larger lineage segments. For example, if members of a *tar* of one clan move across a clan boundary onto the lands claimed by a *tar* of an opposing clan, both *utar* can count on the military backing of all the members of their respective clans. At the boundaries between clans or other large lineage segments, conflict is therefore likely to be both intense and lethal even though the compounds involved may be neighbors geographically, and their residents may know one another better than they do other members of their own clans who live further away. At the highest level, the tribe as a whole may unite against neighboring tribes in land disputes. Thus, the Tiv admonish members of adjacent *utar* not to take land from one another "because they are brothers" but exhort each other to take land from foreigners since "all Tiv are brothers."[38] The Tiv tribe has therefore consistently expanded its territory at the expense of its hapless neighbors, both by infiltration and direct conquest.

Attempts to seize additional land are the direct result of lineage growth and subsequent fission. Within the *tar* itself, the groups most likely to fission are patrilineal groups called literally "segments within the hut." These fluctuate widely in numbers and influence. According to the Bohannans, they are "the spheres of most rapid genealogical change and hence of relative importance."[39] In general, the Tiv regard cooperation within the *tar* as valuable only so long as it provides protection and mutual support but does not make excessive demands on them. The most common reason for the fissioning and migration of part of a *tar* is a charge of tyranny directed against the *tar* elders by the fissioning faction. Usually such charges are accompanied by accusations of sorcery since the elders of the community are the only ones with sufficient spiritual power to call upon the *mbatsav*, an evil presence held responsible for all deaths within the *tar*, including those resulting from what Westerners would call natural causes.[40] Although the elders' control of lethal witchcraft is not disputed, dissident factions invariably claim that the *mbatsav*—and, by implication, the elders who control them—have become selfish and are causing deaths for personal reasons rather than for the good of the community. Thus, dissatisfaction over the distribution of power and resources within the *tar* is transformed into a ritual rebellion based on charges of selfish as opposed to altruistic witchcraft. The conflict seldom proceeds to more open hostilities against the elders because expansion by the fissioning group takes place at the expense of genealogically more distant *utar*. In fact, the members of the original *tar* may continue to unite against other lineage segments.

38. Ibid., p. 56.   39. Ibid., pp. 90–92.   40. Ibid., pp. 20–21.

Tiv fission illustrates the same principles as fission among pastoralists: the potential danger from close agnatic relatives, the power of strong lineages, and the tension between agnatic elders and their sons and male descendants. It also has the same results as fission among pastoralists: over time, the separated lineages become increasingly removed genealogically. In Tiv internal politics, this increased genealogical distance is accompanied by a shift from sticks and stones to spears, bows, and arrows in land conflicts. Ultimately, however, Tiv fissioning deprives other tribes, not other Tiv, of land and resources because the progressive massing of higher-order lineage segments in any land dispute and the injunction to take land from foreigners, not from brothers, pushes conflict and migration outward past the boundaries of the tribe.

The precise manner in which fissioning occurs differs from one strong fraternal interest group society to another, but the problem is common to all. Consanguineal and usually agnatic male kin who are the source of military power are also the source of dangerous political opposition: the group most likely to take advantage of its immediate kin and declare itself independent. The growth of any individual family within a lineage increases the lineage's overall military power, but it also provides the increasing family with political leverage within the lineage itself. This inner contradiction leads to hostility and distrust among agnates from different generations and collateral lines. As long as no one lineage achieves complete military supremacy and establishes itself as the ruling dynasty of a nation-state, this dilemma is inherently insoluble. Consanguineal kinsmen must, therefore, continually monitor the flow of mutual aid, community resources, and political power within each lineage segment to anticipate future lines of fission. Among the Tiv, the relative ranking of patrilineal elders is a constant subject of public discussion and debate, and among the Somali, the waxing and waning of family influence is a constant source of gossip. If fission is to occur, it is to the advantage of the head of a large family to learn of it in advance so that he can either defect himself, taking as much of the community patrimony with him as possible, or, alternatively, attempt to assuage the dissident faction, thus winning additional influence with the lineage and, at the same time, maintaining its overall power by preventing the fission. Advance information on fission is especially important for the elders themselves, who must preserve their group's unity for as long as possible and gauge accurately the strength of the fissioning group. But the shifting tides of influence within a lineage and the relative strength of its factions are never matters of perfect information and depend at least as much on propaganda, reputation, and pretense as on actual numbers. There is no way to find out how effective a fissioning unit will be militarily until it actually segments and some degree of open hostilities becomes possible. The personal animosity generated by fission thus comes as much from the ambiguities of the immediate political situation within the lineage as it does from the ultimate fact of fission. Nevertheless, as long as lineages grow, fission is an inevitable problem in strong fraternal interest group societies. The only immediate solutions to the problem are either unworkable in both the long and the short run or workable in the short run only.

SOLUTIONS TO THE DILEMMA OF FISSION

Castration and Centralized Control

At first glance, castration as a solution to the problem of fission may seem absurd. If a lineage patriarch castrates his own sons or convinces his collaterals or descendants to castrate theirs, he "shortens" his own line to the point of extinction and thus violates the basic principle of fraternal interest group politics: be fruitful and multiply. And, in fact, no society has ever used general castration to solve the problem of fission though the reason for its absence is more complex than the simple extinction argument indicates. Logically, it would be quite possible for an influential patriarch to follow the same policy with his sons and other male descendants that he follows with his herds: castration of all but a very few stud animals that provide the necessary fertilization but do not create social-control problems in the herds. A sexually vigorous patriarch might even perform most of the fertilizations himself. Often, strong lineage heads hold more wives than weaker men; this practice serves both to increase the strength of their own lineage group and to reduce the number of women available to younger men who may wish to found competitive family units. If the patriarch could not fertilize all the women himself, he might obtain stud services from slaves, outcasts, or other subordinate groups and lobby for changes in the kinship ideology to support his claims to their offspring. Such a practice is in fact followed by so-called female fathers among the Nuer. A wealthy woman may pay brideprice for another woman, assume the role of sociological father, and hire an impecunious male relative to perform stud services.[41] Thus, there is no logical reason why the father in a strong fraternal interest group society cannot use castration to solve the problem of fission.

The reasons for the absence of this practice are instead political. One of the most important ties between a son and his father is the prospect that the son will be able to start an independent "long"

41. Lucy Mair, *Marriage* (Harmondsworth, England: Penguin Books, 1971), p. 59.

lineage of his own. A father who deprived a son of this hope would be unable to prevent the son's immediate defection since without wives, children, or herds the son would have nothing to protect, nothing to lose, and no reason to remain in a military coalition with his father. The same reasoning applies to higher-order lineage segments, which remain together only so long as the gains in protection and military aid are not offset by costs in obedience and tribute to the clan or lineage elders. The absence of castration in strong fraternal interest group societies actually indicates the political weakness of these systems. Patriarchs must extend the right to ultimate power to their descendants and collaterals in order to win their loyalty even though this means sharing power and, if a lineage fission occurs, losing some. Thus, castration is never regularly employed as a political tactic by societies organized on the basis of kin-group armies.

Historically, the only political use of castration has been the appointment of eunuchs to higher administrative and court positions in centralized agrarian bureaucracies supported by professional armies. Among such societies the practice is widespread, and the political role of the eunuch is central to the administration of the despotic state. Eunuchs played central political roles most notably in China under the Han and T'ang dynasties and in Byzantium in the declining stages of the Roman Empire; they also appear in the courts of Arabia, Mesopotamia, Assyria, Persia, and the Ottoman empire. Although there is some disagreement about the precise role of the eunuchs in the Chinese imperial administrations, their general purpose was to serve the political interests of the despotic ruler. The eunuch, who was often of slave, plebeian, or barbarian origins, was an alien who had no family ties and was, therefore, personally dependent on the emperor. Lewis Coser argues that the principal function of eunuchism was to undercut the power of the bureaucracy, which showed dangerous tendencies toward political autonomy, by creating a group of loyal officials who could take over many of its administrative functions.[42] Coser's emphasis on conflict with the bureaucracy apparently follows that of Weber, who saw the struggle between the Chinese mandarinate and the emperor and his eunuchs as central to an understanding of Chinese history.[43] Other interpretations have emphasized that the eunuch was employed to counteract the power of noble families rather than that of the bureaucracy and that he was attractive to Oriental despots not because of his isolation from the bureaucracy caused by his deformity and plebeian origins but because of his lack

42. Lewis A. Coser, "The Political Functions of Eunuchism," *American Sociological Review* 29 (1964): 880–85.

43. Ibid., p. 882, quoting Max Weber, *The Religion of China*, tr. and ed. Hans Gerth (Glencoe, Ill.: Free Press, 1951), p. 138.

of issue. Karl Wittfogel observes that the emergence of eunuchs as a politically powerful force in the T'ang dynasty "coincided significantly with the establishment of the examination system," the emperor's attempt to weaken the nobility by eliminating aristocratic control over bureaucratic office.[44] This attempt was only partially successful since only a small proportion, usually less than 15 percent, of high bureaucratic positions was held by commoners, and offices frequently became hereditary, if not within individual families, at least within the higher gentry as a whole.[45] Thus, the struggle between the emperor and the bureaucracy was simply another manifestation of the struggle against the hereditary nobility.

If this is the case, then the problems of the imperial despot dealing with his noble office holders parallel the problems of the lineage patriarch dealing with his consanguineal relatives. Like the patriarch, the emperor must reward his nobles with a share of his economic or political power, usually in the form of land or tax farming rights, in order to maintain their loyalty. These rewards create an independent base of dynastic power that may fission and assert its independence against the central administration, diverting larger shares of state revenues for its own use and converting an office into a hereditary fief. If the emperor is to avoid the insoluble dilemma of the fission of noble dynasties, he must find some means of binding high administrators to him other than through the sharing of his own patrimony. As the ruler becomes more powerful, however, he becomes increasingly independent of the noble families and can replace them with eunuchs who pose no threat of dynastic fission. Thus, the greater the central power of the despot, the greater the likelihood of his employing eunuchs in the central administration. Keith Hopkins has pointed out that in the early Roman Empire the emperor was merely *primus inter pares* and often was on intimate terms with the aristocracy, represented by the senate nobility, who continued to hold considerable local administrative power.[46] As centralized authority increased in response to increasing barbarian attacks in the fourth and fifth centuries, the emperor's powers increased accordingly, and imperial bureaucracy, which had originated in the patrimonial estate of Augustus, became the instrument of centralized rule. In Rome as in China, however, the bureaucracy gradually freed itself from imperial control. Hopkins vividly illustrates its growth in power through the case of the *notarii*, a body of shorthand secretaries. Originally a despised occupation filled entirely by plebeians, the *notarii* were first used in the

---

44. Karl A. Wittfogel, *Oriental Despotism: A Comparative Study of Total Power* (New Haven: Yale University Press, 1957), p. 356.

45. Ibid., pp. 351–52.

46. Keith Hopkins, "Eunuchs in Politics in the Later Roman Empire," *Proceedings of the Cambridge Philological Society* 189 (1963): 70.

first half of the fourth century, but by the end of the century they had evolved into still another branch of the hereditary nobility through increasing inheritance of office and intermarriage with the senatorial aristocracy and had become a base of independent dynastic power.

The eunuch did not present this problem since through his emasculation he had renounced any hopes of dynastic succession. It was this physical fact rather than his plebeian origins or stigmatized status that made him useful to the imperial power. As the case of the *notarii* illustrates, plebeians holding imperial power can rapidly become aristocrats, and the stigmatized status of eunuch can actually become honorific if associated with power. Even Coser notes that in later Byzantium, aristocratic families would compete for higher administrative positions by insisting that their sons be castrated, sacrificing dynastic succession for immediate power.[47] Much of the unfavorable commentary on the unreliable character, torpor, indulgence, sycophancy, gluttony, envy, and acquisitiveness of eunuchs seems to have come from the eloquent but frustrated aristocrats who found themselves reduced to political impotence by eunuchs who formed a solid wall around the emperor. The resiliency of the system was such that even if the nobles succeeded in retiring, exiling, or murdering one influential eunuch, his place was invariably taken by another. The attractiveness of eunuchs to the emperors was not their personal ties, not their willingness to subordinate themselves through mutilation, since emperors were quite willing to dispense with long-established personal ties and replace eunuchs with bewildering speed. Their attraction was simply their lack of issue and hence of dynastic ambitions. Thus, it became of critical importance to determine just how emasculated a particular eunuch was. Romans distinguished three types of eunuchs, depending on whether the testicles had been severed or crushed, or the external genitalia had been entirely removed. The latter were preferred for political purposes because there was no opportunity for trickery. This was not an inconsequential problem, and Robert Spencer provides one example of an Arabic court "eunuch" who actually suffered from undescended testicles and succeeded in impregnating a member of the sultan's harem. Since the eunuch was black and the harem girl blonde, and the Koran provided no explanation of how a mulatto could be produced by the imperial loins, the entire harem was drowned. It is a testimony to the immense political power of eunuchs, however, that the offending eunuch by contrast had to stand trial before he could be removed from office.[48]

47. Coser, "Eunuchism," p. 882, note 13.
48. Robert F. Spencer, "The Cultural Aspects of Eunuchism," *Ciba Symposium* 8 (1946), p. 416.

Eunuchs in the imperial courts, therefore, were of value because of their total renunciation of claims to dynastic power and hence their almost total lack of interest in fissioning. In China as well as Byzantium the status of eunuch eventually became honorable although emasculation was hardly the customary means of upward mobility. No bureaucratic system is perfect, however, and any account of the politics of eunuchs would be incomplete without mention of the case of Korea, where, in a period of general decay of monarchial authority, eunuchs not only ran the kingdom and dominated the aristocracy but also authorized legislation permitting them to adopt children and leave estates, thus evading the imperial restrictions on dynastic fission which their emasculation had been designed to guarantee.[49] Curiously enough, the eunuchs adopted only other eunuchs who were alleged to be the result of "accidents" in childhood so that the principle of loyalty through renunciation of progeny remained even if the practice became somewhat attenuated. Nevertheless, most despots were well served by their eunuchs and the system can only be envied by weaker lineage patriarchs for whom castration is not a workable solution to the problem of fission.

The Politics of Circumcision

In strong fraternal interest group societies, influential lineage elders are in no position to demand castration of their descendants or collaterals, nor are they likely to find anyone who is willing to renounce his lineage ambitions by volunteering for the operation. Circumcision, although a dangerous operation especially when performed in later childhood or adolescence, does not inevitably lead to the loss of reproductive capacity and hence does not create the same political problem for fraternal interest group elders as does castration. On the other hand, it does not provide a certain solution to the problem of fission since insofar as the operation is a success and the patient and his penis survive intact, he can continue building a line of sons powerful enough to defect in a lineage fission.

What, then, do the elders gain from circumcision? They gain visible public evidence that the head of a family unit of their lineage is willing to trust others with his and his family's most valuable political asset, his son's penis. If the surgeon's hands are unsteady, they may gain castration or even death, thus eliminating a competitive and potentially fissionable segment within the primary lineage, although no doubt at the cost of considerable bad feeling on the part of the unfor-

49. Cornelius Osgood, *The Koreans and Their Culture* (New York: Ronald Press, 1951), p. 146.

tunate son's father and immediate consanguineal kin. A surgeon who regularly bungled the circumcision operation could expect to earn the enmity of a growing circle of lineage members as each in turn saw its political prospects literally cut short under the knife, and the circumcisor and those he was suspected of working for would no doubt face retaliation from the dissident faction. But if the operation is successful, both sides gain a certain degree of satisfaction. The lineage elders have the satisfaction of knowing that, whatever a given father's future plans for lineage fission, he is sufficiently loyal to his kin to publicly expose the source of his future political power to danger. The father, while resenting the risk to his son, can expect under normal circumstances to gain the continued trust of his consanguineal kin and to retain the reproductive power of his son.

The behavior of father, son, and consanguineal kin during the ceremony provides valuable information both to the father and, more importantly, to his influential elder kinsmen. Like other ceremonies, the circumcision ceremony allows a man both to assess and to influence the opinions of important political allies or enemies. The behavior of other family heads within the lineage or the lineage elders may in turn indicate how anxious they are to assert their authority over the child. Do they bring gifts or help with the ceremony? Do they try to make the operation as easy as possible, for example, by making the sacrifices necessary to ward off evil spirits that might cause the surgeon's hand to slip? Or do they remain aloof, hoping for the worst and perhaps even plotting against the child through secret witchcraft? A father can answer politically vital questions like these with some accuracy after careful observation of the behavior of principals and spectators at a circumcision ceremony.

The ceremony provides even more valuable information to the lineage elders, who have the most to lose from future lineage fissions and the most to gain by preventing fission through early detection of the lines dividing possible factions within the lineage. Reluctance of fathers or sons to submit to the operation, a certain lack of enthusiasm on the part of the father's close kin during the accompanying ceremonies, or excessive concern about how and by whom the operation is to be conducted may all indicate fault lines in the primary lineage segment. The circumcision ceremony in large part addresses the interest of the lineage elders, and it is precisely these men who are most capable of requiring it of every member of the lineage. Even in a relatively egalitarian lineage, however, pressures from consanguines would be enough to ensure that each father demonstrate his loyalty by risking his son's penis.

This line of reasoning suggests that a circumcision ceremony is a surveillance ritual by which members of a strong fraternal interest group, particularly the most influential members, assess and minimize the likelihood of fission by requiring a public demonstration of loyalty of any man who has a son. This hypothesis, like the many that have preceded it, can be evaluated both by examining ethnographic descriptions of circumcision ceremonies and by using quantitative cross-cultural methods. It is our contention that the hypothesis is supported by both kinds of evidence.

Characteristics of Circumcision Ceremonies

The kin-group loyalty hypothesis has implications for the characteristics of circumcision ceremonies that can be checked against ethnographic descriptions of actual ceremonies. First, it implies that the boy who is circumcised is not himself the object of the ceremony, which is, in fact, conducted to impress others; thus, his physical presence is necessary but his conscious participation is not. This implication of the theory is contrary to both psychoanalytic and anthropological interpretations of circumcision, which emphasize that for one reason or another the norms of the society must be firmly imposed on a potentially recalcitrant but presumably impressionable son. In the orthodox psychoanalytic interpretation, circumcision wards off a potential Oedipal rebellion at puberty by terrorizing the boy into submission; in Whiting's neo-Freudian theory, close mother-son bonds make hazing and genital mutilation necessary to establish the boy's identity as an adult male and his loyalty to his patrilineal descent group.In the *rites de passage* theories of Young and Cohen, the child is initiated into his new adult status, with its obligations to a wider kin group or a solidary group of males, and hence must be the object of the psychological pressures of initiation. Even in Allen's sexual antagonism theory, the psychological disturbances created in the growing boy by the fear of women's pollution must be quieted by demonstrating the dominance of males and their secret societies. A partial exception to the child-centered view of circumcision is the adult neuroticism theory proposed by Reik and Róheim since in this case it is the father rather than the son who experiences an unresolved Oedipal dilemma; the growing child is peripherally involved, however, since it is his approaching maturity that reawakens his father's partially repressed Oedipal fears.

Most of these theories stress that the optimum time for circumcision is at or shortly before puberty, when the boy is old enough to appreciate the proceedings. Age at circumcision, however, shows no reliable relationship to puberty. The approved age varies from eight days after birth among the ancient Hebrews to the late teens, well after biological puberty, among the Dahomey. Even within a given culture, there is seldom close agreement about the most desirable age. Among the Riffians, some tribes prefer early infancy, others the age of three months, and still others the age of seven or eight. The Somali show a similar casualness: some members of the tribe circumcise sons shortly after birth and others at puberty. For twenty-one of the twenty-three societies in the study sample that practiced circumcision, the customary age of circumcision could be estimated: less than a third (six) practice it at or approximately at puberty. Four practice it in infancy; ten during early or late childhood; and one (the Dahomey) in young adulthood.[50] This range, and especially the popularity of infant and early childhood circumcision, makes the idea that the purpose of the operation is to impress any particular cultural norm on the child hard to accept.

The only timing element common to all circumcising societies in our sample is that the operation always occurs before marriage. Among the Dahomey, commoners traditionally were circumcised at seventeen to nineteen and could marry three months later, but members of the royal family were circumcised much earlier, at thirteen or fourteen, because they generally married earlier.[51] Among the Egyptian Nubians, circumcision ceremonies closely resemble weddings. The word for circumcision ceremony translates literally as "big wedding," and the principals in the ceremony are referred to as "bride" and "groom."[52] A similar linguistic connection between circumcision and marriage is apparent in Hebrew: the words for bridegroom, son-in-law, and father-in-law "are all derived from the same root, *hatan*, which means in Arabic, 'to circumcise.'"[53] Among the Rwala, circumcision ceremonies are accompanied by spirited courtship rituals in which veiled nubile girls armed with sabres repel the mock advances of suitors.[54] In most societies that practice circumcision, intercourse before as well as after marriage is dependent on demonstrable circumcision, and women in such societies express disgust and contempt for uncircumcised men. Among the Tiv, for example, an uncircumcised man is doomed to the life of a neurotic outcast. No woman will have anything to do with him; he will be unable to marry and father children; and he will have no value whatsoever in Tiv internal politics.

The fact that circumcision must precede marriage (although the period which must elapse before marriage is variable) is difficult to

50. Murdock, *Ethnographic Atlas*, p. 53, col. 37.

51. Melville J. Herskovits, *Dahomey*, vol. 1 (Evanston: Northwestern University Press, 1967), p. 298.

52. John G. Kennedy, "Circumcision and Excision in Egyptian Nubia," *Man* 5 (1970): 181.

53. De Vaux, *Israel*, p. 47.

54. Musil, *Rwala*, pp. 240, 245.

interpret in terms of traditional anthropological or psychoanalytic theories but is consistent with a view of circumcision as a ritual reaffirmation of allegiance to the existing lineage group. When a son marries, his father acquires a descendant who has value and some power in internal lineage politics, namely, a man who can produce and command the loyalty of sons. As a result, community interest in the father's future loyalties is likely to increase, and the etiquette of circumcision anticipates this interest by requiring the father to place his son at risk under the knife before he can finish negotiating his son's marriage contract. Since it is the loyalties of the father rather than those of the son which are the principal concern in the ceremony, the son's age is irrelevant.

The kin-group loyalty theory implies that the circumcision ceremony should be carried out under the scrutiny of the father's immediate consanguineal relatives, particularly his lineage elders or their representatives, since they are the ones who are most interested in the father's behavior during the ceremony and most concerned that the ceremony be carried out. In all twenty-three cases of circumcision in the study sample, the circumcision or the associated feasting or ceremonies are carried out in the presence of the father's consanguineal kinsmen; although affines are sometimes present, the major ceremonial roles are usually assigned to consanguines. In no society does an affine perform the circumcision operation although this role is sometimes delegated to a barber or other specialist whose kinship relationship to the initiate is unspecified. Frequently, however, consanguines order or closely supervise the circumcision, and in some cases they carry it out themselves.

Among the Somali, a boy is circumcised while he is in a camel camp guarding the herds of the members of his *dia*-paying group and, consequently, when he is among his closest agnatic kin.[55] Among the Tiv, the boy is usually circumcised in the house of the head of the *tar* or of some other influential elder.[56] Among the Kurd, the sons of members of a village are frequently circumcised together in a ceremony financed by the most influential man in the village, who is usually, though not invariably, a senior agnatic relative.[57] Among the Tanala, the initiate is sequestered among his close agnatic kin in a ceremonial house, and his agnates remain with him throughout the ceremony.[58] Among the Sotho of Basutoland, a boy circumcised among nonkinsmen is considered untrustworthy and must earn his

55. Lewis, *Pastoral Democracy*, p. 75.
56. Akiga, *Akiga's Story: The Tiv Tribe as Seen by One of Its Members*, tr. and ed. Rupert East (London: Oxford University Press, 1939), p. 45.
57. William M. Masters, *Rowanduz: A Kurdish Administrative and Mercantile Center* (Ann Arbor, Mich.: University Microfilms, 1954).

way into the good graces of his lineage by performing an act of exceptional heroism.[59] Even among the matrilineal but patrilocal Suku, a boy is usually circumcised in a ceremony directed by the senior male of a localized matrilineage, and the boys in a given ceremony are likely to be members of the core lineage of the village.[60]

In most of these cases, although the initiative for the ceremony comes from the boy's father, it is clear that he is under pressure from his consanguines. (Of course, he is also motivated by the knowledge that it would be impossible for his son to marry if he remained uncircumcised.) In societies with more centralized and powerful political structures, participation in circumcision is not left to community pressure. Among the Thonga, the clan chief orders the circumcision ceremony; all boys from ten to sixteen must attend, and force is used to compel them to participate if they refuse. Even older men who have somehow escaped circumcision will be rounded up in the chief's dragnet and forced to undergo the operation.[61] Since the Thonga are patrilineal, the clan chief represents the senior elder in the maximal lineage segment. In the even more centralized society of Dahomey, the ceremony was performed at the command of the king, whose order was transmitted by chiefs representing localized patrilineages.[62] Among the ancient Hebrews, the spiritual unity of the tribal confederation was represented by their allegiance to Yaweh, and it was this patriarchal deity who ordered Abraham to show his loyalty by circumcising himself and his sons, forming a lasting blood covenant between God and his chosen people (Gen. 17). When Moses broke the covenant by failing to circumcise his son, God threatened him with instant death (Exod. 4:24). Similarly, Joshua commanded the tribes of Israel to circumcise themselves before entering the land of Canaan since the practice had apparently lapsed during their wanderings in the wilderness (Josh. 5:2–9). In all these cases in which senior members of a maximal lineage segment compel fathers to circumcise their sons, the initiative clearly comes from the elders, not from the individual fathers themselves. Although Róheim saw in Australian circumcision rites the image of a "furious father" attacking his son's penis, a more common pattern seems to be a lineage elder commanding a reluctant father to circumcise his sons.

58. Ralph Linton, *The Tanala: A Hill Tribe of Madagascar* (Chicago: Field Museum of Natural History, 1933), pp. 289–90.

59. S. M. Guma, "Some Aspects of Circumcision in Basutoland," *African Studies* 24 (1965): 242.

60. Igor Kopytoff, "The Suku of the Southwestern Congo," in *Peoples of Africa*, ed. James Gibbs, Jr. (New York: Holt, Rinehart and Winston, 1965), pp. 456–57.

61. Junod, *South African Tribe*, pp. 74–75.

62. Herskovits, *Dahomey*, p. 297.

In fact, the role of the father in circumcision ceremonies is usually the opposite of that predicted by Oedipal theories. As Bettelheim observed, he more often plays the role of the son's protector than that of his persecutor. (This generalization, unlike most of Bettelheim's theory, applies to circumcision as well as to super- and subincision.) The protective role of the father is perfectly consistent with the kin-group loyalty theory since the father is the person with the greatest interest in his son's reproductive and hence political potential. In ethnographic accounts of circumcision ceremonies, the father is either entirely absent, as in strongly centralized societies like the Thonga in which circumcision is the chief's affair, or appears in a generally protective or supportive role. In only two cases, the Rwala and the Hebrews, does he perform the operation himself, and in the latter case he may delegate the task to a religious specialist. Among the Tiv, the father's principal concern is to protect his son from the numerous spiritual dangers surrounding the operation and to do what he can to mitigate more direct threats to his son's well-being. Akiga provides a detailed account of one Tiv circumcision in which the father played an active but supporting role: he stood beside his son during the operation, urging stoicism during the cutting and assuring him that he could and should bear it like a man; later he asked somewhat frantically that someone do something to stop the bleeding since at this point the boy was hemorrhaging seriously and seemed to be losing consciousness.[63] Among the Kurd, the father stands beside his son while a barber performs the operation and then praises the boy profusely for his courage once the operation is over.[64] Among the Mongo it is the father's responsibility to wash and care for the circumcision wound of postpubertal sons. It is believed that if the father does not remain continent until the wound heals, the wound may become seriously infected.[65] Among the Riffians, the selection of a circumciser is a matter of great parental interest, and since the operation is generally regarded as dangerous and likely to lead to infection, skilled practitioners are sought, though hard to find. Carleton Coon describes an unsuccessful operation in which the itinerant specialist severed the end of the glans penis along with the prepuce; the child died several days later from the loss of blood. Only the intervention of a sheik prevented the enraged father from killing the circumciser on the spot, and the circumciser's family was assessed 500 dollars blood

63. Akiga, *Akiga's Story*, pp. 33–35.
64. Masters, *Rowanduz*, p. 260.
65. Gustave-E. Hulstaert, "Marriage Among the Nkundó," tr. Monika B. Vizedom, *Mémoires de l'Institut Royal Colonial Belge* 8 (1928): 473–74.

money to dissuade the boy's family from seeking blood vengeance.[66] The father's role in protecting the child is even more direct among the Ndembu, where in circumcision ceremonies the father stands just behind the circumciser with an axe ready to deal him a fatal blow if he should fail.[67] Throughout the operation the boy's brothers surround him and act as protectors against the circumciser and his assistants, who are referred to as "murderers" and are regarded as symbolically if not actually threatening the life of the child. It is, in fact, difficult to find any of the "furious fathers" beloved of psychoanalytic theory in any ethnography. Even the Rwala father who circumcises his son himself first distracts him by pretending to show him something and then carries out the operation as swiftly and painlessly as possible.[68] The Orthodox Jewish rite calls for the father or his religious substitute to kiss the bleeding circumcision wound while the child is calmed with a small sip of wine.[69] The brutality and hazing associated with circumcision operations are frequently present, as Whiting observed, but, as in the case of the Thonga cited by Whiting, they are initiated by consanguineal relatives or tribal elders who do not fully share the father's concern for protecting the child from harm. Relatives and elders also stand to lose potential lineage strength if the child is harmed, of course, but their loss is much less direct and acute than that of the father, and as a consequence they have much less ambivalence about the operation. Although the father must permit the operation to satisfy elders and consanguines, he is not required to let them make a human sacrifice out of his son, and in ceremonies where he does have a role, he does his best to minimize risks.

The father's fears for his son's welfare are well founded, given the mortality and morbidity associated with circumcision under less than aseptic surgical conditions, especially when the operation is performed in late childhood or adolescence. Herskovits' observation that "an appreciable mortality is attendant on circumcision"[70] among the Dahomeans seems to hold true for most cases in which ethnographers have inquired into survival rates. Akiga, in his account of circumcision among the Tiv, describes a successful operation in which the prompt application of an herbal styptic and the powerful spiritual protection of a village elder combined to stop the bleeding. Akiga adds matter-of-factly, however, "here, in some cases, the bleeding

66. Carleton S. Coon, "Tribes of the Rif," *Harvard African Studies* 9 (1931): 130.
67. Victor W. Turner, "Three Symbols of Passage in Ndembu Circumcision Ritual: An Interpretation," in *Essays on the Ritual of Social Relations*, ed. Max Gluckman (Manchester: Manchester University Press, 1962), pp. 124–73.
68. Musil, *Rwala*, p. 245.
69. Frank Zimmerman, "Origin and Significance of the Jewish Rite of Circumcision," *Psychoanalytic Review* 38 (April 1951): 104.
70. Herskovits, *Dahomey*, p. 297.

would stop; in others, however, it would go on, till finally the boy died; then it was said that the son of so-and-so had bled to death."[71] Among the Thonga the death of an initiate in the circumcision school is not uncommon, but deaths are carefully concealed by burying the body in a swampy area so that the more extensive spade work of preparing a formal grave, which might attract attention, is unnecessary. The mother of the dead boy learns of his death only when she returns to pick up the wooden bowl in which she has brought him his daily allotment of gruel and finds a notch cut in the rim.[72] The family is forbidden to mourn the death, and the Thonga generally treat circumcision fatalities as if they had never happened. A similar practice is followed by the Sotho, who bury the fatalities within the circumcision lodge; the boy's parents learn of his death only at the conclusion of the school, when they find not their son but only his blanket in his place in the line of initiates.[73] There is also a substantial risk of permanent dismemberment. Circumcision may represent symbolic castration, but in some cases the castration is all too real. As both the orthodox psychoanalytic view and the theories of Whiting suggest, circumcision is an ordeal, and none of the circumcising societies in the study sample regard it as trivial, like perforating the septum or cutting the hair. There is little doubt that circumcision is regarded as a period of trial and danger by fathers and sons alike. The risk is run for the benefit of consanguineal kin or lineage elders, not for the benefit of the father, who does everything possible to ensure his son's survival and to preserve his son's reproductive potential.

Finally, there is considerable evidence of thinly veiled hostility between, on the one hand, the boy, his father, and their immediate kin and, on the other, members of the consanguineal kin group who may be part of the same lineage but are less closely related to the initiate and his father. Akiga observes that "only a brave man would circumcise his son amongst his paternal relatives" even though this is almost a universal practice among the Tiv, "lest the *mbatsav* would bewitch the boy, and he should bleed to death."[74] The *mbatsav*, it will be recalled, are the spiritual congregation of ancestors who are regarded as responsible for all deaths among the Tiv and are controlled by community elders. Thus, a Tiv father must seek out an important man of his *tar* and have the circumcision conducted under his spiritual protection lest other powerful men bewitch him and cause his son's death. The *mbatsav* are also active in lineage fissions, when elders are accused of causing too many deaths through selfish witch-

71. Akiga, *Akiga's Story*, p. 35.
72. Junod, *South African Tribe*, p. 85.
73. Guma, "Basutoland," pp. 247–48.
74. Akiga, *Akiga's Story*, p. 30.

craft, so that in Tiv religious ideology there is a close connection between patrilineal elders, fission, circumcision, and death.

Among the Tanala, the ambivalence of the consanguineal kin breaks into open hostilities during the latter part of the circumcision ceremony. Like the Tiv, the Tanala live in villages divided into primary agnatic lineage segments; fission occurs when one group grows large enough to move away and establish a new homestead.[75] The lines of fission follow lines of primary consanguineal kinship, as among the Tiv. In the Tanala circumcision ceremony, the members of the village are divided into two groups by a rope bisecting the community meeting house. The boy and his close kin are on one side of the rope, and the remaining members of the village, who are more distantly related to him, are on the other side. Before the surgery, the boy, surrounded by close agnatic kin, proceeds to a nearby stream where his penis is bathed. On the way back to the village he is surrounded by warriors, again selected from his half of the village, and these men literally fight their way to the site of the circumcision at the meeting house over the violent resistance of the other half of the village. According to Linton, the ceremony is not a mock battle, and warriors on both sides are sometimes wounded or killed.[76] Thus, consanguineal tensions that the Tiv express indirectly through fears of sorcery are expressed directly by the Tanala through a pitched battle along the primary lineage fault line at a time when one side appears to be gaining a potentially marriageable man and hence is about to pull ahead in the struggle for internal village dominance. A similar split is apparent among the Ndembu, where the circumciser is usually selected from a chiefly family, and he and his assistants confront the brothers of the initiate in a mock battle at the site of the circumcision. Even though the Ndembu circumcisers are referred to as "murderers," actual as opposed to mock combat apparently does not occur.[77]

Thus, the principal elements of a fraternal interest group theory of circumcision are apparent in ethnographic descriptions of circumcision rites. The ceremony is not designed to impress the child since the age at which it occurs varies from infancy to adulthood; as a prerequisite to marriage, it occurs at a time when the father's political and military potential becomes an immediate source of concern to his lineage. The theory states that the primary purpose of the operation is to demonstrate loyalty to agnatic kin in general and to village elders in particular. Representatives from both groups are generally present at the circumcision, often take active roles, and sometimes order that the ceremony be performed. As the theory suggests, the father is reluc-

75. Linton, *Tanala*, p. 24.
76. Ibid., p. 290.
77. Turner, "Ndembu Circumcision," p. 159.

tant to expose his son to the risks of the operation and generally par-
ticipates in a supportive or defensive role if at all, while hazing and
brutality are largely under the control of lineage elders or other consanguineal kin. Despite his reluctance, the father is forced to permit
his son to participate in the ceremony either by direct orders (in centralized political systems) or by social pressure—the stigma attached
to an uncircumcised son and the social prohibition against his marrying. This prohibition means that a father who wishes to expand his
family power base must have his son submit to the operation or forfeit
the son's assistance in continuing his line. Descriptions of the ceremonies indicate that, as earlier theories suggested, they are often
brutal and sometimes result in castration or death, but the fraternal
interest group theory suggests that the brutality is required as a vivid
demonstration of the father's loyalty to his own kin, not the result of
the father's or his son's unresolved psychological conflicts. Finally,
the role of consanguineal kin is, as the theory suggests, ambivalent,
and consanguines frequently take overtly or covertly hostile roles in
the ceremony. The evidence from ethnographic accounts of circumcision, then, supports the contention that they are obligatory demonstrations of fraternal interest group loyalty.

A Ceremony That Almost Failed: A Ndembu Circumcision

As long as the participants in a circumcision ceremony fulfill
their prescribed roles with a minimum of resistance and accept the
political gains and losses associated with them with relative equanim-
ity, tension and political conflict will be concealed beneath festive
good feeling or repressed by the fear of witchcraft or open conflict.
Thus, Thonga parents are expected to forget their dead son; in cases
of accident, the Riffian father must accept blood money in exchange
for his son's penis; and the Tiv father must seek the protection of a
lineage elder to control evil spirits that the elder himself may have
been instrumental in organizing. Just as weddings only occasionally
deteriorate into brawls, circumcision ceremonies only rarely lead to
open political rebellion or attempts at lineage fission. However, an
analysis of circumcision ceremonies and the dynamics of lineage fission in strong fraternal interest groups indicates that such political
conflicts are always just below the surface.

Victor Turner's account of a barely successful circumcision ceremony among the Ndembu provides an illustration of conflicts that are
hidden by the customary etiquette of circumcision ceremonies.[78] The

78. Victor W. Turner, "Ritual Aspects of Conflict Control in African Metropoli-
tics," in *Political Anthropology*, ed. Marc J. Swartz, Victor W. Turner, and Arthur Tuden
(Chicago: Aldine, 1966), pp. 239–46.

Ndembu are a matrilineal, avunculocal society, and their villages, though agamous, usually contain a core of matrilineally related kinsmen. The horticultural economy and the avunculocal residence pattern of the Ndembu make them a strong fraternal interest group society, even though their patterns of lineage segmentation and spatial proximity are considerably less neat than those of, for example, the Tiv. Although most residents of a given village tend to be consanguines and (as with the Tiv) fissioning groups tend to settle near their native villages, the composition of larger political units, which Turner terms "vicinages," is considerably more heterogeneous than the composition of villages. The circumcision ceremony that Turner observed took place a few years after a lineage fission in the most influential village of the vicinage had deprived its patriarch of half the population originally under his control. Around the same time, economic changes caused by the introduction of a money economy had created new residential units that resembled commercial farms more than communal villages and had further undermined the control of the patriarch.

Under these rather strained circumstances, the members of the modern village-and-farm cluster, which Turner terms E_1, E_2, and E_3, called a meeting to discuss holding a circumcision ceremony. Circumcision ceremonies among the Ndembu are held approximately every ten years, and all the boys of a vicinage between the ages of six and sixteen are involved. Although the internal vicinage politics as described by Turner are complex, they centered on the conflict between the patriarch of the dominant village A, which had recently fissioned into two villages, A_1 and A_2, and the E faction led by the village head of E_1. As a descendant of the sister of the Ndembu senior chief, the head of A_1 had traditionally officiated at all circumcision ceremonies in the vicinage and performed the critical role of circumciser himself. The E faction, however, planned to call upon an elder from a nearby village, who did not hold A_1's dominant position but had sufficient claims to chiefly descent to be a suitable circumciser. According to Turner, this revolutionary innovation was attempted in large part because A_1 had come to be regarded as a "has-been" in the time since the fission of A_2 from the village, and his reputation had been further damaged by charges that he had practiced malevolent witchcraft and that his demands for traditional deference were tyrannical. The E faction pressured the A_2 village elders into supporting their plan by arguing that A_1's hands were old and unsteady and that A_2 might very well lose his son through incompetent surgery. A_2 was sufficiently frightened to seriously consider joining the dissident faction even though his village had recently fissioned from A_1 and its residents had many close kinship ties to people still living in A_1 and even though A_1

was in fact A_2's mother's brother. A_1 was not to be outmaneuvered, however, and after giving a dramatic speech on the need for respect for tribal traditions on the eve of the ceremony, he proceeded to assume the role of circumciser and carry out the operations with dispatch and precision. Thus, the revolt of E was effectively squelched; deference had been rendered to the traditionally dominant A_1; and the bonds of loyalty joining A_1 and A_2 had been reaffirmed by A_2's willingness to risk his son's penis under the hands of A_1. But it was a close call for A_1; time, change, and the money economy clearly were not on his side. Future circumcisions, if there are any, may be carried out at the local British hospital and, hence, may lose or perhaps transfer their symbolic meaning as pledges of consanguineal allegiance.

The Ndembu chief's close call indicates the fundamental forces at work beneath the façade of a circumcision ceremony. The struggle over who was to be the circumciser was actually a conflict over lineage loyalties in a situation of recent lineage fission, and the old chief's triumph accomplished a symbolic fusion of the new and old villages that he could not have brought about by direct political means. The fact that the chief was able to continue in his role as circumciser indicated that the males of the vicinage, and particularly A_1's relatives, were still willing to demonstrate their loyalty by risking their lineage's future even though, according to the E partisans, the risk under the hand of the overbearing and doddering A_1 was excessive. The E strategy also reveals the fundamental political character of the circumcision ceremony. Their questioning of A_1's surgical skill played on the basic anxiety of all fathers at circumcision ceremonies: will the sacrifice required to demonstrate loyalty be symbolic or real? By carrying out the operations quickly and successfully, A_1 demonstrated that he could still maintain the unity of his immediate fraternal interest group but that he was not so greedy for power that he would "accidentally" deprive his recently fissioned relatives of their sons.

The Ndembu ceremony, therefore, illustrates all the principal theoretical elements of the fraternal interest group theory of circumcision. The initiates themselves are involved hardly at all in the political intrigues surrounding the arrangements for the ceremony. In fact, they figure in the proceedings only as objects of their father's concern and their elders' political ambitions. The ceremony itself brought together consanguineal kinsmen who not only observed the ceremony but, since A_1 managed to seize the role of circumciser himself, dominated the proceedings. The operation was viewed as potentially hazardous by all, and this was one of the most telling political arguments put forth by the E faction in its attempt to discredit A_1. The E faction also played on the father's concern for his son's welfare, which is common in most circumcision ceremonies, in its attempt to drive a wedge between A_2 and A_1. Finally, it was the fissioning of A_2 from A_1 and the resulting political tension between close consanguineal kin that gave the modernizing E faction its chance to discredit the former chief. Although lineage loyalty was temporarily restored, the ambivalence of A_1's closest relatives and their fear of his witchcraft and tyranny were the principal themes of the political crisis surrounding the circumcision.

The fraternal interest group theory, therefore, accounts for both the principal ritual elements in ethnographic accounts of circumcision ceremonies and the principal lines of political tensions in disputed ceremonies. The theory requires no vague teleological assumptions about the functional necessity to protect the unity of the fraternal interest group in order to keep the society together. These groups can and do divide, and this process of fission is a fundamental political issue. Instead, the ceremonies serve the political interests of individual men and especially those men who have most to gain from adherence to the traditional forms of circumcision and the power to compel others to conform. The Ndembu circumcision described by Turner was conducted not for the good of the society but for the welfare of the aging chief of A_1, who sought continued dominance despite the shifting coalitions of fraternal interest group politics. Even when centralized control of this kind is absent, each man may act as the guardian of the circumcision practice because it is in each man's interest to see that other men with sons declare their loyalty to him by risking their sons' reproductive capacity just as it is in their interest to demand a similar sacrifice of him. The politics of circumcision ceremonies, like politics generally, are based on self-interest; like conventional politics, they proceed as much through appearance, propaganda, and persuasion as through the naked exercise of power. The underlying political realities of fission in strong fraternal interest groups cannot be denied, but they can be manipulated by clever politicians who recognize that a public ceremony provides them with a means for both assessing and reaffirming their position in the opinion of their fellow citizens.

CIRCUMCISION AND FRATERNAL INTEREST GROUP THEORY: AN EMPIRICAL ANALYSIS

Since our theory asserts that circumcision is a political tactic used to assess and minimize the likelihood of fraternal interest group fission and that such fissions have the most serious consequences in strong fraternal interest groups, it must follow that an empirical correlation exists between circumcision and measures of strong fraternal interest groups.

Measures

The existence of this relationship can easily be tested in the study sample of 108 societies by coding the presence or absence of circumcision and correlating this variable with the measure of fraternal interest group strength and its structural antecedents. Although Murdock's *Ethnographic Atlas* provides information on presence or absence of circumcision for each of the societies in the study sample, an independent coding was made, not so much to assess the reliability of Murdock's work as to distinguish cases of circumcision from superincision and subincision since Murdock treats the operations as equivalent. Circumcision is defined as the complete or partial removal of the prepuce by a lateral or circular incision in which the entire glans penis is exposed. It includes cases such as the Masai, where a vestigial remnant of the prepuce is permitted to hang below the glans and the prepuce is, therefore, not totally removed. Superincision is any longitudinal incision in the dorsal aspect of the prepuce although following Harrington's classification, the Wogeo practice of penis slashing has been included in this category.[79] Subincision is any longitudinal incision in the ventral aspect of the penis although the only case, the Arunta, involves the radical form of the operation. Excepting the distinction between circumcision and the other two operations, the only difference between our codings and those of Murdock is the case of the Mbuti, who do not practice the operation themselves but are circumcised by nearby village Bantu. Since the operation is initiated by the latter rather than by the Mbuti themselves the logic of the theory suggests that Bantu rather than Mbuti social structure should be the source of the operation. Following Murdock's coding decision, however, circumcision was considered present in this case. The Nama, as Murdock notes, represent an ambiguous case since some ethnographers report that the excision of one testicle was at one time a regular practice. We have followed Murdock's code in this case as well and coded circumcision absent.

Results

The matrix in Table 9 presents the correlations between circumcision, as opposed to genital mutilations in general, and the principal causal variables in the fraternal interest group model. Variables in Whiting's original status-envy hypothesis are also included in the matrix so that the relative power of each model of circumcision may be tested. The three variables in our model show the same pattern of

---

79. Charles Harrington, "Sexual Differentiation in Socialization and Some Male Genital Mutilations," *American Anthropologist* 70 (1969): 951–56.

TABLE 9. Correlates of Circumcision

Variable	2	3	4	5	6	7	8
1. Resource Base	.31[b]	.66[c]	.26[b]	.22[a]	.07	.10	.54[c]
2. Residence Patterns		.39[b]	.87[c]	.17	.23	.12	.30[b]
3. Strength Index			.38[c]	.30[b]	.18	.14	.53[c]
4. Patrilocality				.16	.22	.10	.31[b]
5. Polygyny					.23	.18	.16
6. Postpartum Taboo (old codes)[1]						.74[c]	.26
7. Postpartum Taboo (new codes)[2]							.18
8. Circumcision							

[a]p<.05.
[b]p<.01.
[c]p<.001.
[1]Dichotomous measure.
[2]Seven-point scale ranging from short to long.

associations with circumcision as they do with menarcheal cere-monies in the previous chapter although in the case of circumcision all correlations are, as predicted, positive rather than negative. After the potential effects of historical diffusion on the statistical results are eliminated, residence, fraternal interest group strength, and economic resource base remain significantly correlated with circumci-sion (r=.30, .53, and .54, respectively). Significant zero-order correla-tions between the presence of valuable economic resource, residence configurations, strong political groups, and circumcision do not, of course, provide a sufficient test of the fraternal interest group theory of circumcision rituals. It must be shown that the effects of residence patterns and resource base on circumcision are mediated by fraternal interest group strength.

When the statistical association between economic resource base and circumcision is computed holding political strength constant, the correlation between resource base and circumcision is reduced from a strong and statistically significant .54 to a nonsignificant .29. Control-ling for political strength of fraternal interest groups, economic resource base accounts for only 8.5 percent of the variance in circum-cision ritual. When strength is not held constant, resource base accounts for 29.2 percent of the variance. Similarly, when the statisti-cal effects of residence configuration on circumcision are computed holding fraternal interest group strength constant, the correlation is reduced from a statistically significant .30 to a nonsignificant .12, demonstrating that a large proportion of the observed relationship between residence patterns and circumcision is accounted for by the strong association of each variable with the strength index. When the effects of resource base as well as fraternal strength are partialed out, the relationship between residence and circumcision is further reduced to .10. This demonstrates that most of the effect of economic resources and residence on circumcision is mediated by fraternal interest group strength as our theory argues. Including residence in the model also does not improve on a model including only resource base and fraternal interest group strength. A three-step model including residence accounts for 35.5 percent of the variance in circumcision ceremonies, but a two-step model reduces the explained variance only slightly to 34 percent. Circumcision, then, can best be interpreted as a ritual response to the threat of fission in societies whose economic resource base permits the development of strong fraternal interest groups. Since fission in these societies, while infrequent, has serious consequences, fraternal interest groups resort to an extreme, sometimes life-threatening, tactic to assess and minimize the likelihood of its occurrence.

The Whiting Model

Whiting's causal model includes an entirely different set of factors to explain circumcision. The relative power of our theory and Whiting's theory can be examined by first inspecting the intercorrelations among circumcision, patrilocal residence, polygyny, and length of the postpartum sex taboo described in Table 9. Residence and family organization codes were taken from Murdock and Wilson and Murdock's 1967 *Ethnographic Atlas*.[80] Two postpartum taboo codes were used so that the effects of changes in the coding of the variable on Whiting's model could be examined. The codes for the length of the taboo in the 1967 *Ethnographic Atlas* are used since they are the codes that Whiting used in the development of his empirical model. Recent recodes of this variable by Herbert Barry and Lenora Paxton[81] were also used to examine the effects of important coding changes on the postpartum taboo, especially the reduction of much of the considerable missing data on this variable. Patrilocal residence in this case includes avunculocal as well as patrilocal residence. Polygyny includes both sororal and nonsororal polygyny, and the original postpartum sex taboo was dichotomized into "long" (lasting a year or more) and "short" (lasting less than one year). The length of the postpartum sex taboo based on the new Barry and Paxton codes was

80. George P. Murdock and Suzanne F. Wilson, "Settlement Patterns and Community Organization: Cross-Cultural Codes 3," *Ethnology* 11 (1972): 254–95; and George P. Murdock, *Ethnographic Atlas* (Pittsburgh: University of Pittsburgh Press, 1967), p. 47, col. 14.

81. Herbert Barry III and Leonora Paxton, "Infancy and Early Childhood Cross-Cultural Codes," *Ethnology* 10 (1971): 466–508.

not dichotomized; the entire seven-point scale is used, with "intercourse expected soon after birth" representing one end of the continuum and "more than two years" representing the other extreme.

The most important relationship in Whiting's model is that between circumcision and the long postpartum sex taboo. The size of the correlation between these two variables on our sample is .26 when the 1967 taboo codes are used. Although Whiting routinely reported the results of tests of significance, he did not calculate strength of association measures. He did, however, regularly publish the data on which his findings were based so that it is possible to calculate correlations from the data themselves. In his 1964 article, the relationship between circumcision and postpartum sex taboo is nearly identical to that reported in Table 9, .25. This relationship, however, is reduced to .18 when the postpartum sex taboo length is measured by the more recent codes.[82] Inspection of the differences in the two codes shows that the original correlation inflates the actual strength of the relationship primarily because of sampling inadequacies. There is a considerable amount of missing data (thirty-two of 108 cases) in the original postpartum variable as coded by Murdock, but the missing data are not distributed randomly but instead tend to cluster in particular regions. Thus, while only 5.5 percent of the African societies in our sample are coded missing data, 60 percent of the Circum-Mediterranean societies lack any code for the postpartum taboo. Since the Circum-Mediterranean is an area in which circumcision tends to be present and the postpartum taboo short, the underrepresentation of cases from this area tends to strengthen Whiting's findings. The new postpartum codes eliminate much of the missing data on the variable and reduce the regional bias in those missing data still present. Using the new codes not only reduces the amount of missing data by half (sixteen of 108 cases) in our sample but eliminates all missing data on Circum-Mediterranean societies. Using a sample of societies entirely different from either Whiting's or this study's, Saucier reports an even lower .15 correlation between the taboo and Murdock's genital mutilation category than the .18 we report.[83] In any case, the finding which has been the occasion for so much heated theoretical debate turns out in fact to have been a rather modest one.

The Whiting model, however, involved not only a single correlation between circumcision and a long postpartum sex taboo but a re-

82. This scale was not dichotomized as were the original codes since use of the total seven-point scale for the new codes led to higher correlations with all Whiting's variables than a dichotomized measure.

83. Jean-François Saucier, "Correlates of the Long Postpartum Sex Taboo: A Cross-Cultural Study," *Current Anthropology* 13 (April 1972): 245.

lated series of correlations with residence and family organization.[84] Whiting argued that the correlations between polygyny and patrilocality and circumcision were actually a spurious result of the correlations of both variables with the postpartum sex taboo and that this variable became "the best candidate for the solution to the problem of the distribution of circumcision rites."[85] According to Whiting, the presence of a long postpartum sex taboo caused men to seek additional wives and hence led to polygyny. Patrilocal residence developed in turn to facilitate the management of polygynous cowives. The diagram in Whiting's 1964 article indicates that not only should each of these variables be correlated with one another but that they should also be ordered in a causal sequence in which postpartum sex taboo leads to polygyny which in turn leads to patrilocality which in turn leads to circumcision. The actual strength of the zero-order correlations between these variables in Table 9 shows that such a causal model is difficult to support empirically, especially when the potential effects of historical diffusion on the results are also considered. As the data in the matrix indicate, not only is there a weak and statistically nonsignificant association between postpartum taboo length and circumcision, but no intervening variables are significantly associated with the taboo or each other, and only one, patrilocality, is associated with circumcision. When circumcision is regressed simultaneously onto the three variables in the Whiting model, only patrilocality exerts a statistically significant effect on circumcision before the effects of diffusion are eliminated. The size of the beta coefficient for patrilocality is nearly as high as the zero-order correlation between patrilocality and circumcision (beta=.28 and $r=.31$), showing that adding the postpartum taboo and polygyny to the model does not lead to much improvement. The entire model accounts for 12.8 percent of the variance in circumcision, a proportion substantially below that of our fraternal interest group model (34 percent).

The basic problem with Whiting's argument is his attempt to string together a series of relatively weak relationships into a long causal chain. In his 1964 article he presents each link of the chain separately but presents no statistical demonstration of relationship among all the variables considered collectively. Whiting can hardly be faulted for his statistical methods, however, since regression and path analysis had not come into general use in cross-cultural analysis at the time of his original work. When these techniques are applied to his

84. John W. M. Whiting, "Effects of Climate on Certain Cultural Practices," in *Explorations in Cultural Anthropology,* ed. W. H. Goodenough (New York: McGraw-Hill, 1964), pp. 511–44.
85. Ibid.

findings, his explanatory model does not account for the known correlates of circumcision. In addition, the recodes of postpartum sex taboo were not published until recently, nor were the appropriate methods to assess the effects of historical diffusion. When new codes and methods are used to test his model, the results show clearly that his model is not a very powerful explanation of circumcision.

Thus, the results of both qualitative and quantitative analysis of the ethnographic evidence indicate that circumcision is a ceremonial solution to the dilemma of fission in strong fraternal interest group societies. In contrast to the problem confronted ritually in menarcheal ceremonies, which is most severe in weak fraternal interest group societies, the problem confronted by circumcision is most severe among the strong. Thus, the relationship between strong fraternal interest groups and circumcision is precisely the reverse of that with menarcheal ceremonies. Strong fraternal interest groups were negatively correlated with the presence of women's menarcheal ceremonies, but are positively correlated with the presence of circumcision. The political power which gives strong fraternal interest groups the ability to control women and potential suitors, to negotiate binding wedding contracts, and to enforce the terms of these agreements is based on their ability to mobilize males of military age. But if the problem of the control and allocation of women is largely solved by force or the threat of force, the problem of controlling the instruments of force, the fraternal interest groups themselves, remains insoluble. If men are to be the guardians of women, who then will be the guardians of men? The massive military power of a strong fraternal interest group is built up from small lineage units and depends on their continued allegiance since present military allies may become future enemies in the shifting world of lineage fission. Circumcision does not solve this problem, but it does enable men to attempt to continue by ceremonial means what political methods have failed to accomplish.

5 The Dilemma of Legitimacy: Birth Practices

THE DILEMMA OF LEGITIMACY

We have argued that the major events in the reproductive cycle create a series of social dilemmas. When a girl reaches menarche, her family, her suitors and their families, and occasionally seducers or abductors all come into conflict over her reproductive value and rights to her fertility. This conflict continues throughout her marriage, with crises at each pregnancy and birth as interested parties contest rights of legitimate paternity and payment for these rights. Legitimacy is, in fact, a major source of dispute in societies in which individual power and prestige are determined largely by the size and solidarity of one's kin group.

Conflict over legitimacy occurs because the right to exert jural authority over a child is determined not by one's biological contribution to the process of conception and birth but by social consensus and contractual agreements. The person with the greatest biological involvement in childbirth, the mother, is rarely given jural rights over her children. Such rights, which may include the rights to expect political allegiance, extract labor service, and transmit wealth, social position, or political or religious office through inheritance, usually rest with a group of men or with one man, who in some cases is neither the child's biological father nor its mother's husband.

GENITOR AND PATER

In discussing paternity in tribal and band societies, one must distinguish between the role of genitor, the biological father, and the role of pater, the sociological father. A pater is an individual who is granted jural rights over offspring. In most societies, the husband of a woman is recognized as both genitor and pater of her children though biological paternity may be challenged by adulterers. But his rights as pater are usually shared to some extent with other men. In patrilineal societies, the husband may be recognized as the sociological father of his wife's children, but other members of his kin group share jural rights. In bilateral and duolineal societies, jural rights over offspring are shared by the mother's and the husband's families so that children are expected to recognize the claims of many kinsmen of both parents on their services and allegiance.

In some societies, the roles of genitor and pater are played by different people. In matrilineal societies, for example, the husband is recognized as genitor of his wife's offspring, but jural rights are retained by the woman's matrilineal kinsmen. Children owe their political allegiance to their mother's matrilineal kinsmen, such as the mother's eldest brother or the head of her lineage, and they will inherit the mother's kinsmen's property and duties instead of the biological father's. A relationship between the child and his biological father does exist, however, and it may become close enough to threaten the traditional rights of matrilineal kinsmen.[1] Biological fathers in matrilineal societies not only have close personal relationships with their children but frequently pass on gifts, magic, and other items as inheritance; in many societies, the genitor also plays a critical role in the choice of his child's marriage partner.[2] The danger that a biological father may challenge and perhaps succeed in gaining his children's political allegiance may account in part for theories of conception among some matrilineal societies that minimize the genitor's role. Informants in these societies assert that women can be impregnated by spirits, the wind, or natural objects.[3] These beliefs

1. The potential for conflict between the husband and his wife's matrilineal kin group over rights to offspring is best analyzed by David Schneider, "Introduction," in *Matrilineal Kinship,* ed. David Schneider and Kathleen Gough (Berkeley: University of California Press, 1962), pp. 1–29, who argues that a husband is in a strong position to subvert the authority of his wife's matrilineal group over his children not only because of his sex role but also because of his independent power base as a member of another lineage and his close emotional relationship with his offspring; see especially p. 23.

2. Marguerite Robinson, "Complementary Filiation and Marriage in the Trobriand Islands: A Re-Examination of Malinowski's Material," in *Marriage in Tribal Societies,* ed. Meyer Fortes (Cambridge: Cambridge University Press, 1962), pp. 128–30.

3. Bronislaw Malinowski, *Magic, Science, and Religion* (New York: Doubleday

have led some anthropologists to argue that preliterate peoples are ignorant of the relation between conception and intercourse.[4] Not only does the widespread use of contraceptives in some groups suggest otherwise, but interviews indicate the informants' awareness of the physiology of sex and birth despite their belief in magical conception.[5] As Edmund Leach argues, "Human beings, wherever we meet them, display an almost obsessional interest in matters of sex and kinship." Statements that suggest an ignorance of reproductive physiology should be interpreted instead as assertions of a cultural ideology indicating something about the organization of social relationships in a society.[6]

The matrilineal Nayar minimize the possibility of competition between genitor and pater over rights to offspring by substituting a ritual husband and a series of temporary liaisons for the recognized marriage of a woman to one man and the formation of a nuclear household unit.[7] As described in Chapter 1, a Nayar woman is ritually married to a man, or symbol of a man, of the appropriate caste during the tali-tying ceremony just prior to menarche. Although the woman's future offspring may observe pollution taboos at the death of this ritual husband, they owe him no political allegiance whatsoever during his lifetime. Instead, as in other matrilineal groups, the woman's children are considered members of her matrilineage. Once she has completed the tali-tying rite, she may conceive legitimate offspring through temporary but socially approved liaisons with vari-

---

Anchor Book, 1954; originally published in 1948), pp. 230–37; and Beatrice Blackwood, *Both Sides of Buka Passage* (Oxford: Clarendon Press, 1934), pp. 132–34. According to Malinowski's initial reports of the Trobriand islanders' conception beliefs, the biological father is denied any role in impregnation or fetal growth whatsoever, and the true genitor of a child is the spirit, *baloma*. The mechanics of sexual intercourse serve merely to open up the woman's genital tract so that the spirit may enter although this can also be done by digital manipulation by the woman herself. Therefore, among the Trobrianders the husband is neither the recognized genitor nor the pater to his wife's offspring. A similar theory is reported for the matrilineal Kurtatchi, who also minimize the significance of the woman's husband in conception by asserting not only that coitus is not necessarily a prerequisite to conception (for example, women can become pregnant by a banana) but also that the physical growth of the fetus is produced entirely from the mother's menstrual blood.

4. A brief summary of anthropological debate on this issue is presented in notes attached to Edmund Leach, "Virgin Birth," *Journal of the Royal Anthropological Institute of Great Britain and Ireland* 96 (1966): 46–47, note 1.

5. Blackwood, *Buka Passage*, pp. 134–35; and Leach, "Virgin Birth," pp. 47–48, note 5, quoting H. A. Powell, "An Analysis of Present-Day Social Structure in the Trobriands," Ph.D. dissertation, Oxford University, 1956.

6. Leach, "Virgin Birth," p. 41.

7. Kathleen Gough, "The Nayars and the Definition of Marriage," in *Marriage, Family, and Residence*, ed. Paul Bohannan and John Middleton (Garden City, N.Y.: Natural History Press, 1968), pp. 49–71.

ous *sambandham*, who are recognized as the genitors of her offspring. None of these men, however, has any rights to these offspring or any obligation to the mother other than to fulfill the custom of providing her with gifts during their association. At the time of childbirth, some man from the appropriate lineage and caste must assert biological paternity by paying the cost of delivery. Otherwise, the woman will be suspected of having been impregnated by a lower-caste male, and both she and the child will be expelled from the lineage or killed. The Nayar, then, retain the roles of genitor and pater but reduce competition for jural authority over a woman's offspring by eliminating the role of husband.

A distinction between the roles of genitor and pater sometimes is made in nonmatrilineal descent systems as well. In some patrilineal societies, the woman's patrilineal kinsmen retain jural authority over one or more of her offspring after marriage. According to Lucy Mair, some patrilineal African societies allow for "poor man's marriages," in which the husband relinquishes jural rights over his wife's offspring to her patrilineal group as compensation in the marriage bargain.[8] Other cases in which the child's genitor does not hold jural rights include leviratic unions, "ghost marriages," and "woman marriages." According to the custom of levirate, any children born to a woman after her legal husband dies are recognized as the decedent's legitimate offspring rather than as the offspring of their actual genitor. The genitor, who is usually the decedent's classificatory brother, acts as the widow's guardian and is obligated to produce offspring in the name of the dead brother. A similar though less common practice is the so-called ghost marriage observed among the Venda, Zulu, Nuer, and other African patrilineages.[9] Like levirate, ghost marriages serve the purpose of producing legitimate heirs for a deceased husband by

8. Among the Higi, a husband may have jural rights over the first two children born but may or may not have rights over subsequent offspring. These "excess children" may go with the mother if she leaves her husband, and if she stays in the marriage, the husband can count them as legitimate heirs only if he makes additional compensation to the woman's father. See Lucy P. Mair, "African Marriage and Social Change," in *Survey of African Marriage and Family Life,* ed. Arthur Phillips (London: Oxford University Press, 1953), p. 135. A. R. Radcliffe-Brown notes a similar practice occurring outside of Africa, specifically in Sumatra and parts of the Malay Archipelago, where a husband may or may not be recognized as the sociological father of his wife's offspring, depending on whether he compensated her father fully in a marriage bargain ("Introduction," in *African Systems of Kinship and Marriage,* ed. A. R. Radcliffe-Brown and Daryll Forde [London: Oxford University Press, 1950]), p. 51.

9. The practice of "ghost marriages" among some African societies has been discussed by Mair, "African Marriage," pp. 15, 55; E. E. Evans-Pritchard, *Kinship and Marriage Among the Nuer* (London: Oxford University Press, 1951), pp. 109–12; and Denise O'Brien, "Female Husbands in African Societies," paper presented at the 71st Annual Meeting of the American Anthropological Association, Toronto, Canada, Nov. 29–Dec. 3, 1972.

some other genitor. In this case, however, offspring are produced for a kinsman who died before he could marry and produce children himself, and the genitor need not be a particular kinsman. In yet another form of ghost marriage, a widow who is barren or for some other reason failed to produce offspring during her marriage can arrange to have another woman produce offspring for her deceased husband.[10]

While the practices of levirate and "ghost marriage" assign the role of pater to the woman's legal husband regardless of the children's biological origin, the custom of "woman marriage" allows a woman to be recognized as pater to another woman's offspring. Under certain circumstances one woman (the "husband") may contract a marriage with another woman (the "wife"). Since the female husband cannot be the genitor of the wife's children, she contracts not only a wife but also a male genitor to impregnate the wife; the resulting offspring are the legitimate heirs of the female husband. At least among African societies, a female husband usually acts as surrogate for a male kinsman. For example, if a man dies leaving only daughters, the eldest daughter may negotiate a marriage with another woman, whose future offspring will be recognized as the legitimate heirs of the female husband's deceased father.[11] Or a woman may inherit her dead brother's wives and property, if he has no male heirs, and thus become legitimate pater to the offspring of those wives. A widow without sons can arrange a marriage for a man she claims as her "son";[12] children produced by this marriage are considered the legitimate offspring of their biological father, but they are also regarded as the "sons-in-law" of the widowed "husband" and her deceased husband. Barren women, women whose children have all died, and married women with only female offspring have also been known to marry a wife in order to obtain legitimate heirs.[13]

The many recognized marriage forms in a single society, the patrilineal Dahomey, illustrate the wide range of individuals that may be recognized as pater to a woman's offspring.[14] In at least five of thirteen types of Dahomean marriages described by Laura Bohannan, jural authority over a woman's offspring is transferred to her husband and his lineage at the time of marriage. There are many instances, however, in which the husband or genitor is not the pater or in which

10. According to O'Brien in "Female Husbands," ghost marriage in response to childlessness has been observed among the Kikuyu, Nandi, Dinka, and Gusii.

11. Max Gluckman, "Kinship and Marriage Among the Lozi of Northern Rhodesia and the Zulu of Natal," in *African Systems*, p. 184.

12. O'Brien, "Female Husbands," pp. 3–4.

13. Ibid., pp. 6–7.

14. Laura Bohannan, "Dahomean Marriage: A Reevaluation," in *Marriage, Family, and Residence*, pp. 85–107.

his jural rights are ambiguous. For instance, when a Dahomean lineage is faced with a shortage of male heirs, it can increase its strength by contracting marriages called "child stay father house," in which a kinswoman brings a husband into the compound to father offspring who will be counted as members of her own patrilineage. Although her kinsmen are morally (but not legally) obligated to relinquish jural rights over some of her children to the husband, they, and not the biological father, transmit inheritance of wealth and position. Among the royal lineages of Dahomey, jural authority over a kinswoman's offspring is never transferred to her husband. Members of the royalty contract what are called "prince child" marriages, and all children of a princess are considered members of her patrilineage. The political purpose of this practice, as summarized by Dahomeans, is as follows: "If the child of a princess were to become a commoner, that child, as a commoner, would be eligible for high political office and yet possibly have connexions with other than the ruling branch of the royal lineage, which might make him disloyal."[15]

In a third form of marriage, called "cloth in woman," an office is recognized as the pater of a woman attached to that office. The holder of the office arranges her marriage to someone as a reward for his services or labor, but the husband can gain jural rights over her offspring only at the wish of the pater, who could decide to retain them. A fourth marriage form is the "woman marriage," which may occur if a woman is barren or is wealthy enough to found her own compound. In order to found a compound, a woman may marry many wives and choose men to act as genitors. The offspring, at least in the first generation, may intermarry since as offspring of mothers and fathers of different sibs they do not violate the incest taboo, and this increases compound solidarity for a time. A final marriage form is "friend custody"; although a form that Dahomeans disparage, it was becoming more common at the time of ethnographic observations. Like an elopement, the "friend custody" marriage lacks the formal approval of families and transfers no jural rights to the biological father.

Jural rights may also be transferred from one pater to another, as in the cases of widow inheritance, adoption, and fosterage. In widow inheritance, a man obtains jural authority over the children of his deceased brother (real or classificatory), including not only the children already produced by the brother and his widow but also any children that the still-living brother and the widow may produce in the future.[16] The practice of adoption differs from widow inheritance in that it transfers jural authority over children from one man to another dur-

15. Ibid., p. 96, note 22.
16. Kathleen Gough, "Variations in Preferential Marriage Forms," in *Matrilineal Kinship*, pp. 626–30.

ing the first man's lifetime. According to recent analyses of adoption practices in Oceania, adoption may shift the primary allegiance of a child to a new pater but need not completely sever the child's ties to the original pater.[17] At least in Oceania, adoption usually occurs among members of the same kin group so that it is possible for the child to maintain contact with his original kin. Elsewhere, however, adoption can occur between different lineages or even different societies so that adopted children are more likely to sever ties with their original kin completely. According to Mary Douglas' analysis for matrilineal groups generally and Ivan Brady's analysis for Oceania, adoption is one way that a man can increase the power of his kin group without relying on the fertility of his wife.[18] As David Schneider points out, it is especially useful in matrilineal societies, since husbands or wives cannot easily use marriage to found a new segment.[19] A third practice in which jural authority is transferred or shared is fosterage. Unlike adoption, fosterage is a temporary transfer; it commonly occurs when a parent dies leaving no one to take care of young children. The practices of "rearing the bride" during betrothal and of sending prepubertal males to live with other families can also be considered forms of fosterage.[20]

CONFLICT AND COMPETITION OVER SOCIAL PATERNITY

No matter how jural rights to offspring are distributed within a society, tensions over paternity persist. In a society without a centralized judicial system, paternity can never be incontestably claimed. Many societies have developed elaborate systems of descent reckoning that describe the ideal relationships between individuals, including the individual or groups who in theory have jural rights over offspring. Descent ideology alone, however, is not sufficient to resolve personal disputes about paternity claims; nor does it prevent the negotiation of paternity arrangements that are not in accord with the ideal system. Paternity arrangements, after all, are influenced as much by political and economic conditions within a society as by its

17. Ivan Brady, "Adoption and Fosterage in Oceania: Problems of Description and Explanation," paper presented at the 71st Annual Meeting of the American Anthropological Association, Toronto, Canada, Nov. 29–Dec. 3, 1972.

18. Mary Douglas, "Is Matriliny Doomed in Africa?" in *Man in Africa*, ed. Mary Douglas and Phyllis M. Kaberry (Garden City, N.Y.: Doubleday, 1971), p. 127; and Brady, "Adoption and Fosterage."

19. Schneider, "Introduction," p. 26.

20. A good analysis of the practice of fosterage in a single society is Esther Goody's "Kinship Fostering in Gonja," in *Socialization: The Approach from Social Anthropology*, ed. Philip Mayer (London: Tavistock Publications, 1970), pp. 51–74.

descent ideology. In practice, the distribution of rights to a particular woman's children depends to a large extent on personal agreements between the parties to her marriage bargain, on their relative power and wealth, and on structural arrangements that give some individuals greater opportunity than others to influence the allegiance of children. Among bilateral societies such as the Twana, in which the kinsmen of a mother and those of her husband in theory are equally entitled to the allegiance of offspring born during the marriage, the actual authority exercised by various individuals depends on which kin group has more wealth and prestige and on the place of residence of the married couple and their children. Kinsmen with more wealth and prestige can use promises of inheritance (including titles as well as wealth) to manipulate ties of allegiance, and the location of the couple near either family can give that group of relatives greater potential control of the offspring's allegiance because it allows for the daily reinforcement of their kinship ties at the expense of ties to relatives residing elsewhere.

In societies with unilineal descent systems too, lineage relationships can be more or less well defined, the lineages of each spouse can differ in size, power, and prestige, and political and economic changes can rearrange allegiance patterns of offspring as they mature. A weak political faction can be strengthened, for example, if a father refuses to relinquish jural rights to his daughter's children or if he adopts the offspring of other families. Traditional norms about who belongs to whom can then be ignored or reinterpreted to suit particular individuals' interests. The fact that social ideology can describe ideal arrangements of jural rights to offspring yet cannot enforce them means that those rights must be defended and can often be challenged successfully.

Marriage bargains, like descent rules, can specify but not enforce paternity rights. Negotiations are only temporarily settled at marriage; both sets of kindred can continue to use any opportunity to renegotiate the bargain to their own advantage, and a shift in the balance of power between families can enable one family to default on the terms to which they agreed. A pater must always defend his jural rights against encroachment by those individuals who share them: his own kin or, in some societies, his wife's kin as well. From the point of view of these kin groups, the pater must be prevented from asserting complete authority over his child and denying them their rightful share of authority. In societies in which marriage arrangements give the roles of pater and genitor to different individuals, the genitor, although denied customary authority over his biological child, can always attempt to win the child's loyalty; this creates tension between genitor and pater. Even in societies in which the husband is customarily recognized as both genitor and pater of his wife's children, his biological paternity can be contested by adulterers because it can never be proved.

Conflict over Social Paternity at Divorce, Death of a Spouse, or Adultery

Conflict over paternity is particularly apparent during divorce proceedings, at the death of a spouse, and in cases of suspected adultery. In divorce proceedings, a husband may have to relinquish his paternity rights or, if unwilling to yield them, to forfeit any marriage compensation previously transferred to the wife's family. If the wife's family can establish that her husband has broken terms of the marriage bargain or otherwise failed to fulfill his marital obligations, the wife's kin group may challenge the husband's rights to offspring and adopt the children into their own kin group or refuse to return any gifts or property originally transferred to them by the husband in return for paternity rights.[21] In patrilineal societies, a divorced husband more commonly retains paternity rights if he has fulfilled the original marriage bargain so that the children remain in his or his kinsmen's custody. Sometimes, however, children are divided between the husband and wife, with males going to the father and females to the mother.

When jural rights over children are shared by the kin groups of the spouses, as in bilateral societies, the problem of how to redistribute rights to children after a divorce can lead to active hostility, especially if the divorce has been initiated by the wife.[22] Among the Twana, for example, feuds can develop between the spouses' families if the wife takes the children back to her natal family and persuades her family to keep them. A common form of aggression in such cases is sorcery used by the husband's kin against the wife and her kin although more literal forms occur as well. Conflict also occurs if the wife is widowed and does not wish to remain in the husband's community or marry a member of his kin group.[23] A widow who does not want a leviratic union may attempt to take the children back to her own village with her.[24] The two kin groups may work out a compromise whereby the wife takes one or more children to live with her

---

21. For example, among the Shilluk a husband may have to relinquish his claims to his offspring entirely if he has not paid the full amount of the marriage payments at the time of divorce. See Charles G. Seligman and Brenda Z. Seligman, *Pagan Tribes of the Nilotic Sudan* (London: Routledge & Kegan Paul, 1932), p. 68.

22. W. W. Elmendorf, *The Structure of Twana Culture* (Pullman: Washington State University Press, 1960), pp. 359–60.

23. Ibid., pp. 350–52.

24. Ibid., p. 351.

and her kin group and leaves the rest in the custody of the deceased husband's kin group, but such compromises tend to be disagreeable to the husband's kinsmen, who believe that the paternal relationship, reinforced by patrilocal residence, outweighs the legitimate claims of the wife's kin group. By kinship reckoning, the wife's kin group has equal ties to the child, but its claims are difficult to enforce in a group with a patrilocal residence pattern. Equally disagreeable to the deceased husband's kinsmen is the remarriage of his widow to a man from a different kin group, especially one with which they are feuding. In such a situation, the allegiance of the children could shift to the new husband and his family, which of course would undermine the authority of the decedent's group.[25]

Conflict over the rights of families to retain control over a man's offspring after his death occurs in many other societies that practice levirate or widow inheritance. In some of them, losing the allegiance of a decedent's children is considered so undesirable that if a widow succeeds in marrying someone outside the decedent's kin group, her new husband may be murdered.[26] More commonly, when a widow has children or is still capable of producing them, either she is forced to marry one of her husband's kinsmen and grant legal guardianship to him or her family is forced to relinquish entirely whatever rights they hold to the children. Widows can also be prohibited from remarrying or from having sex relations; this occurs especially in strong patrilineal societies in which the marriage bargain states specifically that the husband and his kin group hold primary jural authority over any children the woman produces even after the death of the husband.[27]

In societies where the customs of levirate or widow inheritance are not ordinarily practiced, widows may be pressured to remain in the husband's household. Among the Tanala, for example, if a widow marries a man from a kin group different from that of her original

---

25. Elmendorf notes that when the Twana were put on reservations, conflict over jural rights to divorced or widowed women became even more aggravated since the Americans recognized a woman's right to inherit her original husband's property and her right to marry whomever she chose. If a woman remarried, her new husband could claim the paternity rights to her children which would have formerly stayed with the original husband's group (ibid.).

26. Leslie Spier, *Klamath Ethnography* (Berkeley: University of California Press, 1930), pp. 49–50.

27. According to Laura Bohannan and Paul Bohannan, *The Tiv of Central Nigeria* (London: International African Institute, 1953), p. 78, among the Tiv a widow forfeits her children if she refuses to marry a member of her deceased husband's family, and only if her new husband from outside the family pays a brideprice to the decedant's family are such rights relinquished. Similarly, among the Riffians, although a childless widow may return to her family, one with dependent children is expected to marry a close kinsman of her deceased husband or else relinquish her children; see Carleton Coon, "Tribes of the Rif," *Harvard African Studies* 9 (1931): 120.

husband, he is usually compelled to come and live in the deceased husband's village instead of taking the woman to his own community. Tanala informants claim that this practice serves to safeguard the children from the abuse of stepfathers.[28] Among matrilineal societies in which the husband has no jural rights over his biological children, strong pressure may be exerted on a widow to marry a kinsman of her deceased husband, and she may be asked to defer a second marriage until a willing kinsman can be found. Such pressure illustrates the informal powers that a genitor and his family may acquire in these societies even in the absence of jural rights.[29]

No group in our sample condoned adultery, and in many societies husbands are politically strong enough to assert jural authority over offspring regardless of their biological origins. Nevertheless, adultery always allows for ambiguity about paternity, and claims to a woman's offspring can be made by any male who can convince others that he has had sexual access to her. The claimants may be adulterers or, in some societies, may be friends, guests, or kinsmen of the husband who were permitted sexual relations with the wife out of friendship or custom. As we mentioned earlier, avenging illicit claims to a wife's fertility is a major cause of war in preindustrial societies.[30] While illicit access to a wife's fertility can lead to death or mutilation of the adulterer, it can also lead to the dissolution of the original marriage, the rearrangement of jural rights to a woman's children, and the transfer of rights to any future children she produces. Although husbands usually have the right to avenge suspected adultery, they do not always succeed. By swaying public opinion in his favor, for instance, a wife's lover may be able to establish jural rights to the offspring he has fathered. Daryll Forde describes the case in an African society in which a woman had left her husband and produced a son by another man. After a year she returned to her husband, who

28. Ralph Linton, *The Tanala: A Hill Tribe of Madagascar* (Chicago: Field Museum of Natural History, 1933), p. 133.

29. Although a biological father in a matrilineal society has no jural rights over his biological children, through the practice of patrilateral cross-cousin marriage he succeeds in gaining jural rights to his son's biological children by marrying the son to his sister's daughter who is also his sociological daughter. According to the traditions of matrilineal descent, his sister's daughter's children will be considered his matrilineal kin. Although the practice of patrilateral cross-cousin marriage is rare in world societies and although survey analysis by George Homans and David Schneider (*Marriage, Authority, and Final Causes* [Glencoe, Illinois: Free Press, 1955], pp. 31, 34) showed that the practice is significantly more likely to occur among matrilineal societies than among patrilineal ones, some patrilineal societies practice matrilateral cross-cousin marriage, which gives jural rights to offspring of a kinswoman's daughter back to the mother's patrilineage, who lost rights to the first generation.

30. H. U. E. Thoden van Velzen and W. van Wetering, "Residence, Power Groups, and Intrasocietal Aggression," *International Archives of Ethnography* 49 (1960): 169–200.

wanted her back rather than divorcing her or charging her with adultery. To ward off the possibility of violent conflict, however, a tribal council decided that the genitor rather than the husband should be the pater to the child so that twelve years later the grown son returned to the genitor and grew up as his son and member of his patrilineage.[31]

In some societies, husbands are so weak politically that they have little chance of defending claims to their wives' offspring, who may have been fathered by one or more lovers. Thomas Gregor reports that among the Mehinacu of South America, a wife typically has many lovers who have some rights over children they claim as theirs. In fact, all men claiming sexual access to a woman are considered joint fathers of her children; not only do these children call their mother's lovers "papa" but they are prevented from marrying each other by the incest taboo. None of these lovers, however, is publicly recognized as husband to the mother.[32]

Conflict over Social Paternity During Pregnancy and Childbirth

Childbirth is also an occasion for conflicts over legitimacy. Although paternity rights to offspring are theoretically established at marriage, the birth of a child gives them practical significance. Interested parties can seize the opportunity to advance claims of biological and social paternity, challenge the claims of others, or extend rights already allowed them by custom or formal agreement. Tensions over paternity are particularly evident in the customary practices surrounding pregnancy and childbirth: behavioral restrictions on the pregnant woman, surveillance of all parties to a marriage bargain, and couvade. We hypothesize that these practices are rituals used to assert and defend paternity rights in societies which are unable to protect these rights effectively through a strong centralized judiciary.

Strong fraternal interest group societies and societies in which fraternal interest groups are weak or absent should differ in the tactics used to assert and defend paternity rights during pregnancy and childbirth. In strong fraternal interest group societies, explicit marriage bargains, typically involving the transfer of wealth in exchange for rights in women, specify the distribution of paternity rights to the future children of the woman being married. Although such contracts are not legally enforceable since there is no centralized judicial system, agreement terms are backed up by the organized military power

31. Daryll Forde, "Double Descent Among the Yako," in *African Systems*, pp. 291, 293.
32. Thomas A. Gregor, "Publicity, Privacy, and Mehinacu Marriage," *Ethnology* 13 (October 1974): 337.

of the kin groups involved. Rituals during pregnancy and childbirth are therefore surveillance tactics to ensure that the terms of the bargain will be met. The husband's kin must ensure that the woman bears healthy offspring of unquestioned paternity to compensate them for the wealth they have surrendered in the marriage bargain. The woman's kin must avoid being held responsible for accidents of pregnancy or childbirth that might require them to return part or all of the wealth they received in the marriage bargain. While all parties to a bargain monitor each other, the pregnant woman herself is the primary focus of surveillance, which often takes the form of numerous restrictions on her conduct.

Asserting and defending paternity is just as important in societies in which fraternal interest groups are weak or absent, but the strategies used are different. In the absence of explicit paternity bargains and the military force of a large group of loyal kinsmen, a husband must mobilize political support for his paternity claims by dramatizing his plight and the legitimacy of his interests through couvade. The term "couvade" refers to a variety of practices observed by a husband during his wife's delivery and the postpartum period: food taboos, restriction of ordinary activities, and in some cases seclusion. Like menarcheal ceremonies, couvade can be described as a social mobilization ritual.

ASSERTING AND DEFENDING PATERNITY IN STRONG FRATERNAL INTEREST GROUP SOCIETIES

In societies with strong fraternal interest groups, the distribution of paternity rights is typically agreed upon before the birth of offspring through an explicit marriage bargain. In patrilineal societies, the husband usually exchanges wealth for sexual access to a woman and rights of biological and social paternity to her future offspring. The extent of his rights of social paternity depends to a large extent on his ability to pay brideprice; in "poor man's marriages" in African societies, a husband who cannot pay all the brideprice may be forced to give up custody of some of his children to the woman's family.

The payment of a brideprice is also observed among a few matrilineal societies. Since in these societies the husband is not recognized as pater, some researchers have interpreted the brideprice as payment only for the woman's sexual and domestic services or as a device that commits the husband to a stable marriage. Certainly, rights of biological paternity are valuable as a base for expanding claims to a share of social paternity rights. But we suggest that other factors enter into the question of matrilineal brideprice as well. Formal brideprice payments were made in 41.7 percent of the matrilineal societies in our sample. In six (60 percent) of these, the husband could remove his wife from her family's residential community after marriage and live either virilocally or avunculocally. That is, matrilineal societies practicing brideprice were three times more likely to have nonmatrilocal than matrilocal residence. In societies with nonmatrilocal residence, the husband has an advantage over his wife's kin in making claims on offspring simply because he is in daily contact with them and his wife's kin are not. His claims may thus outweigh the theoretical claims of the matrilineage on his children's economic and political allegiance. Through brideprice, the husband pays for this advantage. As in many patrilineal societies, he may have the choice of giving up custody of his children in exchange for the option of not paying part or all of the brideprice. The matrilineal Suku, for example, practice virilocal residence. A woman's sons typically reside with their father until his death although occasionally, if his father mistreats him, a son will move to the residence of his matrilineage.[33] In a marriage, the only rights transferred to the husband are rights to the woman's domestic services, exclusive sexual rights, and the "trusteeship" of her offspring that virilocal residence implies; jural rights to offspring, at least in theory, are retained by the matrilineage. The husband has the option of paying no brideprice and giving up custody of his children to the matrilineage.

The amount of wealth considered equal to rights over a woman's reproductive capacity varies greatly among societies and also within societies depending on the wealth and interests of the families involved. In general, however, the amount is high: Walter Goldschmidt's analysis of brideprice in twenty-seven East African societies shows as many as twenty-seven livestock being transferred for a wife.[34] With such high stakes involved in marriage, it is not surprising to find that some societies have developed highly sophisticated and subtle negotiation procedures. Sometimes men acting as representatives, or lawyers, of each party's interests do a great deal of the actual bargaining, and the terms of the transfer may call for a series of "installments" over a considerable span of time. The actions of all parties to a marriage bargain among the Taita of Africa have been described in detail by Grace Harris and will be summarized here in order to illustrate the dynamics of high stakes marriage bargains.[35]

33. Igor Kopytoff, "Family and Lineage Among the Suku," in *The Family Estate in Africa*, ed. Robert Gray and P. H. Gulliver (Boston: Boston University Press, 1964), p. 104.

34. Walter Goldschmidt, "The Economics of Brideprice Among the Sebei and in East Africa," *Ethnology* 13 (1974): 325.

35. Grace Harris, "Taita Bridewealth and Affinal Relationships," in *Marriage in Tribal Societies*, pp. 61–67.

Taita Marriage Bargains

In Taita, negotiations concerning the transfer of rights to women's fertility and the brideprice objects can take years. In some cases they are never entirely completed. For about two years before the husband takes the wife to his own household, certain rights are gradually transferred to him in return for certain livestock, foods, and services. For example, payment of the livestock portion of the brideprice explicitly allows the man rights to the wife's reproductive capacity; once that portion has been paid, her future offspring are recognized as his heirs and members of his lineage, his property will pass to her sons, and any brideprice obtained through her daughters' marriages belongs to him. Each animal presented during this and subsequent stages has special significance and involves different members of the kin group most intimately interested in the marriage.

The most important single animal transferred is an unborn heifer calf called *kifu*, or "womb." For this particular transaction to be considered complete, the calf must reach maturity and itself bear a calf. If it dies before giving birth, another heifer must be substituted. Between the time the heifer calf is born and the time it bears its own calf, the husband has certain rights and is a kind of "pater-elect." He is allowed sexual access to the woman during this period although she still lives with her father. If she becomes pregnant, it is not considered shameful, but the man must relinquish another animal "for having made her a woman before her time."[36]

Permission for the man to remove the woman from her father's household to his own may be given whenever her parents wish, but the actual move is contingent on other livestock payments. One bull, called *mlisha*, "the herder," as well as smaller stock must be paid to the woman's father. In some cases (if he has contributed a goat to the woman's initiation ceremonies, for instance), the woman's mother's brother also receives a bull, called *kivavuye*, "thing of the mother's brother." Anyone else who helped rear the woman must get an animal called *vulela*, "nurture." Other animals are slaughtered, and the meat is distributed to kinsmen. One bull, called *horo*, is slaughtered and divided between the two fathers, who in turn divide the meat among their close kinsmen. Sometimes this slaughter does not occur until the woman has borne a child, purportedly so that the child may also share the meat. Another goat or bull is given to the wife's family to be distributed only to their kinsmen. At the termination of the woman's reproductive cycle, a final bull is transferred to signify the completion of the contract. Besides livestock payments, there are many foods, objects, and even labor services that the husband and his

36. Ibid., p. 61.

kinsmen must provide as part of the brideprice, most of them before the woman moves to her husband's homestead. In addition, the husband is continually dunned for gifts and service throughout the marriage. The demands seem to vary with the in-laws, however. In some cases, the woman's father may actually attempt to forestall or evade payments by the husband, not only to keep his son-in-law substantially in his debt but also as an excuse for not paying his own debts. This tactic provides the father with what Harris terms an "insured savings account."[37] Not only can he insist to his creditors that he cannot pay them because of his son-in-law's failure to pay; he can also be fairly sure he will be able to call in the necessary valuables when the time comes to strike a suitable marriage bargain for his own sons. If payment is not forthcoming when the father requests it, he may demand that his daughter return to his home, give the brideprice already collected back to the husband, and perhaps even begin negotiating another marriage bargain for her with a wealthier or more cooperative suitor. If the marriage is terminated before any children are born, a father must return all the property received. If it is terminated after children are born, the husband retains rights to them but does not get back what he has paid to the father by the time of the termination and is still required to pay any livestock debts outstanding. Alternatively, the husband can relinquish paternity rights to offspring, which would then be transferred to his wife's father or brother, and in return get back the brideprice payments.[38]

Compensation for Default

In strong fraternal interest group societies, parties to a bargain can use their political power to enforce the bargain's terms. Their enforcement power makes it possible for them to demand compensation

37. Ibid., p. 66.
38. That paternity rights are the major focus of most brideprice bargains is also illustrated by the Bohannans' description of the marriage arrangements among the Tiv used to substitute for woman exchange. *Kem* marriage, as it is called, is a transfer of a woman's fertility through cumulative brideprice payments as each offspring is produced. The total amount (as of the 1949 value of the pound) relinquished by a husband for a woman who has never before been married is estimated at about twenty-five pounds. Payment schedules depend largely on the number of children actually produced during the marriage although once it seems that the woman will stay with the husband, her guardian may first demand about six to ten pounds and then may continue dunning the husband whenever he is in financial need. To meet the payments, the husband may turn to someone else for assistance, usually the husband of the woman for whom *he* stands as guardian. Each child born is valued at about two to four pounds; among some lineages girls are worth a pound more than boys. If the number of children born exceeds the number paid for by the brideprice initially agreed upon, the husband must pay more. By this system, the Tiv attempt to simulate as closely as possible the kind of bargain they would have had in the ideal exchange marriage that is still preferred; see Bohannan and Bohannan, *The Tiv,* p. 72.

if the other side defaults. In a marriage bargain, a husband is essentially investing in a woman's potential offspring. If she fails to produce healthy offspring of unambiguous paternity, the husband and his kin may view her failure as a default on the original marriage bargain requiring return of part or all of the brideprice. Therefore, any irregularity during pregnancy or delivery—death of the infant or mother, rumors of adultery, prematurity, prolonged labor, breach birth, infant illness, infant deformity—can cause renewed haggling over the fairness of the bargain's terms. In the end, the husband may get back part or all of the brideprice, or he may get none of it. He may even be forced to pay additional compensation to the woman's kin. Who pays and the amount paid for an accident of birth depend on where the blame is eventually assigned. The assignment of blame is seldom a simple matter. A woman's miscarriage, for example, may be considered her own fault for having committed adultery or attempted abortion, her husband's fault for having overworked or injured her during her pregnancy, her lover's fault for having committed adultery with her, her kin group's fault for having given in marriage a woman who is congenitally unable to reproduce, or the fault of any of these people for having practiced witchcraft, broken taboos, or neglected to observe pregnancy and birth rituals properly. Parties to the bargain may make these and many other accusations and counteraccusations.[39]

The fine distinctions determining the distribution of blame for accidents of birth in strong fraternal interest group societies illustrate the high financial stakes involved and the enforcement power for obtaining compensation. Among the Nuer, for example, if a wife dies during her first pregnancy or delivery, the husband is blamed and is given no compensation. But if she dies after the expulsion of the afterbirth, her family is held responsible and required to return the brideprice cattle.[40] The Nkundó Mongo have an explicit set of procedures to determine who is responsible if a woman dies during pregnancy.[41] They perform an autopsy to ascertain the cause of the woman's death and also a Caesarian section to remove the fetus. The

39. Among the Goajiro, for example, the wife's family demands compensation from the husband if the wife complains of any suffering or discomfort during delivery though if the wife dies in childbirth, it is the husband who can demand compensation from the wife's family (Gustaf Bolinder, *Indians on Horseback* [London: Dennis Dobson, 1957], p. 97; and Johannes Wilbert, *Survivors of Eldorado* [New York: Frederick Praeger, 1972], p. 103). Similarly, among the Suku any accident of birth or the death of the infant causes the wife's family to accuse the husband of some form of misconduct, such as the breaking of taboos or laxity in performing the appropriate rituals (Kopytoff, "Family and Lineage," p. 103).

40. E. E. Evans-Pritchard, *The Nuer* (London: Oxford University Press, 1969), pp. 167–68.

41. Gustave-E. Hulstaert, *Le mariage des Nkundó* (Brussels: G. van Campenhout, 1928), pp. 444–61.

responsibility for the death is usually found to rest with the husband. When this happens, he can attempt to shift blame elsewhere by using the evidence of the autopsy, using magic, or convincing the community that his wife had a lover. When a lover is held responsible, he must pay a fine equivalent to the brideprice. Sometimes the deceased woman is accused of having caused her own death, thereby eliminating conflict between the interested parties. Observers at the autopsy may agree, for example, that her "stomach" is peculiar: too large or formed in an unusual way. The Nkundó Mongo believe that only animals have "peculiar" stomachs; in a human, they are a sign of evil. If the decedent is proved not to have caused her own death and no other individual can be held responsible, the fetus may be blamed, in which case it is likely to be killed. If the child dies after delivery, the death is blamed on the mother's bad milk, which in turn is blamed on the husband. Since the woman's kinsmen have nothing to lose by the death of the child, there is little dispute; the husband has merely "wronged himself" through his misdeed.

Maternal Restrictions and Ritual Surveillance

Irregularities of pregnancy and birth clearly have serious financial and political repercussions in strong fraternal interest group societies. It is in the interest of parties to a marriage bargain to monitor each other carefully throughout the birth process so that if there is some accident of birth, each party will have evidence to assign blame to the others. Individuals will also try to conduct themselves in a way that will place them above accusation and suspicion. Among the Tallensi, for example, a husband must be careful about the kinds of activities in which he engages during his wife's pregnancy so that he cannot be held responsible in any way for injury to her or the child.[42] He avoids any connection with death, such as attendance at a funeral, and he may reduce the amount of time he devotes to subsistence activities. He also consults diviners to help prevent miscarriage and offers special sacrifices to his ancestors as a way of putting his wife in their care. The husband's close kinsmen keep watch over the pregnant woman to ensure that she does not overexert herself physically or break any of the food taboos she is supposed to observe. The husband's father consults a diviner, and he and the wife's father may both appeal to their ancestors for assistance. Late in the pregnancy, the wife's mother sends one of her co-wives to give her daughter a special covering for her genitals. All these ritual gestures demonstrate

---

42. Meyer Fortes, *The Web of Kinship Among the Tallensi* (London: Oxford University Press, 1949), pp. 162–66.

the motivation of interested parties to ensure a successful birth and eliminate the possibility of accusation should the birth fail in any way.[43]

In many societies, women are watched carefully for any expression of pain or difficulty during pregnancy or delivery since such behavior is taken to indicate that the child does not belong to the husband. It is often considered a husband's right to demand an abortion if the biological paternity of the fetus is ambiguous. Among the Solomon Islanders, for example, a woman suspected of adultery may be forced either to name the adulterer or to abort the pregnancy at great risk to her own life. If the pregnancy is allowed to proceed and the birth proves difficult, this is taken as an almost certain sign of adultery, and immediate efforts are made to discover the name of the genitor through divination. Should someone confess, he must pay a fine and the birth is allowed to proceed normally.[44] Among the Azande, the husband will consult the *benget* to find out whether his pregnant wife is actually carrying his child. If the *benget* states that the pregnancy is the consequence of adultery, the husband has the right to force an abortion and then bring a divorce suit against his wife.[45]

While dietary and occupational restrictions of pregnant and parturient women are widespread across world societies, strong fraternal interest group societies in particular are likely to manifest the most socially restrictive customs, such as secluding the woman or requiring her to avoid numerous social contacts and activities. For example, in many societies the pregnant woman is considered unclean, dangerous, and likely to contaminate anyone who approaches her— especially men and often even her own husband. Where she should live during pregnancy and at whose homestead she should deliver

43. Among the Tiv, members of the two kin groups participate in pregnancy rituals that involve periodic visits by husband and wife to the wife's kinsmen once conception is recognized. The husband buys goats and chickens to be sacrificed in a ritual called *idyugh* and a purging ritual. The wife's marriage guardian takes part in both of these rituals. Once the time of delivery approaches, the woman must be at her husband's homestead and bear the child there. Her mother is usually present, along with her mother's mother, her mother's co-wives, the husband's mother, and a midwife. Generally no man is present. If the woman shows any signs of pain, observers suspect adultery, which she must confess to before the delivery can proceed. A diviner may be brought in to discover information about the adultery by observing special symptoms. See Akiga, *Akiga's Story: The Tiv Tribe As Seen By One of Its Members* tr. and ed. Rupert East (London: Oxford University Press, 1939), pp. 296–301, and Bohannan and Bohannan, *The Tiv*, p. 63.

44. Hutton Webster, *Taboo: A Sociological Study* (Stanford, Calif.: Stanford University Press, 1942), pp. 139–40.

45. Ashanti husbands can also force an abortion if adultery is suspected. On the basis of his cross-cultural survey of abortion practices, Devereux concludes that ambiguity about the biological origins of a fetus is one of the most common causes for abortion throughout the world (George Devereux, *A Study of Abortion in Primitive Societies* [New York: Julian Press, 1955], pp. 16–17).

the child are topics of debate in many societies; sometimes, as among the Thonga, oracles or diviners must be consulted before a decision can be reached.[46] In some societies, a pregnant woman is sent back to her natal household during pregnancy and is returned to her husband for the delivery. A woman may be required to stay inside her dwelling or a special enclosure for part or all of her pregnancy, delivery, and postpartum. Attendance at the delivery is usually restricted to birthing assistants and specially designated members of the woman's or the husband's kin groups. An early account of the Araucanians, or Mapuche, for example, describes how women were not allowed to give birth within the village since doing so would cause disease. When the time for delivery approached, a woman had to leave the village area and deliver the infant near a stream or lake. On her return, she entered a specially built hut where she remained for about a week watched over by another woman.[47] Among the Ganda, a pregnant woman is also considered dangerous and is forbidden to touch any man or his possessions. She is usually segregated in a special house throughout her pregnancy, and she remains in seclusion for nine days after delivery while a series of purification rites is held. Not until the child is weaned is she allowed to see her husband.[48]

These rules of social avoidance and seclusion facilitate the surveillance and control of the mother and her kin, the husband and his kin, and potential competing claimants to paternity rights. Restricting and confining the mother limits the possibility that the birth will be disrupted through abortion, infanticide, or kidnapping. Sending a pregnant woman back to her natal household may be seen as her husband's way of shifting responsibility for any accident of birth to the woman's own kin. Segregation from men limits the possibility that men other than the husband, such as unsuccessful suitors or adulterers, can claim paternity. Confinement and isolation also mean that contact with the mother can be limited to the agents of the kin groups with a legitimate interest in the birth. When agents of both kin groups are present at delivery, they can monitor not only the mother but also each other. In all these ways, parties to a bargain can attempt to limit conflict over compensation and ensure that blame is not unjustly assigned.

46. Henri Junod, *The Life of a South African Tribe* (New Hyde Park, N.Y.: University Books, 1962), II, 319, 433ff.
47. R. E. Latcham, "Ethnology of the Araucanos," *Journal of the Royal Anthropological Institute of Great Britain and Ireland* 39 (1909): 259f.
48. George P. Murdock, *Our Primitive Contemporaries* (New York: Macmillan, 1934), pp. 536–37.

Nkundó Mongo Surveillance Tactics

One of the most detailed descriptions of the surveillance practices in a society whose marriage contracts transfer paternity rights to the husband through wealth exchange is that of Gustave Hulstaert on the Nkundó Mongo.[49] He describes not only the birth procedure in general but the potential for conflict between parties to the marriage bargain when manipulation is suspected or when either the woman or the infant dies. During the third trimester of pregnancy, interest begins to increase markedly, and an important ceremony called the *bakeka* occurs. To celebrate the beginning of this last phase of pregnancy, the pregnant woman's mother smears her with red paint, which traditionally cannot be removed for three or four weeks. After this ritual, the pregnant woman must stop eating bananas, chicken, and eggs since these foods would stop the fetus from growing.

Both sets of kinsmen are supposed to attend the *bakeka*, and the woman's father and her husband's kinsmen feel very strongly about being present. Hulstaert relates an incident in which the woman's mother began smearing her with red paint when the woman's husband and his kinsmen were not there. Furious, they told the woman's family that because of this, they refused to be held liable for anything that might happen to mother or child during the rest of the pregnancy or delivery. In other words, the husband now had an excuse to disclaim responsibility for paying compensation to his affines for any damage they might accuse him of causing, and he had paved the way for demanding compensation from them instead.

Throughout the final trimester, the Nkundó Mongo take great pains to avoid seduction of the pregnant woman by adulterers and to prevent contact between her and any past adulterers. The husband too must be circumspect in his behavior during this period in order to avoid accusations of rule infringement. According to Hulstaert, any behavior that is even remotely connected with procreation is avoided. Not only must both the woman and her husband avoid touching any part of a person with whom there has been a past adulterous association but they must not eat with them, sit next to them, look at them, or even enter a place where they are present. They cannot sit on someone else's bed or allow any other person to sit on their bed. Violation of these social restrictions is believed to lead to death of the pregnant woman or the infant.

It is the husband who is most vulnerable to charges of misconduct during the pregnancy and birth, and he is most often held responsible for accidents to the wife or child. Any lapse in behavior can immediately lead to conflict, and the rules of conduct are so numer-

49. Hulstaert, *Le mariage*, pp. 444–53.

ous that they can easily be broken inadvertently. To minimize this possibility, the husband sends his wife to live in her father's household until just before the delivery, and he gives his affines a pledge that he has done no misdeeds and does not want to injure his wife.

During delivery, the woman must be at the husband's residence. Although her mother and the husband's female kin are present, the husband stays as far away as possible, perhaps to avoid any blame in case the birth does not proceed normally. If mother or infant dies, the kin groups follow an explicit set of rules, described earlier, to determine how the blame should be assigned. If the delivery is successful, the good news is immediately sent throughout the community. Anyone who has witnessed the delivery or seen the newborn must observe certain taboos until the child's umbilical cord falls off, lest he or she be accused of causing a mishap. Both sets of kin perform additional rituals, such as bodily scarification and the taking of special concoctions at the request of the husband. With a male child, the father takes his place at the entrance to the delivery hut in front of the child, holding a spear over the child and shouting and behaving like a warrior. He takes the child's hand and folds it around the spear, saying, "Be a strong man, make war bravely."[50] The mother remains strictly secluded inside the hut for at least two or three weeks and must follow a set of rituals pertaining to her meals and the care of the hut. The end of seclusion is marked by a ceremony in which both the woman and her husband take part.

The Nkundó Mongo, then, use many rituals of surveillance that require the presence of kin group members involved in the marriage bargain and allow everyone involved to monitor each other's actions and intentions. There is a strong connection between surveillance rituals and charges of liability for irregularities of the birth process. Extreme restrictions on the pregnant woman are clearly related to protection against charges of adultery.

ASSERTING AND DEFENDING PATERNITY IN WEAK FRATERNAL INTEREST GROUP SOCIETIES

In societies in which fraternal interest groups are weak or absent, a man seeking to claim paternity rights to a woman's offspring cannot rely on a large and loyal group of kinsmen to back up his claim. Explicit contracts involving large transfers of valuable resources cannot be made because the resources are not available and contracts cannot be enforced. Paternity rights, therefore, cannot be explicitly agreed upon in marriage bargains prior to childbirth, and

50. Ibid., p. 452.

marriage typically takes the forms of groom service, reciprocal gift exchanges, a symbolic brideprice of little value, or implicit and informal arrangements involving no labor service or transfer of valuable goods. Ritual surveillance in these societies would be difficult to maintain and would in fact have little point. Children are just as important in these societies as in societies with strong fraternal interest groups, but without the power and wealth to engage in contractual agreements before birth or to demand compensation if no offspring are produced, an interested claimant must resort to less effective tactics to gain social recognition of paternity. Like a father sponsoring a menarcheal ceremony, he must use social mobilization rituals to create a temporary political faction and gauge the extent of community support for his claims.

Ritual Bargaining: Couvade

The best-known group of pregnancy and birth rituals is that of couvade: a husband's observance of food taboos, restriction of ordinary activities, and in some cases seclusion during his wife's delivery and postpartum period. Among the Ainu, for example, although the husband cannot be present at the delivery, he joins his wife afterwards in postpartum seclusion, where he observes a series of taboos and remains wrapped up near his hearth as if he were ill.[51] The Witoto of the northwestern Amazon in South America have a similar practice: the husband rests for a week or more in his hammock, observes food taboos, and receives the congratulations of his friends while the new mother is almost ignored. During this couvade, which is practiced until the child's navel is healed, he cannot eat meat or touch his weapons.[52]

The Kurtatchi, whose menarcheal ceremony was described in detail in Chapter 3, also practice couvade, and one such ritual was observed by Beatrice Blackwood, their major ethnographer.[53] The mother was assisted in giving birth by her husband's mother and other matrilineal kinsmen of the husband while the husband secluded himself in a hut close by. During the delivery and for six days thereafter, he remained in seclusion, abstaining from certain foods, ignoring his normal subsistence chores, and not handling sharp tools. For three days he was not allowed to see his newborn child. But on the infant's fourth day of life, he made a medicinal concoction, took it to the place where the mother and infant were secluded, and offered

51. Murdock, *Our Primitive Contemporaries*, pp. 178–79.
52. Ibid., p. 464.
53. Blackwood, *Buka Passage*, pp. 146, 150–51, 159–60.

it to the child to make him strong. The husband, Blackwood observed, was eager to end his couvade at this point, but the village women insisted that it was too soon. On the sixth and final day the ritual that released him from the couvade was performed. The husband entered his wife's seclusion hut once more, this time carrying a large knife, and proceeded to slash at the infant as if he were about to sever its limbs and head. Blackwood argues that the ritual is an acknowledgment of a husband's role in the birth.

Couvade can be interpreted as a form of ritual bargaining rather than as magical activities intended to control a biological process or as consequences of unconscious psychodynamics as other theorists have argued. The political circumstances that lead husbands to perform couvade are the same as those that lead fathers to engage in ritual bargaining at the time of their daughters' menarche. When a father cannot depend on strong fraternal allies to protect his daughter's fertility, he must attempt to develop a temporary political faction that will hold together at least long enough for him to negotiate a good marriage for his daughter. In societies in which fraternal interest groups are weak or absent, the ritual tactics used by a husband to gain social recognition as pater to a woman's offspring are similar to the tactics used by a father to protect his daughter's fertility prior to marriage. Although couvade rituals do not always include the giving of a feast, as menarcheal rites usually do, the political effects of the two ritual activities are the same. Avoiding foods, refraining from critical subsistence activities like hunting, gardening, and fishing, refusing to engage in warfare, and isolating oneself for days at a time all clearly disrupt the daily economic and political life of the community. When others encourage these behaviors, they demonstrate implicit or explicit support for and recognition of the man's paternity rights. The man can therefore turn to them when he needs support in disputing the paternity claims of adulterers. Furthermore, his persistence in continuing couvade against his own more immediate economic and political interests may help convince others that his paternity claims are indeed legitimate.

Ritual Rejection of Social Paternity

Failure to perform couvade when it is customary implies that a man does not want paternity rights to a woman's child. Although the political subtleties of couvade are not always adequately described by ethnographers, an incident that Allan Holmberg witnessed during his stay with the Siriono does illustrate this point.[54] Among the Siriono,

54. Allan R. Holmberg, *Nomads of the Long Bow* (Garden City, N.Y.: Natural History Press, 1969), pp. 177–84, 192–94.

as among many other societies, husbands are not always successful in preventing other men from seducing their wives, and paternity cannot be unambiguously determined. Among the Siriono, however, the husband has a priori claims as the legitimate father of a woman's children, which he must demonstrate through a ritual that includes cutting the umbilical cord, a three-day seclusion with mother and infant, and extensive food and work taboos. On the first day after the birth, the husband is scarified and then proceeds to scarify his wife. On the second day, both husband and wife are ornamented with feathers. On the third day, or whenever the navel string falls off the infant, couvade ends, and the termination is dramatized by the relatives' placement of necklaces on husband and wife. After this, the couple walks into the forest to gather firewood and spread ashes. Upon returning home, they resume their usual domestic routine and the ritual is ended.

In the case of one birth, Holmberg reports that the woman's husband refused to show any interest in the delivery and instead went into the forest to hunt. The birth occurred in the morning, and the relatives and the mother waited all day for the husband to return and cut the umbilical cord. After sunset he finally returned, but he left the umbilical cord uncut, increasing the chances of infection or death. When Holmberg himself felt he must intervene by suggesting that someone else cut the cord, the woman's relatives said it was imperative that no one but the husband perform this task. The husband completely ignored the mother and the newborn, instead going to his other wife and preoccupying himself by taking a thorn out of his foot with her help. This took approximately half an hour and clearly indicated to everyone that he intended never to cut the cord. One of the husband's relatives then announced that the husband did not want to claim the child and had in fact "divorced" the woman some time before. Eventually an implicit compromise was made between the husband and the woman's relatives. As Holmberg describes it,

> one of the mother's female relatives came forward and publicly demanded that he cut the cord. He paid no attention whatsoever to her but continued to lie in his hammock and smoke his pipe. The mother of the infant took no part in the proceedings but continued to sit on the ground with the child. Darkness set in. . . . Finally, after about an hour, he got up from his hammock . . . and took a hasty bath. He then stooped down . . . and severed the cord, thereby recognizing the child as his. Before doing so, however, he emphatically stated that the child was not his and that he was cutting the cord only to prevent the death of the child.[55]

55. Ibid., p. 194.

The husband's reluctance to accept paternity was further demonstrated by his refusal to observe the normal postpartum taboos, to be
scarified, or to remain in seclusion.

Couvade by Competing Claimants

If couvade is a ritual tactic to claim paternity, then claimants
competing with the husband should resort to ritual as well. Competition over paternity rights through multiple couvade rituals is rarely
described in the literature although two cases in our sample could be
so interpreted. Among the Gé-speaking people in South America,
Julian Steward and Louis Faron have noted, any men claiming to
have had sexual relations with the mother observe a series of food
and occupational restrictions like those observed by the woman's
husband.[56] A husband normally joins his wife in postpartum ritual
seclusion behind a partition in their dwelling for at least forty days
after the delivery or until the infant's navel string has dropped off.
They may not decorate themselves, cut their hair, or scratch themselves with their fingers. They must observe many food taboos and
are allowed to eat only a limited variety of vegetables and manioc
cakes. The husband does not engage in any work or exert himself
physically. After this period of seclusion, the husband goes on a hunting trip, and a birth ceremony is held for the kinsmen of both spouses
and the husband's age set. If the child's mother admits to having had
sexual relations with any other men besides her husband during the
pregnancy, she must name those men so that they can perform
couvade rituals as well.[57]

The Timbira believe that for the welfare of the infant, the mother
must name all possible genitors at the time of delivery, and no man

56. Julian Stewart and Louis C. Faron, *Native Peoples of South America* (New York:
McGraw-Hill, 1959), p. 370. One of the societies to which they may have been referring
is the Eastern Timbira, among whom Curt Nimuendajú describes couvade rituals as
performed not only by the husband but by any man recognized as having had sexual
access to the pregnant woman.

57. Nimuendajú observed one instance of this after a woman in the community
gave birth to her first child. She acknowledged that another man should perform the
couvade rituals by going into seclusion at the same time as her husband. After the
husband ended his seclusion, he was directed by the wife's maternal uncle to go hunting as the last part of his ritual. The husband brought the game back to his wife's
maternal kin, who cooked it and made it into three meat pies. These pies were then
distributed to certain members of the community, such as members of the husband's
age class. On the day of the meat pie distribution, the new mother went to the house of
her lover and invited him to take part in the distribution as well. The lover went to the
woman's matrilineal household and there received a slice of meat pie, which he took to
his mother. Thus the possibility that some man other than the woman's husband could
be recognized as pater to her newborn was ritually acknowledged (Curt Nimuendajú,
The Eastern Timbira, tr. and ed. Robert Lowie [Berkeley: University of California Press,
1946], pp. 78, 106–08).

who has been named would dare not perform couvade even if he were also married. Each of these "co-fathers" enters ritual seclusion at his mother's house instead of with the woman, who is in seclusion with her husband. One Timbira woman named four men in addition to her husband who could be the child's father. (The villagers considered this rather out of the ordinary.) The co-fathers, however, were proud of their paternity recognition. As Curt Nimuendajú describes it, "Several times when the parents of a person were under discussion, some Indian would thrust himself forward unbidden, declaring, 'I, too, am his father!' " In this society, co-paternity is also taken into consideration in the giving of names.[58] In the case of a birth Nimuendajú observed, both the husband and the woman's lover were assigned the role of sociological father to her child, and the woman's name was later given to her lover's granddaughter; according to Timbira practice, that granddaughter would inherit from the woman. Among the Timbira, daughters inherit from their mothers, sons from their fathers. The practice of encouraging men other than the legal husband to acknowledge social paternity can thus benefit the woman's matrilineal kin group, who can use these acknowledgments to extend their group beyond children produced by their daughters alone.

A second instance of ritual competition over claims to a woman's fertility, recorded for the Tiv, shows that intrasocietal variations in marriage bargains can lead to different ritual practices at childbirth. As described earlier, the Tiv usually engage in exchange marriages, in which paternity rights are transferred to the husband, and during childbirth, surveillance of the mother rather than couvade by the father is the rule. Some Tiv clans, however, practice what is called "companion" or "sister" marriage, which is more similar to a love affair than to marriage in that each party can practice the exchange, or *kem*, marriage later.[59] These liaisons most frequently occur when a woman has not yet been claimed in the exchange system and thus may "marry" a man in her own compound. This man does not gain paternity rights to the woman's children although the personal relationship between the so-called sibling husband and sibling wife is extremely close and can persist after they are legally married to other spouses, when the man is allowed to resume his relationship with the woman any time she is in her natal compound. Such a situation offers considerable potential for dispute over rights to the woman's fertility and offspring.

Such conflict, as Akiga describes it, is ritually demonstrated

58. Ibid., p. 78.
59. Bohannan and Bohannan, *The Tiv*, p. 75.

when the woman becomes pregnant during her exchange marriage to the second man.[60] In the Tiv clan called the Maser, "companion" marriages have even greater significance than in other clans. Taking a lover from within the compound is urged on women once they have reached puberty. If the woman is legally married through the customary system and becomes pregnant, she accompanies her new husband back to her natal compound for a special "purging" ceremony, and a ritual competition between her lover and her new husband takes place. It resembles in some ways the classic couvade rituals performed by competing males in other societies.

On the day of the purging ceremony, the woman's "local husband" prepares gifts for presentation to her before the ceremony in a calabash bowl that he has carefully carved. In the evening, a piece of black cloth that has been specially shined with a snail shell is tied around the waist of each competitor. The gathered kinsmen of each man and the pregnant woman decide which man is the winner, depending on who has the shiniest cloth. The kinsmen of each are also judged: their dancing ability determines which man has the superior relatives. During the main ceremonial event, the purging of the pregnant woman, the lover or local husband accompanies her instead of her new legal husband, who remains in the background. After the ceremony, her husband takes her back to his compound. Tiv paternity claims, then, in this case take the form of male ritual. The "local husband" had only implicit rights to the pregnant woman through his companionship marriage. He had no formal or legal claims to her offspring, which her kinsmen relinquished to the new husband.

CLAIMING PATERNITY THROUGH BOTH SURVEILLANCE AND COUVADE

In some societies, both couvade and maternal surveillance rituals are performed. In others, the husband is watched as carefully as his pregnant wife though he may have no part in the birth ceremonies. Societies in which both birth practices are observed typically have the characteristics that we are arguing predict couvade and also those that predict maternal surveillance rituals. That is, joint rituals are most common among societies in which wealth is exchanged at marriage through reciprocal gift exchanges and in which enforcement power is low as a consequence of unreliable fraternal interest group loyalty. These societies tend to be those with highly unstable political factions, in which the allegiance of individuals to kin-group objectives is difficult to reinforce. Although they may be wealthy enough to con-

---

60. Akiga, *Akiga's Story*, pp. 127–29.

tract for property exchanges at marriage, it is not certain that these bargains will be fulfilled since parties to them cannot count on the continuing loyalty of a strong military force.

A bargain negotiated at marriage need not, of course, be a bargain fulfilled at childbirth. These societies (typically shifting cultivators, salmon fishermen, buffalo hunters, and cultivators of tree fruits and pigs) all control wealth of considerably less value than that of pastoralists and hoe or plow agriculturalists, who usually make explicit paternity bargains in the form of brideprice and rarely practice couvade. Fraternal interest groups that are wealthy enough to engage in explicit bargains through gift exchange but too unstable politically to assure that paternity rights will be acknowledged at birth are interested in monitoring the birth process, but they are weak enough so that husbands must resort to ritual bargaining in an attempt to establish rights to the child in the eyes of the community.

Of the fifteen societies in our sample that practiced both couvade and maternal surveillance, eleven were among the most unstable politically. One such society is the Marquesans, who arrange marriages through a series of gift exchanges and do not engage in unilineal descent reckoning. In fact, the absence of clearly established claims to wives and children has been the subject of much discussion, especially their widespread practice of adoption and the possibility of polyandry. Whether Marquesan marriages are truly polyandrous or are better described as a system of "adoption" of poorer couples by richer ones is a matter of debate, but whichever way the debate is resolved, it seems clear that their marriage and adoption practices allow for much ambiguity about claims both to a wife's fertility and to her offspring. Since the practice of adoption assists men's political careers by adding members to their political factions through bargains with other fathers, during the birth process a woman's husband should have an interest in establishing whatever claims he has to the newborn, just as competing claimants have an interest in protecting whatever bargain over rights to the children was previously negotiated.

During pregnancy and birth, a Marquesan woman's behavior is carefully monitored, and her husband is also ritually involved; for example, he enters seclusion with his wife during her pregnancy.[61] The woman is considered *tabu* during her pregnancy and also extremely vulnerable to the influence of evil spirits and individuals in the community. People are not even supposed to walk along roads that may bring them into contact with a pregnant woman for fear of

---

61. E. S. C. Handy, *The Native Culture in the Marquesas* (Honolulu: Bernice P Bishop Museum Bulletin, 1923), pp. 71–74.

contaminating her and the fetus, and they are careful to perform a special ritual on entering a dwelling that she occupies. During the pregnancy, a special birth hut is built on a platform adjacent to the sleeping house; well before delivery, the woman moves into the hut, where she observes food and work taboos. If any accident should occur during this period, both the birth hut and the sleeping house must be burned.

The husband secludes himself in the birth hut with his wife and awaits the delivery. A Marquesan husband takes an active role in the delivery, sometimes holding the mother during the birth. Soon after the delivery, he has sex relations with her, although her blood is considered taboo, in order to stop the flow of blood from the womb. On the day of the birth, people gather to find out who will claim the child—whether it will be adopted or remain with its parents—and a feast is held in which kinsmen of both spouses play a prominant role. Pig meat is shared among the relatives, and the mother's brother and husband's sister cut their hair and give it to the newborn.[62]

Ritual strategies that prevent a woman's husband from establishing claims to her offspring have also been described, particularly among matrilineal societies, in which the legitimate claimants, the matrilineal kinsmen, not only closely monitor the activities of the pregnant woman but also appear to be monitoring those of the genitor-husband. In such cases, the behavior of the matrilineal kinsmen can be interpreted as "paternal surveillance." Among many matrilineal societies in our sample, especially those in which a husband makes some kind of wealth bargain at marriage in order to secure rights to a wife, the woman's matrilineal kinsmen play a prominent role in ceremonies to which a husband is not even invited. Instead, the husband may be sent away during the pregnancy or postpartum period or even guarded closely to ensure that he makes no ritual claims that might threaten the wife's kin's legitimate right to the child.[63]

62. Both couvade and maternal surveillance are observed among the Fur, the Eyak, and many other societies characterized by fairly valuable resources but highly unstable political factions. See A. C. Beaton, "The Fur," *Sudan Notes and Records* 29 (1948): 14–15; Robert Felkin, "Notes on the Fur Tribe of Central Africa," *Proceedings of the Royal Society of Edinburgh* 13 (1884–86): 226–27, 234, 260–61; and Kaj Birket-Smith and Frederica de Laguna, *The Eyak Indians of the Copper River Delta, Alaska* (Copenhagen: Levin & Munksgaard, 1938), pp. 159–60.

63. Practices among the Saramacca and Goajiro of South America could be interpreted as paternal surveillance by matrilineal claimants though they are most clearly observed among the more unstable political groups in Oceania, such as the Palauans and the Trobrianders. Saramacca birth practices which seem to minimize the husband's participation are best described by Melville Herskovits and Frances Herskovits in *Rebel Destiny* (New York: McGraw-Hill, 1934), pp. 220, 223. Goajiro practices are well described in Virginia Gutiérrez de Pineda's "Organización social en la Guajira," *Revista del Instituto Etnológico Nacional* 3 (1950): 5–9, 129–30.

Among the politically unstable Palauans, as H. G. Barnett reported in 1949, a pregnant woman was secluded for the entire duration of her pregnancy in the household of her maternal uncle.[64] During a first pregnancy, the husband was obliged to live in the uncle's house throughout the period as well. Both remained secluded from public view, leaving the house only at night. If the uncle was wealthy, a servant was assigned to watch over the couple and care for their needs. At the sixth month of pregnancy, a critical ritual called "breaking open the stomach or womb" was performed by the husband's sister. During this ritual, which determined the outcome of the pregnancy, the child was paid for by a financial backer of the husband, usually his own father. Among the Palauans, the rights being bought from the mother's brother were not jural rights but rights to the services of offspring. Although sons typically returned to the land of the matriclan when they reached maturity, there were many exceptions to this pattern, and a biological father could encourage sons to remain with him and even to inherit his wealth and titles by tying the son into his domestic economy. In practice, Palauan sons could become allegiant to various men in adulthood in addition to the men of their matrilineage and the biological father. Therefore, on receipt of payment or the child, the maternal uncle was quick to reciprocate with plentiful gifts of food.

After the delivery, the husband was released from his confinement in his wife's uncle's dwelling, but the wife remained there for about nine more months, during which time no contact with her husband was allowed. During subsequent pregnancies, the husband did not usually move in with the maternal uncle although the wife still lived there both before and after the birth. Among the Palauans, then, the behavior of the husband as well as that of the pregnant woman were monitored carefully by the maternal uncle with whom both lived during the entire pregnancy.

The Trobriand Islanders' pregnancy practices also illustrate the potential for conflict between matrilineal claimants and the genitor-husband.[65] During each pregnancy, a woman leaves her husband during the seventh or eighth month and goes to live with her biological father. For the delivery, however, she enters a birth hut at her maternal uncle's home, and a watch is kept outside the hut by her maternal kinsmen (armed with spears) and her husband. As Malinowski described it, "It is the duty of the husband to carry out the watch, but in this he is never trusted alone, and the male relatives

64. H. G. Barnett, *Palauan Society* (Eugene: University of Oregon Publications, 1949), pp. 100–11.

65. Bronislaw Malinowski, *The Sexual Life of Savages* (New York: Harcourt, Brace and World, 1929), Chap. 8, especially pp. 228–29.

of the pregnant woman not only assist *but also control him*."[66] During her postpartum seclusion too, the woman is carefully protected, and no men are allowed to come into contact with her, not even her husband. She and her husband can "only speak together through the door and glance at each other now and then. On no account must they eat together or even partake of the same food. Sexual intercourse is strictly taboo for a much longer time, at least until the child can walk. . . . A breach of any of these rules would bring about the death of the child."[67]

Thus, although a husband can attempt to dramatize his claims to offspring by observing taboos and joining his wife in ritual seclusion, other interested claimants can continue to monitor the birth process in spite of him and even attempt to prevent him from engaging in ritual bargaining. Since such ritual tactics cannot be easily prevented, they can seriously jeopardize any paternity agreement established earlier.

Establishing legitimate rights to a woman's children produces a social dilemma in all societies. This dilemma is an inevitable consequence of the fact that sociological paternity is determined by ideology, social opinion, and individual contracts and not by the father's biological contribution to the formation of the fetus. Regardless of how paternity is theoretically established, at the time of a child's birth, it is critical that such rights be unambiguously established and recognized by all interested parties. Claimants who have the backing of strong fraternal interest groups can engage in explicit contractual agreements concerning paternity rights, and they also have the political power to prevent or penalize default. If a paternity bargain calls for compensation in the absence of offspring, the focus of interest throughout the birth process is ritual surveillance of the mother and all parties to the bargain to ensure that nothing happens to upset the agreement. Often, ritual surveillance is facilitated by rules stipulating where the woman may live, whom she may see during pregnancy, and the participation of kinsmen of both spouses in ceremonies that dramatize to all participants the distribution of paternity rights specified in the bargain.

In the absence of a strong fraternal interest group, paternity rights must be established by implicit bargaining tactics at the time of childbirth. Under such conditions, interested claimants resort to couvade in an effort to develop public support for their paternity claims. Couvade, then, is a ritual strategy that serves a purpose similar to that of menarcheal ceremonies. In both cases, the public

66. Ibid., p. 229; emphasis ours.
67. Ibid., p. 233.

αemonstration is a risky but potentially successful mechanism for developing temporary public support. Competing claimants are too weak to prevent ritual paternity claims although they may attempt to assert their own claims by monitoring both the birth and the behavior of the husband. Couvade and maternal surveillance practices, then, are interpreted as alternate mechanisms by which paternity rights are asserted and defended in tribal societies.

BIRTH PRACTICES AND FRATERNAL INTEREST GROUP STRENGTH: AN EMPIRICAL ANALYSIS

Measures of Birth Practices

The customary birth practices of mothers and their husbands were coded from primary ethnographic sources on each society according to the same procedure used to code all original variables in this study, described in Chapter 2. Only observable changes in behavior during the birth process, not beliefs and myths about childbearing practices, were used as indicators of actual practices.

The rituals and taboos of both men and women could be ordered into Guttman-type scales. The ordering of each set of practices and their cumulative frequencies are presented in Table 10. The Maternal Restrictions Scale measures the degree of constraint on women's behavior during pregnancy and childbirth. Customary restrictions are arranged along a five-point scale that has a coefficient of reproducibility of .93.[68] As Table 10 indicates, all societies restrict women's behavior to some extent during pregnancy or after delivery, the most common restrictions being the avoidance of ugly objects that purportedly could damage the unborn infant physically or psychologically; the wearing of certain kinds of clothing, including special charms to protect the mother and the child; and limitations on daily activities such as working. If only these common customs were present in the society, the society received a score of 1. In nearly all of the societies in our sample, women were forbidden to eat certain foods either during pregnancy, postpartum, or both. Even though, as Barbara Ayres has pointed out,[69] the number of foods tabooed varies considerably cross-culturally, we counted a society as having food re-

68. See B. White and E. Saltz, "The Measurement of Reproduceability," in *Problems in Human Assessment*, ed. Douglas Jackson and S. Messick (New York: McGraw-Hill, 1967), pp. 241–57, for computational research.

69. Barbara Ayres, "Pregnancy Magic: A Study of Food Taboos and Sex Avoidances," in *Cross-Cultural Approaches: Readings in Comparative Research*, ed. Clellan Ford (New Haven: HRAF Press, 1967).

TABLE 10. **Measures of Birth Practices**

	Custom Category	Score	Cumulative Frequency (percentages)	Custom Category Description
	Maternal Restrictions Scale[a]			
Social (high)	Structural Seclusion	5	24.3	Confined to dwelling during pregnancy at least 2 weeks before delivery; secluded in special hut.
	Social Avoidance	4	48.6	Contact with people, especially men, restricted during pregnancy. Pregnant women avoided and believed to be unclean and dangerous, evil.
Personal (low)	Sex Taboo	3	63.1	Sexual relations with husband restricted for at least 2 months before delivery.
	Food Taboo	2	82.9	Eating certain foods during either pregnancy or postpartum is restricted.
	Minor	1	100.0	Restrictions on looking at ugly objects, wearing certain clothing, working too hard, etc.
	Husband Involvement Scale[b]			
Couvade (high)	Seclusion	5	16.2	Secluded in dwelling during pregnancy or postpartum with or without mother and child. May also be considered unclean. Avoids others.
	Postpartum Work Taboo	4	29.7	Refrains from performing normal tasks during postpartum period. Must remain close to home; contact with others minimized.
	Food Taboo	3	44.1	Refrains from eating certain foods during pregnancy or postpartum.
Minor (low)	Minor Observances	2	64.0	Minor ritual observances such as seeking a vision, performing birth-related sacrifices. May help wife with daily chores.
	No Observances	1	100.0	Residual category: no changes in normal behavior. No ritual observances.

[a]Coef. of reproducibility = .93 (missing case: Amahuaca).
[b]Coef. of reproducibility = .96 (missing case: Rhade).

strictions if at least one food was taboo. Consideration of the number of foods tabooed did not add to the sensitivity of the scale, and the reliability of ethnographic reports on the exact number of foods restricted was questionable: some included detailed lists of restricted foods as reported by informants, but many others indicated only that "many" or "certain" foods were tabooed. In our sample, 17.1 percent of the societies restricted only women's foods and the minor activities included in the score of 1. Food taboos were given a score of 2 on the scale. The third score was the presence of a pregnancy sex taboo for at least two months before delivery. While most societies began restricting sex relations when labor began or a week or two before delivery, in this sample most of the societies instituted an extended sex taboo (purportedly to assist the growth and development of the fetus) usually during the last one or two trimesters but in some cases during only the first trimester.

Although these three scores for customs do represent some restrictions on women during pregnancy and childbirth, they represent only moderate attempts to monitor the birth and to protect previously negotiated contracts compared with the most elaborate two categories—social avoidance and structural seclusion. A society was scored as having social avoidance customs during pregnancy with a 4 if a pregnant woman was specifically restricted from coming into contact with members of the community, especially men. If only special classes of people, such as shamans or chiefs, were to be avoided, general restrictions on women's social contacts were not considered present. Similarly, a prohibition against certain individuals' observing the delivery was not considered a social avoidance procedure since some form of restriction on who could be present at the delivery occurred in almost all the societies. Husbands rarely could be present, and usually male relatives or friends were restricted. Frequently, however, members of both the wife's and the husband's kin groups sent representatives to observe the birth, and a shaman, or even the husband, would be brought in if delivery was difficult. Of those societies coded as having social avoidance customs during pregnancy, most also believed that pregnant women were unclean, dangerous, and evil and that they should keep away from others in the community. A score of 5 was given to practices that resulted in the structural seclusion of women for at least two weeks prior to delivery, such as putting them in a specially built birth hut or menstrual hut, confining them in their own households, or moving them to another community. This extreme form of maternal restriction occurred in 24.3 percent of the societies in the sample.

For purposes of analysis, the scores of 4 and 5 were collapsed into a single score indicating the presence of significant social and structural restrictions on pregnant women. The remaining three scores were also collapsed into a single score, "personal restrictions." The intercoder reliability coefficient was .83, with most errors resulting from scorers' confusion on how to classify social avoidance customs and some errors resulting from minimal information on the length of the pregnancy sex taboo.

The Husband Involvement Scale measures the degree to which husbands change their behavior in ways that indicate an active ritual involvement in the birth process. Like the Maternal Restrictions Scale, the Husband Involvement Scale is arranged along a five-point Guttman scale; it has a coefficient of reproducibility of .96. The lowest two scores (1 and 2) indicate the absence of significant ritual behavior during pregnancy or postpartum, with a score of 1 being the residual category (no ritual observances) and a score of 2 including minor observances that could not be classified as couvade, such as the giving of a birth feast for friends and relatives after a successful birth, helping the wife with her daily chores during pregnancy or labor, seeking a vision to ensure successful delivery, or avoiding looking at certain objects. In most societies, men observed either minor or no ritual behavior during the pregnancy and postpartum periods.

Customs traditionally classified as couvade in the literature were divided into three categories. The observance of food taboos during pregnancy, postpartum, or both was scored 3. A score of 4 was given to postpartum behavioral changes such as work taboos, hunting and fishing restrictions, and the custom of staying within the community close to home for varying lengths of time. A score of 5 was given to behaviors often described as classic, or prototypical, couvade: the custom of husbands' going into ritual seclusion during pregnancy or postpartum. In either case, the society was scored 5, whether the husband entered into seclusion alone or with his wife, and whether he stayed in his own household (while the wife entered the birth hut or went about her normal activities) or secluded himself in the men's house.

Since only the three highest scores include practices typically described as couvade, these scores were collapsed into one, as were the lowest two scores. The scale as it is used in the analysis, therefore, indicates simply the presence or absence of couvade in a particular society. The intercoder reliability coefficient was .86 for the full scale, with most of the error resulting from some inability to differentiate between scores 4 and 5 and between scores 1 and 2. The distribution of scores on each scale among the societies in the sample is presented in Appendix I.

A measure of *compensation demands* was developed from the original ethnographic sources. Compensation demands were coded as present when the husband or his kinsmen demanded or expected payments of gifts or return of some or all of the wealth exchanged at marriage in cases of barrenness, infanticide, or abortion. They were also coded present when barrenness, infanticide, or abortion were grounds for divorce and when divorce led to compensation demands.

By far the most common reason for demanding compensation was barrenness. There were also numerous cases in which compensation was demanded of a wife's lover, especially when pregnancy occurred; such compensation demands were not included in the present index because they do not show that parties to a marriage agreement have the ability to protect against default.

Results

The correlations in Table 11 show that, with one exception, both maternal restrictions and couvade are significantly associated with each of the proposed antecedent conditions. After the effects of diffusion are taken into account, maternal restrictions are significantly positively correlated with compensation demands ($r=.40$), fraternal interest group strength ($r=.29$), resource base ($r=.23$), and residence patterns promoting the formation of fraternal interest groups ($r=.34$). As predicted, ritual involvement in the birth by husbands (couvade) is significantly negatively associated with each of the measures of fraternal interest groups: $r= -.49$ with resource base, $-.35$ with residence, and $-.48$ with fraternal strength. Although couvade is also negatively associated with compensation demands ($r= -.23$), the correlation is not statistically significant. The model for couvade, however, does not require a strong association with this variable since we argue that compensation demands should only be made when the payoffs of marriage bargains are substantial, as in the case of brideprice.

The causal model accounting for maternal restrictions proposed that fraternal interest group strength and its structural antecedents should lead to ritual surveillance of mothers during pregnancy and birth only if the terms of explicit marriage bargains specify that parties investing wealth in the wife's reproductive capacity are to be compensated if no offspring are produced. The transfer of wealth, such as brideprice, in a society implies that compensation is expected and does not provide a direct measure of explicit marriage bargains being contingent on the production of offspring. The moderate positive association between maternal restrictions and compensation demands supports this hypothesis. The correlation matrix shows that the compensation demand measure is also moderately correlated with fraternal interest group strength ($r=.48$). The hypothesis that compensation demands mediate the effects of strong fraternal interest groups and the two antecedents on maternal restrictions can be tested, first, by examining how much of the correlation between fraternal strength and maternal restrictions is accounted for by the com-

TABLE 11. **Correlates of Birth Practices**

Variable	2	3	4	5	6
1. Resource Base	.31[b]	.66[c]	.47[c]	.23[a]	−.49[c]
2. Residence Patterns		.39[b]	.35[b]	.34[c]	−.35[c]
3. Strength Index			.48[c]	.29[a]	−.48[c]
4. Compensation Demands				.40[c]	−.23
5. Maternal Restrictions					−.32[b]
6. Couvade					

[a] $p < .05$.
[b] $p < .01$.
[c] $p < .001$.

mon association of each variable with compensation demands. When the effects of compensation demands are held constant, the partial correlation between strength and maternal restrictions is .12, a figure substantially lower than the zero-order correlation of .29. Fraternal strength alone explains 8.4 percent of the variance in maternal restrictions, but when the effects of compensation demands are partialed out, strength accounts for only 1.4 percent—a substantial and significant reduction in explained variance. Fraternal interest group strength, then, leads to ritual surveillance of the birth process primarily because the marriage bargains made in societies with strong fraternal interest groups are likely to include contingency clauses that specify compensation if no offspring are produced.

The results of a multiple partial correlation test show that the zero-order correlation between residence patterns and maternal restrictions could also be explained by the effects of residence configurations on fraternal interest group strength and compensation demands. The correlation between residence pattern and maternal restrictions is reduced from .34 to .21 when both intervening variables are held constant, representing a reduction in explained variance from 11.6 percent to 4.4 percent. Additional statistical analysis showed that the effects of residence pattern on maternal restrictions were mediated primarily by compensation demands rather than by fraternal interest group strength. When only the strength index is held constant, the variability in maternal restrictions explained by residence is reduced to 4 percent. Therefore, the 4.4 percent of variance explained by residence that results when both intervening variables are held constant is due almost entirely to the mediating influence of compensation demands.

These analyses show that fraternal interest group strength and its structural antecedents affect maternal restrictions by determining whether or not parties to a paternity bargain expect compensation in case of default. Compensation demands alone, however, do not explain the extensiveness of maternal restrictions during the birth process as completely as does the fraternal interest group model as a whole. The presence of compensation demands alone explains 16 percent of the variance in maternal restrictions whereas the entire model explains 24 percent. Ritual monitoring of the birth process provides a mechanism for assessing the legitimacy of compensation claims in case of birth accidents or suspected malfeasance by interested parties. Compensation demands by strong fraternal interest groups and individuals are most likely in societies whose residence patterns cluster related males (and thus those who share an interest in the outcome of a pregnancy) in the same community. Residence pattern plays a much more significant role in explaining maternal restrictions than does resource base. In fact, including resource base in the model has an insignificant effect on the variance in maternal restrictions explained; its major influence is indirect through its effects on strength.

The model for explaining ritual involvement of husbands in the birth process is the reverse of the maternal restrictions model. The correlation matrix in Table 11 shows that all three components of the fraternal interest group model were significantly negatively associated with couvade and that, as expected, the effects of compensation demands were statistically nonsignificant. Couvade, it is hypothesized, is a form of ritual bargaining at childbirth by which a man claiming rights to a woman's offspring attempts, in the absence of strong fraternal interest groups, to develop a temporary political faction that will support his claims.

The partial correlations between the two structural indicators of fraternal interest groups and couvade when strength is held constant demonstrate the crucial role of fraternal interest group strength as a mediator between residence and resource base on the one hand and couvade on the other. The correlation between resource base and couvade is reduced from $-.49$ to $-.26$ when the effects of strength on the association are partialed out. Therefore, even when the effects of residence are allowed to vary, the variance in couvade rituals explained by the economic resource base is reduced from 24 percent to 6.9 percent, with the latter proportion being statistically nonsignificant once the effects of diffusion are considered. Similarly, the relationship between residence and couvade is reduced from $-.35$ to $-.20$ when the effects of their common association with fraternal strength are partialed out (and resource base is allowed to vary), with a corresponding reduction in explained variance from 12.3 percent to only 4 percent. Clearly, a large proportion of the association between residence and couvade and between resource base and couvade is accounted for by the effects of fraternal interest group strength. When both residence and resource base are held constant, the partial correlation between strength and couvade is .19, and the amount of explained variance is 3.6%.

Fraternal interest group strength, however, is not as adequate an explanation of couvade as the complete fraternal interest group model. Strength alone accounts for a substantial 23 percent of the variance in couvade cross-culturally. However, the complete model accounts for 31.8 percent, representing an 8.8 percent increase in explained variance. This increase is statistically significant even when the effects of diffusion are eliminated (t_{diff}=2.185, p<.025).

These results provide strong empirical support for our bargaining theory of birth practices although the model for maternal restrictions is less powerful than that for couvade.

Alternate Explanations

With the exception of Ayres's hypothesis about maternal food and sex taboos, the relative merits of our model and studies making predictions about the cross-cultural variability in birth practices can be tested on our sample of societies. As described in Chapter 1, Frank Young hypothesized that maternal birth practices and couvade should be explained by the presence of exogamous and clan organization since the high solidarity of societies with these organizations necessitates an elaborate dramatization of the new parental status of couples. Neither practice was shown to be significantly related to clan organization in Young's own study, and in our sample neither practice is significantly associated with types of community organization as coded by Murdock. Inspection of birth practices among three types of community organization showed that couvade was equally likely in each type of community, and maternal restrictions were only slightly more likely to occur in exogamous communities than in agamous or endogamous ones (see Table 12). When community organizations are dichotomized into "exogamous" and "nonexogamous," the correlation between exogamy and maternal restrictions is a nonsignificant .12, between exogamy and couvade, −.07.

Burton and Whiting suggested that couvade is performed in societies in which men are likely to identify strongly with the female role. They hypothesized that such societies should be those having matrilocal residence and exclusive mother-child sleeping arrangements during infancy. To test this hypothesis, we observed the relationships between couvade, sleeping arrangements, and matrilocal

TABLE 12. **Relationship between Birth Practices and Community Organization**

Extensiveness of Birth Practices	Exogamous	Agamous	Endogamous
		Maternal Restrictions	
High (social)	56.2%	51.7%	37.0%
	(27)	(15)	(10)
Low (personal)	43.8%	48.3%	63.0%
	(21)	(14)	(17)
Total	100.0%	100.0%	100.0%
	(48)	(29)	(27)
		Couvade	
Present	41.7%	42.9%	53.8%
	(20)	(12)	(14)
Absent	58.3%	57.1%	46.2%
	(28)	(16)	(12)
Total	100.0%	100.0%	100.0%
	(48)	(28)	(26)

residence separately and also the relationship between couvade and the interaction between sleeping arrangements and matrilocality. Burton and Whiting suggested that couvade should be most likely to occur when a society possessed both structural characteristics promoting female identification in men although they did not test this prediction. In our sample, the correlation between couvade and the presence of exclusive mother-child sleeping arrangements is virtually zero ($r = -.02$) when Barry and Paxton's new codes for sleeping arrangements are used.[70] Although there is a relationship ($r = .24$) between matrilocal residence and couvade, we found that bilocal and neolocal societies are even more likely to practice couvade than matrilocal societies. Whereas our theory predicts that neolocal and bilocal societies should behave like matrilocal ones, Burton and Whiting's theory predicts that they should behave like patrilocal ones since female identification in these societies should not be strong. Not only is our residence dichotomy more strongly associated with couvade, but Burton and Whiting's matrilocality-couvade correlation is rendered statistically insignificant after the effects of diffusion are considered. We also found no association at all between couvade and the combination of matrilocal residence and exclusive mother-child sleep-

70. Herbert Barry III and Leonora Paxton, "Infancy and Early Childhood: Cross-Cultural Codes," *Ethnology* 10 (1971): 466–508.

ing arrangements. Although only six societies in our sample showed both these characteristics, the two together predicted couvade no better than one or the other characteristic alone, or neither. Neither Young's nor Burton and Whiting's theories are supported by our data, and both are clearly weaker than the fraternal interest group/ compensation demands model.

6 Menstrual Restrictions and Sex Segregation Practices

Perhaps no other event in the female reproductive cycle evokes as negative an emotional response as the periodic appearance of menstrual bleeding. It is this negative affect toward menstruation that has led psychoanalytic thinkers to focus on the psychodynamic origins of menstrual taboos. Orthodox Freudians have generally interpreted social restrictions associated with menstruation as behavioral expressions of men's castration anxiety in response to genital bleeding although some psychoanalysts have theorized that these restrictions are a mechanism for protecting men from women's own unconscious pre-Oedipal conflicts, reactivated by each menstrual period.

It must also be recognized, however, that menstruation provides crucial information about a woman's reproductive status. We have already discussed the widespread recognition in tribal societies of menarche as an indicator of potential fertility. Similarly, the regular appearance of menstrual bleeding after each pregnancy provides crucial evidence that a woman remains fertile. An obsessive concern with menstruation may well reflect men's need to assess women's ability to continue producing offspring.

The importance of menstruation as an indicator of a woman's continuing capacity to conceive is clearly recognized in tribal societies. Inspection of the numerous ethnographic accounts of theories of menstruation and of theories of conception shows widespread agreement that menstrual bleeding is a natural biological process by which the womb is cleansed in preparation for future conception and that this same blood is used during pregnancy to help develop and nourish the fetus.[1] As a Navaho informant put it, "The menstruation is to make the baby."[2] Although theories of conception vary considerably cross-culturally in the relative emphasis they give to sperm and menstrual blood in the development of the fetus, with matrilineal societies tending to emphasize menstrual blood and patrilineal societies tending to emphasize sperm,[3] in most conception theories uterine blood is acknowledged as necessary, if not sufficient, for the production of offspring.

The significance of periodic menstrual bleeding as the indicator of continued fertility is further illustrated by the various remedies and rituals used to bring on a delayed menses. Women attempt to induce late or absent menstrual periods through dreaming, avoiding strong emotions, seeking visions, taking hot baths, and drinking special herbal concoctions.[4] Among the Tinne, a woman will wear a special cloth harness that has been soaked in the menstrual blood of another woman to enhance her fertility.[5] Many words for menstruation have been recorded to describe differences in the color, texture, and duration of menstrual flow, differences between retarded, irregular, and missed periods, and menstrual periods signifying the end of the reproductive span,[6] all of which convey information about a woman's reproductive status, how soon she will be able to conceive, and the sex and health of the future fetus. Husbands have also been known to insist on proof of menstruation if they suspect a wife of infidelity. Numerous cases have been recorded of wives' being accused of adul-

1. See, for example, Flora Bailey, "Some Sex Beliefs and Practices in the Navaho Community," *Papers of the Peabody Museum of Archaeology and Ethnology* 40 (1950): 18; L. S. B. Leakey, "Some Notes on the Masai of Kenya Colony," *Journal of the Royal Anthropological Institute of Great Britain and Ireland* 60 (1930): 198; Margaret Mead, *Growing Up in New Guinea* (New York: Dell Publishing, 1968), p. 235; and Johannes Wilbert, *Survivors of Eldorado* (New York: Frederick Praeger, 1972), p. 180.

2. Bailey, "Sex Beliefs," p. 18.

3. See especially Bronislaw Malinowski's discussion of Trobriander beliefs about the insignificant role of a woman's husband in conception in *The Sexual Life of Savages* (New York: Harcourt, Brace and World, 1929), pp. 179–86; Edmund Leach's "The Virgin Birth," *Journal of the Royal Anthropological Institute of Great Britain and Ireland* 96 (1966): 39–49; and Audrey Richards, "Some Types of Family Structure Amongst the Central Bantu," in *African Systems of Kinship and Marriage*, ed. A. R. Radcliffe-Brown and Daryll Forde (London: Oxford University Press, 1950), pp. 222–23. Monica Wilson describes the differences in beliefs about the importance of sperm versus menstrual blood expressed by two informants, one representing a patrilineal society and the other a matrilineal society, in *Rituals of Kinship Among the Nyakyusa* (London: Oxford University Press, 1957), p. 299.

4. Janet Schreiber, "Cross-Cultural Study of Menstrual Perceptions," World Health Organization Task Force Report on the Acceptability of Fertility Regulating Methods, AFT 3:6, April 1974.

5. J. Jette, "On the Superstitions of the Jen'a Indians," *Anthropos* 1 (1911): 257, 403.

6. Schreiber, "Menstrual Perceptions."

tery if they miss a menstrual period or do not menstruate soon after a husband's return from a lengthy war or hunting expedition.[7] Generally, in tribal societies, a wife's marital status remains secure as long as she continues to menstruate and produce viable offspring; if menstruation is not forthcoming, whether because of barrenness, menopause, or adulterous pregnancy, she can be divorced and returned home in shame.

Despite the importance of menstruation as proof of a wife's continued fertility, throughout world societies menstruating women are subject to numerous taboos and social restrictions. The menstrual taboos of the ancient Hebrews, described in the Old Testament, are often cited to illustrate extreme contempt for women; but similar menstrual taboos and postmenstrual purification rituals are the norm in world societies rather than the exception. In most of the societies in our sample, husbands are supposed to refuse to sleep with a menstruating wife, refuse to eat the food she has cooked, and prohibit her from coming near their property, animals, or gardens during this dangerous period.

Most theorists agree that menstrual practices reflect a widespread belief in female pollution, especially the belief that contact with sexually mature women during menstruation and at any time in their reproductive cycle is dangerous to men. In many societies men avoid contact with their wives not only during menstruation but throughout their marriage. Married couples may sleep and eat separately, avoid the use of each other's personal names, and avoid overt demonstrations of affection in public.[8] Contact with women, especially sexual contact, is believed to lessen men's ability to perform in war and to succeed on hunting expeditions or in other subsistence activities, and in many societies men must avoid their wives during these and other important community events such as harvests, funerals, and ceremonies.

Premenarcheal and postmenopausal women are rarely believed to endanger men and are not subjected to social and personal restrictions aimed at controlling pollution. Before menarche, women's social activities are not severely curtailed, and many societies place no restrictions on their contact with male peers and require no special taboo observances. After menopause, many women acquire a special status in the community, taking on ceremonial roles such as supervisor of menarcheal ceremonies; becoming midwives, herbalists, or shamans; or monitoring the behavior of younger, fertile wives in the community. They may be called by a different name to distinguish

7. Ibid.
8. John W. M. Whiting and Beatrice B. Whiting, "Aloofness and Intimacy of Husbands and Wives: A Cross-Cultural Study," *Ethos* 3 (1975): 183–207.

them from the more polluting fertile women, and in some cases they even participate alongside men in religious and political activities.

Social avoidance practices pertaining to husbands and wives throughout the reproductive cycle, then, could be interpreted as expressions of the same belief in female pollution that leads to special restrictions applied to menstruating women. Menstruation may be the focus of special attention because of its significance as proof of continuing fertility, but an analysis of female pollution must consider the range of sex segregation practices throughout the cycle of menstrual periods, pregnancies, and births. The most elaborate sex segregation practices cross-culturally take the form of communal men's houses, sex-segregated living arrangements, and secret men's clubs that severely restrict social contact between spouses throughout their marriage. Many ethnographic accounts describe how men spend much of their daily lives in their communal houses or sweathouses, gossiping about the evils of women, purifying themselves from female pollution, and guarding sacred objects that they believe their wives are trying to steal from them. The obsession with female pollution and the elaborate male segregation practices of the Mundurucu of South America were described in Chapter 1. The Mundurucu believe that the sex that controls the sacred musical instruments also controls the society and that originally women controlled the instruments. Although men eventually wrested control from women, women are constantly attempting to retrieve it and resume their once-dominant social position. The instruments, then, are strictly guarded from women, who are permitted neither to see them nor to hear them played. Mundurucu husbands say that if a woman were to see the instruments she would be dragged into the bush and forced to submit to gang rape.[9] Among the Arapesh, similar sacred instruments are designed specifically to guard a husband against his wife's pollution.[10] The sacred objects that are vulnerable to female pollution are not always instruments, such as flutes or bullroarers, but also include the "sacred bundles" of many North American societies that are kept hidden in lodges of men's societies.

Just as exclusively male institutions such as men's houses, sweathouses, and secret clubs represent the most elaborate male form of sex segregation in tribal and band societies, so does the physical segregation of women represent the most elaborate form of menstrual restrictions. Most cross-cultural studies of menstrual restrictions have ordered practices and taboos along a Guttman-type scale, with the

9. Robert F. Murphy, "Social Structure and Sex Antagonism," *Southwestern Journal of Anthropology* 15 (1959): 89–98.
10. Margaret Mead, "The Mountain Arapesh. II. Supernaturalism," *Anthropological Papers of the American Museum of Natural History* 37 (1940): 426.

segregation of menstruating women appearing at the end of the scale representing the most severe restriction. In this analysis, menstrual practices are dichotomized to separate public practices from relatively private ones. Ritual practices must be public if they are to influence and gauge community opinion. Prohibitions that forbid a menstruating woman to cook for her family, collect water or firewood, and touch or sleep with her husband are within the private or semiprivate domain of the domestic household, observed by her husband, children, and sometimes members of the extended family but not by the community at large. Requiring a menstruating wife to remain entirely secluded for a week or more, however, is a practice that cannot help attracting public attention. Like couvade, the segregation of menstruating wives is a highly public event: it prevents a woman from participating in daily community affairs for an extended period, an absence that is bound to be noticed in the intimate social environment of most tribal and band communities. When women are segregated in a community menstrual hut, their seclusion is even more obvious, especially if the menstrual hut is placed so that everyone passes by it during their daily routines. William Lessa's ethnographic account of the Ulithi menstrual practices includes a photograph of the menstrual hut. It is a large and impressive structure placed next to the seashore under a cluster of palms.[11] Although the "nerve center" of the village is the men's house, which is even more imposing than the menstrual hut, Lessa notes a distinctive characteristic of the menstrual hut in the village he was studying.

> As one walks through a village, one notices that all the houses are built at right angles to the shore—except the menstrual house, which is parallel to the shore. Whatever the original reason for this orientation, its position certainly serves to warn the male visitor of its nature and to remind him to observe the strict rules against trespass.[12]

Similarly, among the Ifaluk, who live on an atoll neighboring the Ulithi, the menstrual house is placed in a prominent location in the village for all to see. As the ethnographers record, "Everyone knows, of course, when a woman is menstruating because she is in the menstrual hut."[13] The public attention menstrual seclusion receives was also illustrated by a speech made by the most prominent man in the community at the island's general meeting. In the speech, the man reminded women to go to the menstrual hut when their

11. William Lessa, *Ulithi: A Micronesian Design for Living* (New York: Holt, Rinehart, and Winston 1966), p. 6.
12. Ibid.
13. Edwin G. Burrows and Melford Spiro, *An Atoll Culture* (Ann Arbor, Mich.: University Microfilms, 1969), p. 290.

menstrual flow appeared and not to leave the hut until it had ceased. Menstrual segregation, then, is an extreme form of menstrual restrictions, but it is also qualitatively different from other menstrual restrictions in that it draws public attention to a woman's reproductive status.

Both menstrual segregation and male segregation practices can be interpreted as elaborate public expressions of the belief in the polluting nature of fertile women. In our sample, 35 percent of the societies practiced menstrual segregation but not male segregation, and 32.3 percent practiced male segregation but not menstrual segregation. Both forms of segregation occurred in 18.9 percent of our sample societies.

THE DILEMMA OF A WIFE'S CONTINUING FERTILITY

If menarcheal ceremonies can be interpreted as ritual attempts to establish a favorable marriage bargain for a daughter, male circumcision as a response to the dilemma of fission, and birth practices as a response to the dilemma of legitimacy, then what explains elaborate public demonstrations of fear and contempt of fertile women? Our theory of ritual politics argues that these practices are a response to the dilemma that a woman's fertility creates for her husband. As preceding chapters have made clear, in all societies control over women's reproductive capacity is the basis for acquiring wealth and power. As a wife continues to bear children and her husband's power increases, the balance of power in the community begins to shift. Both the husband's affines and his consanguineal kinsmen begin to feel threatened.

Response of Affines to a Wife's Continuing Fertility

A wife's continuing fertility as evidenced by pregnancies and regular menstrual periods is explicit proof that her family is fulfilling their side of the marriage bargain. Her fertility therefore safeguards them against accusations of default on the original contract, which might lead to economic loss or dispute with the husband's kin group. At the same time, however, it makes possible a shift in the balance of power between the wife's family of orientation and the newly created family of procreation headed by her husband.

When a man's political power is based largely on his ability to produce a large family, the greater the fecundity of his wife or wives the greater the capacity of his domestic unit to undermine the ties with affines implied by the original marriage contract. While the Mae-Enga concept "We marry those we fight" is most apparent among exogamous patrilineal groups, losing affinal control over a daughter's offspring is risky in cognatic and matrilineal groups as well. Among patrilineal groups in which children produced by a man's wife add not only to his personal power but to the power of his fraternal kin group as a whole, the advantages of a husband's new procreative unit over his wife's family are most apparent. Children are counted as members of their father's lineage and are expected to take up arms with them in any feud, even against their mother's family. But the potential for the defection of an increasingly powerful husband within matrilineal groups has also been acknowledged in the literature on matrilineal kinship.[14] A husband who gains enough wealth and prestige (either through the introduction of new sources of wealth, such as cash wages for labor on colonial plantations, or through inheritance from a wealthy matrilineal brother) may contest the ideological claims of his wife's lineage upon his biological offspring. He may even remove his sons from the lineage homestead or adopt them into his own matrilineage. In the discussion of the matrilineal Bemba in Chapter 1, the concern of a wife's kinsmen about her in-marrying husband's potential power over the wife and her children was, according to Audrey Richards, based on a high frequency of actual defections: husbands often did remove both their wives and their children to their own natal communities. Similarly, in societies with cognatic descent in which a husband and his in-laws theoretically share rights over a woman's reproductive capacity, the proximity between a husband and his children during their youth may reinforce father-child ties to the detriment of the in-laws.

The ambivalence of a married woman's natal family toward her continuing fertility is best reflected in the beliefs and practices by which the family attempts to exert some influence over her childbearing. For example, a father's reluctance to relinquish control over his daughter and her future offspring to a man of another kin group is indicated by the Tallensi's strictly observed taboo against sexual relations between husband and wife while living in the wife's father's household or even in his village. According to Meyer Fortes, sex relations between a husband and wife during visits to her father are considered a "particularly heinous case of 'polluting the room' of a father-in-law by a son-in-law."[15] Furthermore, a woman is pro-

14. See especially David M. Schneider, "The Distinctive Features of Matrilineal Descent Groups," in *Matrilineal Kinship*, ed. David M. Schneider and Kathleen Gough (Berkeley: University of California Press, 1962), pp. 1–29; and Mary Douglas, "Is Matriliny Doomed in Africa?" in *Man in Africa*, ed. Mary Douglas and Phyllis M. Kaberry (Garden City, N.Y.: Doubleday, 1971), pp. 123–37.

15. Meyer Fortes, *The Web of Kinship Among the Tallensi* (London: Oxford University Press, 1949), p. 124.

hibited from bearing a child in her father's house so that a wife is encouraged not to visit her father's home near the end of pregnancy. Fortes reports, "I have known a man to be so angry with a wife who disobediently went to her father's house . . . and gave birth there that he refused at first to have her back."[16] In any other circumstance, with the exception of the first few months of marriage, Tallensi wives have no restrictions on visits to their natal village, and, in fact, such visits are very frequent.

Affines may also attempt to manipulate the occurrence of menstrual periods after a daughter's marriage. In Chapter 3 we described how the Kurtatchi's ambivalence about their daughters' fertility after marriage is evidenced by their sometimes "forgetting" to take down from the rafters the ritual containers used during the daughter's menarcheal ceremony to "fasten her belly," that is, to prevent pregnancy before marriage. The containers are supposed to be broken up and dispersed at sea once the marriage is consummated, in order to "unfasten" her belly, permitting menstruation and conception. Similarly, the Nambicuara and Tupinamba practice of giving daughters special medicinal concoctions to prevent menstruation may be viewed not only as a public gesture to show that the daughter's parents wish to prevent illegitimate pregnancies but also as a signal that they have the power to control their daughter's menstrual periods throughout her marriage and may resort to using it.

Response of Consanguineal Kinsmen to a Wife's Continuing Fertility

A woman's continuing fertility threatens not only her own kin but also her husband's consanguineal kin. No matter how a society's customary descent rules regulate the distribution of authority over offspring, a man's ability to develop a large, procreative unit simultaneously enhances and threatens the power and wealth of his kin group.

Among patrilineal and cognatic kin groups, continuing fertility of each kinsman's wife represents the continuing production of offspring who will be counted as members of the kin group as a whole, increasing the group's potential economic and political power; yet at the same time it creates the potential for weakening a man's allegiance to his consanguineal kinsmen. Since a man's primary authority over his wife and his sole rights as genitor to her offspring give considerable political leverage, he may eventually acquire enough power to fission and form his own lineage. Fortes' analysis of the inevitability of fission was summarized in Chapter 4.

16. Ibid., p. 125.

In some groups, the significance of a wife's continuing fertility for a man's ability to break away from his kin group is reflected in accusations of witchcraft directed at the wife, whose fertility is recognized as a wedge between the husband and his consanguineal kin. Both the Swazi and the Thonga of Africa believe that witchcraft is inherited through women and is brought into a group by in-marrying wives, who pass it on to their daughters (not their sons).[17] Max Gluckman contends that among the Zulu accusations of witchcraft and other evils by a wife's in-laws reflect their anxiety about her role as producer of children, the potentially competitive heirs for social power, position, and property within the lineage. Hence the saying, "it is the wives who marry into the group that ultimately, by producing children, will lead to its breakup."[18] At the same time, however, a wife's primary responsibility is to produce many children, and barrenness is cause for divorce. Thus, a woman who fulfills her duty to bear many children to maintain the patrilineal group also sows the seeds of dissension in the group.[19] The most common accusers of wifely witchcraft are men in competition with her husband and mothers-in-law, who represent the husband's natal family. Gluckman also recognizes that Zulu beliefs in the polluting qualities of a wife's menstruation are an even clearer example of the kin group's ambivalence about her continuing fertility. Menstruating women among the Zulu are blamed for social crises and are particularly degraded by men.[20]

The threat that a wife's continuing fecundity creates for her husband's kin is also severe in matrilineal groups. As David Schneider and Mary Douglas[21] point out, the husband's primary loyalties can always shift from his matrilineage to the local domestic unit headed by his wife's family. Douglas contends, however, that the potential for a husband in a matrilineal society to develop a large family is less than that of a husband in a polygynous patrilineal society.[22] Douglas believes that matrilineal systems are at a disadvantage in comparison to patrilineal societies in that they cannot expand or recruit additional members solely on the basis of their kinswomen's reproductive capacity. Although a woman cannot reproduce indefinitely through multiple marriages, men of course can do so, either through serial monogamy or, even better, by polygyny, which is most common among patrilineal societies.

17. Max Gluckman, *Politics, Law, and Ritual in Tribal Society* (New York: New American Library, 1965), pp. 256–57.

18. Ibid., p. 257.

19. Ibid., pp. 257–58.

20. Ibid., p. 257.

21. Schneider, "Matrilineal Descent Groups"; and Douglas, "Is Matriliny Doomed?"

22. Douglas, "Is Matriliny Doomed?" p. 127.

Even though a rapid buildup of an individual procreative unit is not as likely within a matrilineal system, the institutions of sororal polygyny and adoption occasionally make it possible. Further, the husband may build a large kin group through wealth acquired from newly introduced economies. Jack Goody has remarked that the maintenance of matrilineal systems depends on a poor but egalitarian economic system.[23] Any changes that give some men greater access to wealth and property than others, such as work on a colonial plantation, create the potential for a husband to set up his own independent domestic unit rather than choosing to maintain his own matrilineage through the adoption of his biological sons. The husband may pass on his added wealth and property to his biological sons, who are likely to remain in residence on their father's land after their marriage rather than to live matrilocally. The resulting unit resembles a patrilineal-patrilocal one built on the defection of an individual kinsman who passes on his inheritance to biological sons. The dissolution of matrilineal systems or their gradual adoption of patrilineal characteristics through such a process is well known in Africa.[24]

Wives in matrilineal systems, like those in patrilineal systems, are subject to menstrual taboos and accusations of pollution. Matrilineal wives are as likely as patrilineal ones to drive a wedge between a husband and his consanguineal kinsmen through their continuing fertility.

THE HUSBAND'S ALTERNATIVES

A wife's fertility gives a man economic and political power, but it confronts him with the dilemma of how to represent his power to others. If he deemphasizes it, he may gain the good will and trust of his affines and consanguineal kin, but he puts himself at a disadvantage in bargaining over rights to women and children and other economic and political resources. If he makes a great show of his power, he may make himself respected, gain more power, and improve his bargaining position, but he also stands to alienate and threaten others. Whereas powerful men in a complex state may be able to stay in power despite their unpopularity with the majority of citizens because of their firm control of the centralized military, the legal system, and valuable economic resources, powerful men in tribal societies are far more dependent on the good will of others in the community since their control over resources and military force is

23. Jack Goody, "The Mother's Brother and the Sister's Son in West Africa," *Journal of the Royal Anthropological Institute of Great Britain and Ireland* 89 (1959): 61–86.
24. See descriptions of this process in Douglas, "Is Matriliny Doomed?" p. 126; and Douglas and Kaberry, *Man in Africa*, pp. 125–26.

never secure. Advantages in wealth and power are seldom large or permanent enough to keep a powerful man safe from competitors' attempts to bring him down. The more a man sets himself above others, the more he places himself at risk.

Conditions That Intensify the Dilemma of a Wife's Continuing Fertility

While all societies share the dilemma of a wife's continuing fertility, they do so to varying degrees. Societies with a stable and valuable resource base (pastoralists and hoe and plow agriculturalists) and societies without any valuable resources (hunter-gatherers) generate a less serious dilemma than societies with valuable but unstable resources (salmon fishermen, buffalo hunters, digging-stick shifting cultivators). In societies with a stable and valuable resource base that allows for the formation of strong fraternal interest groups, the husband is not faced with a serious dilemma about how to represent his power. His power outside his fraternal interest group is largely determined by the strength of his group as a whole. Since he can rely on the group's assistance automatically regardless of his individual wealth, influence, or political position, he has little need to resort to self-aggrandizement to acquire a faction in time of need. Within the group, his power is determined by such ascriptive characteristics as seniority or membership in a senior or high-ranking branch of kin and by the size of the family or lineage of which he is the head. While fission occurs in these societies and can have drastic consequences, it occurs less often than in other societies because the scarcity and military vulnerability of the highly valuable economic resources binds younger men to their elders. Thus, a man's power within his kin group as well as outside of it is stable enough so that he does not need to display it continually to win and maintain others' allegiance. In societies without valuable resources to hold factions together, displays of individual power are hardly possible and disclaimers of power hardly necessary since no one can control wealth or the allegiance of others even temporarily. Leaders in hunting and gathering societies typically have no more wealth or privilege than their followers, can be deserted or replaced at any time, and make decisions for the group only by assessing community opinion and then proclaiming it.[25]

Societies with unstable and valuable resources are likely to generate the most severe dilemma of a wife's continuing fertility because

25. See, for example, descriptions of leadership among the Nambicuara and the Kung in Claude Lévi-Strauss' *A World on the Wane* (New York: Criterion Books, 1971), pp. 300–05; and Lorna Marshall's *The !Kung of Nyae Nyae* (Cambridge: Harvard University Press, 1976), pp. 191–95.

they have a highly unstable distribution of political power. The resources are valuable enough to permit the development of medium-
sized coalitions during periods of surplus but too fluctuating and
perishable to maintain coalitions on a more or less permanent basis.
Men can build up factions from a core group of kin but can never rely
on automatic kin-group support. In these societies, a husband must
meet two contradictory requirements. He must build up his own
power as much as possible through provision of goods and services,
charisma, manipulation, and puffery, making a show of his wealth
and prestige in order to maintain and increase his following. Simultaneously he must deemphasize his power to keep from stirring up
antagonism and suspicion in his community, especially among his affines and consanguineal kin.

The ritual solution to this dilemma is the tactic of ritual disinterest. As a man builds up his power, he publicly proclaims his lack of
interest in power, his ordinary status, and his "equality" with other,
less powerful men. He holds feasts and potlatches to display his
wealth, while simultaneously declaring disinterest in wealth by giving it away in large amounts. Similarly, he adheres to elaborate and
public pollution practices to proclaim the continuing fertility of his wife
while simultaneously declaring disinterest by avoiding her, abstaining from sex with her, and leaving her unprotected so that rights to her
fertility may be claimed by adulterers.

UNSTABLE RESOURCE BASES

In Chapter 2 we described the three kinds of economic systems
that should be most likely to produce the political conditions that
most intensify the dilemma of a wife's continuing fertility: buffalo hunting, salmon fishing, and digging-stick shifting cultivation. Among societies based on buffalo hunting or salmon fishing, adult males have the
potential to control abundant wealth in the form of numerous salmon
or large herds of buffalo. Such wealth is perishable, however; the
supply fluctuates from one season or year to the next; and wealth can
be obtained by any man or group of men lucky enough to be located
on the right stream or clever enough to predict where the buffalo
will migrate. In shifting cultivation economies, cleared land is exhausted in a few years and any man can clear his own plot.

Buffalo can be hunted on the plains only during the summer
months. When they migrate, the common practice of killing as many
as possible, sometimes by driving an entire herd over a cliff, provides
a sudden overabundance of meat and hides.[26] Because the wealth is

26. Ruth M. Underhill, *Red Man's America* (Chicago: University of Chicago Press,
1971), Chap. 3.

for the most part perishable, a successful hunter could not possibly use all of it himself. By sharing his wealth with others, he translates his surplus economic resource into a political resource: social indebtedness. His recipients become, at least temporarily, political and military allies. Since affines as well as consanguines will be happy to be attached to a man who can provide food and thus some economic security, the hunter can also expand his faction by translating his perishable economic surplus into reproductive capital. The greater a hunter's success, the bigger the giveaways and the larger his domestic unit and group of political allies.

The economy of salmon fishing produces a similar political dynamic. Villagers can never be sure if or when the salmon will appear in their rivers. As Marvin Harris points out, the failure of a salmon run in a village stream some year could seriously threaten the very survival of a village while a nearby village's streams might be overstocked.[27] Men from villages with an abundance of salmon in their part of the stream are in the same political situation as successful buffalo hunters. No one domestic unit can possibly consume all the salmon it catches, so it distributes the surplus to less fortunate families who are thereby placed in the position of debtors. Giving surplus food to threatened households in impoverished villages is not only a type of insurance against one's own future impoverishment, as Harris argues, but also a means of increasing one's circle of friends and allies. The large potlatches and special "first salmon" ceremonies among salmon fishermen occur in times of large food surpluses and have become the textbook example of ritual politics, as described in Chapter 2.

The wealth accrued by clever or merely lucky individuals, however, is only transient, and so is the political following produced by the distribution of surpluses. A man's coalition can easily dissolve and regroup around newly successful providers. Economies that provide periodic abundance of perishable wealth, then, are "unstable" and produce political conditions that are equally unstable.

Marshall Sahlins has described digging-stick shifting cultivation as producing a "fragile equilibrium" between people and resources.[28] The system requires the continual depletion of land resources, and the fragmentation of local communities is inevitable as families move away in search of more land. The addition of pig raising to the activities of some digging-stick cultivators produces an even more fragile equilibrium. Pigs compete with human beings for food and therefore require periodic slaughtering, the preparation of additional garden plots, or both. Digging-stick shifting cultivation does produce

27. Marvin Harris, *Culture, People, Nature* (New York: Thomas Y. Crowell, 1975), p. 294.

28. Marshall Sahlins, *Tribesmen* (Englewood Cliffs, N.J.: Prentice-Hall, 1968), p. 32.

a continuous yield, and according to some studies slash-and-burn garden plots are capable of producing a surplus.[29] Two critical problems confront economies based primarily on the continual preparation of new garden plots. Once a garden plot has become exhausted, it is easier to let it lie fallow and eventually reclear the secondary growth than to clear the primary growth of more virgin land. As a result, while a plot is being cultivated, it is worth protecting and may need military defense against others, who would also rather prepare gardens from secondary growth. Andrew Vayda's analysis of Maori warfare illustrates the need for a military force to defend garden plots against raiders.[30] He argues that a principal cause of warfare among the Maori of New Zealand was the raiding of other groups' gardens in preference to clearing virgin land. Second, the resources produced by these garden plots are not valuable enough to provide incentives for the formation of large and stable fraternal interest groups. A son does not need to depend on his father for access to wealth. Sons may inherit gardens from fathers or affines, but they also have the opportunity to prepare their own without mediation. Thus, the impermanence and availability of garden plots prepared by digging-stick shifting cultivation inhibit the development of strong, enduring political coalitions, but the need to defend plots currently under cultivation promotes the development of temporary coalitions.

UNSTABLE POLITICAL POWER

We have argued throughout this study that the crucial, intervening link between economy and ritual is the strength of fraternal interest groups. If societies with unstable economic resources are strong enough to form political factions but too weak to ensure their stability, then they should fall within the middle range on our scale of fraternal interest group strength. Inspection of societies with unstable economic systems shows that they are much stronger politically than hunter-gatherers and much weaker than hoe and plow agriculturalists and pastoralists. The average size of their effective political unit is ninety-three, compared with only twelve among hunter-gatherers and 8,174 among the three economies producing the strongest fraternal interest groups. Similarly, 20 percent of the societies with unstable economic

29. See, for example, Roy Rappaport, *Pigs for the Ancestors* (New Haven: Yale University Press, 1974), Chap. 3.

30. Andrew P. Vayda, "Expansion and Warfare Among Swidden Agriculturalists," in *Environment and Cultural Behavior*, ed. Andrew P. Vayda (Garden City, N.Y.: Natural History Press, 1969), Chap. 10.

systems engage in brideprice marriage bargains, compared with only one (5.3 percent) of the hunter-gatherers and 72.1 percent of the three strong systems. Among most unstable societies, if wealth is exchanged for rights to women's reproductive capacity, it is rarely as valuable as the property exchanged in the marriage bargains of strong fraternal interest group societies. Instead of transferring large animals, capital goods, or valuable land, parties frequently engage in a series of gift exchanges of food and ritual objects. If the three additional forms of marriage arrangements that transfer wealth (token brideprice, gift exchange, and sister exchange) are included with brideprice, the unstable systems again occupy the middle range, with 53.3 percent engaging in wealth bargains as compared with 15.8 percent of the hunter-gatherers and 86.1 percent of the strong systems. Unstable societies are somewhat more likely to be patrilineal than hunting-gathering societies (although the difference, 22.2 percent versus 15.8 percent, is not significant) and considerably less likely than hoe and plow agriculturalists and pastoralists (22.2 percent versus 65.9 percent). Unlike hunter-gatherers, among whom the largest political subunit is the family with no resources to distribute in return for political allegiance, men in societies with unstable resources can acquire political power based on success in continually mobilizing political allies through distribution of goods and services. Unlike hoe and plow agriculturalists and pastoralists, however, they cannot promise inheritance of valuable property or political positions in return for political allegiance.

"Big man" (faction leader) politics are best known from ethnographic accounts of Melanesian societies, analyzed by Sahlins in his classic paper "Poor Man, Rich Man, Big Man, Chief."[31] While Sahlins does not attempt to link "big man" politics to an unstable resource economy, he does argue elsewhere that the political dynamics he describes for the Melanesian shifting cultivators should apply to the buffalo hunters of the Great Plains and the salmon fishermen of the Northwest Coast as well.[32] Ethnographic descriptions of all these unstable societies, as well as those of shifting cultivators in other world regions, show that unstable resource base societies share several distinctive political features.

In unstable societies, a leader cannot count on recruiting all the members of his kin group. Political factions are developed on the basis of individual implicit (or occasionally explicit) agreements be-

31. Marshall Sahlins, "Poor Man, Rich Man, Big Man, Chief: Political Types in Melanesia and Polynesia," in *Cultures of the Pacific*, ed. Thomas G. Harding and Ben J. Wallace (New York: Free Press, 1970), pp. 203–15.
32. Sahlins, *Tribesmen*, Chap. 3.

tween a leader and potential followers, whatever their kin-group affiliation. Even though the initial core of followers may be recruited on
the basis of close ties of consanguineal kinship, the faction expands to
include nonrelatives as well. Michael Young's lengthy discussion of
faction building among the Kalauna of Goodenough Island includes
statistical data to show that 90 percent of the "helpers" in each of
thirteen leaders' factions were the leaders' agnatic kinsmen. Young
also notes, however, that the members of a Kalauna community are
for the most part members of a single patrilineage. Even though members of the patrilineage also live in nearby communities, the extent of
support that a leader can receive from kin outside his community is
an unknown quantity.[33] In unstable societies practicing matrilocal or
neolocal residence, a "big man" may attract many followers in the community who are not agnatically related to him.

Individual agreements made with followers usually involve the
exchange of the potential leader's goods or services for the recipient's
loyalty and political assistance. Although an aspiring politician's personal skills, such as shrewdness, oratory, and charisma, help him
achieve success as a political leader, access to economic resources is
usually critical. As Shelly Errington points out, while "big man" politics can be described as "personal" in that the existence of the faction
depends upon the personal power of its leader, the leader's power is
not so much personal appeal as the ability to put individuals in his
debt economically.[34] In theory, leadership can be achieved by any ambitious male, but the importance of access to economic resources puts
practical limits on the possible number of "big men" in a community.
An aspirant must begin his political career with enough wealth to provide loans and gifts to potential followers. Frequently, therefore, the
young aspirant is the son or protégé of a "big man" or other wealthy
elder who gives or loans him the necessary resources.

Among the Kwakiutl, for example, boys begin their political careers even before puberty by entering an elaborate blanket-exchange
system with the help of a loan from an older man in the community.
This system requires boys to keep redistributing increasing numbers
of blankets in order to pay back high interest rates to the men who
lent them blankets originally. While some participants in the exchange
go deeply into debt, others succeed not only in paying back their
original loans but also in acquiring enough surplus wealth to offer

33. Michael W. Young, *Fighting with Food* (Cambridge: Cambridge University
Press, 1971), Chap. 5.
34. Shelly Errington, "Order and Power in Karavar," in *The Anthropology of
Power*, ed. Raymond D. Fogelson and Richard N. Adams (New York: Academic Press,
1977), pp. 23–43.

loans themselves and thereby begin acquiring followers.[35]

In most unstable societies, contracting a marriage bargain is an essential step in a man's political career. Men who already have political influence often obtain new followers by financing the marriage bargains of suitors who cannot afford the required marriage gifts or brideprice payments. The gifts or payments are implicitly exchanged for the new husband's allegiance. Cora Du Bois describes how many Alorese husbands begin their marriages deeply in debt either to their relatives or to some other wealthy member of the community who provided the marriage gifts. Their indebtedness can continue for years since gift exchanges between a husband and his affines are expected to go on indefinitely.[36] Among the Karavar as well, financing a marriage bargain is beyond the ability of many young men. If his father cannot provide the necessary brideprice, a suitor must attach himself to a "big man" who will provide it. In this way the suitor gains a wife and the "big man" gains a new political ally.[37]

If a young man marries well, he may be able to turn to his affines for both economic support and political allegiance. As Sahlins notes, during the early phase of faction building an aspiring leader relies heavily on the contributions of both affines and close consanguineal kin.[38] If he succeeds in gaining their support, he then begins to widen his sphere of influence by attaching more distant relatives, neighbors, and other community members. By sponsoring ceremonial feasts and giveaways, he demonstrates his wealth and the size of his following, while putting more community members in his debt to obtain their allegiance. Through the well-known competitive feasts and potlatches, he may attempt to reduce or eliminate competition from other "big men" or potential "big men" either inside or outside his community by publicly shaming them and luring away their followers.

Preparing and holding ceremonies also enables a "big man" to assess his current political strength. As we have argued elsewhere, sponsoring an elaborate ceremony that requires the services of many people can show a man how many allies he actually has at any given moment. Before a man attempts to sponsor a ceremony, he often harangues his following in order to stir up and assess their enthusiasm. If he cannot mobilize them in this way, he does not go on with the ceremony since, as Douglas Oliver says of the Siuai, "feasts must be well attended to be effective; pork-hungry as they are, most Siuai

---

35. Franz Boas, *Kwakiutl Ethnography* (Chicago: University of Chicago Press, 1966), pp. 92–93.
36. Cora Du Bois, *The People of Alor* (Cambridge: Harvard University Press, 1969), pp. 84–93.
37. Errington, "Order and Power," pp. 26–27.
38. Sahlins, "Poor Man, Rich Man," pp. 207–08.

men will stay away from feasts whose hosts they do not respect."[39] If followers work long hours preparing food, making costumes, and constructing equipment, and if the ceremony is well attended, the "big man" can be at least temporarily secure in his reliance on a faction to support him in political crises.

Achieving leadership is not always based solely on distribution of economic goods to one's followers. In some societies, the provision of such services as military protection and carrying out revenges for others may also be essential. Among the Jivaro, for example, a man acquires the status of *unta*, or "big man," not only by giving parties and gaining a reputation for generosity but also by obtaining renown as a killer. As Michael Harner puts it, leadership among the Jivaro is acquired "literally through life-and-death struggle."[40] A man begins his killing career by going on war parties led by others. As he gains a reputation for success in killing, he begins organizing his own war parties and then leading the war parties of other men. Eventually he may become so famous that even his enemies approach him with requests to kill someone.[41]

Michael Young notes that before the elaborate food exchanges replaced intervillage warfare and interclan feuds among the Kalauna, the "bossman" of a faction derived his political power from his success in battle. He would plan raids and lead groups into battle, and he was expected to be the most reckless and courageous warrior in the group. After a battle it was his job to distribute the bodies of captured enemies for consumption in cannibal feasts.[42]

Unstable societies that emphasize achieved leadership through success in war are typically characterized by a group of practices that we have termed "ritual war": public displays or ceremonies involving cannibalism, headhunting, scalping, or taking other body parts as trophies. Through such displays a "big man" demonstrates his prowess, just as feasts and giveaways demonstrate the wealth of their sponsor. The displays, like feasts and giveaways, also allow the "big man" to assess the extent of his support in the community. Because military alliances may cut across ties of kinship, some members of a war leader's faction may be fighting their own kinsmen residing in another community. If these faction members are required to participate in cannibalistic feasts or victory ceremonies that involve the display of enemy heads, their reaction to the proceedings gives the war leader clear evidence about the direction of their loyalties.

39. Douglas Oliver, *A Solomon Island Society* (Boston: Beacon Paperback, 1967), p. 362.

40. Michael J. Harner, *The Jivaro* (Garden City, N.Y.: Anchor Books, 1973), p. 111.

41. Ibid., p. 112.

42. Young, *Fighting with Food*, p. 79.

DISPLAYS OF RITUAL DISINTEREST IN POWER

If, as we argue, ritual disinterest in a wife's fertility is a demonstration of ritual disinterest in obtaining the wealth and power that her fertility represents, and if this ritual disinterest is a tactic for resolving the dilemma of how to represent personal power that is most intense in unstable societies, then unstable societies should be characterized by elaborate public displays of ritual disinterest in both political power and the fundamental basis of that power, women's fertility.

Ethnographic accounts of unstable societies indicate that ritual disinterest in wealth and power is one of the distinguishing features of unstable resource base politics. Leaders must minimize and deny the status differences between them and their followers. Conspicuous consumption of wealth attracts hostility, and "generosity" is the trait to which political success is most commonly attributed. Among the Kapauku, for example, a rich man wears the same clothes as others do, eats only a little better, and when he kills a pig, distributes all of the meat without eating any himself.[43] It is believed that the only justification for acquiring wealth is to redistribute it among the less fortunate. Wealthy men who fail to abide by this requirement are severely reprimanded and may even be killed. Leonard Pospisil describes an incident concerning a rich man who became unpopular in the community because of his lack of generosity. The people in the community murdered him, saying, "You should not be the only rich man, we should all be the same, therefore you only stay equal with us."[44] In Lesu, ambitious men must disparage themselves and belittle their contributions at ceremonies in public speeches. As Hortense Powdermaker describes it, "When men give contributions at a funeral, they say, 'I have brought a few pigs and I am quite ashamed of them,' and 'I am not an important person. I am just an ordinary or "small" fellow.' "[45] If a man parades his wealth and power too ostentatiously, he is ridiculed and eventually he loses his following. The Alorese assume that all men are competing for political power and prestige but will not admit any differences in wealth openly and have no formal terms for individual differences in wealth.[46] The Iban of Borneo similarly compete for wealth and prestige but deny the existence of any status differences.[47] This professed egalitarianism, common to many unstable societies, is perhaps best illustrated by a Marquesan

43. Leonard Pospisil, *Kapauku Papuans and Their Law* (New Haven: HRAF Press, 1971), p. 80.

44. Ibid., p. 81.

45. Hortense Powdermaker, *Life in Lesu* (New York: W. W. Norton, 1971), pp. 215–16.

46. Du Bois, *People of Alor*, pp. 117–18.

47. J. D. Freeman, *Iban Agriculture* (London: H. M. Stationery Office, 1955), p. 10.

man's response to an ethnographer's questions about leadership: "You are king, I am king, we are all kings."[48]

While ceremonies like potlatches and feasts proclaim the wealth and power of the sponsor and win him allies, they are on the surface gestures of generosity and a complete lack of interest in accruing wealth. Among both the Kwakiutl and the Alorese, wealth contests between "big men" rivals may involve the destruction of huge amounts of property.[49] Intriguingly enough, the Alorese demonstrate some belief in the polluting quality of wealth. As Du Bois describes it,

> Any large accumulation of gongs and mokos [Alorese currency] . . . is considered dangerous. Young children are chased away from it, and adults must be protected by throwing away one of the pieces of smaller value to the wealth-bringing spirits. . . . Should this precaution or some similar one be omitted, the owner of the wealth will fall sick and die within a day.[50]

DISPLAYS OF RITUAL DISINTEREST IN A WIFE'S FERTILITY

The elaborate pollution practices of unstable societies can be interpreted as tactics of ritual disinterest in a wife's fertility that are part of a larger complex of tactics of ritual disinterest in wealth and power. A man's willingness to segregate his wife during her menstruation or to segregate himself from her throughout her reproductive span implies to others that his interest in the growth of his conjugal unit is not so complete as to preclude attention to social obligations and contractual agreements. His adherence to these customs reassures his affines and consanguines of his respect for their rights to share control over his wife's fertility and authority over her offspring and therefore of his continued allegiance toward the larger social group.

Of course, neither sexual avoidance customs nor menstrual restrictions actually interfere with a man's ability to impregnate his wife. Sex between spouses is a private affair, and a public display of disinterest by no means guarantees that a man will also display disinterest in private. Just as men in unstable societies covertly pursue power while overtly declaring disinterest in power, so do they continue to build up their conjugal unit despite public demonstrations of fear and contempt toward their fertile wives. Further, avoiding a wife

48. E. S. C. Handy, *The Native Culture in the Marquesas* (Honolulu: Bernice P. Bishop Museum, 1923), pp. 35–36.

49. See Ronald P. Rohner and Evelyn C. Rohner, *The Kwakiutl Indians of British Columbia* (New York: Holt, Rinehart and Winston, 1970), pp. 103–05; and Du Bois, *People of Alor*, pp. 121–23.

50. Du Bois, *People of Alor*, p. 150.

during menstruation does not lessen her chances of becoming pregnant since women cannot conceive during menstruation. Although informants occasionally attempt to convince ethnographers (and perhaps even members of their own society) that conception can take place only during menstruation, the most widely held belief cross-culturally is that conception occurs either immediately after menstruation or at some unspecified point in between menstrual periods.

Since adherence to sexual avoidance customs or menstrual restrictions does not prevent a man from continuing to impregnate his wife and build up a faction, these practices cannot solve the dilemma of a wife's continuing fertility. They are token gestures of willingness to fulfill obligations to the larger community. Failure to abide by them may indicate unwillingness to abide by more important social obligations as well.

Customs of menstrual segregation, by leaving a wife unprotected during her menstruation, suggest to other men in the community that her husband is not only disinterested in exploiting her fertility but also disinterested in protecting it from the claims of adulterers. Among the Saramacca, for example, a menstruating wife is sent to a specially built hut at the edge of the village where she is exposed not only to the advances of men in the community but also to all visitors who go by on the path beside which the hut is located.[51] Among the Warrau as well, the menstrual hut is on the outskirts of the village.[52] Although a husband may be able to keep watch on the hut from the village, he still runs the risk that his wife will be seduced or raped by a stranger outside the village who passes by the hut. The Warrau even spread the tale that spirits can go into menstrual huts and take menstruating wives as their own.[53] In other societies, a husband may leave his wife at home and take up residence with kinsmen or club members for a week or more, leaving her just as exposed to adulterers as he would by sending her to a menstrual hut.

The risk of these dramatic gestures of disinterest is somewhat lessened by proclamations about the dire consequences of sex with menstruating women—proclamations which may dissuade some potential adulterers. For example, Ifaluk men are warned of the dangers of either social or sexual contact with a menstruating woman in the hut.[54] Although a woman's husband or son may enter the hut if necessary, entry is prohibited to all other men in the community.

51. Morton Kahn, *Djuka: The Bush Negroes of Dutch Guinea* (New York: Viking Press, 1931), p. 130.
52. María Suárez, *Los Warao* (Caracas: Instituto Venezolano de Investigaciones Científicas, 1968), p. 206.
53. Ibid.
54. Burrows and Spiro, *An Atoll Culture*, p. 290.

Should a man violate this prohibition, he would bring disaster to the entire community through a typhoon or the death of vegetation and fish. All men, including the woman's husband, would fall ill and die if they violated the sex taboo. According to one Ifaluk informant, if a drop of menstrual blood falls on a man, his hair will fall out, he will acquire a perpetual stomach-ache, and he will become insane.

The elaborate male segregation practices of some societies are riskier gestures of disinterest since men in these societies may spend most of their married lives in men's houses, leaving their wives relatively unprotected for long periods of time. While men in most tribal societies show disinterest in the daily activities of wives and spend the day in the company of other men, they are never too far away or too ignorant of their wives' whereabouts to ward off potential adulterers. Moreover, in most societies men and women either share the same dwelling unit or live close in adjacent dwellings, frequently in an enclosed compound. But in societies practicing male segregation, husbands display a total lack of interest in guarding their wives' fertility. The account by Yolanda Murphy and Robert Murphy of marital relations among the Mundurucu, for example, describes a small debate about whether the dwelling of one woman should be referred to as belonging to her or to her husband since he lived in the communal men's house and only made occasional visits to her dwelling.[55] The limited contact between spouses that results from male segregation can result in men's losing claims to their wives, as indicated by the high divorce rates not only among the Mundurucu but among many of the Oceanic societies which practice male segregation. The Murphys state that a Mundurucu woman could expect to be married to two or three different husbands during her reproductive span, and the divorce rates reported for other highly segregated societies in the New Guinea Highlands suggest equally high rates of sequential marriage.[56]

Despite these risks, men are willing to retreat to a sex-segregated dwelling or to place their wives in a prominently located menstrual hut because the ritual gains from such gestures of disinterest exceed the expected loss from the defection of some wives. In the coalition politics of unstable resource societies, things are never as they seem; a man must appear to renounce power in order to claim it and disclaim interest in his wife's offspring in order to possess them. Ritual politics in the world of unstable resource societies depend on neither the ritual surveillance of the strong nor the ritual mobilization of the weak but rather on ritual expressions of disinterest. Sex segre-

55. Yolanda Murphy and Robert F. Murphy, *Women of the Forest* (New York: Columbia University Press, 1974), p. 116.
    56. Ibid., pp. 154–55.

gation practices, like the other ritual practices we have examined, ultimately depend on a society's political economy although our argument emphasizes the intermediate position of unstable resource societies rather than the strong/weak dichotomy on which our earlier analyses were based. The argument is, nevertheless, amenable to the same kinds of empirical tests in our sample of societies even if some additional measures must be constructed.

UNSTABLE RESOURCES, UNSTABLE POLITICS, AND SEGREGATION PRACTICES: AN EMPIRICAL ANALYSIS

Measures

The intensity of female pollution beliefs in a society was measured by the presence or absence of two forms of sexual segregation practices—physical segregation of menstruating women and exclusively male social institutions. "Big man" political dynamics in a society were indicated by the presence or absence of three related political variables: the attainment of positions of leadership through wealth distribution, the importance of individually sponsored ceremonies and distributive exchanges of property at community ceremonies, and the existence of ritualized warfare. Each variable was coded from the ethnographic sources on each sample society listed in Appendix III. These sources are the same ones used to develop all other original measures in this study.

Segregation Practices

The measure of segregation practices used in the statistical analysis combines the scores obtained by each society for each form of segregation. A society obtained a score of 0 if neither menstrual nor male segregation was practiced. If one form of segregation was present, the society received a score of 1; if both forms were present, the society received a score of 2. The measures used for each of the two segregation practices are summarized in Table 13.

Our measure of *menstrual segregation* differs in two important ways from the measures developed by William Stephens and by Frank Young and Albert Bacdayan,[57] which were discussed in Chapter 1. First, instead of arranging menstrual restrictions along a Guttman-type scale, we used a dichotomous measure that distinguished between menstrual segregation customs and other menstrual restrictions. Cooking, personal, and sex taboos were all assigned a

57. William Stephens, "A Cross-Cultural Study of Menstrual Taboos," *Genetic Psychology Monographs* 64 (1961): 385–416, cols. 13, 14; and Frank Young and Albert Bacdayan, "Menstrual Taboos and Social Rigidity," *Ethnology* 4 (1965): 225–40.

TABLE 13. **Measures of Menstrual and Male Sex Segregation Practices**

Custom Category	Percentage (*n*)	Custom Description
Menstrual Segregation[a]		
Menstrual Hut	19.2% (19)	Specially constructed seclusion hut or seclusion camp mentioned.
Structural Segregation	16.2% (16)	Structural isolation: menstruating women isolated from men in special room, hammock, special part of house with separate entrance. Social isolation: must avoid contact with community members.
Total	35.4% (35)	
Cooking, Domestic, Personal Taboos	64.6% (64)	Cooking, domestic, and personal taboos (e.g., special clothing or tattoos), sex taboo; women's menstruation believed unclean and engaged in purification rites.
Male Segregation Practices[b]		
Men's House	12.5% (12)	Communal men's house prohibited to wives and used primarily by married men (not bachelor or warrior houses).
Sex-Segregated Living Units	1.0% (1)	Sleeping and living arrangements of entire community arranged by sex rather than uterine or family units.
Male Clubs	13.5% (13)	Male associations, sweathouses, sex-segregated fraternities, or other secret societies prohibiting women in absence of communal men's houses or segregated living arrangement.
Sacred Objects Only	5.2% (5)	Flutes, bullroarers kept away in special but unspecified place from women.
Total	32.3% (31)	
Minor	67.7% (65)	Informal or formal daily spouse avoidance customs; segregation a consequence of polygyny only; sweathouses or other male structures or societies open to women; general beliefs or legends about female inferiority; segregated ceremonies.

[a]Missing data: Goldi, Iban, Fur, Palauans, Amahuaca, Tupinamba, Lapps, Lamet, Saulteaux.
[b]Missing data: Miskito, Bribri, Amahuaca, Tupinamba, Suku, Luguru, Baiga, Burusho, Goldi, Rhade, Aleut, Tarasco.

score of 0, denoting the absence of segregation practices. (It should be mentioned, however, that thirty-two of the thirty-five societies in our sample that segregated menstruating women also practiced cooking, personal, and sexual restrictions during the segregation period.) Although menstrual restrictions among societies in our sample could have been arranged according to a Guttman-type scale, an empirical test of our theory required only that we distinguish between practices that segregate women from the community and those that do not since segregation is the only type of menstrual restriction that is public. Second, we used a broader measure of menstrual segregation. A score of 1 was assigned not only to societies with menstrual huts but to those with other practices that entail the physical segregation of menstruating women from the community.

When our ethnographic sources gave ambiguous information about the possibility of segregation, as through references to menstruating women sleeping on sleeping benches or near the fire, these references were not considered to indicate physical segregation. Unless other menstrual practices were also described, these ambiguous cases were assigned a missing data code and excluded from the analysis. When our sources indicated that husband and wife lived in the same room during menstruation but slept in separate areas (as among the Thonga), the society was given a score of 0, as were polygynous societies in which husbands simply refrained from visiting the dwelling units of menstruating wives.

Of the ninety-nine societies in our sample on which information about menstrual practices could be obtained, 64.6 percent did not practice menstrual segregation. The remaining 35.4 percent did segregate menstruating women: in 19.2 percent of the societies, they were secluded in specially built menstrual huts; in 16.2 percent, either menstruating women were prohibited from leaving their dwelling, hammock, or special part of the household, or their social activities were restricted to such an extent that the women were clearly physically isolated. Intercoder reliability for our dichotomous measure was .78, with the major source of error being differences in scoring of restrictions on menstruating women's social contacts.

Our measure of *male segregation* is also dichotomous. We scored male segregation as present if a society had at least one of the following exclusively male social institutions:

1. Community men's houses prohibited to women and used primarily by adult males. In some societies, prostitutes or nubile lovers were permitted to enter the men's house, but unless other women were also allowed, these groups received a score of 1. Bachelors' quarters, warrior houses, and quarters for political council meetings were not classified as men's houses.

2. Exclusively male clubs, sweathouses, secret societies, or other fraternal organizations. Frequently, females in the same society formed similar clubs or sweathouses for their own use. Men's houses, clubs, and secret societies were often associated with cults in which an ideology of female pollution was central, and the men's house or meeting place often contained ritual objects believed to be vulnerable to female pollution. When our ethnographic sources showed that a society had sweathouses but did not indicate whether they were for men only or not, we obtained that information from the Cultural Elements Distribution Codes.[58]

3. Sacred objects, such as flutes or bullroarers, kept in a special place (whether specified or not) so that women could not see or touch them. In keeping with Robert Murphy's analysis of the significance of these objects as signs of sex antagonism,[59] societies that have them were scored as practicing male segregation. If the objects were not considered pollutable by women at the time the authors of our ethnographic sources did their fieldwork, as in many groups they were not, the group was not scored as practicing male segregation.

4. Sexually segregated living arrangements. In one case, all males, married and unmarried, lived in one section of a longhouse, and all females lived in another. This group was scored as practicing segregation.

Not coded as indicating male segregation were domestic sex segregation practices such as daily spouse-avoidance customs, the segregation of wives in separate dwellings when it resulted from the practice of polygyny, the existence of sweathouses used by both sexes, or general beliefs or legends about women's pollution and social inferiority. Societies with such practices were scored 0, as were societies in which women were not allowed to participate in certain community ceremonies.

As Table 13 shows, of the ninety-six societies about which there was adequate information on male segregation practices, 32.3 percent had one or more of the institutions that we have coded as male segregation and 67.7 percent did not. Communal men's houses were present in 12.5 percent of the societies; in a substantial proportion of these cases, the men's houses contained sacred objects that could be contaminated by women, and members perpetuated legends about female pollution. An additional 13.5 percent of the societies had exclusively male associations or sweathouses, and 5.2 percent had

58. See references to Cultural Elements Distribution Codes in Alfred E. Kroeber's "Culture Elements Distribution. 11. Tribes Surveyed," *University of California, Anthropological Records* 2 (1940): 438–40.

59. Robert F. Murphy, "Social Structure and Sex Antagonism," *Southwestern Journal of Anthropology* 15 (1959): 89–98.

sacred objects that were clearly believed to be vulnerable to female pollution, although the place they were hidden was not specified by the ethnographers. Only one society practiced community-wide sex-segregated living arrangements.

The relationship between menstrual segregation, male segregation, and the *combined segregation index* is described in the correlation matrix in Table 14. After the effects of historical diffusion are taken into account, the correlation between menstrual segregation and male segregation practices is not large but positive and statistically significant ($r=.31$, $p<.01$). Of the ninety societies on which there was information about both forms of segregation, 31.1 percent practice either menstrual segregation or male segregation and 18.9 percent practice both forms. The two types of segregation practices contribute almost equally to the total segregation index, with menstrual segregation correlated .82 with the index and male segregation practices correlated .80.

Unstable Political Power

A summary index of unstable political power in a society was developed by adding together the scores on each of three critical measures: (1) the ability to acquire positions of political leadership through wealth distribution, (2) developing and maintaining a political faction through social indebtedness, and (3) ritualized warfare. The index arranges societies along a four-point scale so that each society's score depends on the number of characteristics indicating unstable political power that are present. Of the 108 societies in the sample, eighty-eight contained codable information on all three indicators comprising the index.

The measure of *achieved leadership through wealth distribution* was an attempt to quantify Sahlins' definition of the process by which males become "big men" in a society. We distinguished between societies in which men became political leaders by developing political coalitions primarily through wealth distribution (feasts, giveaways, loans) and societies in which men became leaders through inheritance or through personal skills such as arbitration or hunting ability. In societies with leadership through inheritance or personal skills other than wealth manipulation, leaders might distribute wealth but did not achieve and maintain their position by distributing wealth. In societies with leadership through wealth distribution, a leader's political power fluctuated with his ability to distribute wealth. Societies with achieved leadership through wealth distribution were assigned a score of 1 on this measure. Societies with leadership through other personal skills or through inheritance were scored 0. A detailed description of this code is given in Appendix I.

According to Sahlins, one of the primary tactics by which "big men" mobilize a coalition is by creating *social indebtedness* through the sponsorship of large feasts, potlatches, and other community ceremonies. Although men may create indebtedness in other ways as well, as by making loans, the sponsorship of large feasts and ceremonial exchanges of goods is the most characteristic strategy and the most reliable measure of social indebtedness in a society. The creation and maintenance of political coalitions through social indebtedness was measured by the combination of two codes already developed by Murdock and Wilson.[60] One code described the most prominent ceremonial activity in a society: calendrical (determined by economic cycles, ritual calendars, or astronomical observations), rites of passage, magical or religious rites, or individually sponsored feasts such as potlatches. The second code described six dominant elements of any community-wide ceremonies: cannibalism and other ceremonial killings, distribution and exchange of property other than food, music and dancing, nonhuman sacrifices, and self-torture or comparable masochistic behavior. If either individually sponsored rites or the distribution of property at community-wide celebrations was coded as dominant, social indebtedness was considered a dominant characteristic of the political community. Rites sponsored by individuals rather than by groups or by the community as a whole can be interpreted as an implicit mechanism for creating social indebtedness since the individual host provides entertainment, food, and perhaps gifts for many guests who have no immediate opportunity to reciprocate. Community-wide ceremonies in which property distribution is the dominant element also create social indebtedness, at least on those occasions when the exchanges between individuals are unequal. Both kinds of ceremonies provide opportunities for a leader to mobilize a political coalition through demonstrations of generosity, power, and wealth while simultaneously allowing him to gauge the current and potential strength of his coalition by observing which and how many males participate in the ceremonies.

A second implicit tactic by which men may mobilize and monitor a political coalition is through *ritual warfare*. The behavior of community members at cannibalistic feasts may involve eating the enemies of a leader or potential leader, and headhunting expeditions or wars may involve scalping a leader's enemies or taking other body parts for display as trophies. Although many societies engaged in more than one form of ritual war, the presence of ritual war was scored as 1 if at least one form was practiced: cannibalism, headhunt-

60. George P. Murdock and Suzanne F. Wilson, "Settlement Patterns and Community Organization: Cross-Cultural Codes 3," *Ethnology* 11 (1972): 254–95.

ing, scalping, or taking other body parts as trophies. All these practices had to involve public display to be counted as ritual war. Therefore, placing body parts outside one's own dwelling or wearing them on the body was counted as ritual war as well as the eating of human flesh in public view. The cannibalism codes developed by Murdock and Wilson could not be used because they do not distinguish between cannibalism and other forms of ritual human killings that may not involve enemies. Eating of a child who died at birth or in early infancy was not counted as cannibalism, nor was the eating of close kinsmen who died in battle or by natural causes. Cannibalism involving community members, such as in-marrying wives or husbands, was scored as ritual war if the ethnographic data made clear that it was a consequence of intracommunity feuding or an act of vengeance against the person's own kinsmen residing elsewhere.

The matrix in Table 14 gives the correlations between each of our three indicators of unstable political power and the correlation of each indicator with the total index of unstable political power. Achieved leadership is significantly associated with both the measure of social indebtedness ($r=.45$) and with the measure of ritual war ($r=.49$), even after the effects of historical diffusion are taken into account. Although these two ritual mechanisms by which political leaders and aspiring leaders may mobilize and assess coalitions are significantly associated with each other ($r=.21$), the correlation is not as high as is the association of each mechanism with achieved leadership. This suggests that ritual war and social indebtedness through feasting and property distribution, in many societies, are alternative mechanisms for building a political career. Of the forty-four societies on which ethnographic data indicated that one or both mechanisms were present, ten (22.7 percent) practiced both forms. Inspection of the correlations of all three indicators with the total index shows that the measure of achieved leadership makes the largest contribution to the total index, followed by ritual war and social indebtedness. All correlations, however, are large and statistically significant after the effects of diffusion are taken into account.

Results

The intercorrelations between unstable economic resources, unstable political power, and segregation practices offer strong empirical support for our theory. The index of unstable political power is correlated .68 with unstable economic resource base, a figure which is statistically significant at the .001 level after the effects of diffusion are controlled. The combined index of segregation practices is correlated .57 with unstable economic resources and .49 with the unstable politi-

TABLE 14. **Correlates of Elaborate Segregation Practices**

Variable	2	3	4	5	6	7	8
1. Unstable Economic Base	.68[c]	.65[c]	.36[c]	.51[c]	.44[c]	.52[c]	.57[c]
2. Unstable Political Power Index		.85[c]	.70[c]	.77[c]	.36[b]	.44[c]	.49[c]
3. Achieved Leadership			.45[c]	.49[c]	.28[a]	.32[a]	.39[b]
4. Social Indebtedness				.21[a]	.20[a]	.31[b]	.29[b]
5. Ritual War					.29[a]	.42[c]	.44[c]
6. Menstrual Segregation						.31[a]	.82[c]
7. Male Segregation Practices							.80[c]
8. Combined Segregation Index							

[a] $p<.05$.
[b] $p<.01$.
[c] $p<.001$.

cal power index. Both correlations are significant at the .001 level after the effects of diffusion are taken into account. The matrix also shows that both unstable economic resources and unstable political power are somewhat more highly correlated with male segregation practices than with menstrual segregation, although the correlations with both components of the segregation index are large and statistically significant. Menstrual segregation is correlated .44 with unstable economic resources and .36 with unstable political power, while male segregation practices are correlated .52 with unstable economic resources and .44 with unstable political power.

If segregation practices are more likely to occur in societies with unstable economic resources because of the effects of unstable resources on the society's internal political dynamics, as we hypothesize, then the correlations between unstable economic resources and segregation practices reported in the matrix should be accounted for to a large extent by their common association with unstable political power. Again, the power of the intervening variable in the model is shown by the size of the reduction in the amount of variance in segregation practices explained by unstable economic resources when the political variable is held constant. The correlation between the economic variable and the combined segregation index is reduced substantially from .57 to .37 when the effects of the political variable are held constant. That is, there is more than a twofold reduction in the amount of variance in segregation practices explained by economic resources when the effects of unstable political power are held constant (a reduction in explained variance from 32.5 percent to 14 percent). Clearly, the observed association between unstable economic resources and the combined segregation index is largely due to the relationship of both variables to unstable political power. These results confirm our hypothesis that segregation practices are a ritual response to the particularly acute dilemma of a wife's continuing fertility in unstable societies, in which a husband must simultaneously display his power in order to enhance and maintain it and disclaim his power to keep from alienating affines, consanguineal kin, and the community as a whole.

The importance of unstable political power as the critical link between economics and ritual is clear when each segregation practice is considered separately. The observed association between unstable economic resources and menstrual segregation is .44 so that 19.4 percent of the variance in menstrual segregation seems to be explained by economics alone. Both variables are highly correlated with unstable political power; partialing out the effects of the political variable reduces the variance in menstrual segregation explained by economics to 7.7 percent, more than a twofold reduction. The results are the same when male forms of sexual segregation are considered: a substantial reduction in explained variance when the effects of the political variable are partialed out. The amount of variance in male segregation practices explained by unstable economic resources is only 11.3 percent when the role of unstable political power is ignored, suggesting that the substantial proportion of the observed variance explained by economics (27 percent) is due to the strong association of politics with both the independent and the dependent variable.

Our two-step model explains 35 percent of the variance in the combined segregation practices, 20 percent of the variance in menstrual segregation, and 28.8 percent of the variance in male segregation, when the multiple R^2 is calculated in those cases for which there were data on all three variables in the model.

Alternative Explanations

Both the psychoanalytic and the structural perspectives on reproductive rituals have proposed testable hypotheses about the causes of worldwide variation in segregation practices. Empirical support for the psychoanalytic theory is provided by Stephens, who argues that menstrual restrictions are a ritual consequence of male castration fears, which vary in intensity depending on patterns of childrearing practices.[61] Theorists within the structuralist tradition have proposed that both menstrual restrictions and male segregation practices symbolize the sexual tension produced by exogamous marriage practices although the theories are based on the behavior of individuals in single cultural areas or descent systems. M. J. Meggitt, for example, suggests that the practice of marrying women from hos-

61 Stephens, "Menstrual Taboos."

tile groups, as among some Oceanic patrilineal societies, is the critical cause whereas M. R. Allen suggests that it is the combination of uni-local residence and unilineal descent.[62] Murphy stresses the impor-tance of a "separate but equal" sexual division of labor in a society, arguing that the control over resources by a solidary female work group poses a threat to male authority. This male dominance hy-pothesis is similar to those proposed by Mary Douglas and Alice Schlegal.[63]

Psychoanalytic Theory: Castration Anxiety

The most convincing evidence for a psychoanalytic inter-pretation of segregation practices is William Stephens' attempt to demonstrate an empirical association between elaborate menstrual restrictions and measures of the intensity of castration anxiety in a sample of seventy-one world societies. If ritual restrictions imposed on menstruating women are mechanisms by which men attempt to control unconscious castration fears exacerbated by the periodic appearance of female genital bleeding, then the more intense the castration anxiety among men, the more elaborate the menstrual restrictions should be. Since psychological states (such as the level of castration anxiety) cannot be measured directly in cross-cultural sur-vey research, Stephens uses an indirect measure based on a positive association between the childrearing patterns most likely to create in-tense castration anxiety and the elaborateness of menstrual restrictions.

Stephens measured the elaborateness of menstrual restrictions by a five-item Guttman scale, with the presence of menstrual huts being the most elaborate restriction followed (in descending order) by cooking taboos, "other" taboos, the belief that menstruating women are dangerous to men, and the sex taboo; the absence of any men-strual taboos represents the low end of the scale. Since Stephens was interested not only in testing his castration-anxiety hypothesis but in distinguishing among a variety of taboos and beliefs about menstruating women, he used a five-item scale rather than a di-chotomous measure like ours, but the two measures are assessing similar practices nonetheless. In fact, the correlation between the two indices is .804 when Stephens' scale is dichotomized into the pres-ence or absence of huts, even though he does not code segregation in the absence of huts, as we do.

62. M. J. Meggitt, "Male-Female Relationships in the Highlands of Australian New Guinea," in *Cultures of the Pacific*, ed. Thomas G. Harding and Ben J. Wallace (New York: Free Press, 1970), pp. 125–43; and H. R. Allen, *Male Cults and Secret Initiations in Melanesia* (Victoria: Melbourne University Press, 1967).
63. Murphy, "Sex Antagonism"; Mary Douglas, *Purity and Danger* (London: Pelican, 1966); and Alice Schlegal, *Male Dominance and Female Autonomy* (New Haven: HRAF Press, 1972).

Stephens' independent variable measures childrearing practices that most nearly reflect the conditions which, according to psychoanalytic theory, determine the intensity of male castration anxiety, such as the degree of sexual arousal of the child by the mother (indicated empirically by the length of the postpartum sex taboo), diffusion of nurturance, punishment for a child's sexual activity, and the nature and severity of punishment for rivalrous behavior of the child toward the father (as measured by severity of aggression training, obedience training, and severity of punishment for disobedience, strictness of father's obedience demands, and whether or not father is the main disciplinarian). Most of these measures of psychodynamically relevant childrearing practices had been devised by Whiting and his colleagues for use in related research. Stephens combines these ten indicators and gives each society an average score ranging from +4 to −4 along a bipolar scale. Given the substantial amount of missing data on many of the items in the index, only societies with information on at least six of the ten items were used in his analysis, thereby reducing the effective sample size to fifty-five cases. Using a nonparametric test of association between his castration-anxiety index and the menstrual taboo scale, Stephens concludes that, as he hypothesized, the childrearing conditions determining the intensity of castration anxiety are a powerful predictor of the extensiveness of menstrual taboos (rho=.53, p<.000001). This powerful statistical association suggests that the childrearing index could provide a social-psychological linkage between the structural conditions of a society and ritual practices, and an important competing explanation for at least one form of segregation practice in world societies.

There are serious logical and methodological problems with Stephens' study, however: in particular, the construct validity of his independent variable, the method by which he produced a statistical relationship, and sampling bias. Each will be examined below by reanalyzing the relationships in Stephens' sample and those in our own sample.

First, if his childrearing index measures conditions determining the intensity of male castration fears, then not only should it predict genital mutilations, as Whiting and Freud himself have postulated, but it should also be associated with the other antecedent conditions, which, according to Whiting, produce variations in the intensity of the Oedipal complex, specifically polygyny, patrilocal residence, and exclusive mother-child sleeping arrangements. The extent to which Stephens' index was associated with each of these variables in his own sample was examined by simply recomputing the mean score on his index for each society and comparing the differences between means among societies with and without genital mutilations, polygyny, patrilocality, and exclusive mother-child sleeping arrangements. Before this and subsequent analyses on Stephens' data were carried out, however, one item in his index—the overall severity of sex training—was eliminated. An item in this subscale also appears as a single item in the overall index (severity of punishment for masturbation) so that this item is given greater weight in the overall index than each of the others. (Since Stephens does not weigh differentially each of the items in the index, a better estimate of the association of the index with other variables should eliminate repeated items.) We chose to eliminate the overall sex training severity item rather than the punishment item because it produced a lower association with the menstrual restriction scale, and to retain the item that favored Stephens' argument.

Comparing the mean differences in castration-anxiety-producing childrearing practices between societies with and without genital mutilations, polygyny, patrilocal residence, and exclusive mother-child sleeping arrangements produced no statistically significant differences. Societies in which exclusive mother-child sleeping arrangements were present scored only slightly lower on the castration index (M=.471) than those without exclusive sleeping arrangements (M=.524). Similarly, societies with patrilocality scored nonsignificantly higher, on the average, on the castration-anxiety-producing index than nonpatrilocal ones (M=.483 versus M=.481), and societies with polygynous marriages scored nonsignificantly higher on the index than those without polygyny (M=.545 versus M=.416). These measures of Oedipal-producing conditions developed by Whiting and associates do have a modest association with other ritual practices (male genital mutilations), but they do not correlate with menstrual taboos. Neither Stephens' independent variable nor his dependent variable correlates with the preconditions measured by the Whiting school.

A second problem with Stephens' study is the biased sample of world societies upon which he based his analysis. As Table 15 indicates, the sample upon which Stephens bases his empirical analysis is not an adequate representation of world regions when his proportions are compared with the recent SCCS. It overrepresents Africa, the Insular Pacific, and North America and underrepresents the Circum-Mediterranean, East Eurasia, and South America. Therefore, to compare the relative power of Stephens' theory of menstrual taboos and our own theory, we first corrected his data to reduce the effects of sampling bias on his correlations. We then compared the new correlations between childrearing practices and menstrual restrictions produced by Stephens' weighted sample with our own correlations between unstable economic base, politics, and menstrual segregation.

TABLE 15. **Proportional Distribution of Societies in Stephens' Sample ($n=71$) across World Regions Compared with SCCS (percentages)**

	SCCS	Stephens	Differences in Regional Representation
Africa	15	19.4	+4.4
Circum-Mediterranean	15	1.4	−13.6
East Eurasia	18	13.9	−4.1
Insular Pacific	17	29.2	+12.2
North America	18	26.4	+8.4
South America	17	9.7	−7.3

The procedure used to weight Stephens' scores on both his independent and dependent variables was as follows. Scores on each of the societies within each of the six world regions were weighted according to the extent that that region was over- or underrepresented in the Stephens sample. The numerical weight then was derived by dividing the proportion of societies in a world region included in the Stephens sample by the proportion of societies in that region contained in the SCCS. For example, all scores on African societies in Stephens' sample were given a weight of 1.29, which was produced by dividing 19.4 percent (the proportion of African societies in Stephens' sample) by 15 percent (proportion in SCCS).

The original correlation produced between Stephens' index of castration-anxiety-producing childrearing practices (minus one item) and the dichotomized measure of menstrual restrictions was .31, which is statistically significant after the effects of diffusion are taken into account. When his variables were weighted to correct for sample bias, however, this correlation was reduced to .17, which is not statistically significant. Comparing this relationship with our own multiple correlation between unstable economic base, politics, and menstrual segregation demonstrates that Stephens' theory accounts for only 3 percent of the variability in menstrual segregation whereas our theory accounts for 20 percent. Our model, then, is a substantial improvement over Stephens'. If male segregation practices are interpreted as expressions of the same cultural beliefs as menstrual restrictions, then our model is a vast improvement over Stephens' model, explaining 35 percent of the variance in both forms of segregation.

A full examination of the possible effects of each major indicator of Oedipal-related childrearing practices included in the complete Whiting model was carried out on our own study sample, with the results reported in Table 16. None of the antecedent variables in the Whiting model (patrilocality, polygyny, postpartum taboo, and exclusive mother-child sleeping arrangements) is significantly associated with our combined measure of segregation practices or with either of

TABLE 16. Correlations between Segregation Practices and Indices of Castration Anxiety

Segregation Practices	Patrilocality	Polygyny	Postpartum Sex Taboo[a]	Circumcision	Exclusive Mother-Child Sleeping Arrangements
Menstrual Segregation	−.22	−.01	−.09	−.34[b]	−.16
Male Segregation	−.10	+.01	+.12	−.35[b]	+.01
Combined Segregation Practices	−.17	−.02	+.02	−.43[b]	−.11

[a]As measured by the Barry and Paxton seven-point scale.
[b]p<.01 after correcting for effects of diffusion.

its two components. In fact, most of the correlations are negative rather than positive. Equally interesting are the strong negative correlations between segregation practices and Whiting's crucial indicator of castration anxiety, circumcision. After the effects of diffusion have been taken into account, circumcision is significantly negatively associated with menstrual segregation ($r = -.34$), male segregation practices ($r = -.35$), and the combined segregation index ($r = -.43$). This indicates, as we would predict, that circumcision and segregation practices tend not to occur in the same societies: the opposite result from what a psychoanalytic theory of Oedipally derived rituals would predict. If segregation practices and circumcision both reflect unconscious anxieties about castration, then the two sets of rituals should be positively associated. Segregation practices, like male circumcision, are therefore not adequately explained within the modified Freudian framework originally proposed by Whiting.

Structural Theories

The hypotheses proposed by Meggitt and Allen need not apply only to the Oceanic societies to which their theories were directed but could also apply to world societies generally. Specifically, the extent to which exogamous marriage practices, intensity of internal war and feuding, unilocal residence, and unilineal descent explain segregation practices measured here may be tested on our study sample.

According to Meggitt's theory, a combination of patrilineal descent, exogamous marriage practices, and internal war should lead to expressions of sexual pollution beliefs.[64] If our measures of menstrual segregation and male segregation practices can be interpreted as indicating intense pollution beliefs, then according to Meggitt's theory they should be most common among societies in which all three antecedent conditions occur. In order to test the Meggitt hypothesis, the ethnographic data on our sample societies were coded for the presence or absence of internal wars and feuds. Internal wars and feuds were distinguished from other forms of war and aggression on the bases of the anthropological literature on tribal warfare.[65] Marriage

64. Meggitt, "Male-Female Relationships."

65. Cross-cultural studies of feuds, warfare, and mechanisms for minimizing internal conflict that were helpful in distinguishing internal war and feuds from other forms of violence were those by Keith F. Otterbein and Charlotte Swanson Otterbein, "An Eye for an Eye, a Tooth for a Tooth: A Cross-Cultural Study," *American Anthropologist* 67 (1965): 1470–82; Keith F. Otterbein, "Internal War: A Cross-Cultural Study," *American Anthropologist* 70 (1968): 277–89; Elbert W. Russell, "Factors of Human Aggression: A Cross-Cultural Factor Analysis of Characteristics Related to Warfare and Crime," *Behavior Science Notes* 4 (1972): 275–312; John W. M. Whiting, "Sorcery, Sin, and the Superego: A Cross-Cultural Study of Some Mechanisms of Social Control," in *Nebraska Symposium on Motivation*, ed. M. R. Jones (Lincoln: University of Nebraska Press, 1959), pp. 174–97; and Robert F. Murphy, "Intergroup Hostility and Social Cohesion," *American Anthropologist* 59 (1957): 1018–35.

practices were coded according to the codes given each sample society by Murdock and Wilson, or Murdock.[66] Societies considered both
"strictly" and "predominantly" exogamous according to these codes
formed a combined measure of the presence of exogamous marriage
practices; all other intercommunity marriage practices were coded as
exogamy "absent." The measure of patrilineal descent is the same one
used throughout this study.[67]

Table 17 presents the proportional distribution of the combined
index across each marriage and warfare combination among both patrilineal and nonpatrilineal societies. If Meggitt's theory about Oceania
applied to world societies, it would be expected that segregation practices would be significantly more likely in societies in which all three
antecedent conditions were present. Inspection of the table, however,
indicates quite a different pattern. In fact, societies that practice both
patrilineal descent and exogamy, regardless of internal warfare incidence, tend *not* to have elaborate segregation practices; societies that
practice other combinations of variables do tend to practice segregation. When the relations between each antecedent variable and segregation practices are examined separately, again there is no support for
the Meggitt hypothesis. Segregation practices are present among 42.4
percent of patrilineal societies and 69.2 percent of nonpatrilineal
societies, a trend that is the reverse of that proposed by Meggitt. Similarly, segregation practices are more likely to be present in nonexogamous societies (73.3 percent) than in exogamous ones (42.5
percent). Finally, 53.7 percent of the societies with internal war have
segregation practices, a figure only slightly less than the 67.7 percent
of societies without internal war. In short, Meggitt's explanation of
the conditions producing segregation practices for a single cultural
area does not hold up when tested on a world sample.

Allen's modification of Meggitt's thesis was also tested and the
results are presented in Table 18. Allen hypothesized that a combination of unilocal residence and unilineal descent was the primary
exogenous feature in explaining segregation practices, specifically
male segregation. Therefore we compared the proportional distribution of our combined segregation index among each combination of
warfare and marriage conditions among societies with and without
this descent-residence combination. We have already shown that
neither warfare alone nor exogamy alone produces the pattern proposed in the "Oceanic" version of the structural-functional model. As
the data in the table indicate, replacing Meggitt's causal variable with
Allen's does not improve matters. Among unilocal-unilineal societies

66. Murdock and Wilson, "Settlement Patterns," p. 262; and George P. Murdock,
Ethnographic Atlas (Pittsburgh: University of Pittsburgh Press, 1967), p. 48, col. 19.
67. Murdock and Wilson, "Settlement Patterns," pp. 261–62, col. 16.

TABLE 17. Relationship between Exogamy, Internal Warfare, and Combined Segregation Practices in Patrilineal and Nonpatrilineal Societies[a]

Combined Segregation Practices	Patrilineal Descent				Nonpatrilineal Descent			
	Exogamous Marriage Practices				Exogamous Marriage Practices			
	Present		Absent		Present		Absent	
	Internal Warfare		Internal Warfare		Internal Warfare		Internal Warfare	
	Present	Absent	Present	Absent	Present	Absent	Present	Absent
Present	17.6% (3)	00.0% (0)	80.0% (8)	75.0% (3)	77.8% (7)	58.3% (7)	61.1% (11)	84.6% (11)
Absent	82.4% (14)	100.0% (2)	20.0% (2)	25.0% (1)	22.2% (2)	41.7% (5)	38.9% (7)	15.4% (2)
Total	100.0% (17)	100.0% (2)	100.0% (10)	100.0% (4)	100.0% (9)	100.0% (12)	100.0% (18)	100.0% (13)

[a]There were twenty-three societies without information on combined segregation practices or internal warfare.

TABLE 18. **Relationship between Exogamy, Internal Warfare, and Combined Segregation Practices in Societies with and without a Unilineal Descent-Unilocal Residence Combination**[a]

Combined Segregation Practices	Unilineal-Unilocal Combination Present				Unilineal-Unilocal Combination Absent			
	Exogamy Present		Exogamy Absent		Exogamy Present		Exogamy Absent	
	Internal Warfare		Internal Warfare		Internal Warfare		Internal Warfare	
	Present	Absent	Present	Absent	Present	Absent	Present	Absent
Present	23.5% (4)	50.0% (2)	40.0% (6)	100.0% (6)	75.0% (6)	45.5% (5)	57.1% (8)	70.0% (7)
Absent	76.5% (13)	50.0% (2)	60.0% (9)	00.0% (0)	25.0% (2)	54.5% (6)	42.9% (6)	30.0% (3)
Total	100.0% (17)	100.0% (4)	100.0% (15)	100.0% (6)	100.0% (8)	100.0% (11)	100.0% (14)	100.0% (10)

[a]There were twenty-three societies without information on combined segregation practices or internal warfare.

the results again show just the opposite trend from that hypothesized. Among these societies, the presence of exogamy and warfare is *less* likely to produce segregation practices than is their absence. Among unilocal-unilineal societies, regardless of the presence or absence of exogamy, segregation practices are *less* likely in the presence of internal warfare than in its absence although these differences are not statistically significant. Only in the *absence* of the unilocal-unilineal structural conditions is there an interesting but perplexing trend: in the presence of exogamy, internal warfare increases the likelihood of segregation practices. Among societies with the unilocal-unilineal condition absent, 75 percent of the societies with both exogamy and internal warfare have segregation practices, compared with 45.5 percent of societies with exogamy but without internal warfare. These proportions, however, are not significant given the small number of cases in each cell. In the absence of exogamy, the presence or absence of internal war does not predict segregation practices. When the effects of descent-residence combination alone on segregation practices are inspected, the results show that 42.9 percent of the unilocal-unilineal societies have the extreme forms of segregation practices coded in our study sample, compared with 60.5 percent of societies with all other residence-descent combinations.

These tests of the Meggitt and Allen hypotheses demonstrate the superiority of our own theory of world patterns of segregation practices. The most elaborate forms of segregation practices of both sexes are better accounted for empirically by considering the internal political dynamics of a society produced by the economic resource base.

Two "male dominance" theories of segregation practices can also be tested on a world sample. Each of these argues that pollution beliefs and their ritual expressions reflect male concern with curbing female social power.

Murphy argues that a critical structural condition producing a threat to male dominance and therefore an intense concern with female pollution is the sexual division of subsistence labor in a society.[68] Subsistence economies that require the daily cooperation of men and women, but whose activities create sex-segregated work groups, facilitate the development of female sociopolitical power. This hypothesis can be tested on our study sample by using Murdock's published codes for the sexual division of economic labor for each society[69] and inspecting the ability of this variable to account for world patterns of segregation practices.

68. Murphy, "Sex Antagonism."
69. Murdock, *Ethnographic Atlas*, pp. 54–55, cols. 42–62.

Murdock provides codes of a sexual division of economic labor similar to that which Murphy argues leads to sexual antagonism. For each of five subsistence activities, Murdock specifies whether the activity was done completely or primarily by one sex, by both sexes working equally on some activity but on separate tasks, or by both sexes working together on each task. Sex-segregated work groups were considered present if 50 percent or more of all subsistence activities in a society were carried out exclusively or predominantly by one sex or the other or if 50 percent or more of the activities were performed by both sexes working at separate tasks. We chose 50 percent as the critical cutoff point for two reasons. First, in nearly all the societies in the sample, sex-exclusive work groups carry out some proportion of subsistence activities. Therefore, there is no worldwide variation although a substantial number of societies lack sex-exclusive work groups carrying out a *majority* (50 percent or more) of the subsistence activities. Second, a 50 percent cutoff point is theoretically meaningful because the presence of sex-exclusive work groups carrying out a majority of the subsistence activities best measures the possibility of women's forming potentially powerful political units based on their daily association in work—a possibility that Murphy argues leads to sex antagonism. There is virtually no difference in the segregation practices among societies with and without sex-exclusive work groups performing a majority of subsistence tasks. Even the construction of alternative measures of subsistence groups did not produce differences in segregation practices (that is, raising the cutoff point to 70 percent and 100 percent or considering only the impact of having exclusively female groups performing 50 percent or more of the subsistence chores).

Alice Schlegal's tabular data on the relationship between husband and brother dominance and menstrual restrictions in a sample of sixty-six matrilineal societies was described in Chapter 1.[70] Schlegal's theory proposed that in matrilineal societies, women's social status (of which one measure is the severity of menstrual taboos) should be greatest when marriage patterns prevent either her in-marrying husband or her kinsmen (classificatory brothers) from becoming dominant. The measure of male dominance was preferred cousin marriage, with matrilateral cross-cousin marriage increasing husband dominance, and patrilateral cross-cousin marriage increasing the authority of lineage brothers and minimizing the husband's dominance. Mixed or random marriage preferences reduce the likelihood of either husbands or brothers becoming dominant.

70. Schlegal, *Male Dominance.*

TABLE **19.** Relationship between Husband or Brother Dominance and Menstrual Restrictions in Schlegal's Sample

Schlegal's Distribution (axes reversed)			
Menstrual Restrictions	Husband Dominant	Neither	Brother Dominant
Seclusion	5	6	7
Cooking	5	1	2
Other	4	3	2
Sex	5	1	3
Total	19	11	14

	Reanalysis	
Menstrual Segregation	Husband Dominance Present	Husband Dominance Absent
Present	26.3%	52.0%
	(5)	(13)
Absent	73.7%	48.0%
	(14)	(12)
Total	100.0%	100.0%
	(19)	(25)

$r=.26$, $\phi^2=.06$, $p<.06$.

Table 19 compares Schlegal's original distribution of menstrual restrictions when either the husband or brother is likely to be dominant and when neither is dominant. The second part of the table examines the probability of menstrual segregation being present or absent in societies in which husband dominance is present or absent. These data show some relationship between menstrual segregation and husband dominance.

We then tested the hypothesis that the presence of husband dominance (as indicated by matrilateral cross-cousin marriage preference) may mediate the effects of an unstable economic base on the segregation practices of both sexes rather than our measure of unstable political power although the low association between husband dominance and menstrual segregation suggests that this variable alone is not as powerful as our own model. Empirical tests were conducted only on matrilineal societies that appeared both in our study sample and in Schlegal's because we had not coded cousin marriage in our sample. The results of the analyses thus apply most specifically to matrilineal societies.

As Table 20 shows, there is a statistically significant relationship between husband dominance and unstable economic base in the matrilineal sample. Husband dominance is present in 77.7 percent of the societies with an unstable resource base but in only 43.2 percent of the societies without unstable resources. The phi coefficient produced by

TABLE 20. **Relationship between Husband Dominance and Unstable Economic Resources in Shared Sample of Societies.**

Husband Dominance	Unstable Economic Resources	
	Present	Absent
Present	77.8% (21)	43.2% (16)
Absent	22.2% (6)	56.8% (21)
Total	100.0% (27)	100.0% (37)

$X^2 = 7.63$, $r = .345$, $\phi^2 = .119$, $p < .01$.

TABLE 21. **Relationship between Segregation Practices and Unstable Economic Resources in Matrilineal Societies Shared by Schlegal and Current Study Sample**

Segregation Practices	Unstable Economic Resources	
	Present	Absent
Menstrual Segregation[a]		
Present	72.7% (8)	25.0% (2)
Absent	27.3% (3)	75.0% (8)
Total	100.0% (11)	100.0% (10)
Male Segregation Practices[b]		
Present	63.6% (7)	25.0% (2)
Absent	36.4% (4)	75.0% (6)
Total	100.0% (11)	100.0% (8)
Combined Segregation Practices[c]		
Present	91.7% (11)	28.6% (2)
Absent	8.3% (1)	71.4% (5)
Total	100.0% (12)	100.0% (7)

[a] $X^2 = 5.84$, $\phi = .53$, $p < .02$.
[b] $X^2 = 2.77$, $\phi = .38$, $p < .10$.
[c] $X^2 = 8.15$, $\phi = .66$, $p < .01$.

this distribution is .345, indicating that among matrilineal societies nearly 12 percent of the variance in marriage practices producing husband dominance is accounted for by the presence of an unstable economic base. Table 21 shows that, among matrilineal societies, each of our segregation indices is strongly associated with unstable economic resources. In fact, the associations between the economic variable and menstrual segregation and the combined index are stronger for this matrilineal sample than for our complete sample although the association between economics and male segregation is lower.

These results show that although husband dominance is negatively associated with one form of segregation—menstrual segregation—among matrilineal societies, unstable economic resources is *positively* associated with husband dominance, as well as with each of our measures of segregation practices. The results presented in Table 22, then, should not be surprising: among matrilineal societies with unstable economic resources, there is no relationship between husband dominance and segregation practices. Husband dominance, then, is an unlikely mediator between economy and segregation practices.

These tests of the major alternative explanations of elaborate menstrual and male forms of sexual segregation seem to confirm the superiority of our own model. The critical test of a psychoanalytic explanation for these practices—the practice of circumcision in association with segregation practices—produced strong negative correlations rather than positive ones, and none of the childrearing practices that produce variations in castration fears were significantly associated with either form of segregation. Similarly, when the structural-functional theories are subjected to empirical tests, the results are negative. Meggitt's and Allen's theories may indeed explain pollution fears and segregation practices within Oceania, and Murphy's theory may explain Mundurucu practices, but our results suggest that they do not explain world patterns.

The least quantifiable alternate to our model, Schlegal's "male dominance" theory, is the one that suggests world trends most accurately, according to our reanalysis. We agree with Schlegal's conclusion that menstrual restriction is probably not a valid indicator of women's social status in world societies although the association between husband dominance and menstrual segregation should be investigated further in a sample of societies including all forms of descent reckoning. It is possible that marriage customs producing husband dominance provide an alternative to unstable economics and internal politics as a precondition of sex-segregation practices.

TABLE 22. **Relationship between Combined Segregation Practices, Husband Dominance, and Unstable Economic Resources among Societies Shared by Both Samples**

Combined Segregation Practices	Unstable Economic Resources			
	Present		Absent	
	Husband Dominance			
	Present	Absent	Present	Absent
Present	80.0%	100.0%	25.0%	33.3%
	(4)	(7)	(1)	(1)
Absent	20.0%	00.0%	75.0%	66.7%
	(1)	(0)	(3)	(2)
Total	100.0%	100.0%	100.0%	100.0%
	(5)	(7)	(4)	(3)

7 Summary and Implications for Complex Societies

Our theory proposes that reproductive rituals are bargaining tactics to resolve critical sociopolitical dilemmas produced by events in the human reproductive cycle. Ritual behavior is a bargaining strategy employed out of political self-interest when more potent tactics are unavailable. In societies that lack a strong centralized state apparatus, an independent military, and a judicial system to make binding decisions about family matters, control over women's reproductive capacity is specified by bargains between interested parties that can never be completely enforced. Parties therefore resort to ritual to declare their intentions, assess each other's intentions, and influence and gauge public opinion. Unlike other theories, ours argues that ritual is performed for the community of observers and not for the performer of the ritual (such as the father or husband) or the person on whom the ritual is performed (such as the menarcheal, pregnant, or menstruating woman).

The hypotheses derived from our general theoretical model all link a society's dominant form of ritual bargaining during critical reproductive dilemmas with the principal sources of political and economic power. In the basic model, the dominant economic resource base and residential patterns of a society are the exogenous variables, and the ritual behavior of individuals or groups are the dependent variables. Each of the hypotheses about reproductive rituals derived from the general theory expresses the relationships among the political power that economic resources provide (as measured by the

strength of fraternal interest groups), the social dilemmas that reproductive events create, and the nature of the reproductive rituals used
to solve these dilemmas.

Briefly, we argued that the human reproductive cycle produces
social dilemmas in all societies, including our own, but that these dilemmas are especially acute in preindustrial societies. Since kinship is
the major source of wealth and power in preindustrial societies,
women's biological capacity to produce new members for a kin group.
is an important capital asset for any individual or group who controls
it. The incest prohibition forces those with original authority over a
woman's reproductive capacity—her father or other legal guardian,
brothers, and close kinsmen—to transfer rights to sexual access and
therefore rights of biological paternity to her children to some man
outside the domestic unit. But a man not bound by incest prohibitions
is also a potential political competitor and enemy since his allegiance
is to men other than the woman's own close kinsmen. Jural rights to a
woman's offspring are, therefore, seldom transferred completely.
Rights to women and their children are distributed by bargains, both
implicit and explicit, between a woman's kinsmen and the kinsmen of
the potential husband. All societies develop codes to specify the distribution of rights and obligations to women and offspring. Without
an independent judicial system, however, ideal codes cannot eliminate the potential for manipulation, default, and coercion in bargains
over women's reproductive capacity. Bargains are negotiated and renegotiated throughout a woman's reproductive span and are especially likely to be challenged at critical reproductive events.

Four of these events are particularly likely to lead to dispute:
menarche, male puberty, childbirth, and menstruation. The dilemmas
that these events intensify and the tactics used to resolve them are the
focus of each of the substantive chapters. In each case, the intensity of
the dilemmas and the tactics used to resolve them depend on the
strength of fraternal interest groups. We will review briefly ritual
strategies that strong and weak fraternal interest group societies use
to try to resolve each of the major social dilemmas produced by
human reproductive events.

DILEMMAS AND RITUALS AMONG THE STRONG

Societies with strong fraternal interest groups are those in which
the subsistence economy is based primarily on pastoralism, the hoe,
the plow, or irrigation agriculture and in which male kinsmen are
localized in single communities. Under these conditions, binding
agreements over claims to women's reproductive capacity can be negotiated explicitly since military action can be used to enforce contract

compliance. Explicit bargains typically involve the transfer of substantial amounts of property in return for rights to women and offspring. The social dilemmas produced by events in the human reproductive cycle, however, are by no means absent in such societies. In the absence of a strong centralized authority and independent military, breach of contract and the defection of segments of the fraternal interest group are always possible. Rituals in these societies, therefore, take the form of surveillance, or monitoring, of parties to bargains to ensure that the terms of contracts are not violated and that kin-group allegiance is maintained.

Attempts to resolve the dilemma produced by a daughter's menarche take the form of close surveillance of her social encounters with men. Among strong fraternal interest group societies, a father need not depend on the unpredictable timing of menarche to complete a profitable marriage arrangement; his kin-group backing allows him to arrange a marriage when it is most convenient financially and politically. Strong fathers can hold out for the suitors who offer the highest brideprice or the best political connections. Similarly, suitors in strong fraternal interest group societies can insist on explicit evidence of a woman's virginity or sexual maturity before closing a marriage bargain. Such procedures as infibulation and virginity tests assure a suitor that seducers will not challenge his rights of paternity.

The dilemma produced by the sexual maturity of sons is especially critical among strong fraternal interest groups. A sexually mature son represents another potential competitor for women's reproductive capacity and as such can upset the established relationships of power and authority among adult males. In the absence of a centralized authority, defection of segments of a kin group is always possible. The sexual maturity of a son represents the possible beginning of an independent power base that could eventually fission from the group. While fission is a problem in all societies, it has especially serious consequences in strong fraternal interest groups, where it may involve great losses in manpower and resources. The dilemma in strong fraternal interest groups, then, is that lineage elders must extend the right to ultimate political power and potential independence to descendents in order to win their loyalty but that by doing so they ultimately lose that loyalty through lineage fission. Circumcision is a ritual attempt to solve this dilemma by ascertaining the continuing loyalty of kin-group members. By subjecting sons to a dangerous operation which could result in castration or death, the lineage elders gain evidence that the head of a family unit in their faction is willing to entrust them with his most valuable political asset—his son's penis. Circumcision offers public evidence that a father is sufficiently loyal to the fraternal interest group to risk publicly his future basis of power.

The dilemma of legitimacy becomes most pronounced at birth, when previously negotiated marriage bargains involving wealth transfer take on practical significance. Parties to a marriage bargain are intent on ensuring that nothing happens during the birth process to upset their agreement. Birth rituals, therefore, take the form of monitoring the mother through social and structural segregation and monitoring the behavior of all parties to the marrriage bargain. The critical determinants of surveillance rituals at birth are the size of marriage bargain payments and the ability to demand compensation in case of default on the agreement.

The dilemma of marriage is the problem of keeping men with expanding households from taking advantage of their wives' fertility by defaulting on contract obligations or defecting from their kin groups. In strong fraternal interest group societies, explicit bargains over paternity rights and rewards of inheritance in return for loyalty to kinsmen reduce, but by no means eliminate, this dilemma; they offer maximum certainty that a husband will comply with marriage bargains and remain allegiant to his kin group. Under these conditions, pollution rituals used to resolve the dilemma of marriage are present but not elaborate; they most frequently take the form of menstrual sex taboos, domestic and cooking taboos, and other personal restrictions on wives. A husband has little need to dramatize his loyalty to affines and agnates when he is in no position to default or defect in the first place.

DILEMMAS AND RITUALS AMONG THE WEAK

Among societies in which the economic resource base does not permit the formation of strong fraternal interest groups, recognition and transfer of rights to women must depend on implicit agreements since there are no effective political means of establishing or defending binding agreements. Without access to stable and valuable resources, incentives for fraternal interest group loyalty are greatly diminished. Men have little incentive to protect communally those few assets available—hunting territories, fishing grounds, or tropical forests converted into temporary agricultural plots—since these are not valuable enough to be continually defended militarily. Further, since these resources are available for anyone's use, a kin group cannot withhold them at will or give them as rewards for kin-group loyalty. The absence of valuable economic assets both diminishes the power to enforce explicit bargains and prevents the accumulation of capital resources of great enough value to be used in negotiating explicit bargains.

In these societies, rituals attempt to establish temporary political factions at critical points in a woman's reproductive cycle and gain at least temporary support for claims to a woman's fertility. Such rituals can be interpreted as a form of psychological warfare to evaluate community consensus, create social indebtedness, and establish a temporary military force to protect claims from the challenges of competitors.

The timing of a daughter's sexual maturity produces a much more serious dilemma for the weak than for the strong since weak fathers lack the military power of a large loyal kin group to protect their newly fertile daughter's honor and virginity. While fathers in strong fraternal interest group societies can afford to wait for some period after menarche to arrange a marriage, fathers in weak fraternal interest group societies must arrange a daughter's marriage before seducers make illicit claims to her fertility. In the absence of a large and loyal political faction to protect his interests, a father in a weak society is forced to develop a temporary political faction that can protect his bargaining position long enough for him to contract a suitable marriage.

A menarcheal ceremony is a ritual means of protecting a daughter's newly acquired fertility. The public ceremony, by involving the participation of many people and displaying and distributing wealth, allows the father to demonstrate his power and prestige in the community toward anyone with illegitimate intentions toward the daughter. It also allows him to garner support by creating indebtedness and to gauge the extent of his support by assessing the willingness of others to participate. If a father is too weak to give a successful menarcheal ceremony or if such a dramatic attempt at coalition formation would upset the current power relationships within the community, an alternate ritual tactic to protect a daughter's marriage value is simply to put her in physical seclusion until a suitable marriage partner is found.

The sexual maturity of sons in weak societies is considerably less problematic than the sexual maturity of daughters. Weak societies do not have stable economic resources that are militarily vulnerable, controlled by adult males, and inaccessible to individuals except through allegiance to kinsmen. Large lineages are therefore less likely to develop, making the dilemma of lineage fission less intense. Demonstrations of kin-group loyalty through the ritual of circumcision are neither necessary nor possible to accomplish. Among politically weak societies, fathers and other adult members of kin groups have no means of ensuring their sons' loyalty. Ritual attempts to reinforce the sons' loyalty, such as vision quests, hazing, or extended ceremonies of initiation into age sets or men's associations, do occur in these societies, but such rituals rarely include a surgical operation that could eliminate a son's reproductive capacity. In weak societies, kinsmen have everything to gain by a son's reproductive capacity and little to lose by his defection and formation of an independent faction. Therefore, ritual puberty practices that do not include circumcision are weak attempts to create incentives for kin-group loyalty of sons instead of ritual demonstrations of a father's loyalty to his consanguineal relatives.

The lower likelihood of lineage fission in weak societies does not diminish the dilemma of legitimacy. In the absence of important economic resources to reinforce the allegiance of other adult males or to arrange explicit financial bargains over paternity rights, husbands in weak societies must resort to the same tactics to establish paternity claims as fathers do to protect their daughters' fertility at menarche. Through ritual demonstrations of involvement in a wife's pregnancy and delivery, such as couvade, husbands attempt to establish and defend claims to their wives' offspring. In some societies, adulterers competing with the husband for social recognition of paternity perform competing rituals during childbirth.

The severity of the dilemma of marriage, or of a wife's continuing fecundity, differs substantially *among* politically weak societies depending on the nature of the dominant subsistence activity. Extractive societies have no valuable economic resources that can be used to develop political factions through social indebtedness. Since the poverty of the resource base does not allow individuals to acquire significant or lasting advantages of wealth or power over others in the community, a husband has little need either to display his power to draw followers or to reassure others that he is disinterested in power. Elaborate ritual displays of disinterest in a wife's continuing ability to reproduce—represented by her menstruation—are therefore rare in extractive societies.

In societies with strong fraternal interest groups and stable, valuable resources, some individuals can acquire advantages of wealth and power that are both significant and lasting. But since their power is so often obtained from attachment to a powerful kin group or hereditary political office rather than their own efforts to develop a faction and become powerful and respected, they are not faced with a serious dilemma of how to represent their power to others. They do not need to make a show of power to attract and maintain a following, and they do not need to deemphasize their power to avoid alienating and threatening others because their secure position renders them relatively independent of public opinion.

The continuing fertility of wives creates the most severe dilemma in societies that share problems of both weak and strong fraternal interest group societies. These are societies in which the economic base (buffalo, salmon, yams, and pigs) permits the development of political coalitions around single individuals but does not provide the stable economic assets necessary for the development of strong fraternal interest groups. Men base coalitions on a core kinship group but expand them to nonrelatives through personal charisma, manipulative skill, and wealth distribution. Members of a "big man's" faction must be continually rewarded lest they defect to the faction of a competing politician. Men must display their power to others to develop a reputation as a "big man." Yet they must simultaneously deemphasize their power to avoid alienating and threatening others such as affines and consanguines since the instability of the economic base makes even the most powerful leader vulnerable to public opinion. Leaders and potential leaders solve this dilemma through displays of ritual disinterest. They sponsor feasts and ceremonies to dramatize the extent of their wealth and political influence but simultaneously declare disinterest in their power by redistributing their wealth on a lavish scale or even destroying it. Similarly, by segregating a wife during her menstruation and thereby ostentatiously refraining from intercourse with her as well as leaving her unguarded, a man proclaims his wife's continuing fertility while simultaneously declaring disinterest in his rights to her fertility that are the basis of obtaining power. In some societies, men go even further in their declaration of ritual disinterest in the wealth and power that women's fertility affords; they may reside in separate living quarters from women, spend most of their time in men's clubs or men's houses forbidden to their wives, and proclaim that fertile women are dangerously polluting to men not only during menstruation but throughout their reproductive span. With few exceptions, elaborate pollution practices are observed only in those societies in our sample in which access to women's fertility is the keystone to men's ability to gain influence and power and in which unstable economic and political conditions make the representation of individual power a problem that can be resolved only through tactics of ritual disinterest.

DIRECTIONS FOR FURTHER RESEARCH

The argument that rituals are attempts to persuade others, assess others' intentions, gauge public opinion, and manipulate perceptions assumes psychological characteristics linking political and economic conditions with ritual behavior. With the exceptions of psychoanalysis and the Whiting school, most theoretical traditions are content with establishing a connection between social or economic conditions and ritual or merely describing the cultural symbolic meaning of the ritual performance itself.

But rituals are performed by individuals and have emotional significance for both observers and participants. The data we gathered and the method we used to test our theory did not permit us to measure individual psychological responses to ritual. Our theory does assume, however, that an individual's decision to use a certain ritual is strategic and is constrained by the economic and social resources at his disposal. We have presented a model of cognitive behavior; the process by which emotions become attached to ritual remains unresolved. A ritual could not be very successful, whatever the intentions of its participants and observers, if it did not arouse emotion. Perhaps George Homans, whose general theoretical perspective we share, has provided the best attempt so far to explain the role of affect in ritual. As we described in Chapter 1, Homans attempts to combine the theories of ritual of both Malinowski and Radcliffe-Brown. According to his compromise, individuals become emotionally aroused under conditions of uncertainty and perform ritual to reduce anxiety; if the ritual is not performed according to social expectations, however, individuals will continue to be anxious. The issue of how emotions become attached to ritual, specifically the developmental process by which individuals attach affective meaning to rituals, requires further theory and research.

A second issue our theory does not address is the problem of the incest taboo. Our model rests on the assumption of universal incest prohibitions among members of a conjugal unit. The problems of menarche, fission, legitimacy, and a wife's continuing fertility exist because fathers and brothers cannot exploit the valuable reproductive assets that their daughters and sisters represent. In fact, the internal stability of a strong fraternal interest group frequently rests on its male members' renunciation of interest in one another's daughters and sisters. Although kin-group solidarity may be an important correlate of the incest taboo, our task has been to explain some of the consequences, not the causes, of this taboo.

The theory does not, of course, explicitly address the problem of reproductive rituals in complex societies with strong, effective state organization. Yet even in an advanced industrial society like the United States, several practices accompanying reproductive events may be viewed as ritual by Jack Goody's definition. Men are still circumcised; many couples refrain from sexual intercourse during menstruation, pregnancy, and the postpartum period; and hospital births are accompanied by several unnecessary or even dangerous procedures. While the medical establishment has justified many of these practices on the grounds of health or hygiene, recent studies have demonstrated their failure to achieve their purported ends. Current research also shows that the beliefs in the polluting quality of female sexuality and fertility that we have examined in preindustrial societies flourish in complex states today even though their expression may take less dramatic forms. Social scientists have barely begun to consider reproductive beliefs and practices in a political and economic context. But circumcision, birth, menarche, and menstruation have substantial ritual elements in this society as in others even if the ultimate causes may be different.

Circumcision

Male circumcision in the United States has been almost completely ignored in social science literature. Within the medical profession, however, it has become a topic of considerable controversy. Both the 1957 and 1968 editions of Dr. Spock's manual for infant care advise that parents circumcise their sons mainly because it makes a boy feel "regular" if his peers are also circumcised but also for "cleanliness and practicality."[1] But beginning in the mid-1960s, arguments for and against circumcision have been appearing regularly in American medical journals,[2] most probably sparked by a critical article in 1965 in the *Journal of the American Medical Association* entitled "The Rape of the Phallus."[3] This short and somewhat satirical essay reviews the various reasons that have been advanced in favor of circumcision and judges them unsound. Medical rationales have included the prevention of phimosis, paraphimosis, venereal disease, and cancer; aesthetic reasons; and the enhancement of sexual pleasure. Morgan refutes each rationale, arguing, for example, that phimosis is all but unknown in infancy; that any physician with experience in the Middle

1. Benjamin Spock, *Baby and Child Care* (New York, 1957), pp. 154–55.
2. See E. Noel Preston, "Whither the Foreskin?" *Journal of the American Medical Association* 213 (September 1970): 1853–58; William K. Morgan, "The Rape of the Phallus," *Journal of the American Medical Association* 193 (July 1965): 123–24; Thomas Szasz, *The Manufacture of Madness* (New York: Dell Paperback, 1970), pp. 180–206; Committee on Fetus and Newborn, "Report of the Ad Hoc Task Force on Circumcision," *Pediatrics* 56 (October 1975): 610–11; *New York Times*, "Incompetent Surgery Is Found Not Isolated," January 27, 1976, p. 1; E. Le Duc, "Value of Common Medical Procedures," *New England Journal of Medicine* 292 (March 1975): 538; A. Philip, "Urologist's Views Challenged," *Pediatrics* 56 (1975): 338; Gary Carpenter and A. Hervada, "More Criticism of Circumcision," *Pediatrics* 56 (1975): 338–39; Morris Sorrells, "Still More Criticism," *Pediatrics* 56 (1975): 339; George Demetrakopoulos, "A Different View of the Facts," *Pediatrics* 56 (1975): 339–40; R. Burger and T. Guthrie, "Why Circumcision?" *Pediatrics* 54 (1974): 362–64; Charles Reiser, "Should Circumcision Be Done Routinely?" *Medical Aspects of Human Sexuality* 1 (1967): 27–28; Fred Rosner, "Circumcision: Attempt at Clearer Understanding," *New York State Journal of Medicine* 66 (November 1966): 2919–22; C. Garven and L. Persky, "Circumcision: Is It Justified in Infancy?" *Journal of the National Medical Association* 58 (July 1966): 233–38; and Harold Speert, "Circumcision of the Newborn: An Appraisal of Its Present Status," *Obstetrics and Gynecology* 2 (August 1953): 164–71.
3. Morgan, "Rape."

East, where circumcision is universally practiced, should know that in this world region the venereal disease rate is "second to none"; that penile cancer is extremely rare ("appendicitis causes many more deaths . . . than does cancer of the penis, but nobody yet recommends routine appendectomy"); and that as for hygiene, "soap and water work wonders with the body's other orifices and appendages and there would seem no reason to doubt their efficacy with respect to the foreskin; the pinnae also collect dirt but removal of the external ears does not find favor as a routine measure of hygiene."[4] This critique and those that followed also argue that in fact circumcision inhibits rather than enhances sexual pleasure.[5]

The most heated debate has focused on circumcision's effectiveness in preventing penile and cervical cancer. In 1970 an analysis of prevalence rates for penile cancer demonstrated that the purported causal relationship between circumcision and lowered cancer risk for males was spurious.[6] Another well-designed empirical investigation demonstrated no difference in cervical cancer rates among wives of circumcised versus uncircumcised husbands.[7] By this time, health insurance companies were beginning to make inquiries to the American Academy of Pediatrics, the American Urological Association, and other medical associations about why they should continue covering male circumcision;[8] after all, according to one 1971 estimate, the practice of circumcision was costing insurance companies $200 million annually,[9] and according to Blue Cross/Blue Shield estimates in Texas, the average physician's fee for circumcision was between fifty and seventy-five dollars.[10] Finally, in 1975 an ad hoc committee of the American Pediatrics Society concluded that "there are no valid medical indications for circumcision in the neonatal period," that the decision should be left up to parents after they have been advised of the benefits and risks of surgery, and that "circumcision . . . cannot be considered an essential component of adequate total health care."[11] In 1976 the *New York Times* carried a front page story on questionable surgical practices in which they described in detail the risks associated with circumcision.[12] Based on intensive investigation of American surgical practices, it found that circumcision, the most common medical procedure in the United States, could result in such complications as local infection which could progress to septicemia (an infection

    4. Ibid., p. 124.
    5. See also Preston, "Whither the Foreskin?"
    6. Ibid.
    7. M. Terris, F. Wilson, and J. Nelson, "Relation of Circumcision to Cancer of the Cervix," *American Journal of Obstetrics and Gynecology* 117 (December 1973): 1056–66.
    8. Burger and Guthrie, "Why Circumcision?" p. 362.
    9. Demetrakopoulos, "A Different View of the Facts," p. 340.
    10. R. Burger, "Dr. Burger Replies," *Pediatrics* 56 (1975): 339.
    11. Committee on Fetus and Newborn, "Task Force on Circumcision," p. 610.
    12. *New York Times*, "Incompetent Surgery."

throughout the body), hemorrhage, and mutilation. Recent empirical studies within developmental psychology are for the first time assessing the effects of circumcision on neonatal behavior.[13]

Circumcision has been so commonplace in the United States that data on its prevalence are impossible to obtain. Rates within certain hospitals and some insurance statistics do give some indications of its prevalence in the recent past. According to one study, 98 percent of infant males were circumcised in 1951, and a survey of eighteen teaching hospitals in 1976 reported a rate of 83 percent.[14]

The perplexing question is why the medical establishment has decided at this time in history to take a stand against male genital surgery. One factor that may have influenced the timing is the interest of health companies due to high costs of covering circumcision. In Great Britain, where circumcision was never as widespread as in the United States, a substantial reduction in circumcision rates was reported after the introduction of the National Health Service.[15] In England and Wales, less than one percent of males born in 1972 were circumcised compared with an estimate of 20 percent in 1949.[16] It is not clear, however, why the medical necessity of circumcision has been challenged when many other questionable surgical procedures have not. It is also unclear why some countries, such as the United States and Australia, have high circumcision rates while others, such as European and South American countries, do not.[17]

It should be noted that female genital surgery is being performed in the United States for the first time in decades. Female circumcision is currently being performed in New York City, where a major proponent justifies it on the grounds that it cures women of frigidity. Plastic surgeons are now making surgical alterations in women's genitals to "align the clitoris and to lengthen vaginal muscle." Blue Shield, however, has just announced that these procedures will no longer be given insurance coverage.[18]

13. T. Anders and R. Chalemian, "The Effects of Circumcision on Sleep-Wake States in Human Neonates," *Psychosomatic Medicine* 36 (March–April 1974): 174–79; Luther Talbert, E. Kraybill, and H. D. Patter, "Adrenal Cortical Response to Circumcision in the Neonate," *Obstetrics and Gynecology* 48 (August 1976): 208–10; and M. Richards, J. F. Bernal, and Yvonne Brackbill, "Early Behavioral Differences: Gender or Circumcision," *Developmental Psychobiology* 9 (January 1976): 89–95.

14. M. Hovespan, "Pros and Cons of Routine Circumcision," *California Medicine* 75 (1951): 359; and Richards, Bernal, and Brackbill, "Early Behavioral Differences."

15. Burger, "Dr. Burger Replies."

16. Richards, Bernal, and Brackbill, "Early Behavioral Differences," pp. 91, 93, note 3.

17. F. R. Fredman, "Neonatal Circumcision: A General Practitioner Survey," *Medical Journal of Australia*, January 18, 1969, pp. 117–19.

18. Leo Wollman, "Female Circumcision," *Journal of American Psychosomatic Dentistry and Medicine* 20 (1974): 130–31; Leo Wollman, "Hooded Clitoris: Preliminary Report," *Journal of American Psychosomatic Dentistry and Medicine* 20 (1973): 3–4; *Vogue Magazine*, "Operation Orgasm," May 1977; and *San Francisco Chronicle*, "Blue Shield Won't Pay for 28 Procedures," May 19, 1977.

Historical accounts of medical practices do not say exactly when circumcision of either sex began in Europe or the United States, but there is good evidence that these rituals began during the nineteenth century as a consequence of the popular belief that aberrant behavior, particularly insanity, was caused by masturbation.[19] It was not until the early 1800s in Europe that masturbation became defined as a psychiatric disease needing medical treatment, and ritual genital surgery to cure masturbation in both sexes seems to have begun in the mid-nineteenth century in both Europe and the United States. Although apparently the notion that masturbation was a major cause of insanity began to die down a few decades later, medical efforts to prevent and treat masturbation mania actually increased and continued into the present century. There were several bizarre treatments for male masturbation, including locking men in chastity belts. By the 1890s, male circumcision was beginning to be used as a treatment, as an 1891 European medical text, *Circumcision as Preventive of Masturbation*, indicates. American psychoanalytic and pediatric texts were advocating it as a treatment for masturbation as late as the 1940s.[20] Female genital surgery in the form of clitoridectomy, excision, and circumcision specifically to cure masturbation, nymphomania, epilepsy, hysteria, and other disorders thought to be caused by female sexuality began in Europe at least as early as 1858 and in the United States in the 1860s.[21] While male circumcision continues to be practiced at least in the United States, female genital surgery seems to have lost popularity in England in about 1866 and in the United States around the turn of the century (although we noted earlier that there are today doctors who believe that the practice should be resumed). Thomas Szasz argues that both the ideology of masturbation mania and its expression in the form of ritual surgery are due at least in part to "medical imperialism," a mechanism by which the rising medical profession could obtain control over the diagnosis and treatment of bodily and psychological ailments once mystical explanations of such ailments lost supporters. He suggests that beginning in the eighteenth century, the concept of insanity replaced beliefs in witchcraft as the cause of antisocial behavior. The traditional source of evil, the devil, had to be replaced by a new source, masturbation. Why a sexual organ and sexual activity should be the focus of the new ideology and surgery is explained by Szasz as partly due to the rise of

19. See especially historical reviews by Szasz, *Madness*, Chap. 11; and G. J. Barker-Benfield, "The Spermatic Economy: A Nineteenth-Century View of Sexuality," in *The American Family in Social-Historical Perspective*, ed. Michael Gordon (New York: St. Martin's Press, 1973), pp. 336–72.

20. Szasz, *Madness*, pp. 191–99.

21. Ibid., p. 191; Barker-Benfield, "Spermatic Economy," pp. 353–54.

psychoanalytic theory. Within the American context, G. J. Barker-Benfield suggests a more broadly based origin. He argues that female genital surgery was an attempt to define women's social status in a changing economy and that both male and female surgery served to enforce the principle that sexuality was solely for the production of children and that women's sole function was to reproduce. Genital surgery also expressed the American ethos of ambition, individualism, and self-control. In the nineteenth century, the body was seen as a machine whose energy had to be conserved. Sexual energies had to be controlled because sexual activity and fantasies weakened mind and body. As Thoreau expressed it in 1854, "The generative which when we are loose, dissipates and makes us unclean, when we are continent invigorates and inspires us."[22] Barker-Benfield argues that the ideology of controlling sexual energies developed to help men direct their mental energies toward work and achievement, to keep men from being distracted by eroticism, and to prevent women from distracting men from their ambition through sexual demands.

The view that circumcision of both sexes is a ritual expression of beliefs about sexuality, body physiology, the role of women, and the causes of insanity seems justified on the basis of historical documentation, but the social, political, and economic bases of the ideology still need to be investigated. Szasz's hypothesis linking circumcision to the rise of the medical profession suggests a connection between fundamental socioeconomic trends that began in the nineteenth century, changes in the nature of occupations and professions, and the development of belief systems about women, sexuality, and the importance of hard work. Why circumcision continues today in the United States and not in other industrialized countries is baffling, however. The extent to which these differences in circumcision practices can be interpreted within a ritual bargaining model must await further research on the social, political, and economic historical trends associated with the practice and especially the effects of these trends on family structure and dynamics.

Birth Practices

Before industrialization, the birth of a child in the United States, as in other preindustrial societies, was a family event. The mother delivered either in her house or in a nearby "borning room," assisted by female relatives and friends with only minimal physical intervention by the local midwife. During the second stage of labor (fetal expulsion), the mother assumed an upright position, often aided by a

---

22. Quoted in Barker-Benfield, "Spermatic Economy," p. 341.

"birth stool" to support her back.[23] At the turn of the century, only 5 percent of women delivered in hospitals, but by World War II the proportion had reached nearly 50 percent, and by 1955 nearly all deliveries were performed in hospitals.[24] A similar transition occurred in Europe though it began later and is proceeding more slowly. In 1971 in the Netherlands, 58 percent of births took place at home, and a substantial number of home births still occur in England, particularly in rural areas.[25] The transition of delivery from home to hospital did not proceed without conflict, as male midwives and eventually licensed practitioners training in medical schools competed with the local female midwives and eventually eliminated their profession, often by legislative tactics.

Most women today deliver under the complete authority of hospital staff with nurses, obstetricians, and anesthesiologists in attendance. There is abundant evidence that many standard delivery practices are "rituals," if Goody's definition described in Chapter 2 is applied; of those that cannot be correctly termed rituals, at least there are serious questions about their health benefits and the necessity for their use in every delivery. Hospital deliveries treat every delivery as if it were an emergency requiring scientific technology, highly trained specialists, and surgery. The first stage of labor, in which the expectant mother is placed in a special labor room awaiting the transfer to the delivery room for fetal and placental expulsion (the second and third stages), involves three standard practices of ritual rather than medical value: the complete shaving of the pubic hair, prohibitions against eating and drinking, and the enema. Numerous studies indicate that none of these is necessary for health preservation and that all cause considerable psychological and physical discomfort.[26]

---

23. Richard W. Wertz and Dorothy C. Wertz, *Lying-In: A History of Childbirth in America* (New York: Free Press, 1977), Chap. 1, pp. 7–39.

24. Ibid., p. 144; Louis M. Hellman and N. J. Eastman, *Williams' Obstetrics*, 13th ed. (New York: Appleton-Century-Crofts, 1966).

25. Doris Haire, "Cultural Warping of Childbirth," *Journal of Tropical Pediatrics and Environmental Child Health* 19 (June 1973): 172–91 (a special issue); and Helen C. Chase, "The Position of the United States in International Comparisons of Health Status," *American Journal of Public Health* 62 (1972): 581–89, contain discussions of the reliability of statistics on infant mortality. See also Suzanne Arms, *Immaculate Deception* (Boston: Houghton Mifflin, 1975), pp. 255–91, for a description of obstetrical services and midwifery in England, Denmark, and Holland; and Aiden MacFarlane, *The Psychology of Childbirth* (Cambridge: Harvard University Press, 1977), p. 29, for a description of the Dutch birth process.

26. R. C. Burchell, "Predelivery Removal of Pubic Hair," *Obstetrics and Gynecology* 24 (1964): 272; Herman Kantor, Robert Rember, Pablo Tibio, and Ronald Buchanon, "Value of Shaving the Pudendal Perineal Area in Delivery Preparation," *Obstetrics and Gynecology* 24 (April 1965): 509–12; and William Sweeney, *Woman's Doctor* (New York: Morrow, 1969), p. 28.

Hospital delivery of the fetus and placenta involves five practices of questionable medical value that may be harmful to both mother and newborn. Considerable evidence suggests that the lithotomy (supine) position, the use of general or regional anesthesia and drugs to induce or delay labor, the surgical procedure called episiotomy, used to widen the vaginal opening, and early clamping of the umbilical cord after fetal expulsion are all unnecessary in a large majority of births.[27] Each of these procedures, however, makes delivery less time-consuming for doctors and substantially increases the financial costs. We argue that this is why the medical profession insists on continuing such practices despite empirical evidence of their lack of effects or potential harm and that this accounts for the new interest in a return to home deliveries and increased public regulation of obstetrical practice.

Empirical evidence from both the United States and the Netherlands demonstrates the safety of home births, at least among low-risk mothers if properly supervised. The American medical profession's response to the home birth movement, however, has been to claim that home birth is unsafe.[28] A return to home births on a massive scale would, of course, seriously jeopardize and even eliminate the authority of hospitals and obstetricians over American births by demonstrating the dubious need for elaborate technology, heavy medication, and routine ritual procedures of hospitals for the vast majority of births. It would also clearly reduce the cost of bearing children. The fee for a delivery and forty-eight-hour stay in an "alternative" birth unit in San Francisco, for example, is only $350[29] compared with the average cost of $2,200 for a standard obstetrical birth in the same city in 1976.[30] The safety of home births in the United States has recently been examined carefully in a study comparing 1,000 home births and 1,000 hospital births among women with similar social and reproductive characteristics.[31] The study reported that delivering at home did not affect the health of either mother or infant and in many important

27. J. A. Pritchard and P. C. MacDonald, *Williams' Obstetrics*, 15th ed. (New York: Appleton-Century Crofts, 1976), pp. 187–88; Hellman and Eastman, *Williams' Obstetrics*, 13th ed., pp. 259, 429; J. O. McCall, "The Lamaze Lament," *Transactions of the Pacific Coast Obstetrical and Gynecological Society* 42 (1975): 129; Arms, *Immaculate Deception*, p. 81; and R. Caldeyro-Barcia, quoted in Arms, *Immaculate Deception*, p. 56.
28. Wertz and Wertz, *Lying-In*, p. 244.
29. Judith Anderson, "Home Birth at the Hospital," *San Francisco Chronicle*, June 8, 1976, p. 15.
30. Anderson, "Home Birth," p. 15.
31. Lewis E. Mehl et al., "Home Birth Versus Hospital Birth: Comparisons of Outcomes of Matched Populations," paper presented at 104th Annual Meeting, American Public Health Association, Miami Beach, October 1976, as summarized by Wertz and Wertz, *Lying-In*, pp. 245–46.

respects actually reduced medical hazards. Among the home birth sample, fewer anesthesia and labor-speeding drugs were used, there were fewer occasions on which forceps were used, and there was a much lower likelihood of episiotomy and use of the lithotomy position. Physical damage to the mother, such as perineal tears and wounds and postpartum hemorrhage, was also reduced.

Within the last two decades in the United States there has been much interest in what is now termed "natural childbirth." Participation in special training classes and husband involvement in the birth process have become so widely adopted among middle-class couples that they have been termed a social movement challenging standard medical birth practices. It has been estimated that between a third and a half of pregnant women and their husbands participate in "natural childbirth."[32] Initially the medical profession was outraged at the idea of modifying delivery procedures through such techniques as teaching breathing patterns, reducing medication during delivery, and allowing paternal participation. They argued, for example, that the special training techniques were hazardous to both mother and infant, causing "perineal battering" and a "shocky" newborn requiring resuscitation, as well as a "gaping vaginal barrel" in the mother that was both physically unattractive and sexually dissatisfying.[33] Doctors have been most concerned about the presence of the husband in the delivery room, probably for good reason. As one doctor warned, the husband, as a "layman witness," would present serious problems for the defense in malpractice suits,[34] and another advised that the "management of complications in delivery now requires that the doctor not panic in the presence of a mentally alert patient and husband-father."[35]

An inspection of the natural childbirth literature suggests that these techniques by no means represent a serious challenge to the medical control of childbirth. The increasing acceptance of modifications advocated by "natural childbirth" proponents is most likely due to the recognition that these modifications are really minor—that they do not alter the most commonly used obstetrical procedures,

32. See especially MacFarlane, *Psychology of Childbirth*; C. D. Davis and F. A. Marrone, "An Objective Evaluation of a Prepared Childbirth Program," *American Journal of Obstetrics and Gynecology*, November 1, 1962, pp. 1196–1201; and C. E. Werts, S. H. Gardener, K. Mitchell, J. Thompson, and J. Oliver, "Factors Related to Behavior in Labor," *Journal of Health and Human Behavior* 6 (Winter 1975): 238–42.

33. McCall, "Lamaze Lament," pp. 128, 130.

34. John H. Morton, "Fathers in the Delivery Room—An Opposition Standpoint," *Hospital Topics* 44 (January 1966): 103.

35. C. Y. Shu, "Husband-Father in Delivery Room?" *Hospitals* 47 (September 1973): 94.

challenge doctors' control of the delivery process, or—perhaps most important—lower costs of delivery. While the "natural childbirth movement" has reduced the use of heavy medication, it does not question the nutritional taboos, enemas, genital shaving, episiotomy, timing of cord clamping, or the right of doctors to perform Caesarian section, use anesthesia, or use forceps. All of these techniques represent additional expense beyond the average $2,200 estimate.

The major innovation of "natural childbirth" is paternal participation in delivery. Although husband involvement in the birth process is not uncommon in preindustrial societies, as we showed in Chapter 5, the emerging American practice of having the husband present at the delivery itself is almost unique in world societies. The increasing popularity of this new form of "couvade" in the United States is particularly intriguing theoretically and represents an unexplored issue in social-psychological research.

Female Pollution Practices

Several surveys of contemporary attitudes and practices surrounding menarche, menstruation, pregnancy, and the postpartum period indicate a continuing belief in the polluting quality of female sexuality and fertility. Male and female attitudes of fear, contempt, or shame about female reproductive events have generally been explained psychoanalytically or justified medically, but only recently have they begun to be examined sociologically. In Chapter 1 we described psychoanalytic theories about male and female responses to menstrual bleeding. In general, psychoanalysts have viewed female reproductive events—menarche, menstruation, pregnancy, delivery, and postpartum—as psychological crises during which women regress to earlier stages of development and reexperience infantile fantasies that revive disappointment, fear, and hostility toward men.[36] These crises are said to explain female negative affect toward reproductive events. Male negative affect may be explained either as the result of male infantile fantasies evoked by female genital bleeding or as a self-protective response to women's dangerous emotional state during reproductive events.

---

36. See literature reviews by Karen Paige, Elisabeth Magnus, Susan Hahn, and Cher Carrie, eds., *The Female Reproductive Cycle: An Annotated Bibliography* (Boston: G. K. Hall, forthcoming); Karen Paige, "The Effects of Oral Contraceptives on Affective Fluctuations Associated with the Menstrual Cycle," Ph.D. dissertation, University of Michigan, 1969; Mary Parlee, "The Pre-Menstrual Syndrome," *Psychological Bulletin* 80 (1973): 454–65; and Julia Sherman, *On the Psychology of Women* (Springfield, Ill.: C. C. Thomas, 1971), pp. 125–42.

In their attempt to challenge and modify orthodox Freudian theory about female psychosexuality, neo-Freudians such as Helene Deutsch, Karen Horney, and Marie Bonaparte have argued that among women the reproductive stages are as critical determinants of psychic conflicts and the organization of personality as the Freudian psychosexual stages. Endocrine researchers' discovery of the fluctuations in estrogen and progesterone throughout the reproductive cycle gave neo-Freudians a biological energizing force motivating psychological development that could supplement the role of libidinal energy in the Freudian model of personality organization and change.[37] The causal connection between hormonal shifts and reproductive psychodynamics is most fully developed by Thérèse Benedek.[38] While more recent researchers have placed less emphasis on the unconscious forces associated with endocrine activity, Benedek's biopsychological theoretical framework forms the basis of much current empirical research. Estrogen and progesterone in her model have profound and complicated psychological effects. Their fluctuations over the reproductive cycle directly affect women's psychodynamics and behavior toward others. Thus, psychological changes during the menstrual cycle are caused by changes in hormone levels; the emotional state of pregnant women is caused by the consistently high levels of steroids throughout pregnancy; postpartum depression is caused by a dramatic decrease in steroid levels after delivery; and the emotional state at menopause is caused by estrogen depletion.

Most psychological research on female reproductive events has attempted to discover possible biochemical linkages between steroid levels and female psychology and behavior. It is frequently argued that women's depression, elation, hostility, or anxiety expressed during menarche, menstruation, ovulation, pregnancy, birth, postpartum, and menopause are biologically determined responses and that men's social adjustments to women during these events are a direct response to women's changing behavior. More elaborate biological models now hypothesize that steroids influence the activity of other biochemical agents, such as the level of MAO enzymes, electrolyte balance, adrenalin, and androgens, that may provide a more direct link to behavior.[39] Recently, however, some researchers have begun to challenge the causal relation of endocrine fluctuation to psycholog-

---

37. See especially Juliet Mitchell's critique of the female psychoanalytic modifications of orthodox theory in *Psychoanalysis and Feminism* (New York: Doubleday, 1975).

38. Thérèse Benedek, "Sexual Functions in Women and Their Disturbance," in *American Handbook of Psychiatry*, ed. Sylvano Arieti (New York: Basic Books, 1959).

39. Mary Parlee, "Psychological Aspects of Menstruation, Childbirth, and Menopause," paper presented at the NIMH-NSF Seminar on the Psychology of Women, Madison, Wisconsin, June 1975; Paige, "Effects of Oral Contraceptives"; and Sherman, *Psychology of Women*, Chap. 9.

ical status. This relationship has never been empirically established, and the possibility that men's and women's negative affect toward female reproductive events may be produced by the social context of these events has not yet been thoroughly examined.

Menarche

The scant research available on menarche in contemporary American society suggests that emotional reactions to it are strong but that their expression takes a precisely opposite form from their expression in preindustrial societies. The onset of menstruation is marked not by public announcement but by privacy and concealment. It is known only by other close female relatives, some friends, and the family doctor. Fathers often remain ignorant of their daughters' menarche and may even be the last to be told.[40] Paula Weideger argues that the very privacy of the event and the avoidance of the subject of menstruation during child socialization instruct young women in the "rules of the game" and "encourage the young women to believe the taboo is just."[41] Virginia Ernster has reviewed themes in novels that describe the shame, mystique, fear, and necessity for secrecy associated with menarche.[42] Two or three recent empirical studies confirm these literary themes, demonstrating that by late childhood both girls and boys have acquired negative attitudes about menarche. The fear and sense of secrecy expressed by late childhood could be partly influenced by school instruction on menstruation. Boys are rarely formally instructed, but girls are given "health" information about the physiology of the menstrual cycle and particularly the necessity of taking "hygienic" precautions. L. Whisnant and L. Zeguns' study of the attitudes of girls of menarcheal age has led them to argue that menarche in our society represents a "hygienic crisis," given the instructional emphasis on keeping clean.[43] In Ernster's study of 152 Girl Scouts of menarcheal age, the most common responses to a sentence completion question about how one would feel at first menstruation were "strange" (23 percent), "sick" (17 percent), and "scared" (17.8 percent); only 9.9 percent responded "happy."[44] Similarly, one study showed that as early as fifth grade,

40. According to data in three surveys (J. Rake, "Menstruation and Growing Up Female," University of California, Berkeley, Department of Anthropology, 1971; Paige, "Effects of Oral Contraceptives"; and Virginia Ernster, "Attitudes and Expectations About Menstruation Among Girls of Menarcheal Age," Ph.D. dissertation, Columbia University, 1977), a father is less likely to be told of the event than siblings, female friends, and relatives.

41. Paula Weideger, *Menstruation and Menopause* (New York: Knopf, 1976), p. 171.

42. Ernster, "Attitudes and Expectations," pp. 63–67.

43. L. Whisnant and L. Zeguns, "A Study of Attitudes Towards Menarche in White Middle-Class American Adolescent Girls," *American Journal of Psychiatry* 138 (1975): 809–14.

44. Ernster, "Attitudes and Expectations," p. 121, Table 17.

both boys and girls had developed expectations that menstruation was a source of negative moods and painful physical symptoms and that it affected performance of school work. Beliefs about the psychological and behavioral effects of menstruation became even more negative with increased age.[45] A content analysis of conversations with groups of menarcheal age girls strongly suggests that by this age young women are beginning to internalize the contradictory expectations in this culture about appropriate behavior before marriage and especially during menstruation. Members of the Girl Scout sample were very aware of such pollution taboos as the need to avoid swimming during menstruation, the potential dangers associated with washing hair or bathing, and the potential necessity for altering daily social routine by staying home, avoiding sports, and avoiding "fancy dancing." Particularly salient were the fears that menstrual blood would appear on clothing, that menstrual pads would be unavailable in an emergency, and that ridicule would result in case of "accidents."[46] The response of the young women when the experimenter passed around a tampon and "sanitary napkin" for all to handle are especially revealing of emerging pollution beliefs.[47] The initial response of the young women to the thought of even touching the objects was revulsion: many refused to touch them, some physically retreated, and one actually screamed. Ernster's summary of the emotional responses of her sample focuses on four themes: fear of being unprepared to prevent exposure of menstrual blood; fear of male ridicule; shame, embarrassment, and social humiliation; and the horror of inserting tampons into a somewhat mysterious and tabooed organ.[48]

Menstruation

More abundant research is available on social beliefs and practices associated with menstruation. Ernster has collected a large number of euphemistic terms colloquially used for menstruation in the United States.[49] The two major classes of euphemisms reported were "on the rag" and its variants and "flying the flag" and its variants. Women reported several euphemisms indicating shame and embarrassment about menstruation and the materials used to conceal it (for example, "the curse," "a weeping womb," "wearing red shoes

45. Diane Ruble and J. Brooks, "Adolescents' Attitudes About Menstruation," paper presented at the Biennial Meeting, Society for Research in Child Development, New Orleans, March 1977.
46. Ernster, "Attitudes and Expectations," Chap. 6.
47. Ibid., pp. 174–76.
48. Ibid.
49. Virginia Ernster, "Menstrual Expressions," *Sex Roles* 1 (1975): 3–13.

today," "riding a cotton pony," and "mouse mattresses"). Men were especially likely to use expressions reflecting beliefs about the polluting quality of sex during menstruation, such as "manhole cover," "coyote sandwich," and "too wet to plow." That such expressions reflect current menstrual sex taboos is indicated by the results of a series of studies by the senior author of this volume. A survey of 352 unmarried college women showed that a large proportion of respondents endorsed the notion that sexual intercourse during menstruation would be personally embarrassing, unsanitary, repugnant to their male partners, and otherwise distasteful and unenjoyable.[50] A sizable number also engaged in social practices similar to those observed among women in preindustrial societies, such as avoiding bathing and swimming, taking special naps, and remaining at home during the menses.

There is empirical evidence that premarital endorsement of sexual pollution beliefs and practices leads to sexual taboos after marriage and that women's emotional response to menstrual bleeding may be due to prevailing social values about menstrual pollution rather than endocrine-produced affect. Data on a sample of 102 married women showed that 52 percent had never had sex during menstruation.[51] Those women who adhered to the menstrual sex taboo were shown to be more anxious during menstruation than women who rejected the taboo. Additional analysis of the unmarried college sample demonstrated that adherence to sexual pollution beliefs in our society depends on one's social background, particularly the religious affiliation of one's family of origin. Expressions of negative affect during menstruation within three different religious groups—Jews, Protestants, and Catholics—were shown to be expressions of different attitudes about appropriate female behavior. Among Orthodox Jews, the intensity of menstrual distress was associated with the degree of adherence to menstrual sex taboos and associated social avoidance practices. Among Catholic women, the intensity of negative affect associated with menstruation was associated with the degree of conservatism about the role of women as mothers and wives and with premarital sexual activity: Catholics who were not virgins but held traditional beliefs about women's family role reported more intense menstrual distress than virginal Catholics. Neither familism and virginity nor menstrual taboos predicted the emotional response of Protestants to menstruation.[52]

50. Karen Paige, "Women Learn to Sing the Menstrual Blues," *Psychology Today,* September 1973.

51. Paige, "Effects of Oral Contraceptives."

52. Paige, "Menstrual Blues."

Pregnancy and Postpartum

Other studies have indicated that pollution beliefs and practices extend to pregnancy and postpartum in our society as well. Social avoidance of pregnant women, for example, has been observed in a recent field experiment measuring the degree of social distancing that occurred in the presence of pregnant and nonpregnant women in an elevator.[53] A strong and statistically significant preference was revealed for standing next to the nonpregnant women, with most of the avoidance behavior accounted for by men; women were substantially less likely to avoid the pregnant woman. Research has also documented numerous personal taboos observed by pregnant American women, most of which are precisely those observed by pregnant women in the preindustrial sample.[54] Among the 284 pregnancy prohibitions recorded were food taboos; avoidance of the ugly, sick, and deformed; minimizing physical exertion and social activities; avoiding evil thoughts; and the pregnancy and postpartum sex taboo.

The practice of avoiding sex during pregnancy and postpartum as well as menstruation most clearly suggests that the widespread notion of sexual pollution is shared by Americans. Adherence to sex taboos during both pregnancy and the postpartum has been documented in several studies. In their famous sex research studies, for example, Masters and Johnson found that sex taboos were complicating their progress in collecting data on the sex responses of men and women during pregnancy.[55] Of the 101 pregnant women in their study, 77 percent had been advised by their doctors to avoid sex during the third trimester of pregnancy, and 21 percent followed their doctors' advice. Other studies have reported similar findings, all of which show that sexual activity during pregnancy continually decreases, with 50 percent of one large sample abstaining during the third trimester[56] and 59 percent of another sample abstaining completely through the ninth month.[57] Another study found that 33 percent of the couples in the survey were observing a postpartum sex taboo eight weeks after delivery and that sexual activity seven months later was still below the pre-pregnancy average.[58] The apparent

53. S. Taylor and E. Langer, "Pregnancy: A Social Stigma?" unpublished paper, 1975.

54. Lucille Newman, "Folklore of Pregnancy," *Western Folklore* 27 (1969): 112–35.

55. R. Brecher and E. Brecher, eds., *An Analysis of Human Sexual Response* (New York: Signet-New American Library, 1966).

56. Boston Children's Medical Center, *Pregnancy, Birth, and the Newborn Baby* (New York: Delacorte, 1972), p. 14.

57. D. Solberg, J. Butler, and N. Wagner, "Sexual Behavior in Pregnancy," *New England Journal of Medicine* 288 (1973): 1098–1103.

58. Celia Falicov, "Sexual Adjustment During First Pregnancy and Postpartum," *American Journal of Obstetrics and Gynecology* 117 (1971): 991–1000.

pregnancy and postpartum sex taboos in this society are reflected in medical advice, which, according to analyses of medical texts and surveys among doctors, advocates a four-to-eight-week pregnancy taboo (last trimester) and a four-to-eight-week postpartum taboo. The ritual status of these proscriptions is evident from several studies showing an absence of health hazards of sexual activity during these periods.[59]

Most female pollution practices in our society are private, as opposed to the dramatic public displays of preindustrial societies. Clearly, they cannot be similarly interpreted as ritual attempts to influence and assess community opinion. Nevertheless, circumcising an infant, abstaining from sex during menstruation, or avoiding pregnant women in an elevator are customary behaviors which are nonempirical or irrational; they are, according to the definition with which we began this analysis, rituals. And like the rituals which we have examined in earlier chapters, their causes must be sought in social dilemmas posed by the major biological events of the human reproductive cycle.

59. See especially SEICUS, *Sexuality and Man* (New York: Scribner, 1970), pp. 50–51; A. Clark and R. Hale, "Sex During and After Pregnancy," *American Journal of Nursing* 74 (1974): 1430–31; Brecher and Brecher, *Human Sexual Response;* and Falicov, "Sexual Adjustment."

Measures

CODEBOOK

Menarcheal Ceremonies

1   Present if onset of menstruation associated with either elaborate or limited rites:

a. Elaborate. Onset of menstruation marked by either (1) ritual seclusion, observance of taboos, and avoidance of men for more than one week; or (2) public feasting and ceremonials; or (3) both 1 and 2. Customary guarding or segregating female children and adolescents not included.

b. Limited. Onset of menstruation marked by ritual seclusion, taboos, and male avoidance only during length of flow (less than one week). Parents may also observe taboos. No public feasting recorded.

0   Absent if onset of menstruation not marked by special public ritual:

a. Other Rites. Attainment of sexual maturity not marked by special public ritual, but (1) unmarried females may play role in male rites or lineage rites; or (2) marriage requires clitoral excision or ritual observances (e.g., wearing veil, tying up hair) but occurrence not in association with menarche.

b. None. No special ritual practices associated with attainment of puberty. Category includes cases of rites observed only by special classes of females (e.g., royalty).

9   Missing data.

Circumcision

1   Circumcision. Complete or partial removal of the prepuce by means of a lateral or circular incision in which the entire glans penis is exposed.

0   Superincision. Longitudinal incision in the dorsal aspect of the penis including slashing; or
Subincision. Longitudinal incision in the ventral aspect of the penis; or
Absent. No circumcision, superincision, or subincision.

9   Missing data.

Maternal Restrictions

1   Present if:
a. Confined to dwelling during pregnancy at least one week prior to delivery; secluded in special hut; moved to another community during birth process; or
b. Contact with people, especially men, is restricted during pregnancy. Pregnant women avoided and believed to be unclean, dangerous, or evil.

0   Absent if a and b are absent but:
c. Sexual relations with husband restricted for at least two months before delivery; or
d. Eating certain foods during either pregnancy or postpartum is restricted; or
e. Restrictions on looking at ugly objects, wearing certain clothing, working too hard, etc.; or
f. No restrictions are present.

9   Missing data.

Husband Involvement Scale (Couvade)

1   **a.** Seclusion. Secluded in dwelling in pregnancy or postpartum with or without mother and child; may be considered unclean; avoids others; or
b. Postpartum Work Taboo. Refrains from performing normal tasks during postpartum; must remain close to home; contact with others minimized; or
c. Food Taboo. Refrains from eating certain foods during pregnancy or postpartum.

0   **a.** Minor Observances. Minor ritual observances such as seeking a vision, performing birth-related sacrifices; may help wife with daily chores; or
b. Informal. No changes in normal behavior; no ritual observances.

9   Missing data.

Menstrual Segregation

1   Present if one of the following is reported and not limited to first menstruation:
a. Menstrual Hut. Specially constructed seclusion hut mentioned.
b. Structural Isolation. Menstruating women isolated from men in special room, hammock, or special part of house with separate entrance, or segregation mentioned but not elaborated.

0   Absent. Cooking, domestic, and personal taboos (e.g., special clothing or tattoos), sex taboo; women's menstruation believed unclean.

9   Missing data.

Male Segregation Practices

1   Present if one of the following is reported:
a. Communal men's house prohibited to wives and used primarily by married men (not bachelor or warrior houses).
b. Sleeping and living arrangements of entire community arranged by sex rather than by uterine or family units.
c. Male associations, sweat houses, sex-segregated fraternities or other secret societies used primarily by married men.
d. Sacred objects such as magic flutes or bullroarers kept away from women in special place.

0   Absent or Minor. Informal or formal daily spouse avoidance customs; segregation a consequence of polygyny only; sweat houses or other male structures or societies open to women; general beliefs or legends about female inferiority; segregated ceremonies.

9   Missing data.

Combined Segregation Practices

1   Present. Either menstrual segregation or male segregation practices coded present.

0   Absent. Neither menstrual segregation nor male segregation practices coded present.

9   Missing data on both menstrual segregation and male segregation practices, or one variable coded absent and the other missing data.

Compensation Demands

1   Present. Husband or his kinsmen demand payment of gifts or return of some or all of the bridewealth in cases of infanticide, abortion, or barrenness; or barrenness, infanticide, and abortion are grounds for divorce, and divorce leads to compensation demands.

0   Absent.

9   Missing data.

Fraternal Interest Group Size
(largest effective kin-based political subunit; number of members male and female; decimal notation)

This unit must have the following characteristics:

a. Corporate. The leaders of the kin group must meet periodically to consider kin-group affairs. These meetings include formal councils of elders, ceremonial gatherings, audiences with kin-group heads, courts presided over by a single lineage group head or informal meetings of localized groups of kinsmen even when such meetings are not regularly scheduled or organized. The leadership may consist of one man or many, but it must periodically consider the welfare of the kin unit. Moieties and implicit exogamous marriage groups which order marriage choice but do not have a corporate existence or make decisions from time to time are not corporate kin groups. The leadership of a corporate kin group must be selected largely or entirely on the basis of ties of consanguineal kinship, or such kinship must exercise veto power over selection. In many cases the members of the kin group itself may constitute the leadership.
b. Decision Making. The kin group must make decisions in one or both of the following areas: (1) the adjudication of disputes within the kin group or the collective responsibility for obedience to the dictates of higher authorities; or (2) the military organization and operations of the kin groups in internal warfare with other groups (feuding).

Fraternal Interest Group Strength

(presence or absence of brideprice and patrilineality in a society and a trichotomized measure of size of effective kin-based political subunit)

0   Both brideprice and patrilineality are absent, and size of effective kin-based political subunit is less than 100.

1   Only one of the following conditions present: brideprice; patrilineality; size of political subunit between 100 and 999.

2   **a.** Size of political subunit is 1,000 or greater, and brideprice and patrilineality are absent; or
b. Size of political subunit is less than 100 and both brideprice and patrilineality are present; or
c. Size of political subunit is between 100 and 999 and either brideprice or patrilineality is present (but not both).

3   **a.** Size of political subunit is between 100 and 999, and both brideprice and patrilineality are present; or
b. Size of political subunit is 1,000 or greater, and either brideprice or patrilineality is present (but not both).

4   Size of political subunit is 1,000 or greater, and both brideprice and patrilineality are present.

9   There is missing data on one or more of the three measures, brideprice, patrilineality, and size of effective kin-based political subunit.

Resource Base

(from *Ethnographic Atlas*, cols. 7, 28, 39; Murdock and White "level of political integration" code; presence of metal hoe original code)

0   Low
a. Foraging. Hunting and gathering predominant. *EA* gathering 0-9; hunting 0-9; fishing less than or equal to 4; sum of scores for animal husbandry and agriculture cannot exceed 2; mounted hunting absent.

1   Unstable:
a. Fishing. *EA* fishing greater than or equal to 5 (excluding pursuit of aquatic mammals), sum of scores for animal husbandry and agriculture cannot exceed 2.
b. Mounted Hunting. *EA* hunting greater than or equal to 4; fishing less than or equal to 3; sum of scores for animal hus-

bandry and agriculture cannot exceed 2; mounted hunting from the backs of horses, camels, or reindeer predominates.

c. Simple Horticulture. *EA* sum of animal husbandry and agriculture greater than or equal to 3; col. 28 casual, extensive horticulture in the absence of metal hoes; includes advanced horticultural societies where the sum of animal husbandry and agriculture is equal to 3 or 4.

2   High:

a. Pastoralism. *EA* animal husbandry greater than or equal to 3; agriculture less than or equal to 2; col. 39, B, C, D, S.

b. Advanced Horticulture. *EA* col. 28, intensive (I) and irrigated (J) agriculture or extensive cultivation when metallic hoes are employed or any combination of these techniques; sum of animal husbandry and agriculture must exceed or equal 5.

c. Agriculture. Sum of agriculture and animal husbandry must equal or exceed 3; plow and animal traction reported in col. 39. Murdock and White level of political integration I, J, K.

d. Peasant Agriculture. Sum of agriculture and animal husbandry must exceed or equal 3, and plow and animal traction are reported in col. 39. Murdock and White level of political integration equals L (large state).

9   Missing data.

Residence Pattern
(Ethnology 11, col. 9, *EA* col. 16 for alternates)

1   Favoring formation of fraternal interest groups:

a. Avunculocal Residence. With or near the maternal uncle or other male matrilineal kinsmen of the husband, including cases where men preferentially and typically marry a MoBrDa and reside matrilocally (*EA* A, C where matrilateral cross-cousin marriage preferred).

b. Patrilocal or Virilocal Residence. With or near the male patrilineal kinsmen of the husband (*EA* P, V).

c. Optionally Patrilocal or Avunculocal Residence (*EA* D).

0   Not favoring formation of fraternal interest groups:

a. Matrilocal or Uxorilocal Residence. With or near the female matrilineal kinsmen of the wife (*EA* M, U).

b. Ambilocal Residence. Optionally with or near the parents of either the husband or wife depending upon personal choice or circumstances, where neither alternative exceeds the other in actual frequency by a ratio greater than two to one (*EA* B).

c. Neolocal Residence. Where spouses establish a common household at a location not determined by the kin ties of either (*EA* N).

9   Missing data.

Ritual Warfare

1   Present. In warfare, enemy dead or prisoners are cannibalized in a public ceremony; or their scalps, heads, or other body parts are taken by individual warriors for trophies; or there is a practice of "counting coup."

0   Absent. None of the above practices is mentioned in accounts of warfare.

9   Missing data.

Achieved Leadership Through Wealth Distribution

1   Acts of wealth distribution which bring prestige to the giver are one of the most important factors in attaining and maintaining the highest degree cf political power in the society—that is, the greatest influence over the greatest number of people in initiating policy and swaying the outcome of decisions, whether or not this influence is exerted in a formal office. Should it be exerted in a formal office, this office must not be hereditary—that is, competition for it must not be restricted to a single kinship subgroup of the population led—and if it is theoretically hereditary but there are instances of individuals who lack the hereditary qualifications attaining office through wealth distribution, the society shall be coded as 1.

0   Acts of wealth distribution which bring prestige to the giver are not one of the most important factors in attaining and maintaining the highest degree of political power in the society (as defined above). Those individuals with the greatest political power may distribute wealth, but neither the attaining of their position nor the range of their powers is dependent on these acts. The factors on which their power depends are, instead, either (a) hereditary: if the highest degree of political power is exerted in a formal office, competition for this office is restricted to a single kinship subgroup of the population led, and no wealth distributor lacking the hereditary qualifications can attain office;

or (b) personal characteristics such as advanced age, hunting ability, bravery in war, skill in arbitration, and magico-religious powers.

9   Missing data.

Social Indebtedness
(*Ethnology* 11, cols. 13, 14, and own codes for unlisted societies)

1   **a.** The most prominent ceremonies in the community are individually sponsored rites other than rites of passage which are normally attended by the community at large, e.g., potlatches, "feasts of merit," votive sacrifices (col. 13, I); or
b. The feature or element most strongly emphasized in community ceremonies is distribution or exchange of property other than food (col. 14, D); or
c. Both a and b.

0   None of the above.

9   Missing data.

Unstable Political Power Index
(a summary measure based on codes for ritual warfare, achieved leadership, and social indebtedness)

0   All three variables—ritual warfare, achieved leadership, and social indebtedness—have a score of 0.

1   Only one of the three variables has a score of 1; the other two score 0.

2   Two of the variables have a score of 1; the other has a score of 0.

3   All three variables have a score of 1.

9   One, two, or three of the three variables have a score of 9.

SP	Society	MC	Ci	MR	Co	MS1	MS2	CS	CD	Si	St	RB	Res	RW	Ach	UP
AFRICA																
1	Nama	1	0	1	0	0	0	0	1	1	2	2	1	0	0	0
2	Kung	1	0	1	0	0	0	0	0	0	0	0	0	0	0	0
3	Thonga	0	1	1	0	0	0	0	1	2	4	2	1	1	0	1
6	Suku	0	1	0	9	0	9	9	1	0	1	2	1	0	0	0
7	Lamba	1	0	0	0	0	0	0	0	0	0	2	1	0	0	0
9	Nyakyusa	1	0	1	1	1	0	1	1	0	2	2	0	0	0	0
11	Luguru	1	1	0	0	0	9	9	1	1	2	2	0	0	0	0
13	Ganda	1	0	1	0	0	0	0	1	2	4	2	0	0	0	0
14	Mongo	0	1	1	0	0	0	0	1	9	9	2	1	9	0	9
15	Mbuti	1	1	0	1	0	0	0	1	0	0	0	1	0	0	0
19	Dahomey	1	1	1	0	1	0	1	1	2	4	2	1	0	0	0
20	Ashanti	1	0	1	0	1	0	1	1	2	3	2	1	1	0	1
24	Bambara	0	1	1	0	0	0	0	1	2	4	2	1	0	0	0
26	Tallensi	0	0	1	1	0	0	0	1	2	4	2	1	0	0	0
29	Tiv	0	1	1	0	0	0	0	1	2	3	2	1	1	1	2
33	Azande	0	1	1	0	0	0	0	1	0	2	2	1	0	0	0
37	Shilluk	0	0	1	0	0	0	0	1	1	3	2	1	0	0	0
38	Masai	0	1	1	0	0	0	0	1	2	4	2	1	0	0	0
CIRCUM-MEDITERRANEAN																
28	Hausa	0	1	1	0	0	0	0	1	0	2	2	1	1	0	2
32	Fur	0	1	1	1	9	0	9	1	1	2	2	0	0	0	0
41	Somali	0	1	1	0	0	0	0	1	2	4	2	1	0	0	0
46	Tuareg	0	1	1	0	0	0	0	1	1	2	2	1	0	0	0
47	Riffians	0	1	0	0	0	0	0	1	1	3	2	1	0	0	0
51	Hebrews	0	1	1	0	0	0	0	9	2	4	2	1	0	0	0
52	Rwala	0	1	1	0	0	0	0	1	2	4	2	1	0	0	0
55	Gheg	0	0	0	0	0	0	0	1	0	2	2	1	0	0	0
58	Lapps	0	0	1	0	9	0	9	0	0	0	2	1	0	9	9
62	Kurd	0	1	0	0	0	0	0	9	2	4	2	1	0	0	0
EAST EURASIA																
63	Basseri	0	1	9	0	0	0	0	0	1	3	2	1	0	0	0
66	Vedda	0	0	0	0	0	0	0	0	0	0	0	0	9	9	9
67	Chenchu	0	0	0	0	0	0	0	0	0	2	0	0	9	9	9
68	Baiga	0	0	0	0	0	9	9	0	1	3	2	1	9	9	9
70	Burusho	0	1	1	0	0	9	9	9	0	1	2	1	0	0	0
72	Kazak	0	1	0	0	0	0	0	0	2	4	2	1	0	0	0
73	Yurak Samoyed	1	0	1	0	0	0	0	9	0	2	2	1	9	0	9
76	Chukchee	0	0	1	0	0	0	0	9	0	0	2	1	0	9	9
78	Ainu	9	0	0	1	0	0	0	0	0	0	0	1	0	0	0
81	Goldi	0	0	1	0	9	9	9	1	1	3	1	1	9	9	9
85	Lepcha	0	0	0	1	0	0	0	9	0	2	2	1	0	9	9
87	Garo	0	0	0	1	1	0	1	1	1	1	1	0	1	1	2
88	Lakher	0	0	0	0	0	1	1	9	1	3	2	1	9	9	9
90	Lamet	0	0	0	1	9	1	9	9	0	2	1	1	9	9	9
92	Andamanese	1	0	0	1	0	0	0	9	0	0	0	0	0	0	0
96	Rhade	0	0	0	9	0	9	9	9	0	9	0	0	9	9	9
8	Tanala	0	1	0	0	0	0	0	1	1	2	2	1	0	0	0

SP	Society	MC	Ci	MR	Co	MS1	MS2	CS	CD	Si	St	RB	Res	RW	Ach	UP
INSULAR PACIFIC																
101	Iban	9	0	0	9	9	0	9	0	0	0	1	0	1	1	2
104	Balinese	0	0	1	0	1	0	1	9	0	1	2	1	0	0	0
107	Alorese	0	0	0	1	0	0	0	1	0	2	1	1	1	1	2
108	Murngin	1	1	0	0	0	0	0	1	0	0	0	1	0	0	0
109	Arunta	1	0	1	0	0	1	1	0	0	9	0	1	0	0	0
112	Kiwai	1	0	1	1	1	1	2	1	1	2	1	1	1	1	3
113	Wogeo	1	0	1	1	1	1	2	1	0	0	1	1	0	1	2
114	Kapauku	1	0	0	0	0	0	0	0	1	3	1	1	0	1	2
115	Palauans	0	0	1	0	9	1	9	1	0	1	1	1	0	0	1
116	Yapese	1	0	1	1	1	1	2	1	0	0	1	1	1	1	3
117	Ifaluk	1	0	0	1	1	0	1	0	0	0	1	0	0	0	0
118	Marshallese	1	0	1	0	1	1	2	0	1	1	0	0	0	0	0
120	Manus	1	0	1	0	0	1	1	9	9	9	1	1	1	1	3
121	Lesu	1	0	1	0	0	1	1	0	0	1	1	0	1	1	2
122	Trobrianders	0	0	1	0	0	0	0	0	0	0	1	1	0	1	2
123	Kurtatchi	1	0	0	1	0	1	1	9	0	1	1	0	1	0	1
124	Ontong Java	0	0	0	0	0	1	1	9	0	0	1	0	9	1	9
125	Tikopia	9	0	1	0	1	1	2	9	1	2	1	1	0	0	0
128	Lau Fijians	0	0	1	1	0	1	1	1	0	1	1	1	1	0	2
129	Samoans	1	0	0	0	1	1	2	0	0	0	1	1	1	1	2
130	Maori	0	0	1	0	1	1	2	9	1	1	1	1	1	1	2
131	Marquesans	1	0	1	1	0	1	1	0	9	9	1	0	1	1	2
NORTH AMERICA																
132	Aleut	1	0	1	0	0	9	9	9	9	9	1	1	1	9	9
133	Cop. Eskimo	0	0	0	1	0	0	0	0	0	0	0	0	0	0	0
136	Eyak	1	0	1	1	1	0	1	0	0	0	1	1	0	1	2
138	Kaska	1	0	0	1	1	0	1	0	0	0	1	0	1	1	3
139	Kwakiutl	1	0	1	1	1	1	2	9	0	0	1	1	1	1	3
140	Twana	1	0	1	1	1	0	1	1	0	0	1	1	0	1	2
141	Hupa	1	0	0	1	1	1	2	1	0	1	1	1	0	1	1
142	Klamath	1	0	1	0	1	0	1	1	0	0	1	1	1	1	2
144	Yokuts	1	0	0	1	0	0	0	0	9	9	0	1	0	0	0
146	Paiute	1	0	0	1	1	0	1	0	0	0	0	0	1	9	9
149	Sanpoil	1	0	1	1	1	0	1	0	0	0	1	1	0	0	0
150	Gros Ventre	0	0	1	0	1	1	2	9	0	1	1	1	1	1	3
152	Micmac	1	0	1	0	1	0	1	0	9	9	0	0	1	0	1
153	Saulteaux	1	0	0	9	9	0	9	0	0	1	0	1	0	0	0
154	Hidatsa	0	0	0	0	1	1	2	9	0	0	2	0	1	0	2
157	Creek	1	0	0	1	1	1	2	9	0	0	1	0	1	9	9
159	Pawnee	0	0	0	1	1	1	2	1	0	0	1	0	1	1	2
161	Apache	1	0	0	0	0	1	1	0	0	0	1	0	1	1	2
162	Navaho	1	0	0	1	1	1	2	9	0	0	2	0	0	0	1
163	Papago	1	0	1	1	1	0	1	0	0	1	2	1	0	0	0
165	Tarasco	0	0	9	9	0	9	9	0	9	9	2	1	0	0	0

SP	Society	MC	Ci	MR	Co	MS1	MS2	CS	CD	Si	St	RB	Res	RW	Ach	UP
SOUTH AMERICA																
168	Miskito	1	0	1	1	1	9	9	1	0	0	1	0	1	0	1
169	Bribri	1	0	1	1	1	9	9	0	9	9	1	0	9	9	9
170	Cuna	1	0	0	1	0	0	0	0	0	0	1	0	0	0	0
172	Goajiro	1	0	1	0	0	0	0	1	1	2	2	0	0	0	0
173	Callinago	1	0	0	1	1	0	1	0	0	0	1	0	1	0	1
175	Warrau	1	0	0	1	1	1	2	9	0	0	0	0	9	0	9
178	Carib	1	0	0	1	1	0	1	0	0	0	1	0	9	0	9
179	Saramacca	0	0	0	0	1	1	2	1	2	3	2	1	1	0	1
180	Mundurucu	1	0	0	1	0	1	1	0	0	1	1	0	1	0	1
182	Witoto	0	0	0	1	0	1	1	0	1	2	1	1	1	0	1
183	Jivaro	1	0	0	1	0	0	0	0	0	0	1	1	1	1	3
184	Amahuaca	0	0	9	0	9	9	9	9	0	0	1	1	9	0	9
187	Siriono	1	0	0	1	0	0	0	9	0	0	0	0	0	0	0
188	Nambicuara	1	0	0	1	0	1	1	0	0	0	0	1	0	0	0
190	Timbira	0	0	0	1	1	1	2	0	0	0	1	0	0	0	0
191	Tupinamba	1	0	0	1	9	9	9	0	1	1	1	0	1	0	1
194	Aweikoma	9	0	0	1	0	0	0	0	0	0	0	0	0	0	0
196	Lengua	1	0	0	1	0	0	0	0	0	0	0	0	0	0	0
198	Mapuche	0	0	1	0	0	0	0	1	0	2	2	1	1	0	1
200	Yahgan	1	0	1	1	0	0	0	9	0	0	0	1	0	0	0

SP   Sampling Province
MC   Menarcheal Ceremonies
Ci   Circumcision
MR   Maternal Restrictions
Co   Couvade
MS1   Menstrual Segregation
MS2   Male Segregation Practices
CS   Combined Segregation Practices
CD   Compensation Demands
Si   Fraternal Interest Group Size
St   Fraternal Interest Group Strength
RB   Resource Base (low, unstable, high)
Res   Residence Patterns
RW   Ritual Warfare
Ach   Achieved Leadership
UP   Unstable Political Power Index

Similarity Coefficients for Each Reproductive Ritual and Each Predictor Variable in Theoretical Model

Menarcheal Ceremonies	.36
Circumcision	.45
Maternal Restrictions	.25
Couvade	.09
Menstrual Segregation Practices	.36
Male Segregation Practices	.51
Combined Segregation Practices	.52
Compensation Demands	.12
Fraternal Interest Group Strength	.42
Bridgeprice	.34
Fraternal Interest Group Size	.28
Patrilocality	.22
Residence Pattern Favoring Formation of Fraternal Interest Groups	.19
Resource Base (low-high)	.50
Resource Base (stable-unstable)	.51
Ritual War	.08
Achieved Leadership	.36
Social Indebtedness	.004
Unstable Political Power Index	.18

Description of Sample

AFRICA

Nama

Sampling Province 1 (Hottentots)
Ethnographic Atlas: Aa3
Language: Khoisan (Southern)
Location: The Gei/Khauan tribe, 27°30'S, 17°E
Time: Reconstructed for 1860, just prior to their decimation and
 loss of independence in the Herero War
Authorities: Schultze, Schapera (secondary)

Kung

Sampling Province 2 (Bushmen)
Ethnographic Atlas: Aa1
Language: Khoisan (Southern)
Location: The Agau Kung of the Nyae Nyae region, 19°50'S,
 20°35'E
Time: In 1950, when the Marshalls began their study of this
 still unacculturated group
Authority: L. Marshall

Thonga

Sampling Province 3 (Southeastern Bantu)
Ethnographic Atlas: Ab4
Language: Niger-Congo (Bantoid)
Location: The Ronga subtribe around Lourenco Marques,
 25°50'S, 32°20'E
Time: In 1895, at the beginning of Junod's missionary field
 work
Authority: Junod

Suku

Sampling Province 6 (Western Central Bantu)
Ethnographic Atlas: Ac17
Language: Niger-Congo (Bantoid)
Location: The Suku of Feshi territory, 6°S, 18°E
Time: In 1920, just prior to their loss of independence
Authorities: Kopytoff, Torday and Joyce

Lamba

Sampling Province 7
Ethnographic Atlas: Ac5
Language: Niger-Congo (Bantoid)
Location: The Lamba near the Kafue River, 13°S, 28°E
Time: In 1920, in the later years of Doke's missionary field
      work
Authority: Doke

Nyakyusa

Sampling Province 9
Ethnographic Atlas: Ad6
Language: Niger-Congo (Bantoid)
Location: The Nyakyusa near towns of Mwaya 9°35'S, 34°10'E
      and Masoko 9°20'S, 34°E
Time: In 1934, at the beginning of the Wilsons' field work
Authority: M. Wilson

Luguru

Sampling Province 11
Ethnographic Atlas: Ad14
Language: Niger-Congo (Bantoid)
Location: The Luguru of west central Morogoro District 6°25'
      to 7°25'S, 37°20' to 38°E
Time: In 1925, the last date of the traditional political
      organization
Authorities: Beidelman, Scheerder and Tastevin

Ganda

Sampling Province 13
Ethnographic Atlas: Ad7
Language: Niger-Congo (Bantoid)
Location: The Ganda of Kyaddondo district 0°20'N, 32°30'E
Time: In 1875, just prior to the founding of Kampala and the
      initiation of significant administrative changes
Authorities: Roscoe, Mair

Mongo

Sampling Provinces 14/16
Ethnographic Atlas: Ae4
Language: Niger-Congo (Bantoid)
Location: The Mongo of the Ilanga subtribe 0°15' to 1°15'S,
      18°35' to 19°45'E
Time: In 1930, the approximate date of Hulstaert's description
Authority: Hulstaert

Mbuti

Sampling Province 15
Ethnographic Atlas: Aa5
Language: Niger-Congo (Bantoid)
Location: The Epulu net hunters of the Ituri Forest 1°30' to
      2°N, 28°25'E
Time: In 1950, just prior to Turnbull's field work
Authorities: Turnbull, Schebesta

Fon

Sampling Province 19
Ethnographic Atlas: Af1
Language: Niger-Congo (Kwa)
Location: The Fon in the vicinity of Abomey 7°12'N, 1°56'E
Time: In 1890, prior to the conquest of the Dahomean kingdom
      by the French
Authorities: Herskovits, Le Herissé

Ashanti

Sampling Province 20
Ethnographic Atlas: Af3
Language: Niger-Congo (Kwa)
Location: The Ashanti of the state of Kumasi 6° to 8°N,
         0° to 3°W
Time: In 1895, just prior to British conquest
Authorities: Rattray, Fortes

Bambara

Sampling Province 24
Ethnographic Atlas: Ag1
Language: Niger-Congo (Mande)
Location: The Bambara along the Niger River from Segou to
         Bamako 12°30' to 13°N, 6° to 8°W
Time: In 1902, at approximately the beginning of Henry's field
      experience as a missionary and Monteil's as an
      administrator
Authorities: Monteil, Henry, Pacques (secondary)

Tallensi

Sampling Provinces 26/27
Ethnographic Atlas: Ag4
Language: Niger-Congo (Voltaic or Gur)
Location: The small Tallensi tribe as a whole 10°30' to 10°45'N,
         0°30' to 0°50'W
Time: In 1934, at the beginning of the field work of Fortes
Authority: Fortes

Tiv

Sampling Provinces 29/30
Ethnographic Atlas: Ah3
Language: Niger-Congo (Bantoid)
Location: The Tiv of Benue province 6°30' to 8°N, 8° to 10°E
Time: In 1920, prior to extensive organizational changes
      wrought by the British
Authorities: L. and P. Bohannan, East (Akiga)

Azande

Sampling Provinces 33/34
Ethnographic Atlas: Ai3
Language: Niger-Congo (Eastern)
Location: The Azande of the Yambio chiefdom 4°20' to 5°50'N,
    27°40' to 28°50'E
Time: In 1905, just prior to British conquest and the collapse of
    the Avongara political system
Authority: Evans-Pritchard

Shilluk

Sampling Province 37
Ethnographic Atlas: Ai6
Language: Chari-Nile or Sudanic (Eastern)
Location: The politically unified Shilluk as a whole 9° to
    10°30'N, 31° to 32°E
Time: In 1910, the date of the field work by Westermann and
    the Seligmans
Authorities: C. and B. Seligman, Westermann

Masai

Sampling Province 38
Ethnographic Atlas: Aj2
Language: Chari-Nile (Eastern)
Location: The Kisonko or Southern Masai of Tanzania 1°30' to
    5°30'S, 35° to 37°30'E
Time: In 1900, about the time of Merker's field work
Authorities: Merker, Jacobs

CIRCUM-MEDITERRANEAN

Hausa

Sampling Province 28
Ethnographic Atlas: Cb26
Language: Afroasiatic or Hamito-Semitic (Chadic)
Location: The Zazzagawa Hausa 9°30' to 11°30'N, 6° to 9°E
Time: In 1900, just prior to the advent of British rule
Authority: Smith

Fur

Sampling Province 32
Ethnographic Atlas: Cb17
Language: Furian
Location: The Fur of western Darfur around Jebel Marra
          13°30'N, 25°30'E
Time: In 1880, prior to effective Egyptian subjugation
Authorities: Felkin, Beaton

Somali

Sampling Province 41
Ethnographic Atlas: Ca2
Language: Afroasiatic (Eastern Cushitic)
Location: The Dolbahanta subtribe 7° to 11°N, 45°30' to 49°E
Time: In 1900, subsequent to the earliest descriptions but prior
      to the later and fuller accounts
Authority: Lewis

Amhara

Sampling Province 42
Ethnographic Atlas: Ca7
Language: Afroasiatic (Semitic)
Location: The Amhara of the Gondar district 11° to 14°N, 36° to
          38°30'E
Time: In 1953, at the beginning of Messing's field work
Authority: Messing

Tuareg

Sampling Province 46
Ethnographic Atlas: Cc9
Language: Afroasiatic (Berber)
Location: The Ahaggaren or Tuareg of Ahaggar 21° to 25°N, 4°
          to 9°E
Time: In 1900, prior to the French military occupation of the
      Sahara
Authorities: Nicolaisen, Lhote

Riffians

Sampling Provinces 47/48
Ethnographic Atlas: Cd3

Language: Afroasiatic (Berber)
Location: The Riffians as a whole 34°20′ to 35°30′N, 2°30′
to 4°W
Time: In 1926, at the beginning of Coon's field work
Authority: Coon

Hebrews

Sampling Province 51
Ethnographic Atlas: Cj3
Language: Afroasiatic (Semitic)
Location: The kingdom of Judah 30°30′ to 31°55′N, 34°20′ to
35°30′E
Time: In 621 B.C., the date of promulgation of the
Deuteronomic laws
Authorities: Old Testament, De Vaux (secondary)

Rwala

Sampling Province 52
Ethnographic Atlas: Cj2
Language: Afroasiatic (Semitic)
Location: The Rwala Bedouin of south central Syria and
northeastern Jordan 31° to 35°30′N, 36° to 41°E
Time: In 1913, early in the periods of field work of Musil and
Raswan
Authorities: Musil, Raswan

Gheg

Sampling Province 55
Ethnographic Atlas: Ce1
Language: Indo-European (Albanian)
Location: The Mountain Gheg of northern Albania 41°20′ to
42°N, 19°30′ to 20°31′E
Time: In 1910, just prior to the expulsion of the Turks in the
two Balkan Wars
Authorities: Coon, Durham

Basques

Sampling Province 56
Ethnographic Atlas: Ce4
Language: Basque

Location: The mountain village of Vera de Bidasoa 43°18'N,
1°40'W
Time: In 1934, the date of the field work by Caro Baroja
Authority: Caro Baroja

Lapps

Sampling Province 58
Ethnographic Atlas: Cg4
Language: Uralic (Finnic)
Location: The Konkama Lapps of Karesuando parish in
northern Sweden 68°20' to 69°5'N, 20°5' to 23°E
Time: In 1950, during the period of Pehrson's field work
Authorities: Pehrson, Whitaker

EAST EURASIA

Kurd

Sampling Province 62
Ethnographic Atlas: Ci11
Language: Indo-European (Iranian)
Location: The Kurd of the town and environs of Rowanduz
36°30'N, 44°30'N
Time: In 1951, the date of the field work by Masters
Authorities: Masters, Leach

Basseri

Sampling Province 63
Ethnographic Atlas: Ea6
Language: Indo-European (Iranian)
Location: The nomadic Basseri 27° to 31°N, 53° to 54°E
Time: In 1958, during the period of Barth's field work
Authority: Barth

Vedda

Sampling Province 66
Ethnographic Atlas: Eh4
Language: Indo-European (Indic)
Location: The Danigala group of Forest Vedda 7°30' to 8°N, 81°
to 81°30'E
Time: In 1860, the date of the observations by Bailey made
prior to intensive acculturation
Authorities: C. and B. Seligman, Bailey

Chenchu

Sampling Province 67
Ethnographic Atlas: Eg1
Language: Dravidian
Location: The Chenchus of Hyderabad of the Amrabad
            Plateau, 16°N, 79°E
Time: In 1940, during von Fürer-Haimendorf's field work
Authority: von Fürer-Haimendorf

Baiga

Sampling Province 68
Ethnographic Atlas: Eg9
Language: not given
Location: The Baiga near the Maikala Range, 22°N, 81°E
Time: In 1930
Authorities: Elwin, Nag (secondary)

Burusho

Sampling Provinces 70/71
Ethnographic Atlas: Ee2
Language: Burushaski
Location: The Burusho of Hunza state 36°20′ to 36°30′N, 74°30′
            to 74°40′E
Time: In 1934, during the period of the Lorimers' field work
Authorities: D. and E. Lorimer

Kazak

Sampling Province 72
Ethnographic Atlas: Eb1
Language: Altaic (Turkic)
Location: The Kazak of the Great Horde 37° to 48°N, 68° to 81°E
Time: In 1885, the approximate time of Grodekov's field work
Authorities: Grodekov, Hudson

Yurak Samoyed

Sampling Province 73
Ethnographic Atlas: Ec4
Language: Uralic (Samoyedic)
Location: The Tundra Yurak 65° to 71°N, 41° to 62°E

Time: In 1894, during the periods of observation by Englehardt
        and Jackson
Authorities: Jackson, Englehardt

Chukchee

Sampling Province 76
Ethnographic Atlas: Ec3
Language: Luorawctlan
Location: The Reindeer Chukchee 63° to 70°N, 171°W to 171°E
Time: In 1900, the date of the beginning of the field work by
        Bogoraz
Authority: Bogoraz

Ainu

Sampling Province 78
Ethnographic Atlas: Ec7
Language: Ainu
Location: The Ainu of the basins of the Tokapchi and Saru
            rivers in southeastern Hokkaido 42°40′ to 43°30′N,
            142° to 144°E
Time: Reconstructed for about 1880
Authorities: Watanabe, Watanabe, Munro, Batchelor

Koreans

Sampling Province 80
Ethnographic Atlas: Ed1
Language: Korean
Location: The village of Sondup'o and town of Samku Li on
            Kanghwa Island 37°37′N, 126°25′E
Time: In 1847, the date of Osgood's field work
Authority: Osgood

Tungus

Sampling Province 81
Ethnographic Atlas: Ec9
Language: Altaic (Tungusic)
Location: The Goldi east of the Birarcen area, 47°N, 132°E
Time: In 1920, shortly after Shirokogoroff's field work
Authorities: Shirokogoroff, Lopatin

Lepcha

Sampling Province 85
Ethnographic Atlas: Ee3
Language: Tibeto-Burman (Tibetan)
Location: The Lepcha in the vicinity of Lingthem in Sikkim 27°
        to 28°N, 89°E
Time: In 1937, the date of Gorer's field work
Authorities: Gorer, Morris

Garo

Sampling Province 87
Ethnographic Atlas: Ei1
Language: Tibeto-Burman (Garo)
Location: The Garo of Rengsanggri and neighboring
        intermarrying villages 26°N, 91°E
Time: In 1955, during the period of Burling's field work
Authority: Burling

Lakher

Sampling Provinces 87/88
Ethnographic Atlas: Ei4
Language: Tibeto-Burman (Kuki-Chin)
Location: The small Lakher tribe as a whole 22°20′N, 93°E
Time: In 1930, the approximate date of Parry's field work
Authority: Parry

Lamet

Sampling Province 90
Ethnographic Atlas: Ej1
Language: Tibeto-Burman (Palaung-Wa)
Location: The small Lamet tribe as a whole 20°N, 100°40′E
Time: In 1940, the approximate date of the field work by
        Izikowitz
Authority: Izikowitz

Central Thai

Sampling Province 91
Ethnographic Atlas: Ej9
Language: Thai-Kadai
Location: The Central Thai village of Bang Chan 14°N, 100°50′E

Time: About 1955, the midpoint of the Cornell University
        research project
Authorities: Sharp, L. and J. Hanks

Andamanese

Sampling Province 92
Ethnographic Atlas: Eh1
Language: Andamanese
Location: The Aka-Bea tribe of South Andaman 11°45' to 12°N,
        93° to 93°10'E
Time: In 1860, prior to significant acculturation and
        depopulation
Authorities: Man, Radcliffe-Brown

Rhade

Sampling Province 96
Ethnographic Atlas: Ej10
Language: Malayo-Polynesian (Hesperonesian)
Location: The Rhade of the village of Ko-sier on the Darlac
        plateau
Time: In 1962, the date of Donoghue's field work
Authorities: Donoghue

Tanala

Sampling Province 8
Ethnographic Atlas: Eh3
Language: Malayo-Polynesian (Hesperonesian)
Location: The Menabe subtribe 22°S, 48°E
Time: In 1925, just prior to Linton's field work
Authority: Linton

INSULAR PACIFIC

Iban

Sampling Province 101
Ethnographic Atlas: Ib1
Language: Malayo-Polynesian (Hesperonesian)
Location: The Iban of the Ulu Ai group 2°N, 112°30' to 113°30'E
Time: In 1950, near the beginning of Freeman's field work
Authority: Freeman

Balinese

Sampling Province 104
Ethnographic Atlas: Ib3
Language: Malayo-Polynesian (Hesperonesian)
Location: The village of Tihingan in the district of Klunghung
        8°30'S, 105°20'E
Time: In 1958, the date of the field work of the Geertzes
Authorities: C. and H. Geertz

Alorese

Sampling Province 107
Ethnographic Atlas: Ic2
Language: Malayo-Polynesian (Moluccan)
Location: The village complex of Atimelang in north central
        Alor 8°20'S, 124°40'E
Time: In 1938, at the beginning of the field work by DuBois
Authority: Du Bois

Murngin

Sampling Province 108
Ethnographic Atlas: Id2
Language: Australian
Location: The Naladaer west of Buckingham Bay, 12°S, 136°E
Time: In 1930, immediately after completion of Warner's
        field work
Authorities: Warner, Berndt

Arunta

Sampling Province 109
Ethnographic Atlas: Id1
Language: Australian
Location: The Arunta Mbainda of Alice Springs 23°30'S,
        132°30' to 134°20'E
Time: In 1896, the date of the early field work by Spencer and
        Gillen
Authorities: Spencer and Gillen, Strehlow

Kiwai

Sampling Province 112
Ethnographic Atlas: Ie13

Language: Papuan
Location: Kiwai Island, 9°S, 143°E
Time: In 1920
Authority: Landtman

Wogeo

Sampling Province 113
Ethnographic Atlas: Ie4
Language: Malayo-Polynesian
Location: Wogeo Island, 3°S, 144°E
Time: In 1930, immediately prior to Hogbin's field work
Authority: Hogbin

Kapauku

Sampling Province 114
Ethnographic Atlas: Ie1
Language: Papuan (distinct family)
Location: The village of Botukebo in the Kamu Valley ca.
      4°S, 36°E
Time: In 1955, the date of Pospisil's first field trip
Authority: Pospisil

Palauans

Sampling Province 115
Ethnographic Atlas: If1
Language: Malayo-Polynesian (Hesperonesian)
Location: The village of Ulimang in northern Babelthuap Island
      7°30'N, 134°35'E
Time: In 1947, the date of Barnett's field work
Authorities: Barnett, Krämer

Yapese

Sampling Province 116
Ethnographic Atlas: If6
Language: Malayo-Polynesian (Carolinian)
Location: The island of Yap as a whole 9°30'N, 138°10'E
Time: In 1910, at the close of Müller's period of field work
Authorities: Müller, Schneider

Ifaluk

Sampling Province 117
Ethnographic Atlas: If4
Language: Malayo-Polynesian
Location: Ifaluk atoll, 7°N, 147°E
Time: In 1940, shortly before Burrows' and Spiro's field work
Authorities: Burrows and Spiro, Damm, Krämer

Marshallese

Sampling Province 118
Ethnographic Atlas: If3
Language: Malayo-Polynesian (Carolinian)
Location: The atoll of Jaluit 6°N, 165°30'E
Time: In 1900, the mean date of the early German
       ethnographers
Authorities: Erdland, Krämer and Nevermann

Manus

Sampling Province 120
Ethnographic Atlas: Ig9
Language: Malayo-Polynesian (Melanesian)
Location: The village of Peri 2°10'S, 147°E
Time: In 1929, the date of Mead's first field trip
Authority: Mead

New Ireland

Sampling Province 121
Ethnographic Atlas: Ig4
Language: Malayo-Polynesian (Melanesian)
Location: The village of Lesu 2°30'S, 151°E
Time: In 1930, at the time of Powdermaker's field work
Authority: Powdermaker

Trobrianders

Sampling Province 122
Ethnographic Atlas: Ig2
Language: Malayo-Polynesian
Location: The island of Kiriwina 8°38'S, 151°4'E
Time: In 1914, at the beginning of Malinowski's field work
Authority: Malinowski

Kurtatchi

Sampling Province 123
Ethnographic Atlas: Ig3
Language: Malayo-Polynesian
Location: Buka Island, 5°S, 154°E
Time: In 1930, during Blackwood's field work
Authority: Blackwood

Ontong Javanese

Sampling Province 124
Ethnographic Atlas: Ii5
Language: Malayo-Polynesian
Location: Ontong-Java Atoll, 5°S, 160°E
Time: In 1920
Authority: Hogbin

Tikopia

Sampling Province 125
Ethnographic Atlas: Ii2
Language: Malayo-Polynesian (Polynesian)
Location: The small island of Tikopia as a whole 12°30'S,
        168°30'E
Time: In 1930, at the conclusion of Firth's first field trip
Authority: Firth

Lau Fijians

Sampling Province 128
Ethnographic Atlas: Ih4
Language: Malayo-Polynesian
Location: The Lau Fijians of the dominion of the chief of
        Lakemba, 18°S, 179°E
Time: In 1920
Authorities: Hocart, Thompson

Samoans

Sampling Province 129
Ethnographic Atlas: Ii1
Language: Malayo-Polynesian (Polynesian)
Location: The kingdom of Aana in western Upolu Island 13°48'
        to 14°S, 171°54' to 172°3'W

Time: In 1829, prior to the military defeat of Aana and the
          beginning of intensive European contact
Authorities: Turner, Stair

Maori

Sampling Province 130
Ethnographic Atlas: Ij2
Language: Malayo-Polynesian (Polynesian)
Location: The Nga Puhi tribe of the northern isthmus 34°10′ to
          35°30′S, 174° to 174°20′E
Time: In 1820, prior to European settlement and missionization
Authorities: Earle, Clarke

Marquesans

Sampling Province 131
Ethnographic Atlas: Ij3
Language: Malayo-Polynesian (Polynesian)
Location: The Te-i′i chiefdom of southwestern Nuku Hiva
          Island 8°55′S, 140°10′W
Time: About 1800, at about the time of the earliest reliable
          descriptions
Authorities: Fleurieu, Forster, Langsdorff

NORTH AMERICA

Aleut

Sampling Province 132
Ethnographic Atlas: Na9
Language: Eskimauan (Aleut)
Location: The Unalaska branch of the Aleut 53° to 57°30′N, 158°
          to 170°W
Time: About 1800, prior to intensive acculturation
Authorities: Veniaminov, Sarytschew

Copper Eskimo

Sampling Province 133
Ethnographic Atlas: Na3
Language: Eskimauan (Eskimo)
Location: The Copper Eskimo of the Arctic mainland 66°40′ to
          69°20′N, 108° to 117°W
Time: In 1915, during the period of field work by Jenness
Authorities: Jenness, Rasmussen

Eyak

Sampling Province 136
Ethnographic Atlas: Nb5
Language: Eyak
Location: The small Eyak tribe as a whole 60° to 61°N, 144° to
 146°W
Time: In 1890, prior to full acculturation
Authorities: Birket-Smith and De Laguna

Kaska

Sampling Province 138
Ethnographic Atlas: Na4
Language: Athapaskan (Northern)
Location: The Kaska of the Upper Liard River 60°N, 131°W
Time: Reconstructed for 1900, just prior to intensive
 missionization
Authority: Honigmann

Kwakiutl

Sampling Province 139
Ethnographic Atlas: Nb3
Language: Wakashan
Location: The Kwakiutl of the Coast of British Columbia, 51°N,
 128°W
Time: In 1890
Authority: Boas

Twana

Sampling Province 140
Ethnographic Atlas: Nb2
Language: Salishan
Location: The small Twana tribe as a whole 47°20′ to 47°30′N,
 123°10′ to 123°20′W
Time: Reconstructed for 1860, prior to missionization
Authorities: Elmendorf, Eells

Hupa

Sampling Province 141
Ethnographic Atlas: Nb35
Language: Athapaskan (Pacific)
Location: The Hupa of the lower Trinity River, 41°N, 123°W

Time: Reconstructed for 1860, prior to establishment of a
     reservation
Authority: Goddard

Klamath

Sampling Provinces 142/148
Ethnographic Atlas: Nc8
Language: Sahaptin (Lutuamian)
Location: The Klamath tribe as a whole 42° to 43°15′N, 121°20′
     to 122°20′W
Time: In 1860, prior to intensive acculturation
Authorities: Spier, Gatschet

Yokuts

Sampling Province 144
Ethnographic Atlas: Nc24
Language: Penutian (Mariposan)
Location: The Lake Yokuts 35°10′N, 119°20′W
Time: In 1850, prior to the influx of settlers following the
     gold rush
Authority: Gayton

Paiute

Sampling Provinces 146/147
Ethnographic Atlas: Nd22
Language: Shoshonean
Location: The Wadadika or Harney Valley band of Northern
          Paiute 43° to 44°N, 118° to 120°W
Time: Reconstructed for about 1870, just prior to the
     establishment of the reservation
Authority: B. Whiting

Sanpoil

Sampling Province 149
Ethnographic Atlas: Nd4
Language: Salishan
Location: 48°N, 119°W
Time: Reconstructed for 1870, immediately prior to
     establishment of the reservation
Authority: Ray

Gros Ventre

Sampling Province 150
Ethnographic Atlas: Ne1
Language: Algonkian
Location: The homogeneous Gros Ventre as a whole 47° to
        49°N, 106° to 110°W
Time: In 1880, shortly prior to missionization and the
        disappearance of the buffalo
Authorities: Flannery, Cooper

Micmac

Sampling Province 152
Ethnographic Atlas: Na41
Language: Algonkian
Location: The Micmac of the mainland 43°30' to 50°N,
        60° to 66°W
Time: In 1650, midway in the governorship of Denys
Authorities: Denys, Le Clercq

Northern Saulteaux

Sampling Province 153
Ethnographic Atlas: Na33
Language: Algonkian
Location: The Northern Saulteaux of the Berens River band
        52°N, 95°30'W
Time: In 1930, at the beginning of Hallowell's field work
Authority: Hallowell

Hidatsa

Sampling Province 154
Ethnographic Atlas: Ne15
Language: Siouan
Location: The village of Hidatsa 47°N, 101°W
Time: Reconstructed for 1836, prior to depopulation in a severe
        smallpox epidemic
Authorities: Bowers, Matthews

Creek

Sampling Province 157
Ethnographic Atlas: Ng3

Language: Natchez-Muskogean (Muskogean)
Location: The Upper Creek of Alabama 32°30' to 34°20'N,
          85°30' to 86°30'W
Time: In 1800, prior to Tecumseh's rebellion and removal to
      Oklahoma
Authority: Swanton

Pawnee

Sampling Province 159
Ethnographic Atlas: Nf6
Language: Caddoan
Location: The Skidi or Skiri Pawnee 42°N, 100°W
Time: Reconstructed for 1867
Authorities: Weltfish, Dorsey and Murie

Chiricahua Apache

Sampling Province 161
Ethnographic Atlas: Nh1
Language: Athapaskan (Southern)
Location: The central band or Chiricahua proper 32°N,
          109°30'W
Time: In 1870, immediately prior to the reservation period
Authority: Opler

Navaho

Sampling Province 162
Ethnographic Atlas: Nh3
Language: Athapaskan (Southern)
Location: The Navaho in the vicinity of Monument Valley,
          37°N, 110°W
Time: In 1930
Authorities: Kluckhohn and Leighton, Bailey

Papago

Sampling Province 163
Ethnographic Atlas: Ni2
Language: Piman
Location: The Archie Papago near Sells, Arizona 32°N, 112°W
Time: In 1910, the date of the early observations by Lumholtz
Authorities: Underhill, Lumholtz, Foster

Tarasco

Sampling Province 165
Ethnographic Atlas: Nj8
Language: Tarascan
Location: 19°N, 101°W
Time: In the sixteenth century
Authorities: Beals, Lumholtz

Zapotec

Sampling Province 166
Ethnographic Atlas: Nj10
Language: Zapotecan
Location: The Zapotec of Mitla, 17°N, 96°W
Time: In 1940, following Parson's field work
Authorities: Parsons, Nader

SOUTH AMERICA

Miskito

Sampling Province 168
Ethnographic Atlas: Sa9
Language: Misumalpan
Location: The Miskito in the vicinity of Cape Gracias a Dios
          15°N, 83°W
Time: In 1921, the date of the field work by Conzemius
Authority: Conzemius

Bribri

Sampling Province 169
Ethnographic Atlas: Sa5
Language: Chibchan
Location: The Bribri tribe of the Talamanca nation 9°N, 83°15'W
Time: In 1917, the date of Skinner's field work
Authorities: Stone, Skinner

Cuna

Sampling Province 170
Ethnographic Atlas: Sa1
Language: Chibchan

Location: The Cuna of the San Blas Archipelago 9° to 9°30'N,
     78° to 79°W
Time: In 1927, the date of Nordenskiöld's field work
Authorities: Nordenskiöld, Wafer, Stout

Goajiro

Sampling Province 172
Ethnographic Atlas: Sb6
Language: Arawakan
Location: The homogeneous Goajiro tribe as a whole 11°30' to
     12°20'N, 71° to 72°30'W
Time: In 1947, the date of the field work by Gutiérrez de
     Pineda
Authorities: Gutiérrez de Pineda, Bolinder

Callinago

Sampling Province 173
Ethnographic Atlas: Sb1
Language: Cariban
Location: The Callinago of the island of Dominica 15°30'N,
     60°30'W
Time: Reconstructed for 1650, shortly prior to missionization
Authorities: Breton, Taylor

Warrau

Sampling Provinces 175/176
Ethnographic Atlas: Sc1
Language: Warrauan
Location: The Warrau of the Orinoco delta 8°30' to 9°50'N,
     60°40' to 62°30'W
Time: In 1935, early in the period of missionary field work by
     Turrado Moreno
Authorities: Turrado Moreno, Wilbert

Carib

Sampling Province 178
Ethnographic Atlas: Sc3
Language: Cariban
Location: The Carib along the Barama River in British Guiana
     7°10' to 7°40'N, 29°20' to 60°20'W
Time: In 1932, at the beginning of Gillin's field work
Authority: Gillin

Saramacca

Sampling Province 179
Ethnographic Atlas: Sc6
Language: Indo-European (creolized Romance)
Location: The Saramacca group of Bush Negroes in the upper
basin of the Suriname River 3° to 4°N, 55°30' to 56°W
Time: In 1928, early in the periods of field work of Herskovits
and Kahn
Authorities: Kahn, Herskovits

Mundurucu

Sampling Provinces 180/181
Ethnographic Atlas: Sd1
Language: Tupi-Guarani
Location: The savanna-dwelling Mundurucu of the Rio de
Tropas drainage 6° to 7°S, 56° to 57°W
Time: Reconstructed for about 1850, prior to the period of
increasing assimilation
Authorities: Murphy, Tocantins

Witoto

Sampling Province 182
Ethnographic Atlas: Se6
Language: Witotan
Location: 1°S, 74°W
Time: In 1900, shortly before Whiffen's exploration
Authorities: Whiffen, Steward

Jivaro

Sampling Province 183
Ethnographic Atlas: Se3
Language: Jivaran
Location: The Jivaro proper 2° to 4°S, 77° to 79°W
Time: In 1920, near the beginning of Karsten's field work
Authorities: Karsten, Stirling

Amahuaca

Sampling Province 184
Ethnographic Atlas: Se8
Language: Panoan

Location: The Amahuaca on the upper Inuya River 10° 10' to
           10°30'S, 72° to 72°30'W
Time: In 1960, the date of the beginning of the field work by
       Carneiro and Dole
Authorities: Carneiro, Dole, Huxley and Capa

Aymara

Sampling Province 186
Ethnographic Atlas: Sf2
Language: Kechumaran (Aymaran)
Location: The Aymara of the community of Chucuito in Peru
           16°S, 70°W
Time: In 1940, at the beginning of Tschopik's field work
Authority: Tschopik

Siriono

Sampling Province 187
Ethnographic Atlas: Se1
Language: Tupi-Guarani
Location: The Siriono in the forests near the Rio Blanco 14° to
           15°S, 63° to 64°W
Time: In 1942, during the period of Holmberg's field work
Authority: Holmberg

Nambicuara

Sampling Province 188
Ethnographic Atlas: Si4
Language: Nambicuaran
Location: The Cocozu or eastern Nambicuara 12°30' to 13°30'S,
           58°30' to 59°W
Time: In 1940, shortly prior to the field work of Lévi-Strauss
Authority: Lévi-Strauss

Timbira

Sampling Province 190
Ethnographic Atlas: Sj4
Language: Ge
Location: The Ramcocamecra or Eastern Timbira 6° to 7°S, 45°
           to 46°W

Time: In 1915, near the beginning of Nimuendajú's field work
Authorities: Nimuendajú, Crocker

Tupinamba

Sampling Province 191
Ethnographic Atlas: Sj8
Language: Tupi-Guarani
Location: The Tupinamba near Rio de Janeiro 22°30' to 23°S,
        42° to 44°30'W
Time: In 1550, at the time of Staden's captivity
Authorities: Staden, Thevet

Aweikoma

Sampling Province 194
Ethnographic Atlas: Sj3
Language: Ge (Caingang)
Location: The Aweikoma of the Duque de Caxias reservation
        38°S, 50°W
Time: In 1932, at the beginning of Henry's field work
Authority: Henry

Lengua

Sampling Province 196
Ethnographic Atlas: Sh9
Language: Mascoian
Location: The Lengua in contact with the Anglican mission 23°
        to 24°S, 28° to 29°W
Time: In 1889, the date of the founding of the mission
Authority: Grubb

Mapuche

Sampling Province 198
Ethnographic Atlas: Sg2
Language: Araucanian
Location: The Mapuche in the vicinity of Temuco 38°30'S,
        72°35'W
Time: In 1950, just prior to Faron's field work
Authorities: Faron, Hilger, Titiev

Yahgan

Sampling Province 200
Ethnographic Atlas: Sg1
Language: Yahgan
Location: The eastern and central Yahgan 54°30′ to 55°30′S, 67°
    to 70°W
Time: Reconstructed for 1865, early in the period of missionary
    field work by Bridges
Authorities: Gusinde, Bridges, Lothrop

Ethnographic Source Bibliography

Starred (*) sources are those recommended by George Murdock and Douglas White in "Standard Cross-Cultural Sample," *Ethnology* 8 (1969): 329–69. A single asterisk represents a primary source and a double asterisk a secondary source.

AFRICA

Ashanti

Basehart, Harry W. "Ashanti." In *Matrilineal Kinship*, edited by David Schneider and Kathleen Gough. Berkeley: University of California Press, 1961, pp. 270–97.

Busia, Kofi A. *The Position of the Chief in the Modern Political System of Ashanti*. London: Oxford University Press, 1951.

Christensen, James. *Double Descent Among the Fanti*. New Haven: HRAF Press, 1954.

*Fortes, Meyer. "Kinship and Marriage Among the Ashanti." In *African Systems of Kinship and Marriage*, edited by A. R. Radcliffe-Brown and Daryll Forde. London: Oxford University Press, 1950, pp. 252–84.

*———. *Social Structure*. New York: Russell & Russell, 1963.

*———. "The Ashanti Social Survey." *Journal of the Rhodes-Livingstone Institute* 6 (1948): 1–36.

Habenstein, Robert, and William Lamers. *Funeral Customs the World Over*. Milwaukee: Bulfin Printers, 1963.

Manoukian, Madeline. *Akan and Ga-Adangme Peoples of the Gold Coast*. London: Oxford University Press, 1950.

*Rattray, Robert S. *Ashanti*. London: Oxford University Press, 1923.

*———. *Ashanti Law and Constitution*. London: Oxford University Press, 1929.

*———. *Ashanti Proverbs*. Oxford: Clarendon Press, 1916.

*———. *Religion and Art in Ashanti*. London: Oxford University Press, 1927.

*———— . "Totemism and Blood Groups in West Africa." In *Custom Is King*, edited by David Buxton. London: Hutchinson, 1936, pp. 17–32.

Azande

Brock, R. G. C. "Some Notes on the Zande Tribe as Found in the Meridi District." *Sudan Notes and Records* 1 (1918): 249–62.

Czekanowski, Jan. "Forschungen im Nil-Kongo Zwischengebiet." *Wissenschaftlicht Ergebnisse der Deutschen Zentral Afrika, 1907–1908.* Leipzig: Klinkhardt and Biermann, 1924.

*Evans-Pritchard, E. E. "A Final Contribution to the Study of Zande Culture." *Africa* 35 (1965): 1–7.

*———— . "Cannibalism: A Zande Text." *Africa* 26 (1956): 73–74.

*———— . *Essays in Social Anthropology.* New York: Free Press, 1963.

*———— . "Heredity and Gestation as the Azande See Them." *Sociologus* 3 (1932): 400–14.

*———— . "Social Character of Bridewealth with Special Reference to the Azande." *Man* 34 (1934): 172–75.

*———— . "Some Collective Expressions of Obscenity in Africa." *Journal of the Royal Anthropological Institute of Great Britain and Ireland* 59 (1929): 318–20.

*———— . "Sorcery and Native Opinion." *Africa* 4 (1931): 22–55.

*———— . *The Azande: History and Political Institutions.* Oxford: Clarendon Press, 1971.

*———— . *The Position of Women in Primitive Societies and Other Essays in Anthropology.* New York: Free Press, 1965.

*———— . "The Zande Royal Court." *Zaire* 11 (1957): 361–89, 491–511, 687–713.

*———— . "Witchcraft Among the Azande." *Sudan Notes and Records* 12 (1929): 163–249.

*———— . *Witchcraft, Oracles, and Magic Among the Azande.* Oxford: Clarendon Press, 1937.

*———— . "Zande Blood-Brotherhood." *Africa* 6 (1933): 369–440.

*———— . "Zande Border Raids." *Africa* 27 (1957): 217–30.

*———— . "Zande Warfare." *Anthropos* 52 (1957): 239–62.

Graffen, Enrico, and Eduardo Columbo. "Les Niam-Niam." *Revue Internationale de Sociologie* 14 (1906): 769-99.

Habenstein, Robert, and William Lamers. *Funeral Customs the World Over.* Milwaukee: Bulfin Printers, 1963.

Huntingford, G. W. B. *Ethnographic Survey of East Central Africa.* London: International African Institute, 1969.

Hutereau, Armand. *Notes on the Family and Legal Life of Some Peoples of the Belgian Congo.* Brussels: Ministre des Colonies, 1909.

Lagae, C. R. "Les Azande ou Niam-Niam." *Bibliothèque-Congo* 18 (1926): 1–224.

Larkin, P. M. "An Account of the Zande." *Sudan Notes and Records* 9 (1926): 1–55, and 10 (1927): 85–134.

———. "Impressions of the Azande." *Sudan Notes and Records* 13 (1930): 99–115.

Phillips, J. E. Tracy. "Observations on Some Aspects of Religion Among the Azande ('Niam-Niam') of Equatorial Africa." *Journal of the Royal Anthropological Institute of Great Britain and Ireland* 56 (1926): 171–89.

Seligman, Charles G., and Brenda Z. Seligman. *Pagan Tribes of the Nilotic Sudan.* London: George Routledge & Kegan Paul, 1932.

Bambara

Dieterlen, Germaine. *Essai sur la religion Bambara.* Paris: Presses Universitaires de France, 1951.

*Henry, Joseph. "L'âme d'un peuple Africain: les Bambara." *Bibliothèque Anthropos* 1 (1910): 1–240.

*Monteil, Charles. *Les Bambara du Ségou et du Kaarta.* Paris: LaRose, 1924.

**Pacques, Viviana. *Les Bambara.* Paris: Presses Universitaires de France, 1954.

Fon

Beraud, M. "Note sur le Dahomé." *Bulletin de la Société de Géographie* 12, ser. 5 (1866): 371–86.

Burton, R. F. "The Present State of Dahomé." *Transactions of the Ethnological Society of London* 3 (1865): 400–07.

Foa, Edouard. *Le Dahomey.* Paris: A. Hennuyer, 1895.

Forbes, Frederick E. *Dahomey and the Dahomans.* London: Longmans, Brown, Green, & Longmans, 1851.

Habenstein, Robert, and William Lamers. *Funeral Customs the World Over.* Milwaukee: Bulfin Printers, 1963.

*Herskovits, Melville J. *Dahomey.* 2 vols. New York: J. J. Augustin, 1938.

*Le Herissé, A. *L'ancien royaume du Dahomey.* Paris: LaRose, 1911.

Murdock, George P. *Our Primitive Contemporaries.* New York: Macmillan, 1934.

Ganda

Apter, David. *The Political Kingdom in Uganda.* Princeton, N.J.: Princeton University Press, 1961.

Fallers, M. C. *The Eastern Lacustrine Bantu.* London: International African Institute, 1960.

Felkin, R. W. "Notes on the Waganda Tribe of Central Africa." *Proceedings of the Royal Society of Edinburgh* 13 (1886): 699–770.

Habenstein, Robert, and William Lamers. *Funeral Customs the World Over.* Milwaukee: Bulfin Printers, 1963.

Kagwa, Apolo. *The Customs of the Baganda.* New York: Columbia University Press, 1934.

*Mair, Lucy. *An African People in the Twentieth Century.* London: George Routledge & Sons, 1934.

*———. "Buganda Land Tenure." *Africa* 6 (1933): 187–205.

*———. *Native Marriage in Buganda.* London: Oxford University Press, 1940.

*———. *Primitive Government.* Baltimore: Penguin Books, 1962.

Murdock, George P. *Our Primitive Contemporaries.* New York: Macmillan, 1934.

Richards, Audrey. "The Assimilation of the Immigrants and the Problem for Buganda." In *Economic Development and Tribal Change,* edited by Audrey Richards. Cambridge, England: W. Heffer & Sons, 1954, pp. 161–223.

*Roscoe, John. "Further Notes on the Manners and Customs of the Baganda." *Journal of the Anthropological Institute of Great Britain and Ireland* 32 (1902): 25–80.

*———. "Notes on the Manners and Customs of the Baganda." *Journal of the Anthropological Institute of Great Britain and Ireland* 31 (1901): 117–30.

*———. *The Baganda: An Account of Their Native Customs and Beliefs.* London: Macmillan, 1911.

*———. "The Negro-Hamitic People of Uganda." *Scottish Geographical Magazine* 39 (1923): 145–58.

*———. *Twenty-Five Years in East Africa.* Cambridge: Cambridge University Press, 1921.

*———. "Worship of the Dead as Practiced by Some African Tribes." *Harvard African Studies* 1 (1917): 33–47.

Southwold, Martin. *Bureaucracy and Chiefship in Buganda.* Kampala, Uganda: East African Institute of Social Research, 1961.

———. "The Ganda of Uganda." In *Peoples of Africa,* edited by James Gibbs, Jr. New York: Holt, Rinehart and Winston, 1965, pp. 88–118.

Speke, John H. *Journal of the Discovery of the Source of the Nile.* London: Blackwood & Sons, 1863.

Thomas, Harold B., and Robert Scott. *Uganda.* London: Oxford University Press, 1935.

Wrigley, Christopher. *Crops and Wealth in Uganda.* Kampala, Uganda: East African Institute of Social Research, 1960.

Kung

Bleek, Dorothea F. "Bushmen Terms of Relationship, and Note on Bushmen Orthography." *Bantu Studies* 2 (1924): 57–74.

Fourie, L. "The Bushmen of South West Africa." In *The Native Tribes of South West Africa,* edited by H. P. Smit. Cape Town: Cape Times, 1928.

Lebzelter, Viktor. *Eingeborenen Kulturen in Sudwest-und Sudafrika.* Leipzig: Karl Hiersemann, 1934.

Marshall, John. "Man as Hunter." *Natural History* 72 (1958): 291–309, 376–95.

*Marshall, Lorna. "!Kung Bushman Bands." *Africa* 30 (1960): 325–55.

*———. "!Kung Bushmen Religious Beliefs." *Africa* 32 (1962): 221–52.

*———. "Marriage Among the !Kung Bushmen." *Africa* 29 (1959): 335–65.

*———. "Sharing, Talking, and Giving: Relief of Social Tensions Among !Kung Bushmen." *Africa* 31 (1961): 231–49.

*———. "The Kin Terminology System of the !Kung Bushmen." *Africa* 27 (1957): 1–25.

*———. "The !Kung Bushmen of the Kalahari Desert." In *Peoples of Africa,* edited by James Gibbs, Jr. New York: Holt, Rinehart and Winston, 1965, pp. 241–78.

Oswalt, Wendell. *Other Peoples, Other Customs.* New York: Holt, Rinehart and Winston, 1972.

Schapera, Isaac. *The Khoisan Peoples of South Africa.* London: George Routledge & Sons, 1930.

Thomas, Elizabeth. *The Harmless People.* New York: Knopf, 1959.

Lamba

*Doke, Clement M. "Lamba Folklore." *Memoirs of the American Folklore Society* 20 (1927): 1–570.

*———. *The Lambas of Northern Rhodesia.* London: George Harrap, 1931.

Luguru

*Beidelman, T. O. *The Matrilineal Peoples of Eastern Tanzania.* London: International African Institute, 1967.

Christensen, James. "Utani Joking: Sexual License and Social Obligations Among the Luguru." *American Anthropologist* 65 (1963): 1314–27.

McVicar, Thomas. "Death Rites Among the Waluguru and Wanguru." *Primitive Man* 18 (1945): 26–35.

———— . "Sibs, Privileged Familiarity and Cross-Cousin Marriage Among the Waluguru." *Primitive Man* 8 (1935): 57–67.

———— . "The Position of Woman Among the Wanguru." *Primitive Man* 7 (1934): 17–22.

———— . "The Relations Between Religion and Morality Among the Wanguru." *Primitive Man* 7 (1935): 1–5.

Mzuanda, C. *Historia ya Uluguru.* Dar-es-Salaam, Tanzania: Luguru Native Authority, 1958.

*Scheerder, R., and R. Tastevin. "Les Wa lu guru." *Anthropos* 45 (1950): 241–86.

Wallis, P. "Waluguru Sibs." *Primitive Man* 7 (1935): 58–63.

Masai

Bernardi, B. "The Age System of the Masai." *Annali Lateranensi* 18 (1954): 257–318.

Fosbrooke, H. "An Administrative Survey of the Masai Social System." *Tanganyika Notes and Records* 26 (1948): 1–50.

Fox, D. S. "Further Notes on the Masai of Kenya." *Journal of the Royal Anthropological Institute of Great Britain and Ireland* 40 (1910): 473–82.

Hollis, Alfred. "Note on the Masai System of Relationship." *Journal of the Royal Anthropological Institute of Great Britain and Ireland* 40 (1910): 473–82.

———— . *The Masai: Their Language and Folklore.* Oxford: Clarendon Press, 1905.

Huntingford, G. W. B. *Ethnographic Survey of East Central Africa.* London: International African Institute, 1969.

———— . *The Southern Nilo-Hamites.* London: International African Institute, 1953.

*Jacobs, Alan. "Bibliography of the Masai." *African Studies Bulletin* 8 (1965): 40–60.

Leakey, L. S. B. "Some Notes on the Masai of Kenya Colony." *Journal of the Royal Anthropological Institute of Great Britain and Ireland* 60 (1930): 185–210.

Maguire, R. A. "The Masai Penal Code." *African Society Journal* 28 (1928): 12–18.

*Merker, Meritz. *Die Masai.* Berlin: Dietrich Reimer, 1904.

Sanford, George. *An Administrative and Political History of the Masai Reserve.* London: Waterlow & Sons, 1919.

Thomson, Joseph. *Through Masai Land*. London: Sampson Low, Marston, Searle & Rivington, 1887.
Young, Roland. *Through Masailand with Joseph Thomson*. Chicago: Northwestern University Press, 1962.

Mbuti

Putnam, Patrick. "The Pygmies of the Ituri Forest." In *A Reader in General Anthropology*, edited by Carleton S. Coon. New York: Henry Holt, 1948, pp. 322–42.
*Schebesta, Paul. *Among Congo Pygmies*. London: Hutchinson, 1933.
*————. "Die Bambuti-Pygmäen vom Ituri: Ethnographie der Ituri-Bambuti, Das soziale Leben." *Mémoires de l'Institut Royal Colonial Belge* 2 (1948): 1–551.
*————. "Die Bambuti-Pygmäen vom Ituri: Ethnographie der Ituri-Bambuti, Die Wirtschaft der Ituri-Bambuti." *Mémoires de l'Institut Royal Colonial Belge* 2 (1941): 1–284.
*————. "Die Bambuti-Pygmäen vom Ituri: Geschichte, Geographie, Umwelt, Demographie, und Anthropologie." *Mémoires de l'Institut Royal Colonial Belge* 1 (1938): 1–438.
*————. "Les Pygmées du Congo belge." *Mémoires de l'Institut Royal Colonial Belge* 26 (1952): 1–432.
*————. *My Pygmy and Negro Hosts*. London: Hutchinson, 1936.
*————. *Revisiting My Pygmy Hosts*. London: Hutchinson, 1937.
*————. *Vollblutneger und Halbzwerge*. Salzburg: Anton Pustet, 1934.
*Turnbull, Colin. "Initiation Among the BaMbuti Pygmies of the Central Ituri." *Journal of the Royal Anthropological Institute of Great Britain and Ireland* 87 (1957): 191–216.
*————. *The Forest People*. New York: Simon and Schuster, 1962.
*————. "The Mbuti Pygmies." *Anthropological Papers of the American Museum of Natural History* 50 (1965): 1–282.
*————. "The Mbuti Pygmies of the Congo." In *Peoples of Africa*, edited by James Gibbs, Jr. New York: Holt, Rinehart and Winston, 1965, pp. 279–317.
*————. *Wayward Servants*. Garden City, N.Y.: Natural History Press, 1965.

Mongo

Brown, H. D. "The Nkumu of the Tumba: Ritual Chieftainship on the Middle Congo." *Africa* 14 (1944): 431–46.
Gutersohn, T. H. "Het economisch Leven van den Mongo-neger." *Congo* 1 (1920): 92–105.

*Hulstaert, Gustave-E. "Le mariage des Nkundó." *Mémoires de l'Institut Royal Colonial Belge* 8 (1928): 1–520.

*————. *Les Mongo*. Tervuren, Belgium: Musée Royal de l'Afrique Centrale, 1961.

Maes, Joseph. *Notes sur les populations des bassins du Kasai, de la Lukenie, et du Lac Leopold II*. Brussels: Librarie Falk Fils, 1924.

Van der Kerken, G. "L'ethnie Mongo." *Mémoires de l'Institut Royal Colonial Belge* 3 (1944): 1–1143.

Nama

Habenstein, Robert, and William Lamers. *Funeral Customs the World Over*. Milwaukee: Bulfin Printers, 1963.

Hahn, Theophilus. *Tsuni-//Goam, the Supreme Being of the Khoi-Khoi*. London: Trübner, 1881.

Hoernle, A. Winifred. "Certain Rites of Transition and the Conception of !Nau Among the Hottentots." *Harvard African Studies* 2 (1918): 65–82.

————. "The Social Organization of the Nama Hottentot of South Africa." *American Anthropologist* 27 (1925): 1–24.

Laidter, R. "Magic Medicine Among Hottentots." *South African Journal of Science* 25 (1928): 433.

Murdock, George P. *Our Primitive Contemporaries*. New York: Macmillan, 1934.

Oswalt, Wendell. *Other Peoples, Other Customs*. New York: Holt, Rinehart and Winston, 1972.

**Schapera, Isaac. *The Khoisan Peoples of South Africa*. London: George Routledge & Sons, 1930.

**Schapera, Isaac, and B. Farrington, eds. *Early Cape Hottentots*. Cape Town: Van Riebeeck Society, 1933.

*Schultze, Leonhard. *Aus Namaland und Kalahari*. Jena: G. Fischer, 1907.

*————. "Zur Kenntnis des Körpers der Hottentotten und. Büschmänner." *Denkschriften der Medizinisch-Naturwissenschaftlichen Gesellschaft Zu Jena* 17 (1928): 147–227.

Nyakyusa

Gulliver, P. H. *Land Tenure and Social Change Among the Nyakyusa*. Kampala, Uganda: East African Institute of Social Research, 1958.

Lehmann, F. R. "Notes on the Daily Life of the Nyakyusa." *Sociologus* 1 (1951): 138–48.

Moreau, R. "Joking Relationships in Tanganyika." *Africa* 14 (1943–44): 386–400.

Wilson, Godfrey. "An Introduction to Nyakyusa Society." *Bantu Studies* 10 (1936): 253–91.

——— . "Introduction to Nyakyusa Law." *Africa* 10 (1937): 16–36.

——— . "Nyakyusa Conventions of Burial." *Bantu Studies* 13 (1939): 1–31.

——— . "The Land Rights of Individuals Among the Nyakyusa." *Rhodes-Livingstone Papers* 1 (1938): 1–52.

——— . "The Nyakyusa of South-Western Tanganyika." In *Seven Tribes of British Central Africa*, edited by Elizabeth Colson and Max Gluckman. Manchester: Manchester University Press, 1951, pp. 253–91.

*Wilson, Monica. *Communal Rituals of the Nyakyusa*. London: Oxford University Press, 1959.

*——— . *Good Company*. Boston: Beacon Press, 1951.

*——— . "Nyakyusa Kinship." In *African Systems of Kinship*, edited by A. R. Radcliffe-Brown and Daryll Forde. London: Oxford University Press, 1950, pp. 111–39.

*——— . *Rituals of Kinship Among the Nyakyusa*. London: Oxford University Press, 1957.

Shilluk

Butt, Audrey. *The Nilotes of the Anglo-Egyptian Sudan and Uganda*. London: International African Institute, 1952.

Dempsey, James. *Mission on the Nile*. London: Burns & Oates, 1955.

Evans-Pritchard, E. E. *The Divine Kingship of the Shilluk of the Nilotic Sudan*. Cambridge: Cambridge University Press, 1948.

Howell, P. P. "Observations on the Shilluk of the Upper Nile. Customary Law: Marriage and the Violation of Rights in Women." *Africa* 23 (1953): 94–109.

——— . "Observations on the Shilluk of the Upper Nile. The Laws of Homicide and the Legal Functions of the Reth." *Africa* 22 (1952): 97–110.

Howell, P. P., and W. Thomson. "The Death of a Reth of the Shilluk." *Sudan Notes and Records* 27 (1946): 4–85.

Oyler, D. S. "Nikawng's Place in the Shilluk Religion." *Sudan Notes and Records* 1 (1918): 283–92.

——— . "Shilluk Notes." *Sudan Notes and Records* 9 (1926): 57–68.

——— . "The Shilluk's Belief in the Evil Eye: The Evil Medicine Man." *Sudan Notes and Records* 2 (1919): 122–37.

——— . "The Shilluk's Belief in the Good Medicine Men." *Sudan Notes and Records* 3 (1920): 110–16.

Pumphrey, M. E. C. "The Shilluk Tribe." *Sudan Notes and Records* 24 (1941): 1–45.

*Seligman, Charles G., and Brenda Z. Seligman. *Pagan Tribes of the Nilotic Sudan.* London: George Routledge & Kegan Paul, 1932.

*Westermann, Diedrich. *The Shilluk People, Their Language and Folklore.* Philadelphia: Board of Foreign Missions of the United Presbyterian Church of North America, 1912.

Suku

Cory, Hans. *The Indigenous Political System of the Sukuma.* Nairobi: Eagle Press, 1954.

*Kopytoff, Igor. "Extension of Conflict as a Method of Conflict Resolution Among the Suku of the Congo." *Journal of Conflict Resolution* 5 (1961): 61–9.

*———. "Family and Lineage Among the Suku of the Congo." In *The Family Estate in Africa,* edited by Robert Gray and Philip H. Gulliver. Boston: Boston University Press, 1964, pp. 83–116.

*———. "The Suku of Southwestern Congo." In *Peoples of Africa,* edited by James Gibbs, Jr. New York: Holt, Rinehart and Winston, 1965, pp. 441–77.

*Torday, Emil, and T. A. Joyce. "Notes ethnographiques sur des populations habitant les bassins du Kasai et du Kwango Oriental." *Annales du Musée du Congo Belge* 2 (1922): 1–359.

*———. "Notes on the Ethnography of the Ba-Yaka." *Journal of the Anthropological Institute of Great Britain and Ireland* 36 (1906): 39–58.

Van de Ginste, Fernand. "Le mariage chez les Basuku." *Bulletin des Juridictions Indigènes et du Droit Coutumier Congolais* 1–2 (1947): 17–28, 33–50.

Tallensi

*Fortes, Meyer. *Oedipus and Job.* Cambridge: Cambridge University Press, 1959.

*———. "Social and Psychological Aspects of Education in Taleland." Supplement to *Africa* 11 (1938): 1–64.

*———. *The Dynamics of Clanship Among the Tallensi.* London: Oxford University Press, 1945.

*———. "The Political System of the Tallensi of the Northern Territories of the Gold Coast." In *African Political Systems,* edited by Meyer Fortes and E. E. Evans-Pritchard. London: Oxford University Press, 1940, pp. 238–71.

*———. *The Web of Kinship Among the Tallensi.* London: Oxford University Press, 1949.

Rattray, Robert S. *The Tribes of the Ashanti Hinterland.* Vol. 2. Oxford: Clarendon Press, 1932.

Thonga

*Junod, Henri A. *The Life of a South African Tribe*. 2 vols. New Hyde Park, N.Y.: University Books, 1962.

Tiv

Abraham, Roy C. *The Tiv People*. London: Crown Agents for the Colonies, 1940.

*Akiga. *Akiga's Story: The Tiv Tribe as Seen by One of Its Members*, translated by Rupert East. London: Oxford University Press, 1939.

*Bohannan, Laura. "Political Aspects of Tiv Social Organization." In *Tribes Without Rulers*, edited by John Middleton and David Tait. London: Routledge & Kegan Paul, 1958, pp. 33–66.

*Bohannan, Paul. "Homicide Among the Tiv of Central Nigeria." In *African Homicide and Suicide*, edited by Paul Bohannan. Princeton, N.J.: Princeton University Press, 1960, pp. 154–78.

*———. *Justice and Judgement Among the Tiv*. London: Oxford University Press, 1957.

*———. "Some Principles of Exchange and Investment Among the Tiv." *American Anthropologist* 57 (1955): 60–70.

*———. "The Tiv of Nigeria." In *Peoples of Africa*, edited by James Gibbs, Jr. New York: Holt, Rinehart and Winston, 1965, pp. 513–46.

*———. *Tiv Farm and Settlement*. London: H.M. Stationery Office, 1954.

*Bohannan, Paul, and Laura Bohannan. *A Source Notebook in the Tiv Life Cycle*. New Haven: HRAF Press, 1966.

*———. *Source Notebooks*. 3 vols. New Haven: HRAF Press, 1966.

*———. *The Tiv of Central Nigeria*. London: International African Institute, 1953.

Bowen, Elenore S. *Return to Laughter*. New York: Harper & Row, 1964.

Downes, Roger M. *The Tiv Tribe*. Kaduna: Nigerian Government Printer, 1933.

Temple, Charles. *Notes on the Tribes, Provinces, Emirates, and States of the Northern Provinces of Nigeria*. Lagos: C.M.S. Bookshop, 1922.

CIRCUM-MEDITERRANEAN

Amhara

Bruce, James. *Travels to Discover the Source of the Nile*. Edinburgh: Edinburgh University Press, 1964.

Levine, Donald. *Wax and Gold: Tradition and Innovation in Ethiopian Culture*. Chicago: University of Chicago Press, 1965.

Lipsky, George A. *Ethiopia*. New Haven: HRAF Press, 1962.

*Messing, Simon D. "The Highland-Plateau Amhara of Ethiopia." Ann Arbor, Mich.: University Microfilms, 1957.

Reminick, Ronald A. "Ritual of Defloration: The Symbolic Expression of Authority and Masculinity Within the Institution of Marriage Among the Manze Amhara of Ethiopia." Paper delivered at the 70th Annual Meeting of the American Anthropological Association, New York, November 1971.

Rey, Charles F. *The Real Abyssinia.* London: Seeley, Service, 1935.

———— . *Unconquered Abyssinia.* Philadelphia: J. B. Lippincott, 1924.

Trimingham, J. Spencer. *Islam in Ethiopia.* London: Frank Cass, 1965.

Basques

*Caro Baroja, Julio. *La vida rural en Vera de Bidasoa.* Madrid: Talleres Gráficos E. T., 1944.

*———— . *Los pueblos del norte de la península ibérica.* Madrid: Aldecoa, 1943.

*———— . *Los vascos.* San Sebastián: Biblioteca Vascongada de los Amigos del País, 1949.

Douglass, William A. *Death in Murelaga.* Seattle: University of Washington Press, 1969.

Fur

*Beaton, A. C. "The Fur." *Sudan Notes and Records* 29 (1948): 1–39.

*———— . "Youth Organization Among the Fur." *Sudan Notes and Records* 24 (1941): 181–87.

*Felkin, Robert. "Notes on the Fur Tribe of Central Africa." *Proceedings of the Royal Society of Edinburgh* 13 (1884–86): 205–65.

MacMichael, Harold A. *A History of the Arabs in the Sudan.* Vol. 1. Cambridge: Cambridge University Press, 1922.

Seligman, Charles G., and Brenda Z. Seligman. *Pagan Tribes of the Nilotic Sudan.* London: George Routledge & Kegan Paul, 1932.

Gheg

*Coon, Carleton S. "The Mountains of Giants." *Papers of the Peabody Museum of American Archaeology and Ethnology* 23 (1950): 3–105.

*Durham, M. Edith. *Some Tribal Origins, Laws, and Customs of the Balkans.* London: Allen & Unwin, 1928.

Hasluck, Margaret. "Couvade in Albania." *Man* 39 (1939): 18–20.

———— . "The Albanian Blood Feud." In *Law and Warfare,* edited by Paul Bohannan. Garden City, N.Y.: Natural History Press, 1967, pp. 381-408.

————. *The Unwritten Law in Albania.* Cambridge: Cambridge University Press, 1954.

Pisko, J. "Gebräuche bei der Geburt und Behandlung der Neugeborenen bei den Albanesen." *Mitteilungen der Anthropologischen Gesellschaft zu Wien* 26 (1896): 141–46.

Hausa

Barth, Heinrich. *Travels in Nigeria 1850–1855.* London: Oxford University Press, 1961.

Dry, E. A. "The Social Development of the Hausa Child." *International West African Conference Proceedings* 3 (1949): 164–70.

Greenberg, J. H. "Islam and Clan Organization Among the Hausa." *Southwestern Journal of Anthropology* 3 (1947): 193–211.

————. "The Influence of Islam on a Sudanese Religion." *Monographs of the American Ethnological Society* 10 (1946): 1–73.

Meek, Charles K. *The Northern Tribes of Nigeria.* London: Oxford University Press, 1925.

*Rattray, Robert S. *Hausa Folk-Lore, Customs, Proverbs, Etc.* Oxford: Clarendon Press, 1913.

Robinson, Charles H. *Hausalana, or Fifteen Hundred Miles Through the Central Soudan.* 3rd ed. London: Sampson, Low, 1900.

Smith, Mary F. *Baba of Karo.* New York: Philosophical Library, 1955.

*Smith, Michael G. *Government in Zazzau 1800–1950.* London: Oxford University Press, 1960.

*————. *The Economy of Hausa Communities of Zaria.* London: H.M. Stationery Office, 1955.

*————. "The Hausa of Northern Nigeria." In *Peoples of Africa,* edited by James Gibbs, Jr. New York: Holt, Rinehart and Winston, 1965, pp. 119–55.

*————. "The Hausa System of Social Status." *Africa* 29 (1959): 239–52.

Tremearne, A. J. N. *Hausa Superstitions and Customs.* London: Frank Cass, 1970.

Hebrews

**De Vaux, Roland. *Ancient Israel: Its Life and Institutions.* New York: McGraw-Hill, 1961.

Jerusalem Bible. Garden City, N.Y.: Doubleday, 1966.

Patai, Raphael. *Sex and Family in the Bible and the Middle East.* Garden City, N.Y.: Doubleday, 1959.

Pederson, Johannes. *Israel, Its Life and Culture.* 4 vols. London: Geoffrey Cumberledge, 1926.

Lapps

Bernatzik, Hugo. *Overland with the Nomad Lapps.* New York: Robert McBride, 1938.

Bosi, Roberto. *The Lapps.* London: Thames & Hudson, 1960.

Collinder, Bjorn. *The Lapps.* Princeton, N.J.: Princeton University Press, 1949.

Gjessing, Gutorm. *Changing Lapps.* London: London School of Economics and Political Science, 1954.

Haglund, Sven. *Mitt Lappliv.* Stockholm: Wahlström and Widstrand, 1934.

Itkonen, Toivo. *The Lapps in Finland up to 1945.* Helsinki: Werner Söderström Osakeyhtio, 1948.

Karsten, Rafael. *The Religion of the Samek.* Leiden: E. J. Brill, 1955.

Minn, Eeva. *The Lapps.* New Haven: HRAF Press, 1955.

Paine, Robert. "Changes in the Ecological and Economic Bases in a Coast Lappish District." *Southwestern Journal of Anthropology* 14 (1948): 168–88.

————. *Coast Lapp Society.* Trømso, Norway: Trømso Museums Skrifter, 1957.

*Pehrson, Robert. "The Bilateral Network of Social Relations in Könkäma Lapp District." *International Journal of American Linguistics* 23 (1957): 1–128.

Scheffer, John. *The History of Lappland.* London: Newborough, 1704.

Turi, Johan. "The Story of the Reindeer Lapps." In *A Reader in General Anthropology,* edited by Carleton S. Coon. New York: Henry Holt, 1948, pp. 142–70.

————. *Turi's Book of Lapland.* London: Harper & Bros., 1931.

Vorren, Ørnulv. *Lapp Life and Customs.* London: Oxford University Press, 1962.

*Whitaker, Ian. *Social Relations in a Nomadic Lappish Community.* Oslo: Utgitt av Norsk Folkemuseum, 1955.

Riffians

*Coon, Carleton S. "The People of the Rif." *Journal of the American Museum of Natural History* 35 (1935): 93–106.

*————. "Tribes of the Rif." *Harvard African Studies* 9 (1931): 1–417.

Hart, David M. "An Ethnological Survey of the Riffian Tribe of Aith Wuryaghil." *Tamuda* 2 (1954): 1–86.

Mouliéras, Auguste. *Le Maroc inconnu.* Paris: Augustin Challamel, 1895.

Westermarck, Edward A. *Ritual and Belief in Morocco.* New Hyde Park, N.Y.: University Books, 1968.

Rwala

*Musil, Alois. *The Manners and Customs of the Rwala Bedouins.* New York: Charles Crane, 1928.
*Musil, Alois, and John B. Glubb. "The Complicated Lives of Desert Nomads." In *A Reader in General Anthropology,* edited by Carleton S. Coon. New York: Henry Holt, 1948, pp. 380–407.
*Raswan, Carl. *Black Tents of Arabia.* Boston: Little, Brown, 1935.

Somali

Burton, Richard. *First Footsteps in East Africa.* London: Longman, Brown, Green & Longmans, 1856.
Cerulli, Enrico. *Somalia: scritti vari editi ed inediti.* 2 vols. Rome: Amministrazione Fiduciaria Italiana, 1959.
Drake-Brockman, Ralph E. *British Somaliland.* London: Hurst & Blackett, 1912.
Kirk, J. W. C. "The Yibirs and Midgans of Somaliland." *African Society Journal* 4 (1905): 91–108.
Landberg, Pamela. "Women's Role and Spirit Possession Cults." Paper delivered at the Annual Meeting of the American Anthropological Association, New York, November 1971.
Leroi-Gourham, André. "La Somalie française." *Ethnologie de l'Union Française* (1953): 422–40, 467–68.
*Lewis, Ioan M. *A Pastoral Democracy: A Study of Pastoralism and Politics Among the Northern Somali of the Horn of Africa.* London: Oxford University Press, 1961.
*———. "Clanship and Contract in Northern Somaliland." *Africa* 29 (1959): 274–93.
*———. "Dualism in Somali Notions of Power." *Journal of the Royal Anthropological Institute of Great Britain and Ireland* 93 (1963): 109–16.
*———. "Force and Fission in Northern Somali Lineage Structure." *American Anthropologist* 63 (1961): 94–112.
*———. *Marriage and the Family in Northern Somaliland.* Kampala, Uganda: East African Institute of Social Research, 1962.
*———. "Modern Leadership and Loyalties in Somalia and Somaliland." *Civilizations* 10 (1960): 49–62.
*———. *Peoples of the Horn of Africa.* London: International African Institute, 1955.
*———. "Sufism in Somaliland: A Study in Tribal Islam." *School of Oriental and African Studies Bulletin* 17 (1955): 581–602; 18 (1956): 145–60.
*———. "The Northern Pastoral Somali of the Horn." In *Peoples of Africa,* edited by James Gibbs, Jr. New York: Holt, Rinehart and Winston, 1965, pp. 319–60.

*————. *The Somali Lineage System and the Total Genealogy.* Hargeisa: Somaliland Land Protectorate, 1957.

Paulitschke, Phillip. *Beiträge zur Ethnographie und Anthropologie der Samal, Galla, Harar.* Leipzig: Edvard Baldamus, 1888.

Puccioni, Nello. *Antropologia e etnografie delle genti della Somalia.* Bologna: Niccola Zanichelli, 1936.

Swayne, H. G. C. *Seventeen Trips Through Somaliland and a Visit to Abyssinia.* London: Rowland Ward, 1900.

Trimingham, J. Spencer. *Islam in Ethiopia.* London: Oxford University Press, 1952.

Tuareg

Benhazera, Maurice. *Six mois chez les Touareg du Ahaggar.* Algiers: Typographie Adolphe Jourdan, 1908.

Blanguernon, Claude. *Le Hoggar.* Paris: Arthaud, 1955.

Briggs, Lloyd C. *Tribes of the Sahara.* Cambridge: Harvard University Press, 1960.

*Lhote, Henry. *Les Touaregs du Hoggar.* Paris: Payot, 1955.

Murphy, Robert F. "Social Distance and the Veil." *American Anthropologist* 66 (1964): 1257–74.

*Nicolaisen, Johannes. *Ecology and Culture of the Pastoral Tuareg.* Copenhagen: National Museets Skrifter, 1963.

*————. "Political Systems of Pastoral Tuareg in Air and Ahaggar." *Folk* 1 (1959): 67–131.

Rodd, Francis. *People of the Veil.* London: Macmillan, 1926.

EAST EURASIA

Ainu

*Batchelor, John. *Ainu Life and Lore.* Tokyo: Kyobunkwan, 1927.

*————. "Notes on the Ainu." *Transactions of the Asiatic Society of Japan* 10 (1882): 206–19.

*————. *The Ainu and Their Folklore.* London: Religious Tract Society, 1901.

*————. *The Ainu of Japan.* London: Religious Tract Society, 1892.

Hitchcock, R. "The Ainos of Yezo, Japan." *Smithsonian Institution Annual Report for the Year Ending June 30, 1890,* pp. 429–502.

Holland, S. C. "On the Ainos." *Journal of the Anthropological Institute of Great Britain and Ireland* 3 (1874): 233–44.

Kindaichi, K. "The Ainu." *Proceedings of the Third Pan-Pacific Science Congress* 2 (1926): 2307–22.

Montandon, G. "Résultats d'une enquête ethnologique chez les Ainou." *Proceedings of the Third Pan-Pacific Science Congress* 2 (1926): 2291–97.

*Munro, Neil G., and Brenda Z. Seligman. *Ainu, Creed and Cult.* New York: Columbia University Press, 1963.

Murdock, George P. *Our Primitive Contemporaries.* New York: Macmillan, 1934.

Oswalt, Wendell. *Other Peoples, Other Customs.* New York: Holt, Rinehart and Winston, 1972.

Peng, F. C. C., R. Ricketts, and N. Imamura. "Continuity and Change in a Modern Ainu Community." Human Relations Area Files, 1970.

Pilsudski, Bronislaw. "Der Schamanismus bei den Ainu-Stämmen von Sachalin." *Globus* 95 (1909): 72–78.

———. "Schwangerschaft, Entbindung und Fehlgeburt bei den Bewohnern der Insel Sachalin." *Anthropos* 5 (1910): 756–74.

Sternberg, Leo. "The Inau Cult of the Ainu." In *Boas Anniversary Volume,* edited by Berthold Laufer. New York: G. E. Stechert, 1906, pp. 425–37.

St. John, H. C. "The Ainos: Aborigines of Yeso." *Journal of the Anthropological Institute of Great Britain and Ireland* 2 (1873): 248–54.

Sugiura, K., and H. Befu. "Kinship Organization of the Saru Ainu." *Ethnology* 1 (1962): 287–98.

Sutherland, Ivan. "The Ainu People of Northern Japan." *Journal of the Polynesian Society* 57 (1948): 203–26.

*Watanabe, Hitoshi. "Subsistence and Ecology of Northern Food Gatherers with Special Reference to the Ainu." In *Man the Hunter,* edited by Richard Lee and Irven DeVore. Chicago: Aldine, 1968, pp. 69–77.

*———. "The Ainu." *Journal of Faculty of Science, University of Tokyo* 2 (1964): 1–164.

Andamanese

Cipriano, Lidio. *The Andaman Islanders.* New York: Frederick Praeger, 1966.

*Man, Edward H. "On the Aboriginal Inhabitants of the Andaman Islands." *Journal of the Anthropological Institute of Great Britain and Ireland* 12 (1882–83): 69–175, 327–434.

Oswalt, Wendell. *Other Peoples, Other Customs.* New York: Holt, Rinehart and Winston, 1972.

*Radcliffe-Brown, A. R. *The Andaman Islanders.* New York: Free Press, 1922.

*———. "The Andaman Islanders." In *A Reader in General Anthropology,* edited by Carleton S. Coon. New York: Henry Holt, 1948, pp. 172–213.

Service, Elman. *Profiles in Ethnology.* New York: Harper & Row, 1963.

Temple, Richard. *The Andaman and Nicobar Islands Report on the Census.* Calcutta: Office of the Superintendent of Government Printing, 1903.

Baiga

*Elwin, Verrier. *The Baiga*. London: John Murray, 1939.
*————. "The Functional Character of Baiga Myth." In *Anthropological Society of Bombay Jubilee Volume*. Bombay: 1938, pp. 136–58.
Hutton, John H. *The Baiga*. London: Wyman & Sons, 1939.
*Nag, Daya S. *Tribal Economy: An Economic Study of the Baiga*. Delhi: Bharatiya Adimjati Sevak Sangh, 1958.

Basseri

*Barth, Fredrik. *Nomads of South Persia*. Oslo: Oslo University Press, 1961.

Burusho

Clark, John. *Hunza in the Himalayas*. New York: American Museum of Natural History, 1963.
*Lorimer, David. *The Burushaski Language*. 3 vols. Oslo: H. Aschehoug, 1935–38.
*Lorimer, Emily. *Language Hunting in the Karakoram*. London: Allen & Unwin, 1939.
*————. "The Burusho of Hunza." *Antiquity* 12 (1938–39): 5–15.
Tobe, John. *Hunza: Adventures in a Land of Paradise*. Emmaus, Penna.: Rodale Books, 1960.

Central Thai

Anuman Rajadhon, Phraya. *Life and Ritual in Old Siam*. New Haven: HRAF Press, 1961.
Benedict, Ruth. *Thai Culture and Behavior*. Ithaca: Cornell University Press, 1952.
Bowring, John. *The Kingdom and People of Siam*. London: J. W. Parker & Son, 1857.
Crawford, John. *Journal of an Embassy from the Governor-General of India to the Courts of Siam and Cochin China*. London: Colburn & Bentley, 1830.
Credner, Wilhelm. *Siam: das Land der Tai*. Stuttgart: J. Engelhorn, 1935.
De Young, John. *Village Life in Modern Thailand*. Berkeley: University of California Press, 1955.
Embree, John. "Thailand, a Loosely Structured Social System." *American Anthropologist* 52 (1950): 181–93.
Goldsen, Rose, and Max Ralis. "Factors Related to Acceptance of Innovations in Bang Chan, Thailand." *Cornell University, Department of Asian Studies, Southeast Asia Program, Data Paper* 25 (1957): 1–81.

Graham, Walter. *Siam.* 2 vols. London: A. Moring, 1924.

*Hanks, Jane R. "Maternity and Its Rituals in Bang Chan." *Cornell University, Department of Asian Studies, Southeast Asia Program, Data Paper* 51 (1963): 1–136.

*Hanks, L. M., and Jane R. Hanks. "Thailand: Equality Between the Sexes." In *Women in New Asia,* edited by Barbara E. Ward. Paris: UNESCO, 1961.

*Hanks, L. M., Jane R. Hanks, and Lauriston Sharp, eds. "Ethnographic Notes on Northern Thailand." *Cornell University, Department of Asian Studies, Southeast Asia Program, Data Paper* 58 (1965): 1–94.

Landon, Kenneth. *Thailand in Transition.* Chicago: University of Chicago Press, 1939.

McGilvary, D. *A Half Century Among the Siamese and the Lao.* New York: Fleming Revell, 1912.

Manunet, Banhán. *Siamese Tales, Old and New.* London: N. Douglas, 1930.

Phillips, Herbert. *Thai Peasant Personality: The Patterning of Interpersonal Behavior in the Village of Bang Chan.* Berkeley: University of California Press, 1966.

Seidenfaden, Erik. *The Thai Peoples.* Bangkok: Siam Society, 1958.

*Sharp, Lauriston, Hazel Hauck, Kamol Janlekha, and Robert Textor. *Siamese Rice Village.* Ithaca: Cornell University, Southeast Asia Program, 1953.

Thompson, Virginia. *Thailand, the New Siam.* New York: Macmillan, 1941.

Villa, Walter. *Siam Under Rama III.* Locust Valley, Long Island, N.Y.: I. J. Augustin Monograph of the Association for Asian Studies, 1937.

Young, Ernest. *The Kingdom of the Yellow Robe.* Westminster, England: Archibald Constable, 1898.

Chenchu

Elwin, Verrier. "Primitive Ideas of Menstruation and the Climacteric in the Central Provinces of India." In *Essays in Anthropology Presented to Rai Bahadur Sarat Chandra Roy,* edited by J. P. Mills, B. S. Guha, K. P. Chattopadhayay, D. N. Majumdar, and A. Aiyappan. Lucknow, India: Maxwell, 1942, pp. 141–57.

Oswalt, Wendell. *Other Peoples, Other Customs.* New York: Holt, Rinehart and Winston, 1972.

*Von Furer-Haimendorf, Christoph. *Morals and Merit.* Chicago: University of Chicago Press, 1967.

*———. *The Chenchus.* London: Macmillan, 1943.

Chukchee

Antropova, V. V., and V. G. Kuznetsova. "The Chukchi." In *The Peoples of Siberia*, edited by Maxsim G. Levin and L. P. Potapov. Chicago: University of Chicago Press, 1964, pp. 799–835.
*Bogoraz, Vladimir G. *Chukchee Mythology.* New York: G. E. Stechert, 1910.
*———. "The Chukchee." *Memoirs of the American Museum of Natural History* 11 (1909): 1–732.
Hooper, William. *Ten Months Among the Tents of the Tuski.* London: John Murray, 1853.
Leeds, Anthony. "Reindeer Herding and Chukchi Social Institutions." In *Man, Culture, and Animals*, edited by Anthony Leeds and Andrew Vayda. Washington, D.C.: American Association for the Advancement of Science, 1965, pp. 87–128.
Nordenskiöld, Nils. *The Voyage of the Vega Round Asia and Europe.* Berlin: O. Janke, 1883.
Oswalt, Wendell. *Other Peoples, Other Customs.* New York: Holt, Rinehart and Winston, 1972.
Shklovsky, Izak W. *In Far North-East Siberia.* London: Macmillan, 1916.
Sverdrup, Harald. *With the People of the Tundra.* Oslo: Gyldendal, 1938.

Garo

*Burling, Robbins. "Garo." In *Ethnic Groups of Mainland Southeast Asia*, edited by Frank LeBar, Gerald Hickey, and John Musgrave. New Haven: HRAF Press, 1964, pp. 55–57.
*———. *Rengsanggri.* Philadelphia: University of Pennsylvania Press, 1963.
Choudhury, Bhupendranath. *Some Cultural and Linguistic Aspects of the Garos.* Gauhati, Assam: Lawyer's Book Stall, 1958.
Costa, Giulio. "The Garo Code of Law." *Anthropos* 49 (1954): 1041–66.
Mukherjee, B. "A Magico-Religious Ceremony in Connection with the Disease of a Garo." *Government of India, Department of Anthropology Bulletin* 5 (1956): 11–13.
Nakane, Chie. "Cross Cousin Marriage Among the Garos of Assam." *Man* 58 (1958): 7–12.
———. *Garo and Khasi.* Paris: Mouton, 1967.
Playfair, Major A. *The Garos.* London: David Nutt, 1909.

Kazak

Castagné, J. "Magie et exorcisme chez les Kazak-Kirghizes et autres peuples turks orientaux." *Revue des Etudes Islamiques* 4 (1930): 53–151.

*Hudson, Alfred E. *Kazak Social Structure*. New Haven: Yale University Press, 1938.

Korbe, O. "The Culture and Way of Life of the Kazakh Kolkhoz Village." *Sovetskaia Etnografiia* 4 (1950): 67–91.

Murdock, George P. *Our Primitive Contemporaries*. New York: Macmillan, 1934.

Koreans

Bergman, Sten. *In Korean Wilds and Villages*. London: John Gifford, 1938.

Bishop, Isabella. *Korea and Her Neighbors*. New York: Fleming Revell, 1898.

Clark, Charles A. *Religions of Old Korea*. New York: Fleming Revell, 1932.

Dallet, Charles. *Histoire de l'église de Corea*. Paris: Victor Palmé, 1874.

Griffis, William. *Korea: The Hermit Nation*. New York: Charles Scribner's Sons, 1882.

Habenstein, Robert, and William Lamers. *Funeral Customs the World Over*. Milwaukee: Bulfin Printers, 1963.

Hewes, Gordon W., and Chin Hong Kim. "Korean Kinship Behavior and Structure." *Research Monograph on Korea* 2 (1952): 1–20.

Hulbert, Homer. *The Passing of Korea*. New York: Doubleday, Page, 1906.

———. "The Status of Women in Korea." *Korean Review* 2 (1902): 1–8, and 1 (1901): 529–34.

Kang, Younghill. *The Grass Roof*. New York: Scribner, 1931.

Kim, Anne. "Village Life in Korea." *Journal of Geography* 36 (1919): 24–48.

Landis, E. B. "The Capping Ceremony in Korea." *Journal of the Anthropological Institute of Great Britain and Ireland* 27 (1894): 523–31.

Landor, Arnold. *Corea*. London: W. Heinemann, 1895.

Moose, J. Robert. *Village Life in Korea*. Nashville, Tenn.: Publishing House of the Methodist Episcopal Church, 1911.

Morse, Edward S. "Korean Interviews." *Popular Science Monthly* 51 (1897): 1–16.

*Osgood, Cornelius. *The Koreans and Their Culture*. New York: Ronald Press, 1951.

Rockhill, W. Woodville. "Notes on Some of the Laws, Customs, and Superstitions of Korea." *American Anthropologist* 4 (1891): 177–87.

Rutt, Richard. *Korean Works and Days*. Rutland, Vt.: C. E. Tuttle, 1964.

Saunderson, H. S. "Notes on Corea and Its People." *Journal of the*

Anthropological Institute of Great Britain and Ireland 24 (1894): 299–316.
Turner, Leonard. "The Social and Psychological Role of the Korean Sorceress." Human Relations Area Files, 1950.

Kurd

Barth, Fredrik. "Father's Brother's Daughter." *Southwestern Journal of Anthropology* 10 (1954): 164–71.
———. *Principles of Social Organization in Southern Kurdistan.* Oslo: Brødene Jørgensen, 1953.
Garnett, Lucy M. *Women of Turkey and Their Folklore.* London: David Nutt, 1891.
Hansen, Henny. *The Kurdish Woman's Life.* Copenhagen: National-museet, 1961.
*Leach, Edmund R. *Social and Economic Organization of the Rowanduz Kurds.* London: Percy Lund, Humphries, 1940.
*Masters, William. *Rowanduz: A Kurdish Administrative and Mercantile Center.* Ann Arbor, Mich.: University Microfilms, 1954.
Vinogradov, Amal. "Kurd Cultural Summary." Human Relations Area Files, 1965.

Lakher

Leach, Edmund R. "Aspects of Bridewealth and Marriage Stability Among the Kachin and Lakher." *Man* 57 (1957): 50–55.
*Parry, N. E. *The Lakhers.* London: Macmillan, 1932.

Lamet

Habenstein, Robert, and William Lamers. *Funeral Customs the World Over.* Milwaukee: Bulfin Printers, 1963.
*Izikowitz, Karl. *Lamet.* Göteborg, Sweden: Etnografiska Museet, 1951.

Lepcha

*Gorer, Geoffrey. *Himalayan Village: An Account of the Lepchas of Sikkim.* London: M. Joseph, 1938.
*Morris, John. *Living with Lepchas.* London: W. Heinemann, 1938.
Waddell, L. A. "The 'Lepchas' or 'Rongs' and Their Songs." *International Archiv für Ethnographie* 12 (1899): 41–57.

Rhade

De Berval, René. "Les populations montagnardes du sud-indochinois." *France-Asie* 49–50 (1950): 1–278.

*Donoghue, John D. *People in the Middle: The Rhade of South Viet Nam*. East Lansing: Michigan State University, 1962.

Mole, Robert. *The Montagnards of South Viet Nam*. Rutland, Vt.: C. E. Tuttle, 1970.

Sabatier, Léopold. *Palabre du serment au Darlac*. Hanoi: Imprimerie Française d'Extrème Orient, 1930.

———— . *Recueil des coutumes rhadees*. Hanoi: Imprimerie Française d'Extrème Orient, 1940.

Tanala

Habenstein, Robert, and William Lamers. *Funeral Customs the World Over*. Milwaukee: Bulfin Printers, 1963.

*Linton, Ralph. *The Tanala*. Chicago: Field Museum of Natural History, 1933.

*———— . "The Tanala of Madagascar." In *The Individual and His Society*, edited by Abram Kardiner. New York: Columbia University Press, 1939, pp. 251–90.

Tungus

Lattimore, Owen. *The Gold Tribe, "Fishskin Tatars" of the Lower Sungari*. New York: Kraus Reprint Corporation, 1964.

Levin, Maxsim G., and L. P. Potapov. "The Nanays." In *The Peoples of Siberia*, edited by Maxsim G. Levin and L. P. Potapov. Chicago: University of Chicago Press, 1964, pp. 691–720.

Lopatin, Ivan A. *The Cult of the Dead Among the Natives of the Amur Basin*. The Hague: Mouton, 1960.

Service, Elman. *Profiles in Ethnology*. New York: Harper & Row, 1963.

*Shirokogoroff, Sergei M. *Psychomental Complex of the Tungus*. London: Trübner, 1935.

*———— . *Social Organization of the Northern Tungus*. Shanghai: Commercial Press, 1933.

Vedda

*Bailey, John. "An Account of the Wild Tribes of the Veddahs of Ceylon." *Transactions of the Ethnological Society of London* 2 (1863): 278–319.

*Seligman, Charles G., and Brenda Z. Seligman. *The Veddas*. Oosterhout, The Netherlands: Anthropological Publications, 1969.

Spittel, Richard. *Wild Ceylon*. Colombo: Ceylon Daily News for General Publishers, 1945.

Yurak Samoyed

Dolgikh, B. O. "The Clan Composition and the Geographical Distribution of the Enets." *Sovetskaia Etnografiia* 4 (1946): 109–24.

Donner, Kai. *Among the Samoyed of Siberia.* New Haven: HRAF Press, 1954.

*Engelhardt, Alexander. *A Russian Province of the North.* London: Archibald Constable, 1899.

Hajdú, Peter. *The Samoyed Peoples and Languages.* The Hague: Mouton, 1963.

*Jackson, Frederick. *The Great Frozen Land.* London: Macmillan, 1895.

Kopytoff, Igor. *Subcontractor's Monograph on the Samoyed.* New Haven: HRAF Press, 1955.

Lehtisalo, Toivo. "Hunting Among the Yurak Samoyed." *Suomalais-Vgrilaisen Seuran Aika Kauskirja* 30 (1918): 1–13.

Veniainin, A. "The Samoyed of Mezen." *Vestnik, Imperator-Skago Russkago Geograficheskago Obshchestva* 14 (1855): 77–140.

Von Struve, B. "Einiges über die Samojeden im Norden von Sibirien." *Das Ausland* 103 (1880): 741–44, 774–77, 794–98.

INSULAR PACIFIC

Alorese

*Du Bois, Cora. "Attitudes Toward Hunger and Food in Alor." In *Language, Culture, and Personality,* edited by Leslie Spier, A. Irving Hallowell, and Stanley Newman. Menasha, Wisc.: Sapir Memorial Fund, 1941, pp. 272–81.

*———. "How They Pay Debts in Alor." *Asia* 40 (1940): 482–86.

*———. *The People of Alor: A Social-Psychological Study of an East Indian Island.* Minneapolis: University of Minnesota Press, 1944.

Arunta

Basedow, Herbert. *The Australian Aboriginal.* Adelaide, Australia: F. W. Preece, 1925.

Chewings, Charles. *Back in the Stone Age.* Sydney, Australia: Angus & Robinson, 1936.

DeVidas, J. "Childbirth Among the Aranda." *Oceania* 18 (1947–48): 117–19.

*Gillen, F. J. "Magic Amongst the Natives of Central Australia." In *Report of the Eighth Meeting of the Australasian Association for the Advancement of Science,* edited by T. Hall. Melbourne, Australia: Australasian Association for the Advancement of Science, 1901.

*————— . "Notes on Some Manners and Customs of the Aborigines of the McDonnell Ranges Belonging to the Arunta Tribe." In *Report on the Work of the Horn Scientific Expedition to Central Australia.* Vol. 4, edited by Baldwin Spencer. London: Dulau, 1896.

Mathews, R. "Marriage and Descent in the Arranda Tribe, Central Australia." *American Anthropologist* 10 (1907): 88–102.

————— . "Notes on the Arranda Tribe." *Journal and Proceedings of the Royal Society of New South Wales* 41 (1907): 146–62.

Murdock, George P. *Our Primitive Contemporaries.* New York: Macmillan, 1934.

Radcliffe-Brown, A. R. "The Social Organization of Australian Tribes." *Oceania* 1 (1930–31): 34–63.

Róheim, Géza. *The Eternal Ones of the Dream.* New York: International Universities Press, 1945.

————— . "Women and Their Life in Central Australia." *Journal of the Royal Anthropological Institute of Great Britain and Ireland* 63 (1933): 207–65.

Shulze, Louis. "The Aborigines of the Upper and Middle Furke River." *Royal Society of South Australia, Transactions, Proceedings, and Reports* 14 (1891): 210–46.

*Spencer, Baldwin. *Wanderings in Wild Australia.* London: Macmillan, 1928.

*Spencer, Baldwin, and F. J. Gillen. "The Ancestors Walk." In *A Reader in General Anthropology,* edited by Carleton S. Coon. New York: Henry Holt, 1948, pp. 214–36.

*————— . *The Arunta.* London: Macmillan, 1927.

*————— . *The Native Tribes of Central Australia.* London: Macmillan, 1899.

*————— . *The Northern Tribes of Central Australia.* London: Macmillan, 1904.

*Strehlow, Carl. *Aranda Traditions.* Melbourne, Australia: Melbourne University Press, 1947.

*————— . *The Aranda and Loritja Tribes.* Vol. 5. Frankfurt am Main: Städtisch Völker-Museum, 1920.

*————— . *The Aranda and Loritja Tribes of Central Australia.* Vol. 1. Frankfurt am Main: Städtisch Völker-Museum, 1907.

*————— . *The Social Life of the Aranda and Loritja.* Vol. 4. Frankfurt am Main: Städtisch Völker-Museum, 1913.

Balinese

Belo, Jane. *Bali: Rangda and Barong.* New York: J. J. Augustin, 1949.

————— . "Study of a Balinese Family." *American Anthropologist* 38 (1936): 12–31.

————. "The Balinese Temper." *Character and Personality* 4 (1936): 120–46.

Covarrubias, Miguel. *Island of Bali.* New York: Knopf, 1942.

*Geertz, Clifford. "Form and Variation in Balinese Village Structure." *American Anthropologist* 61 (1959): 991–1012.

*————. *Peddlers and Princes.* Chicago: University of Chicago Press, 1963.

*————. *Person, Time, and Conduct in Bali.* New Haven: Yale University Press, 1966.

*————. "Tihingan: A Balinese Village." *Anthropologica* 6 (1964): 1–33.

*Geertz, Hildred. "The Balinese Village." In *Local, Ethnic, and National Loyalties in Village Indonesia: A Symposium,* edited by G. William Skinner. New Haven: Yale University, Southeast Asia Studies, Cultural Report Series no. 5, 1959, pp. 24–33.

Habenstein, Robert, and William Lamers. *Funeral Customs the World Over.* Milwaukee: Bulfin Printers, 1963.

Mead, Margaret, and F. MacGregor. *Growth and Culture.* New York: Putnam, 1951.

Wertheim, Willem F., ed. *Bali: Studies in Life, Thought, and Ritual.* The Hague: W. Van Hoeve, 1960.

Iban

*Freeman, J. Derek. *Iban Agriculture: A Report on the Shifting Cultivation of Hill Rice by the Iban of Sarawak.* London: H.M. Stationery Office, 1955.

*————. *Report on the Iban.* London: Athlone Press, 1970.

*————. "The Family System of the Iban of Borneo." In *The Developmental Cycle in Domestic Groups,* edited by Jack Goody. Cambridge: Cambridge University Press, 1958, pp. 15–52.

*————. "The Iban of Western Borneo." In *Cultures of the Pacific,* edited by Thomas G. Harding and Ben J. Wallace. New York: Free Press, 1970, pp. 180–200.

Gomes, Edwin. *Seventeen Years Among the Sea Dyaks of Borneo.* London: Seeley, 1911.

Hewitt, Florence E. "Some Sea Dyak Tabus." *Man* 8 (1908): 186–87.

Hose, Charles, and William McDougall. *The Pagan Tribes of Borneo.* 2 vols. London: Macmillan, 1912.

Howell, William. "Dyak Birth and Pregnancy Ceremonies." *Journal of the Royal Asiatic Society* 46 (1906): 125–32.

Low, Hugh. *Sarawak, Its Inhabitants and Productions.* London: Richard Bentley, 1848.

Morris, M. "War, Agriculture, and Religion." *Journal of the American Oriental Society* 25 (1904): 213–47.

Roth, H. Lind. "Natives of Borneo." *Journal of the Anthropological Institute of Great Britain and Ireland* 21 (1892): 110–37, and 22 (1893): 22–64.
Sandin, Benedict. *The Sea Dayaks of Borneo Before White Rajah Rule.* London: Macmillan, 1967.

Ifaluk

Bates, Marston, and Donald Abbott. *Coral Island.* New York: Charles Scribner's Sons, 1958.
*Burrows, Edwin G. "From Value to Ethos on Ifaluk." *Southwestern Journal of Anthropology* 8 (1952): 13–35.
*Burrows, Edwin G., and Melford E. Spiro. *An Atoll Culture.* Ann Arbor, Mich.: University Microfilms, 1969.
*Damm, Hans, and Augustin Krämer. *Zentralkarolinen. Vol. 2. Ifaluk, Aurepik, Faraulip. Sorol, Mogemog.* Hamburg: Friederichsen, De Gruyter, 1938.
*Krämer, Augustin. *Zentralkarolinen. Vol. 1. Lamotrek, Woleai, Fais.* Hamburg: Friederichsen, De Gruyter, 1937.
*Spiro, Melford E. "A Psychotic Personality in the South Seas." *Psychiatry* 13 (1950): 189–204.
*———. "Cultural Heritage, Personal Tensions, and Mental Illness in a South Sea Culture." In *Culture and Mental Health,* edited by Marvin Opler. New York: Macmillan, 1959, pp. 141–71.
*———. "Some Ifaluk Myths and Folktales." *Journal of American Folklore* 64 (1951): 289–302.
U.S. Office of Naval Operations. *West Caroline Islands Civil Affairs Handbook.* Washington, D.C.: Office of the Chief of Naval Operations, 1944.

Kapauku

*Pospisil, Leopold. "Kapauku Papuan Economy." *Yale University Publications in Anthropology* 67 (1963): 1–502.
*———. "Kapauku Papuans and Their Law." *Yale University Publications in Anthropology* 54 (1958): 1–292.
*———. *The Kapauku Papuans of West New Guinea.* New York: Holt, Rinehart and Winston, 1963.

Kiwai

*Landtman, Gunnar. "Folktales of the Kiwai Papuans." *Acta Societatis Scientiarum* 67 (1917): 1–571.
*———. *The Kiwai Papuans of British New Guinea.* London: Macmillan, 1927.

Róheim, Géza. "Psychoanalysis of Primitive Cultural Types." *International Journal of Psychoanalysis* 13 (1932): 1–224.

Kurtatchi

*Blackwood, Beatrice M. *Both Sides of Buka Passage.* Oxford: Clarendon Press, 1934.
*———. "Folk Stories from North Solomons." *Folklore* 43 (1932): 61–120.

Lau Fijians

*Hocart, A. M. *Kingship.* Oxford: Oxford University Press, 1927.
*———. *Lau Islands, Fiji.* Honolulu: Bernice P. Bishop Museum, 1929.
*Thompson, Laura. *Fijian Frontier.* New York: Institute of Pacific Relations, 1940.
*———. *Southern Lau, Fiji: An Ethnography.* Honolulu: Bernice P. Bishop Museum, 1940.
Waterhouse, Joseph. *The King and the People of Fiji.* New York: Institute of Pacific Relations, 1940.

Manus

Fortune, Rev. F. *Manus Religion.* Philadelphia: American Philosophical Society, 1935.
*Mead, Margaret. "An Investigation of Thought of Primitive Children with Special Reference to Animism." *Journal of the Royal Anthropological Institute of Great Britain and Ireland* 62 (1932): 173–90.
*———. *Growing Up in New Guinea.* New York: W. Morrow, 1930.
*———. "Kinship in the Admiralty Islands." *Anthropological Papers of the American Museum of Natural History* 34 (1934): 180–358.
*———. *Male and Female.* New York: W. Morrow, 1952.
*———. "Melanesian Middlemen." *Natural History* 30 (1930): 115–30.
*———. *New Lives for Old.* New York: W. Morrow, 1956.
*———. "The Manus of the Admiralty Islands." In *Cooperation and Competition Among Primitive Peoples,* edited by Margaret Mead. New York: McGraw-Hill, 1937, pp. 210–39.

Maori

Beaglehole, Ernest. *Some Modern Maoris.* Wellington: New Zealand Council for Educational Research, 1946.
Beaglehole, Ernest, and Pearl Beaglehole. "Contemporary Maori Death Customs." *Journal of the Polynesian Society* 54 (1945): 91–116.

Best, Elsdon. *Forest Lore of the Maori.* Wellington, New Zealand: Polynesian Society, 1942.

———— . *Maori Agriculture.* Wellington, New Zealand: Board of Maori Ethnological Research, 1925.

———— . "Maori Medical Lore." *Journal of the Polynesian Society* 14 (1905): 1–23.

———— . "Notes on the Art of War." *Journal of the Polynesian Society* 13 (1904): 1–19.

———— . "The Lore of the Whare-Kohanga." *Journal of the Polynesian Society* 14 (1905): 205–15.

———— . *The Maori.* Vol. 1. Wellington, New Zealand: H. H. Tombs, 1924.

———— . *The Maori.* Vol. 2. Wellington, New Zealand: Polynesian Society, 1941.

Buck, Peter. *The Coming of the Maori.* Wellington: New Zealand Department of Internal Affairs, 1950.

Cruise, Richard A. *Journal of Ten Months Residence in New Zealand.* London: Longman, Hurst, Rees, Orme, Brown, & Green, 1824.

Downes, T. "Maori Etiquette." *Journal of the Polynesian Society* 38 (1929): 148–68.

*Earle, Augustus. *Narrative of a Residence in New Zealand.* Oxford: Clarendon Press, 1966.

Firth, Raymond. *Economics of the New Zealand Maori.* Wellington, New Zealand: Government Printer, 1959.

———— . *Primitive Economics of the New Zealand Maori.* London: George Routledge, 1929.

Gudgeon, Thomas. *The History and Doings of the Maori.* Auckland, New Zealand: H. Brett, 1885.

Habenstein, Robert, and William Lamers. *Funeral Customs the World Over.* Milwaukee: Bulfin Printers, 1963.

Hawthorn, Harry. *The Maori: A Study in Acculturation.* Menasha, Wisc.: American Anthropological Association, 1944.

Keesing, Felix M. *The Changing Maori.* New Plymouth, New Zealand: T. Avery & Sons, 1928.

Makereti. *The Old Time Maori.* Collected and edited by T. K. Penniman. London: Victor Gollancz, 1938.

Metge, A. Joan. "Marriage in Modern Maori Society." *Man* 57 (1957): 166–70.

Polack, J. S. *The Manners and Customs of the New Zealanders.* 2 vols. London: James Madden, 1838.

Reed, Alexander W. *Illustrated Encyclopedia of Maori Life.* Wellington, New Zealand: A. H. and A. W. Reed, 1963.

Shortland, Edward. *Traditions and Superstitions of the New Zealanders.* London: Longman, Brown, Green, Longmans, & Roberts, 1854.

Sutherland, Ivan L., ed. *The Maori People Today*. London: Oxford University Press, 1940.

Vayda, Andrew. "Maori Warfare." In *Law and Warfare*, edited by Paul Bohannan. Garden City, N.Y.: Natural History Press, 1967, pp. 359–80.

Marquesans

*Fleurieu, Charles. *A Voyage Round the World 1790–92 Performed by Etienne Marchand*. Vol. 1. Amsterdam: N. Israel, 1969.

*Forster, John R. *A Voyage Round the World*. Vol. 2. London: J. Nourse, 1772.

Handy, Edward S. C. *Music in the Marquesas Islands*. Honolulu: Bernice P. Bishop Museum, 1925.

——— . *The Native Culture in the Marquesas*. Honolulu: Bernice P. Bishop Museum, 1923.

*Langsdorff, Georg Heinrich von. *Voyage and Travels in Various Parts of the World During 1803, 1804, 1805, 1806, and 1807*. London: H. Colburn, 1813.

Linton, Ralph. "Marquesan Culture." *American Anthropologist* 27 (1925): 474–78.

Lisiansky, Vrey. *A Voyage Round the World in the Years 1803, 1804, 1805, and 1806*. London: John Booth & Longman, Hurst, Rees, Orme, & Brown, 1814.

Otterbein, Keith. "Marquesan Polyandry." In *Marriage, Family, and Residence*, edited by Paul Bohannan and John Middleton. Garden City, N.Y.: Natural History Press, 1968, pp. 287–96.

Porter, David. *A Voyage in the South Seas in the Years 1812, 1813, and 1814*. London: Sir Richard Phillips, 1823.

Suggs, Robert. *Marquesan Sexual Behavior*. New York: Harcourt, Brace and World, 1966.

Tautain, Dr. "Etude sur la dépopulation de l'archipel des Marquises." *Anthropologie* 9 (1898): 298–318.

——— . "Notes sur l'ethnographie des îles Marquises." *Anthropologie* 7 (1896): 542–52.

Williamson, Robert. *Essays in Polynesian Ethnology*. Cambridge: Cambridge University Press, 1939.

Marshallese

*Erdland, P. August. "Die Marshall Insulaner." *Anthropos Bibliothek Ethnological Monographs* 2 (1914): 1–376.

Finsch, Otto. *Ethnologische Erfahrungen und Belegstucke aus der Sudsee*. Vienna: Alfred Holder, 1893.

*Krämer, Augustin. *Hawaii, Ostmikronesien, und Samoa.* Stuttgart: Strecker & Schröder, 1906.

*Krämer, Augustin, and Hans Nevermann. *Ralik-Ratak.* Hamburg: Friederichsen, De Gruyter, 1938.

Mason, Leonard. "Relocation of the Bikini Marshall." Ph.D. dissertation. Yale University, 1954.

Senfft, Arno. "Die Marshall-Insulaner." In *Rechtsverhältnisse von eingebornenen Völkern in Afrika und Ozeanien,* edited by S. R. Steinmetz. Berlin, Springer, 1903, pp. 425–55.

Spoehr, Alexander. *Majuro: A Village in the Marshall Islands.* Chicago: Chicago Natural History Museum, 1949.

U.S. Office of Naval Operations. *Marshall Islands Military Government Handbook.* Washington, D.C.: Office of the Chief of Naval Operations, 1943.

Wedgwood, Camilla. "Notes on the Marshall Islands." *Oceania* 13 (1942): 1–23.

Murngin

*Berndt, Ronald. *Djanggwal: An Aboriginal Religious Cult of North-Eastern Arnhem Land.* London: George Routledge, 1952.

*———. *Kunapipi: A Study of an Australian Aboriginal Religious Cult.* Melbourne, Australia: F. W. Cheshire, 1951.

*Berndt, Ronald, and Catherine Berndt. *Sexual Behavior in Western Arnhem Land.* New York: Viking Fund Publications in Anthropology, 1951.

Mountford, Charles. *Records of the American-Australian Scientific Expedition to Arnhem Land.* Melbourne, Australia: Melbourne University Press, 1956.

Thompsen, D. F. *Economic Structure and the Ceremonial Exchange Cycle in Arnhem Land.* Melbourne, Australia: Macmillan, 1949.

*Warner, W. Lloyd. *A Black Civilization.* New York: Harper & Bros., 1937.

Webb, T. Theodor. "Aboriginal Medical Practice in East Arnhem Land." *Oceania* 4 (1933): 91–98.

———. *The Aborigines of East Arnhem Land, Australia.* Melbourne, Australia: Methodist Laymen's Missionary Movement, 1934.

New Ireland

Brown, George. *Melanesians and Polynesians.* London: Macmillan, 1910.

*Powdermaker, Hortense. *Life in Lesu.* New York: W. W. Norton, 1933.

Williamson, Robert. *Essays in Polynesian Ethnology.* Cambridge: Cambridge University Press, 1939.

Ontong Javanese

*Hogbin, H. Ian. "Education of the Ontong-Java." *American Anthropologist* 33 (1931): 601–14.

*———. *Law and Order in Polynesia*. Camden, Conn.: Shoe String Press, 1934.

*———. "Spirits and Healing of the Sick in Ontong-Java." *Oceania* 1 (1930): 146–66.

*———. "The Sexual Life of the Ontong-Java." *Journal of the Polynesian Society* 40 (1931): 28–29.

*———. "The Social Organization of the Ontong-Java." *Oceania* 1 (1930–31): 399–425.

*———. "Transition Rites at Ontong-Java." *Journal of the Polynesian Society* 39 (1930): 94–112, 201–20.

*———. "Tribal Ceremonies of the Ontong-Java." *Journal of the Royal Anthropological Institute of Great Britain and Ireland* 61–62 (1931–32): 27–55.

Lazarus, D. "Marriage and Birth Rites in Ontong-Java." *Ethnologia Cranmorensis* 1 (1937): 26–30.

Palauans

*Barnett, H. G. *Being a Palauan*. New York: Holt, Rinehart and Winston, 1960.

*———. *Palauan Society*. Eugene: University of Oregon Publications, 1949.

*Krämer, Augustin. *Hawaii, Ostmikronesien, und Samoa*. Stuttgart: Strecker & Schröder, 1906.

U.S. Office of Naval Operations. *West Caroline Islands Civil Affairs Handbook*. Washington, D.C.: Office of the Chief of Naval Operations, 1944.

Useem, John. *Report on Yap and Palau*. Honolulu: U.S. Commercial Co., 1946.

Samoans

Buck, Peter H. *Samoan Material Culture*. Honolulu: Bernice P. Bishop Museum, 1930.

Ember, Melvin. "Political Authority and the Structure of Kinship in Aboriginal Samoa." *American Anthropologist* 64 (1962): 964–71.

Fraser, J. "Folksongs and Myths." *Journal of the Polynesian Society* 5 (1896): 171–88, and 6 (1897): 19–36, 67–76, 107–22.

———. "Folksongs and Myths." *Proceedings of the Royal Society of New South Wales* 24–26 (1892): 264–301.

Hogbin, H. Ian. *Law and Order in Polynesia*. Camden, Conn.: Shoe String Press, 1934.

Keesing, Felix M. *Modern Samoa*. London: Allen & Unwin, 1934.

Krämer, Augustin. *Die Samoa-Inseln*. Stuttgart: E. Schweizerbart, 1902.

Mead, Margaret. *Coming of Age in Samoa*. New York: W. Morrow, 1928.

——— . *Social Organization of Manua*. Honolulu: Bernice P. Bishop Museum, 1930.

——— . "The Role of the Individual in Samoan Culture." *Journal of the Royal Anthropological Institute of Great Britain and Ireland* 58 (1928): 481–95.

Murdock, George P. *Our Primitive Contemporaries*. New York: Macmillan, 1934.

Schultz, E. "The Most Important Principles of Samoan Family Law." *Journal of the Polynesian Society* 20 (1911): 43–53.

*Stair, John B. *Old Samoa*. London: Religious Tract Society, 1897.

*Turner, George. *Nineteen Years in Polynesia*. London: J. Snow, 1861.

*——— . *Samoa: A Hundred Years Ago and Long Before*. London: Macmillan, 1884.

Williamson, Robert. *Essays in Polynesian Ethnology*. Cambridge: Cambridge University Press, 1939.

Tikopia

*Firth, Raymond. "A Dart Match in Tikopia." *Oceania* 1 (1930–31): 64–96.

*——— . "Authority and Public Opinion in Tikopia." In *Social Structure: Studies Presented to A. R. Radcliffe-Brown*, edited by Meyer Fortes. Oxford: Clarendon Press, 1949, pp. 168–88.

*——— . "Ceremonies for Children and Social Frequency in Tikopia." *Oceania* 27 (1956): 12–55.

*——— . "Marriage and the Classificatory System of Relationship." *Journal of the Royal Anthropological Institute of Great Britain and Ireland* 60 (1930): 235–68.

*——— . *Primitive Polynesian Economy*. London: George Routledge, 1939.

*——— . *Rank and Religion in Tikopia*. Boston: Beacon Press, 1970.

*——— . "Report on Research in Tikopia." *Oceania* 1 (1930–31): 105–17.

*——— . *Social Change in Tikopia*. London: Allen & Unwin, 1959.

*——— . "Succession to Chieftainship in Tikopia." *Oceania* 30 (1960): 161–80.

*——— . "The Sociology of 'Magic' in Tikopia." *Sociologus* 4 (1954): 97–116.

*———— . *The Work of the Gods in Tikopia.* London: London School of Economics and Political Science, 1940.

*———— . *Tikopia Ritual and Belief.* London: Allen & Unwin, 1967.

*———— . "Totemism in Polynesia." *Oceania* 1 (1930–31): 291–321, 377–98.

*———— . *We, the Tikopia.* Boston: Beacon Press, 1936.

Rivers, William. *The History of Melanesian Society.* 2 vols. Cambridge: Cambridge University Press, 1914.

Spillius, James. "Natural Disaster and Political Crisis in a Polynesian Society: An Exploration of Operational Research." *Human Relations* 10 (1957): 12–55.

Trobrianders

Fathauer, George. "Trobriand." In *Matrilineal Kinship,* edited by David Schneider and Kathleen Gough. Berkeley: University of California Press, 1961, pp. 234–69.

Hogbin, H. Ian. "The Trobriand Islands, 1945." *Man* 46 (1946): 72.

*Malinowski, Bronislaw. *Argonauts of the Western Pacific.* London: George Routledge & Sons, 1922.

*———— . *Coral Gardens and Their Magic.* New York: American Book, 1935.

*———— . *Crime and Custom in Savage Society.* New York: Harcourt, Brace, 1926.

*———— . *Sex and Repression in Savage Society.* New York: Harcourt, Brace, 1927.

*———— . *Sexual Life of Savages in North-Western Melanesia.* New York: Harcourt, Brace and World, 1929.

*———— . "Traders of the Trobriands." In *A Reader in General Anthropology,* edited by Carleton S. Coon. New York: Henry Holt, 1948, pp. 293–321.

Powell, H. A. "Competitive Leadership in Trobriand Political Organization." *Journal of the Royal Anthropological Institute of Great Britain and Ireland* 90 (1960): 118–45.

Robinson, Marguerite. "Complementary Filiation and Marriage in the Trobriand Islands: A Re-Examination of Malinowski's Material." In *Marriage in Tribal Societies,* edited by Meyer Fortes. Cambridge: Cambridge University Press, 1962, pp. 121–55.

Service, Elman. *Profiles in Ethnology.* New York: Harper & Row, 1963.

Wogeo

*Hogbin, H. Ian. "A New Guinea Childhood: From Weaning till the Eighth Year in Wogeo." *Oceania* 21 (1946): 275–96.

*————. "From Conception to Weaning in Wogeo." *Oceania* 13 (1943): 285–309.

*————. "Mana." *Oceania* 6 (1935–36): 241–74.

*————. "Marriage in Wogeo, New Guinea." *Oceania* 16 (1944): 324–52.

*————. "Native Culture of Wogeo: A Report of Field Work in New Guinea." *Oceania* 5 (1934–35): 308–37.

*————. "Native Land Tenure in New Guinea." *Oceania* 10 (1939): 113--65.

*————. "Puberty to Marriage: A Study of the Sexual Life of the Natives of Wogeo, New Guinea." *Oceania* 16 (1945–46): 185–209.

*————. "Social Reaction to Crime: Law and Morals in the Schouten Islands, New Guinea." *Journal of the Royal Anthropological Institute of Great Britain and Ireland* 68 (1938): 223–62.

*————. "Sorcery and Administration." *Oceania* 6 (1935–36): 1–32.

*————. "The Father Chooses His Heir." *Oceania* 12 (1940–41): 1–39.

*————. *The Island of Menstruating Men.* Scranton, Penna.: Chandler, 1970.

*————. "Tillage and Collection: A New Guinea Economy." *Oceania* 9 (1938–39): 127–51, 286–325.

*————. "Trading Expedition in Northern New Guinea." *Oceania* 5 (1934–35): 375–407.

Yapese

De Beauclair, Inez. "The Stone Money of Yap Island." *Academia Sinica, Institute of Ethnology Bulletin* 16 (1963): 147–60.

Furness, William. *The Island of Stone Money.* Philadelphia: Lippincott, 1910.

Haas, Johann. *Die Karolinen-Insel Jap.* Berlin: W. Süsserott, 1907.

Hunt, Edward, David Schneider, Nathaniel Kidder, and William Stevens. *The Micronesians of Yap and Their Depopulation.* Cambridge: Peabody Museum, Harvard University, 1949.

Müller, Wilhelm. *Yap.* Vol. 2, part 1. Hamburg: Friederichsen, 1917.

Ogata, S. "Traditional Coconut Culture on Yap." *South Pacific Bulletin* 10 (1960): 50–54.

*Schneider, David. "Abortion and Depopulation on Pacific Island." In *Health, Culture, and Community,* edited by Benjamin Paul. New York: Russell Sage Foundation, 1955, pp. 211–35.

*————. "Political Organization, Supernatural Sanctions, and the Punishment for Incest on Yap." *American Anthropologist* 59 (1957): 791–800.

*————. "Yap Kinship Terminology and Kin Groups." *American Anthropologist* 55 (1933): 215–36.

Senfft, Arno. "Ethnographic Contributions Concerning the Carolines Island of Yap." *Petermanns Mitteilungen* 49 (1903): 49–60, 83–87.

Tetens, Alfred, and Johann Kubary. "The Carolines Island Yap or Guap." *Journal of the Museum Godeffroy, Hamburg* 1 (1873): 84–130.

U.S. Office of Naval Operations. *West Caroline Islands Civil Affairs Handbook.* Washington, D.C.: Office of the Chief of Naval Operations, 1944.

Useem, John. *Report on Yap and Palau.* Honolulu: U.S. Commercial Co., 1946.

NORTH AMERICA

Aleut

Antropova, V. V. "The Aleuts." In *The Peoples of Siberia,* edited by Maxsim G. Levin and L. P. Potapov. Chicago: University of Chicago Press, 1964, pp. 884–88.

Coxe, William. *Account of the Russian Discoveries Between Asia and America.* London: Cadell & Davies, 1804.

Dall, William. *On the Remains of Later Pre-Historic Man Obtained from Caves in the Catherina Archipelago, Alaska Territory.* Washington, D.C.: Smithsonian Institution, 1878.

Elliot, Henry. *Our Arctic Province.* New York: Charles Scribner's Sons, 1886.

Ivanov, S. V. "Aleut Hunting Headgear and Its Ornamentation." *International Congress of Americanists Proceedings* 23 (1928): 477–504.

Jochelson, Vladimir. *History, Ethnology, and Anthropology of the Aleut.* Washington, D.C.: Carnegie Institute of Washington, 1933.

Langsdorff, George Heinrich von. *Voyage and Travels in Various Parts of the World During 1803, 1804, 1805, 1806, and 1807.* London: H. Colburn, 1813.

Ransom, Jay E. "Stories, Myths, and Superstitions of Fox Island Aleut Children." *Journal of American Folklore* 60 (1947): 62–72.

*Sarychev, Gavriil. *Account of a Voyage of Discovery to the North-East of Siberia, the Frozen Ocean, and the North-East Sea.* New York: Da Capo Press, 1969.

Shade, Charles. *Ethnological Notes on the Aleuts.* Cambridge: Harvard University Press, 1949.

*Veniaminov, Ivan E. *Notes on the Islands of the Unalaska District.* Vols. 2 and 3. Saint Petersburg: Izdano Izhdiveniem Rossusko-Amerikanskoi Kompanii, 1840.

Chiricahua Apache

Basso, Keith. *Western Apache Witchcraft.* Tucson: University of Arizona Press, 1969.

Casteller, E., and Morris Opler. "Ethnobiology of the Chiricahua and Mescalero Apache." *University of New Mexico Bulletin* 4 (1936): 1–63.

*Opler, Morris. *An Apache Life-Way.* Chicago: University of Chicago Press, 1941.

*————. "An Outline of Chiricahua Apache Social Organization." In *Social Anthropology of North American Tribes,* edited by Frederick Eggan. Chicago: University of Chicago Press, 1937, pp. 171–239.

*————. "Cause and Effect in Apachean Agriculture, Division of Labor, Residence Patterns, and Girls' Puberty Rites." *American Anthropologist* 74 (1972): 1133–51.

*————. "Chiricahua Apache Material Relating to Sorcery." *Primitive Man* 19 (1946): 81–92.

*————. "Myths and Tales of the Chiricahua Apache." *Memoirs of the American Folklore Society* 37 (1942): 1–114.

*————. "Notes on Chiricahua Apache Culture. 1. Supernatural Power and the Shaman." *Primitive Man* 20 (1947): 1–14.

*————. "The Kinship Systems of the Southern Athabaskan-Speaking Tribes." *American Anthropologist* 38 (1936): 620–33.

*————. "Three Types of Variation and Their Relation to Culture Change." In *Language, Culture, and Personality,* edited by Leslie Spier, A. Irving Hallowell, and Stanley Newman. Menasha, Wisc.: Sapir Memorial Fund, 1941, pp. 146–57.

Copper Eskimo

Habenstein, Robert, and William Lamers. *Funeral Customs the World Over.* Milwaukee: Bulfin Printers, 1963.

*Jenness, Diamond. *The Life of the Copper Eskimos.* Ottawa: F. A. Acland, 1922.

*————. *The People of the Twilight.* Chicago: University of Chicago Press, 1928.

*Rasmussen, Knud. *Across Arctic America.* New York: G. P. Putnam's Sons, 1927.

*————. *Intellectual Culture of the Copper Eskimos.* Copenhagen: Gyldendal, 1932.

Roberts, Helen, and Diamond Jenness. *Eskimo Songs: Songs of the Copper Eskimo.* Ottawa: F. A. Acland, 1925.

Service, Elman. *Profiles in Ethnology.* New York: Harper & Row, 1963.

Steffánsson, Vilhjálmur. *My Life with the Eskimo.* New York: Macmillan, 1913.

————. "The Steffánson-Anderson Expedition." *Anthropological Papers of the American Museum of Natural History* 14 (1914): 1–475.

Creek

Hewitt, J. N. B. "Notes on the Creek Indians." *Bulletin of the U.S. Bureau of American Ethnology no. 123* 10 (1939): 119–59.

*Swanton, John. "Religious Beliefs and Medical Practices of the Creek Indians." *Annual Report of the U.S. Bureau of American Ethnology* 42 (1924–25): 473–672.

*————. "Social Organization and Social Usages of the Indians of the Creek Confederacy." *Annual Report of the U.S. Bureau of American Ethnology* 42 (1924–25): 23–472.

Eyak

*Birket-Smith, Kaj, and Frederica de Laguna. *The Eyak Indians of the Copper River Delta, Alaska.* Copenhagen: Levin & Munksgaard, 1938.

Gros Ventre

*Cooper, John. *The Gros Ventres of Montana. Part 2. Religion and Ritual.* Washington, D.C.: Catholic University of America, 1956.

*Flannery, Regina. "Individual Variations in Culture." In *Men and Cultures*, edited by Anthony F. C. Wallace. Philadelphia: University of Pennsylvania Press, 1960, pp. 87–92.

*————. "The Changing Form and Functions of the Gros Ventre Grass Dance." *Primitive Man* 20 (1947): 39–70.

*————. *The Gros Ventres of Montana. Part 1. Social Life.* Washington, D.C.: Catholic University of America, 1953.

Kroeber, Alfred. "Ethnology of the Gros Ventre." *Anthropological Papers of the American Museum of Natural History* 1 (1908): 145–281.

Hidatsa

*Bowers, Alfred. *Hidatsa Social and Ceremonial Organization.* Washington, D.C.: U.S. Government Printing Office, 1965.

Curtis, Edward S. *The North American Indian.* New York: Johnson Reprint Corp., 1970.

Lowie, Robert. "Notes on the Social Organization and Customs of the Mandan, Hidatsa, and Crow Indians." *Anthropological Papers of the American Museum of Natural History* 11 (1917): 1–99.

————. "Societies of the Crow, Hidatsa, and Mandan Indians." *Anthropological Papers of the American Museum of Natural History* 11 (1916): 221–358.

*Matthews, Washington. "Ethnology and Philology of the Hidatsa Indians." *Miscellaneous Publications of the U.S. Geological and Geographical Survey*, no. 7 (1877): 1–239.

Thivaites, Reuben, ed. *Early Western Travels.* Vols. 22–24. Cleveland: Arthur Clark, 1906.

Hupa

Driver, Harold E. "Culture Element Distributions. 10. Northwest California." *University of California Anthropological Records* 1 (1937–39): 294–434.
*Goddard, Pliny E. *Life and Culture of the Hupa.* Berkeley: University of California Press, 1903.

Kaska

*Honigmann, John. "Culture and Ethos of Kaska Society." *Yale University Publications in Anthropology* 40 (1949): 1–365.
*———. "The Kaska Indians: An Ethnographic Reconstruction." *Yale University Publications in Anthropology* 51 (1954): 1–163.
Teit, J. "Field Notes on the Tahltan and Kaska Indians: 1912–15." *Anthropologica* 3 (1956): 39–171.

Klamath

Barnett, S. "The Material Culture of the Klamath Lake and Modoc Indians of Northeastern California and Southern Oregon." *University of California Publications in American Archaeology and Ethnology* 5 (1907–10): 239–92.
*Gatschet, Albert. *The Klamath Indians of Southwestern Oregon.* Washington, D.C.: U.S. Government Printing Office, 1890.
Nash, Philleo. "The Place of Religious Revivalism in the Formation of the Intercultural Community on Klamath Reservation." In *Social Anthropology of North American Tribes,* edited by Frederick Eggan. Chicago: University of Chicago Press, 1937, pp. 377–444.
Pearsall, M. "Klamath Childhood and Education." *Anthropological Records* 9 (1950): 339–51.
*Spier, Leslie. *Klamath Ethnography.* Berkeley: University of California Press, 1930.
Stern, Theodore. *The Klamath Tribe.* Seattle: University of Washington Press, 1965.
Thompson, Lucy. *To the American Indian.* Eureka, Calif.: Cummins Print Shop, 1916.
Voegelin, E. "Northeast California." *Anthropological Records* 7 (1942): 47–252.

Kwakiutl

Benedict, Ruth. *Patterns of Culture.* Boston: Houghton Mifflin, 1934.
*Boas, Franz. "Current Beliefs Among the Kwakiutl." *Journal of American Folklore* 45 (1932): 177–260.

*——— . "Ethnology of the Kwakiutl." *Annual Report of the U.S. Bureau of American Ethnology* 35 (1913–14): part 1, pp. 43–794; part 2, pp. 795–1481.

*——— . *Kwakiutl Ethnography*. Chicago: University of Chicago Press, 1966.

*——— . "Kwakiutl of Vancouver Island." *Memoirs of the American Museum of Natural History* 9 (1909): 301–516.

*——— . *Kwakiutl Tales*. New York: Columbia University Press, 1910.

*——— . *The Social Organization and the Secret Societies of the Kwakiutl Indians*. Washington, D.C.: U.S. Government Printing Office, 1897.

Ford, Clellan. *Smoke from Their Fires*. New Haven: Yale University Press, 1941.

Goldman, Irving. "The Kwakiutl Indians of Vancouver Island." In *Cooperation and Competition Among Primitive Peoples*, edited by Margaret Mead. New York: McGraw-Hill, 1934, pp. 180–209.

Lopatin, I. "Social Life and Religion of the Indians at Kitimat, British Columbia." *University of Southern California Social Science Series* 26 (1945): 3–118.

Rohner, Ronald, and Evelyn Rohner. *The Kwakiutl Indians of British Columbia*. New York: Holt, Rinehart and Winston, 1970.

Micmac

*Denys, Nicolas. "The Description and Natural History of the Coasts of North America." *Publications of the Champlain Society* 2 (1908): 1–625.

Johnson, Frederick. "Notes on Micmac Shamanism." *Primitive Man* 16 (1943): 53–80.

*Le Clercq, Chrestien. "New Relation of Gaspesia." *Publications of the Champlain Society* 5 (1910): 1–452.

Parsons, Elsie. "Micmac Notes." *Journal of American Folklore* 39 (1928): 460–85.

Speck, Frank. "Kinship Terms and the Family Band Among the Northeastern Algonkian." *American Anthropologist* 20 (1918): 143–61.

Wallis, Wilson, and Ruth Wallis. "Culture Loss and Culture Change Among the Micmac of the Canadian Maritime Provinces 1912–1950." *Kroeber Anthropology Papers* 8–9 (1953): 100–29.

——— . *The Micmac Indians of Eastern Canada*. Minneapolis: University of Minnesota Press, 1955.

Navaho

Aberle, David. "Navaho." In *Matrilineal Kinship*, edited by David Schneider and Kathleen Gough. Berkeley: University of California Press, 1961, pp. 96–201.

*Bailey, Flora. "Some Sex Beliefs and Practices in a Navaho Community." *Papers of the Peabody Museum of American Archaeology and Ethnology* 40 (1950): no. 2.

Carr, Malcolm, Katherine Spencer, and Dorianne Woolley. "Navaho Clans and Marriage at Pueblo Alto." *American Anthropologist* 41 (1939): 245–57.

Habenstein, Robert, and William Lamers. *Funeral Customs the World Over.* Milwaukee: Bulfin Printers, 1963.

Hartman, Lillian. "The Life and Customs of the Navajo Women." *Wisconsin Archeologist* 18 (1938): 100–07.

Keith, Anne. "The Navajo Girls' Puberty Ceremony: Function and Meaning for the Adolescent." *El Palacio* 71 (1964): 27–36.

*Kluckhohn, Clyde. "Navaho Witchcraft." *Papers of the Peabody Museum of American Archaeology and Ethnology* 22 (1944): 1–149.

*———. "Personality Formation Among Navaho." *Sociometry* 9 (1946): 128–32.

*———. "Some Aspects of Navaho Infancy and Early Childhood." *Psychoanalysis and the Social Sciences* 1 (1947): 37–86.

*Kluckhohn, Clyde, and Dorothea Leighton. *Children of the People.* New York: Octagon Books, 1969.

*———. *The Navaho.* Garden City, N.Y.: Doubleday, 1946.

Opler, Morris. "The Kinship Systems of the Southern Athabaskan-Speaking Tribes." *American Anthropologist* 38 (1936): 620–33.

Reichard, Gladys. *Dezba: Woman of the Desert.* New York: J. J. Augustin, 1939.

———. *Social Life of the Navajo Indians.* New York: Columbia University Press, 1928.

Roberts, J. "Three Navaho Households." *Papers of the Peabody Museum of American Archaeology and Ethnology* 40 (1951): 1–89.

Service, Elman. *Profiles in Ethnology.* New York: Harper & Row, 1963.

Northern Saulteaux

Barnouw, Victor. *Acculturation and Personality Among Wisconsin Chippewa.* Menasha, Wisc.: American Anthropological Association, 1933.

Cameron, Duncan. "The Nipigon Country." In *Les bourgeois de la campagne du nord-ouest,* edited by L. R. Masson. Quebec: Imprimerie Générale A. Cote, 1890, pp. 227–300.

Densmore, Frances. "Chippewa Customs." *Bulletin of the U.S. Bureau of American Ethnology* 86 (1929): 1–204.

———. *Chippewa Music.* Washington, D.C.: U.S. Government Printing Office, 1913.

Dunning, R. W. *Social and Economic Change Among the Northern Ojibwa.* Toronto: University of Toronto Press, 1959.

Grant, M. Peter. "The Salteaux Indians About 1804." In *Les bourgeois de la campagne du nord-ouest*, edited by L. R. Masson. Quebec: Imprimerie Générale A. Cote, 1890, pp. 308–66.

*Hallowell, A. Irving. "Aggression in Salteaux Society." In *Personality in Nature, Society, and Culture*, edited by Clyde Kluckhohn and H. Murray. New York: Knopf, 1959, pp. 260–75.

*———. *Culture and Experience*. Philadelphia: University of Pennsylvania Press, 1955.

*———. "Fear and Anxiety as Cultural and Individual Variables in a Primitive Society." *Journal of Social Psychology* 9 (1938): 25–47.

*———. "Ojibwa Ontology, Behavior, and World View." In *Culture in History*, edited by Stanley Diamond. New York: Columbia University Press, 1960, pp. 19–52.

*———. "Psychic Stresses and Culture Patterns." *American Journal of Psychiatry* 92 (1936): 1291–1310.

*———. "Shabwan, a Dissocial Indian Girl." *American Journal of Orthopsychiatry* 8 (1938): 329–40.

*———. *The Role of Conjuring in Salteaux Society*. Philadelphia: University of Pennsylvania Press, 1942.

Hilger, M. Inez. *A Social Study of One Hundred Fifty Chippewa Indian Families of the White Earth Reservation of Minnesota*. Washington, D.C.: Catholic University of America Press, 1939.

———. "Chippewa Child Life." *Bulletin of the U.S. Bureau of American Ethnology* 136 (1932): 1–204.

Hoffman, W. J. "The Mide'wiwin or 'Grand Medicine Society' of the Ojibway." *Annual Report of the U.S. Bureau of American Ethnology* 7 (1885–86): 149–300.

Jenness, Diamond. *Ojibwa Indians of Parry Island*. Ottawa: National Museum of Canada, 1935.

Jones, William. "Ojibwa Texts." *Publications of the American Ethnological Society* 7, part 1 (1917): pp. 1–501; part 2 (1919): 1–777.

Kinietz, W. Vernon. *Chippewa Village: The Story of Katikitegon*. Bloomfield Hills, Mich.: Cranbrook Press, 1947.

Kohl, Johann G. *Kitchi-Gami*. London: Chapman & Hall, 1866.

Landes, Ruth. *Ojibwa Sociology*. New York: Columbia University Press, 1937.

———. "The Ojibwa of Canada." In *Cooperation and Competition Among Primitive Peoples*, edited by Margaret Mead. New York: McGraw-Hill, 1937, pp. 87–126.

———. *The Ojibwa Woman*. New York: W. W. Norton, 1971.

Long, John. *Voyages and Travels of an Indian Interpreter and Trader*. Cleveland: Arthur Clark, 1904.

Radin, Paul. *Some Myths and Tales of the Ojibwa of Southeastern Ontario*. Ottawa: Government Printing Bureau, 1914.

Ritzenthaler, Robert. "Chippewa Preoccupation with Health." *Milwaukee Public Museum Bulletin* 19 (1953): 175–257.

Skinner, Alanson. "Notes on the Eastern Cree and Northern Salteaux." *Anthropological Papers of the American Museum of Natural History* 9 (1912): 1–177.

———. "Political and Ceremonial Organization of the Plains-Ojibway." *Anthropological Papers of the American Museum of Natural History* 2 (1916): 475–511.

Paiute

Sapir, Edward. "The Southern Paiute Language." *American Academy of Arts and Sciences Proceedings* 65 (1930): 1–296.

Stewart, Omer. "Culture Elements Distributions: XIV. Northern Paiute." *Anthropological Records* 4 (1941): 361–446.

———. "The Northern Paiute Bands." *Anthropological Records* 2 (1939): 127–49.

*Whiting, Beatrice. "Paiute Sorcery." *Viking Fund Publications in Anthropology* 15 (1950): 1–109.

Papago

Densmore, Frances. "Papago Music." *Bulletin of the U.S. Bureau of American Ethnology* 90 (1929): 1–229.

Joseph, Alice, Rosamond Spicer, and Jane Chesky. *The Desert People.* Chicago: University of Chicago Press, 1949.

*Lumholtz, Carl. *New Trails in Mexico.* New York: Charles Scribner's Sons, 1912.

*Underhill, Ruth. "Autobiography of a Papago Woman." *Memoirs of the American Anthropological Association* 46 (1936): 1–64.

*———. *Papago Indian Religion.* New York: Columbia University Press, 1946.

*———. *Social Organization of the Papago Indians.* New York: AMS Press, 1939.

Pawnee

Densmore, Frances. *Pawnee Music.* Washington, D.C.: U.S. Government Printing Office, 1929.

*Dorsey, George. "The Skidi Rite of Human Sacrifice." *International Congress of Americanists, 15th Session, part 2* (1906): 65–70.

*———. *Traditions of the Skidi Pawnee.* Boston: Houghton Mifflin, 1904.

*Dorsey, George, and James Murie. *Notes on Skidi Pawnee Society.* Chicago: Field Museum of Natural History, 1940.

Grinnell, George. "Marriage Among the Pawnees." *American Anthropologist* 4 (1891): 275–81.

Lesser, Alexander. "Levirate and Fraternal Polyandry Among the Pawnees." *Man* 30 (1930): 98–101.

————. *The Pawnee Ghost Dance Hand Game.* New York: Columbia University Press, 1933.

Linton, Ralph. *Annual Ceremony of the Pawnee Medicine Men.* Chicago: Field Museum of Natural History, 1923.

*Murie, James. *Pawnee Indian Societies.* New York: American Museum of Natural History, 1914.

Wedel, Waldo. *An Introduction to Pawnee Archaeology.* Washington, D.C.: U.S. Government Printing Office, 1936.

*Weltfish, Gene. *The Lost Universe.* New York: Basic Books, 1965.

Sanpoil

Boas, Franz. *Folktales of Salishan and Sahaptin Tribes.* Lancaster, Penna.: American Folk-Lore Society, 1917.

*Ray, Verne. "Sanpoil Folktales." *Journal of American Folklore* 46 (1933): 129–87.

*————. "The Sanpoil and the Nespelem." *University of Washington Publications in Anthropology* 5 (1932): 3–237.

Tarasco

*Beals, Ralph. *Cherán: A Sierra Tarascan Village.* Washington, D.C.: U.S. Government Printing Office, 1946.

*Beals, Ralph, Pedro Carrasco, and Thomas McCorkle. *Houses and House Use of the Sierra Tarascans.* Washington, D.C.: U.S. Government Printing Office, 1944.

Carrasco Pizara, Pedro. *Tarascan Folk Religions.* New Orleans: Tulane University Press, 1952.

Foster, George. *Empire's Children.* Mexico: Imprenta Nuevo Mundo, 1948.

*Lumholtz, Carl. *Unknown Mexico.* Vol. 2. New York: Charles Scribner's Sons, 1902.

Mendieta y Núñez, Lucio, ed. *Los Tarascos.* Mexico: Imprenta Universitaria, 1940.

Twana

*Eells, Myron. "The Twana, Chemakum, and Klallam Indians of Washington Territory." *Smithsonian Institution Annual Report for the*

Year Ending June 30, 1887. Washington, D.C.: U.S. Government Printing Office, 1889.
*Elmendorf, W. W. *The Structure of Twana Culture.* Pullman: Washington State University Press, 1960.

Yokuts

Driver, Harold. "Culture Elements Distributions: VI. Southern Sierra Nevada." *Anthropological Records* 1 (1937): 53–154.
*Gayton, Anna. "Yokuts and Western Mono Ethnography." *Anthropological Records* 10 (1949): 7–45.
*———. *Yokuts—Mono Chiefs and Shamans.* Berkeley: University of California Press, 1930.
Kroeber, Alfred L. *Handbook of the Indians of California.* Berkeley: California Book, 1953.
Latta, Frank. *Handbook of Yokuts Indians.* Bakersfield, Calif.: Kern County Museum, 1949.

Zapotec

De la Fuente, Julio M. *Yalalag: Una villa zapoteca serrana.* Mexico: Museo Nacional de Antropologia, 1949.
Kearney, Michael. *The Winds of Ixtepeji.* New York: Holt, Rinehart and Winston, 1972.
Mendieta y Núñez, Lucio. *Los Zapotecos.* Mexico: Imprenta Universitaria, 1949.
*Nader, Laura. "An Analysis of Zapotec Law Cases." In *Law and Warfare,* edited by Paul Bohannan. Garden City, N.Y.: Natural History Press, 1967, pp. 117–38.
*———. "Talea and Juquila." *University of California Publications in American Archaeology and Ethnology* 48 (1964): 195–296.
*———. "The Zapotec Indians." *Harvard University Committee on Middle American Studies, Working Papers in Ethnology* 1 (1957): 1–28.
*Parsons, Elsie. *Mitla.* Chicago: University of Chicago Press, 1936.
Radin, Paul. "An Historical Legend of Zapotec." *Ibero-Americana* 9 (1935): 1–29.
———. "Zapotec Texts." *International Journal of Linguistics* 12 (1946): 152–72.

SOUTH AMERICA

Amahuaca

*Carneiro, Robert. "Shifting Cultivation Among the Amahuaca of Eastern Peru." *Volkerkundliche Abhandlungen* 1 (1964): 9–18.

*———— . "The Transition from Hunting to Horticulture in the Amazon Basin." *Proceedings of the 8th Congress of Anthropological and Ethnological Sciences* 3 (1968): 244–48.

*Dole, Gertrude. "Endocannibalism Among the Amahuaca Indians." In *You and Others,* edited by A. Kimball Romney and Paul L. Devore. Cambridge: Harvard University Press, 1973, pp. 240–46.

*———— . "The Marriages of Pacho: A Woman's Life Among the Amahuaca." In *Many Sisters: Women in Cross-Cultural Perspective,* edited by Carolyn J. Matthiasson. New York: Free Press, 1974, pp. 3–35.

Farabee, William C. "Indian Tribes of Eastern Peru." *Papers of the Peabody Museum of American Archaeology and Ethnology* 10 (1922): 115–25.

*Huxley, Matthew, and Cornell Capa. *Farewell to Eden.* New York: Harper & Row, 1964.

Steward, Julian, and Alfred Métraux. "Tribes of the Peruvian and Ecuadorian Montana." In *Handbook of South American Indians.* Vol. 3, edited by Julian Steward. Washington, D.C.: U.S. Government Printing Office, 1948, pp. 535–657.

Tessman, Günter. *Die Indianer nordost-Perus.* Hamburg: Friederichsen, De Gruyter, 1930.

Aweikoma

De Paula, José. "Memoir on the Botocudo of Parana and Santa Catarina, Organized by the Indian Protection Service." *International Congress of Americanists, Proceedings* 20 (1922): 117–37.

Habenstein, Robert, and William Lamers. *Funeral Customs the World Over.* Milwaukee: Bulfin Printers, 1963.

*Henry, Jules. *Jungle People.* New York: Vintage Books, 1964.

*———— . "The Personality of the Kaingang." *Character and Personality* 5 (1936): 113–23.

Hicks, David. "A Structural Model of Aweikoma Society." In *The Translation of Culture,* edited by T. O. Beidelman. London: Tavistock, 1971, pp. 141–59.

Métraux, Alfred. "The Caingang." In *Handbook of South American Indians.* Vol. 1, edited by Julian Steward. Washington, D.C.: U.S. Government Printing Office, 1946, pp. 445–75.

Oswalt, Wendell. *Other Peoples, Other Customs.* New York: Holt, Rinehart and Winston, 1972.

Aymara

Bouroncle Carreón, Alfonso. "Contribución al estudio de los Aymaras." *América Indígena* 24 (1964): 233–69.

Forbes, David. "On the Aymara Indians of Bolivia and Peru." *Ethnological Society of London Journal* 2 (1870): 193–305.
La Barre, Weston. "Aymara Folktales." *International Journal of American Linguistics* 16 (1950): 40–45.
————. "The Aymara Indians of the Lake Titicaca Plateau, Bolivia." *Memoirs of the American Anthropological Association* 68 (1948): 1–250.
Métraux, Alfred. "Contribution au folk-lore andine." *Journal de la Société des Américanistes de Paris* 26 (1934): 67–102.
*Tschopik, Jr., Harry. "The Aymara." In *Handbook of South American Indians*. Vol. 2, edited by Julian Steward. Washington, D.C.: U.S. Government Printing Office, 1947, pp. 501–73.
*————. "The Aymara of Chucuito, Peru." *Anthropological Papers of the American Museum of Natural History* 44 (1951): 133–308.

Bribri

Gabb, William. "On the Indian Tribes and Languages of Costa Rica." *American Philosophical Society Proceedings* 14 (1876): 483–602.
Johnson, Frederick. "The Caribbean Lowland Tribes." In *Handbook of South American Indians*. Vol. 4, edited by Julian Steward. Washington, D.C.: U.S. Government Printing Office, 1949, pp. 231–51.
*Skinner, Alanson. "Notes on the Bribri of Costa Rica." *Indian Notes and Monographs* 6 (1920): 37–106.
*Stone, Doris. "The Talamancan Tribes of Costa Rica." *Papers of the Peabody Museum of Archaeology and Ethnology* 43 (1962): 1–108.

Callinago

Bouton, Jacques. *Relation de l'establissement de François depuis l'an 1635.* Paris: Cramoisy, 1640.
*Breton, Raymond. "Observations of the Island Carib: A Compilation of Ethnographic Notes." Human Relations Area Files, 1957.
*Breton, Raymond, and Armand de la Paix. "Relation de l'île de la Guadeloupe." In *Les Caraibe, la Guadeloupe 1635–1656*, edited by Joseph Rennard. Paris: Librairie Générale et Internationale, 1929, pp. 45–74.
Du Tertre, Jean B. *Histoire générale des Antilles habitées par les François.* Paris: T. Jolly, 1667–71.
Hodge, W., and D. Taylor. "The Ethnobotany of the Island Caribs of Dominica." *Webbia* 12 (1957): 513–664.
Rouse, Irving. "The Carib." In *Handbook of South American Indians*. Vol. 4, edited by Julian Steward. Washington, D.C.: U.S. Government Printing Office, 1949, pp. 547–65.

*Taylor, Douglas. "Kinship and Social Structure of the Island Carib." *Southwestern Journal of Anthropology* 2 (1946): 180–212.
*————. *The Caribs of Dominica*. Washington, D.C.: U.S. Government Printing Office, 1938.
*————. "The Meaning of Dietary and Occupational Restrictions Among the Island Carib." *American Anthropologist* 52 (1950): 343–49.

Carib

*Gillen, John. "The Barama River Caribs of British Guiana." *Papers of the Peabody Museum of American Archaeology and Ethnology* 14 (1931–36): 1–274.
*————. "Tribes of the Guianas." In *Handbook of South American Indians*. Vol. 4, edited by Julian Steward. Washington, D.C.: U.S. Government Printing Office, 1949, pp. 799–860.
Kloos, Peter. "Female Initiation Among the Maroni River Caribs." *American Anthropologist* 71 (1969): 898–905.
Roth, W. E. "An Introductory Study of the Arts, Crafts, and Customs of the Guiana Indians." *Annual Reports of the U.S. Bureau of American Ethnology* 38 (1924): 25–720.

Cuna

Borland, Francis. *The History of Darien*. Glasgow: John Bryce, 1779.
Densmore, Frances. *Music of the Indians of Panama*. Washington, D.C.: Smithsonian Institution, 1926.
De Puydt, Lucien. "Account of Scientific Explorations in the Isthmus of Darien in the Years 1861 and 1865." *Royal Geographic Society Journal* 38 (1868): 69–110.
De Smidt, Leon. *Among the San Blas Indians of Panama*. Troy, N.Y.: n.p., 1948.
Habenstein, Robert, and William Lamers. *Funeral Customs the World Over*. Milwaukee: Bulfin Printers, 1963.
Harris, Reginald. "The San Blas Indians." *American Journal of Anthropology* 9 (1926): 17–63.
Krieger, Herbert. "Material Culture of the People of Southeastern Panama." *Bulletin of the United States National Museum* 134 (1926): 1–133.
Marshall, Donald. "Cuna Folk." Master's thesis. Harvard University, 1950.
McKim, Fred. *San Blas: An Account of the Cuna Indians of Panama*. Göteborg, Sweden: Etnografiska Museet, 1947.
*Nordenskiöld, Erland. *An Historical and Ethnological Survey of the Cuna Indians*. Göteborg, Sweden: Etnografiska Museet, 1938.
*————. "Cuna Indian Religion." *International Congress of Americanists Proceedings* 23 (1928): 668–77.

*————. *Picture Writing and Other Documents by Néle, Paramount Chief of the Cuna Indians.* Göteborg, Sweden: Erland Nordenskiöld, 1928.
*Stout, David. "San Blas Cuna Acculturation: An Introduction." *Viking Fund Publications in Anthropology* 9 (1947): 1–121.
*————. "The Cuna." In *Handbook of South American Indians.* Vol. 4, edited by Julian Steward. Washington, D.C.: U.S. Government Printing Office, 1949, pp. 257–69.
*Wafer, Lionel. *A New Voyage and Description of the Isthmus of America.* Oxford: Hakluyt Society, 1934.
Wassén, Henry. "Contributions to Cuna Ethnography." *Etnologiska Studier* 16 (1949): 38–40.

Goajiro

Armstrong, John, and Alfred Métraux. "The Goajiro." In *Handbook of South American Indians.* Vol. 4, edited by Julian Steward. Washington, D.C.: U.S. Government Printing Office, 1949, pp. 369–83.
*Bolinder, Gustaf. *Indians on Horseback.* London: Dennis Dobson, 1957.
*Gutiérrez de Pineda, Virginia. "Organización social en la Guajira." *Revista del Instituto Etnológico Nacional* 3 (1950): 1–225.
Petrullo, Vincenzo. "Composition of 'Torts' in Guajiro Society." *Philadelphia Anthropological Society Publications* 1 (1937): 153–60.
Pineda, Giraldo Roberto. "Aspectos de la magía en la Guajira." *Revista del Instituto Etnológico Nacional* 3 (1950): 1–164.
Santa Cruz, Antonio. "Aspects of the Avunculate in the Goajiro Culture." *Primitive Man* 14 (1941): 1–13.
Simons, F. "An Exploration of the Goajira Peninsula of Colombia." *Proceedings of the Royal Geographical Society* 7 (1885): 781–840.
Turrado Moreno, Angel. *Como son los Guajiros.* Caracas: El Compas, 1950.
Watson, Lawrence. "Guajiro Social Structure: A Reexamination." *Antropológica* 20 (1967): 3–36.
Wilbert, Johannes. "Kinship and Social Organization of the Yekauna and Goajiro." *Southwestern Journal of Anthropology* 14 (1958): 153–60.
————. *Survivors of Eldorado.* New York: Frederick Praeger, 1972.

Jivaro

Bollaert, William. "On the Idol Human Head of the Jivaro Indians, with an Account of the Jivaro Indians." *Transactions of the Ethnological Society of London* 2 (1863): 117–18.
Danielson, Bengt. "Some Attraction and Repulsion Patterns Among Jivaro Indians: A Study in Sociometric Anthropology." *Sociometry* 12 (1949): 83–105.
Dyott, George. *On the Trail of the Unknown in the Wilds of Ecuador and the Amazon.* London: Thornton Butterworth, 1926.

Farabee, William C. "Indian Tribes of Eastern Peru." *Papers of the Peabody Museum of American Archeology and Ethnology* 10 (1922): 115–25.

Habenstein, Robert, and William Lamers. *Funeral Customs the World Over.* Milwaukee: Bulfin Printers, 1963.

Harner, Michael. "Machetes, Shotguns, and Society." Ph.D. dissertation. University of California, Berkeley.

————. *The Jívaro.* Garden City, N.Y.: Anchor Books, 1972.

Hermessen, J. L. "A Journey of the Rio Zamora, Ecuador." *Geographical Review* 4 (1917): 434–49.

*Karsten, Rafael. "Blood Revenge and War Among the Jibaro Indians of Eastern Ecuador." In *Law and Warfare,* edited by Paul Bohannan. Garden City, N.Y.: Natural History Press, 1967, pp. 303–25.

*————. *Blood Revenge, War, and Victory Feasts Among the Jivaro Indians of Eastern Ecuador.* Washington, D.C.: Smithsonian Institution, 1923.

*————. *Civilization of the South American Indians.* London: Dawsons, 1968.

*————. "Contributions to Sociology of Indian Tribes of Ecuador." *Acta Academiae Aboensis* 1 (1920): 1–75.

*————. *The Head Hunters of the Western Amazonas.* Helsinki: Centraltryckeriet, 1935.

Oswalt, Wendell. *Other Peoples, Other Customs.* New York: Holt, Rinehart and Winston, 1972.

Reiss, W. "Ein Resuch bei den Jivaros-Indianern." *Verhandlungen der Gesellschaft für Erdkund zu Berlin* 7 (1880): 325–37.

Rivet, Paul. "Les indiens jivaro: étude géographique, historique et ethnographique." *L'Anthropologie* 18 (1907): 333–68, 583–618; 19 (1908): 69–87, 235–59.

Service, Elman. *Profiles in Ethnology.* New York: Harper & Row, 1963.

Simson, Alfred. "Notes on the Jivaros and Canelos Indians." *Journal of the Anthropological Institute of Great Britain and Ireland* 9 (1880): 385–93.

Steward, Julian, and Alfred Métraux. "The Jivaro." In *Handbook of South American Indians.* Vol. 3, edited by Julian Steward. Washington, D.C.: U.S. Government Printing Office, 1948, pp. 617–27.

*Stirling, Matthew W. *Historical and Ethnographical Material on the Jivaro Indians.* Washington, D.C.: Smithsonian Institution, 1938.

Tessman, Günter. *Die Indianer nordost-Perus.* Hamburg: Friederichsen, De Gruyter, 1930.

Up de Graff, Fritz W. *Head Hunters of the Amazon.* Garden City, N.Y.: Garden City Publishers, 1923.

Vigna, Juan. "Bosquejo sobre los indios shuaras y jíbaros." *América Indígena* 5 (1945): 35–49.

Vite, Felice. "Among the Jivaro Indians, Hunters of Heads." *Revista Geográfica Americana* 4 (1935): 15–22.

Lengua

Baldus, H. "Indianerstudien im nordostlichen Chaco." *Forschungen zur Volkerpsychologie und Soziologie* 11 (1931): 1–239.

*Grubb, W. Barbrooke. *An Unknown People in an Unknown Land*. London: Seeley, Service, 1914.

Hawtrey, Seymour H. C. "The Lengua Indians of the Paraguayan Chaco." *Journal of the Anthropological Institute of Great Britain and Ireland* 4 (1901): 280–99.

Métraux, Alfred. "Ethnography of the Chaco." In *Handbook of South American Indians*. Vol. 1, edited by Julian Steward. Washington, D.C.: U.S. Government Printing Office, 1946, pp. 197–370.

Mapuche

Cooper, John. "The Araucanians." In *Handbook of South American Indians*. Vol. 2, edited by Julian Steward. Washington, D.C.: U.S. Government Printing Office, 1947, pp. 687–760.

*Faron, Louis. "Araucanian Patri-Organization and the Omaha System." *American Anthropologist* 58 (1956): 435–56.

*———. "Mapuche Social Structure." *Illinois Studies in Anthropology* 1 (1961): 1–247.

*———. *The Mapuche Indians of Chile*. New York: Holt, Rinehart and Winston, 1968.

Hallowell, A. Irving. "Araucanian Parallels to the Omaha Kinship System." *American Anthropologist* 45 (1943): 489–91.

*Hilger, M. Inez. *Araucanian Childlife and Its Cultural Background*. Washington, D.C.: Smithsonian Institution, 1957.

Latcham, Richard. "Ethnology of the Araucanos." *Journal of the Royal Anthropological Institute of Great Britain and Ireland* 39 (1909): 334–70.

Padden, Richard. "Cultural Change and Military Resistance in Araucanian Chile, 1550–1730." *Southwestern Journal of Anthropology* 13 (1957): 103–21.

*Titiev, Mischa. "Araucanian Culture in Transition." *Occasional Contributions of the Museum of Anthropology of the University of Michigan* 15 (1951): 1–164.

*———. *Social Singing Among the Mapuche*. Ann Arbor: University of Michigan Press, 1949.

Miskito

*Conzemius, Edward. "Ethnographical Survey of the Miskito and Sumu Indians of Honduras and Nicaragua." *Bulletin of the U.S. Bureau of American Ethnology* 106 (1932): 1–191.

Kirchoff, Paul. "The Caribbean Lowland Tribes." In *Handbook of South American Indians.* Vol. 4, edited by Julian Steward. Washington, D.C.: U.S. Government Printing Office, 1949, pp. 219–29.

Wickham, H. A. "Notes on the Soumoo or Woolwa Indians of Mosquito Territory." *Journal of the Anthropological Institute of Great Britain and Ireland* 24 (1895): 198–208.

Mundurucu

Horton, Donald. "The Mundurucú." In *Handbook of South American Indians.* Vol. 3, edited by Julian Steward. Washington, D.C.: U.S. Government Printing Office, 1948, pp. 271–82.

Martius, Karl. *Beiträge zur Ethnographie Amerika's zumal Brasiliens.* Leipzig: F. Fleischer, 1867.

*Murphy, Robert F. *Headhunters' Heritage.* Berkeley: University of California Press, 1960.

*———. "Intergroup Hostility and Social Cohesion." *American Anthropologist* 59 (1957): 1018–35.

*———. "Matrilocality and Patrilineality." *American Anthropologist* 58 (1956): 414–34.

*———. "Mundurucú Religion." *University of California Publications in American Archaeology and Ethnology* 49 (1958): 1–146.

*———. *The Rubber Trade and the Mundurucú Village.* Ann Arbor, Mich.: University Microfilms, 1954.

*Murphy, Robert F., and Julian Steward. "Tappers and Trappers." *Economic Development and Cultural Change* 4 (1956): 335–55.

*Murphy, Yolanda, and Robert F. Murphy. *Women of the Forest.* New York: Columbia University Press, 1974.

*Tocantins, Antonio. "Estudos sôbre a tribe Mundurucú." *Revista do Instituto Historico Geographico e Ethnographico do Brasil* 40 (1877): 73--161.

Nambicuara

*Lévi-Strauss, Claude. *A World on the Wane.* New York: Criterion Books, 1955.

*———. "La vie familiale et sociale des indiens Nambikwara." *Journal de la Société des Américanistes de Paris* 37 (1948): 1–131.

*———. "The Nambicuara." In *Handbook of South American Indians.* Vol. 3, edited by Julian Steward. Washington, D.C.: U.S. Government Printing Office, 1948, pp. 361–69.

*———. "The Social and Psychological Aspect of Chieftainship in a Primitive Tribe." *New York Academy of Sciences Transactions* 7 (1945): 16–32.

Oberg, Kalervo. "Indian Tribes of Northern Mato Grosso, Brazil." *Publications of the Institute of Social Anthropology* 15 (1953): 82–105.

Vellard, Jehan. "Préparation du curare par le Nambikwara." *Journal de la Société des Américanistes de Paris* 31 (1939): 211–21.

Saramacca

De Groot, Silvia W. *Djuka Society and Social Change*. Assen, The Netherlands: Van Gorcum, 1969.
*Herskovits, Melville, and Frances Herskovits. *Rebel Destiny*. New York: McGraw-Hill, 1934.
*Kahn, Morton. *Djuka*. New York: Viking Press, 1931.

Siriono

*Holmberg, Allan. *Nomads of the Long Bow*. New York: Natural History Press, 1969.
*———. "The Siriono." In *Handbook of South American Indians*. Vol. 3, edited by Julian Steward. Washington, D.C.: U.S. Government Printing Office, 1948, pp. 455–64.
Oswalt, Wendell. *Other Peoples, Other Customs*. New York: Holt, Rinehart and Winston, 1972.

Timbira

*Crocker, William. "Os indios canelas de hoje." *Boletim do Museu Paraense Emilio Goeldi* 2 (1958): 1–9.
Kissenberth, Wilhelm. "Bei den Canella-Indianern in Zentral-Maranhao (Brasilien)." *Baessler-Archiv* 2 (1912): 45–54.
*Nimuendajú, Curt. *The Eastern Timbira*. Berkeley: University of California Press, 1946.
Snethlage, E. "Unter nordost brasilianschen Indianern." *Zeitschrift für Ethnologie* 62 (1930): 111–205.

Tupinamba

D'Abbeville, Claude. *Histoire de la mission des pères Capucins en l'isle de Maragnan et terres circonvoisines*. Paris: A. Franck, 1864.
D'Evreux, Yves. *Voyage dans le nord du Brésil fait durant les années 1613 et 1614 par le père Yves d'Evreux*. Paris: A. Franck, 1864.
Gandavo, Pedro de Magalhães. *Documents and Narratives Concerning the Discovery and Conquest of Latin America*. Vol. 2. New York: Cortes Society, 1922.
Heriarte, Mauricio de. *Descriçam do estado maranham, para eorupa e Rio des Amazonas*. Graz, Austria: Akadëmische Drud und Verlaganstalt, 1964.
Léry, Jean de. "Extracts out of the Historie of John Lerius." *Haklytus Posthumus or Purchas His Pilgrimes* 16 (1906): 518–79.

Métraux, Alfred. *La religion des Tupinamba et ses rapports avec celle des autres tribus Tupi-Guarani.* Paris: E. LeRoux, 1928.

————. "The Tupinamba." In *Handbook of South American Indians.* Vol. 3, edited by Julian Steward. Washington, D.C.: U.S. Government Printing Office, 1948, pp. 95–133.

Soares de Souza, Gabriel. "Tratado descriptivo do Brasil em 1587." *Revista do Instituto Historico e Geographico do Brasil* 14 (1851): 1–423.

*Staden, Hans. *The True Story of His Captivity.* London: Broadway Travellers, 1928.

*Thevet, André. *La cosmographie universelle.* Paris: Pierre L'Huillier, 1575.

*————. *The Peculiarities of French Antarctica.* Paris: Maisonneuve, 1878.

Vasconcellos, Simão. *Chronica da companhia de Jesu do estado do Brasil.* Lisbon: Lopes, 1865.

Warrau

Hilhouse, William. "Memoir of the Warao Land of British Guiana." *Journal of the Royal Geographical Society* 4 (1834): 321–32.

Hill, George, Roberto Lizarralde, James Silverberg, José Silva Michelena, Adelaide G. de Díaz Ungría, Sebastián Mier y Teran, and Jose Díaz Ungría. *Los Guarao del Delta Amacuro.* Caracas: Universidad Central de Venezuela, 1956.

Kirchoff, Paul. "The Warrau." In *Handbook of South American Indians.* Vol. 3, edited by Julian Steward. Washington, D.C.: U.S. Government Printing Office, 1948, pp. 869–81.

Plassard, Louis. "Les Guaraunos et le delta de l'Orénoque." *Société de Géographie de Paris, Bulletin* 15 (1868): 568–92.

Schad, Werner. "A puntes sobre los Guarao." *Boletín Indigenista Venezolano* 1 (1953): 399–422.

Suárez, María. *Los Warao.* Caracas: Departemento de Antropología, Instituto Venezolano de Investigaciones Científicas, 1968.

*Turrado Moreno, Angel. *Etnografía de los indios Guaraunos.* Caracas: Vargas, 1945.

*Wilbert, Johannes. "Die soziale und politische Organisation der Warrau." *Kolner Zeitschrift für Soziologie und Sozialpsychologie* 10 (1958): 272–91.

*————. *Survivors of Eldorado.* New York: Frederick Praeger, 1972.

*————. *Textos folklóricos de los indios Warao.* Los Angeles: University of California Press, 1969.

Williams, James. "The Warau Indians of Guiana and Vocabulary of Their Language." *Journal de la Société des Américanistes de Paris* 20 (1928): 193–252.

Witoto

Farabee, William C. "Indian Tribes of Eastern Peru." *Papers of the Peabody Museum of American Archaeology and Ethnology* 10 (1922): 136–49.

Hardenburg, W. E. "The Indians of the Putumayo, Upper Amazon." *Man* 10 (1910): 134–38.

Koch-Grünberg, T. "Die Indianer stamme am oberen Rio Negro und Yapura." *Zeitschrift für Ethnologie* 28 (1906): 166–205.

———. "Die Uitoto-Indianer." *Journal de la Société des Américanistes de Paris* 7 (1910): 61–83.

———. "Les indiens Ouitotos: étude linguiste." *Journal de la Société des Américanistes de Paris* 3 (1906): 157–89.

Murdock, George P. *Our Primitive Contemporaries.* New York: Macmillan, 1934.

Preuss, Konrad T. *Religion und Mythologie der Uitoto.* Leipzig: J. Hinrichs, 1921.

Schmidt, H. "Die Witito-Indianer." *Journal de la Société des Américanistes de Paris* 3 (1910): 63–85.

*Steward, Julian. "The Witotoan Tribes." In *Handbook of South American Indians.* Vol. 3, edited by Julian Steward. Washington, D.C.: U.S. Government Printing Office, 1948, pp. 749–62.

Tessman, Günter. *Die Indianer nordost-Perus.* Hamburg: Friederichsen, De Gruyter, 1930.

*Whiffen, Thomas. "A Short Account of the Indians of the Issa-Japura District." *Folklore* 24 (1913): 41–62.

*———. *The North-West Amazons.* New York: Duffield, 1915.

Yahgan

*Bridges, Thomas, and Samuel Lothrop. "The Canoe Indians of Tierra del Fuego." In *A Reader in General Anthropology,* edited by Carleton S. Coon. New York: Henry Holt, 1948, pp. 84–116.

Cooper, John. "Temporal Sequence and the Marginal Cultures." *Anthropological Series, Catholic University of America* 10 (1941): 1–69.

———. "The Yahgan." In *Handbook of South American Indians.* Vol. 1, edited by Julian Steward. Washington, D.C.: U.S. Government Printing Office, 1946, pp. 81–106.

*Gusinde, Martin. *The Yamana: The LIfe and Thought of the Water Nomads of Cape Horn.* New Haven: HRAF Press, 1961.

*Lothrop, Samuel. *The Indians of Tierra del Fuego.* New York: Museum of the American Indian, 1928.

Oswalt, Wendell. *Other Peoples, Other Customs.* New York: Holt, Rinehart and Winston, 1972.

Service, Elman. *Profiles in Ethnology.* New York: Harper & Row, 1963.

Index

Abortion, 91, 93, 185, 186
Achieved leadership: measure of, 235, 284–85; relation to unstable political power, ritual war, and social indebtedness, 237, 238 Table 14. *See also* "Big man" politics; Social indebtedness
Adoption, 172–73, 195, 218
Adultery: as basis for claiming paternity rights, 177–78; believed to cause irregularities of birth or pregnancy, 183, 184, 185, 187; suspected, as cause for abortion, 185
Agricultural economy: measure of, 74, 283; using hoe, plow, or irrigation, 56, 57. *See also* Digging-stick shifting cultivation economy
Ainu, birth and pregnancy rituals among, 189
Allen, M. R.: on female pollution and male segregation, 30, 31, 240, 245, 246–47, 253; on male initiation rites, 17–18, 149
Alorese: marriage loans, 225; ritual disinterest in wealth, 228
Andamanese, menarcheal ceremony among, 104
Arapesh, beliefs about female pollution among, 212
Arunta: breast-growing ceremony, 82, 104; defloration ceremony, 104, 105–06; exchange marriage, 63; menarcheal ceremony, 104, 105; subincision, 161
Ashanti: consequences of premarital pregnancy, 93; suspected adultery as cause for abortion, 185n; virginity test, 89n, 91
Ashley-Montagu, M. F., 12, 13
Ayres, Barbara, 37–38, 199
Azande: marriage bargains, 86n; suspected adultery as cause for abortion, 185

Bacdayan, Albert, 33–34
Bachofen, J. J., 40–41
Bambara, virginity test among, 89n
Barker-Benfield, G. J., 266n, 267
Basseri: consequences of seduction, 93; virginity test, 89n, 90
Bemba: *chisungu* ceremony, 23, 24–25; kingroup allegiance of husbands, 215
Benedek, Therese, 272
Bettelheim, Bruno, 7n; on couvade, 35; on male genital mutilations, 11–14, 15, 153; on menstrual restrictions, 28
"Big man" politics, 52–53, 223–26, 261. *See also* Achieved leadership; Ritual war; Social indebtedness; Unstable political power; Wealth contests
Birth and pregnancy:
—in complex societies: home births, 267–68, 269–70; medical rituals of, 268–69; natural childbirth, 270–71; sex taboos, 276–77; social avoidance of pregnant women, 276
—irregularities of, 183–84, 185, 186, 187, 188
—premarital, consequences of, 91–93. *See also* Seduction
—rituals by fathers, 184, 185, 187, 188, 196. *See also* Couvade
—rituals by kin groups of the father and mother: among the Nkundo Mongo, 187–88; among the Tallensi, 184; among the Tiv, 185; as surveillance rituals, 184, 186, 196–99
—rituals by mothers. *See* Maternal restrictions
Bonaparte, Marie, 272
Brady, Ivan, 173
Brideprice, 63–64, 86n; amount, 85, 180; as payment for paternity rights, 179–80; in matrilineal societies, 179–80; loans, 225; token, 61, 189. *See also* Mar-

Designer: Randall Goodall
Compositor: Viking Typographics
Printer: Braun-Brumfield
Binder: Braun-Brumfield
Text: 10/12 VIP Palatino
Display: Typositor Antikva Margaret
Cloth: Holliston Roxite B51567
Paper: 50 lb. P & S Vellum B32